14.95
54p

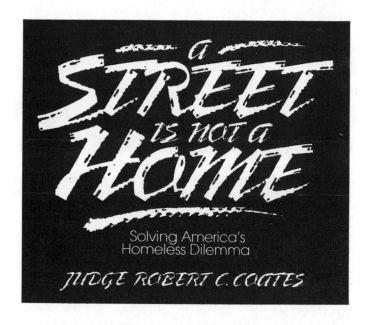

A STREET IS NOT A HOME

Solving America's Homeless Dilemma

JUDGE ROBERT C. COATES

Prometheus Books
Buffalo, New York

A STREET IS NOT A HOME: SOLVING AMERICA'S HOMELESS DILEMMA. Copyright © 1990 by Robert C. Coates. All rights reserved. No part of this book may be reproduced in any manner whatsoever without written permission, except in the case of brief quotations embodied in critical articles and reviews. Inquiries should be addressed to Prometheus Books, 700 E. Amherst Street, Buffalo, New York 14215, 716-837-2475.

94 93 92 91 90   5 4 3 2 1

Library of Congress Cataloging-in-Publication Data

Coates, Robert C., 1938-
    A street is not a home : solving America's homeless dilemma / by
Robert C. Coates.
        p.   cm.
    Includes bibliographical references and index.
    ISBN 0-87975-621-7
    1. Homelessness—United States. I. Title.
HV4504.C63   1990
362.5'0973—dc20   90-43193
                                                                        CIP

Printed in the United States of America on acid-free paper

To
Genevieve T. Coates
and
H Crawford Coates, Jr.
my parents,
whom I have come to know to be not just unique,
but splendid and noble.

Life cannot wait until the sciences have explained the universe. We cannot put off living until we are ready. The most salient characteristic of life is its coerciveness; it is always urgent, "here and now" without any possible postponement. Life is fired at us point blank.

—José Ortega y Gasset

Contents

Foreword   9

Acknowledgments   11

Introduction   19

PLANNING

1   The New Homeless   25
2   Planning Help   29
3   The Mayor's Task Force in the Streets   34

SUBPOPULATIONS OF HOMELESS, SPECIAL SOLUTIONS

4   An Easy Early Step: Public Drunks   51
5   Women and Children   59
6   The Elderly Homeless   71
7   Homeless Veterans   78
8   Runaway and Throwaway Kids   86

THE MAJOR SOLUTIONS

9   Cycling Able-Bodied Homeless into Jobs   95
10   Model Homeless Shelters   112
11   Affordable Housing   128
12   The Homeless Mentally Ill   155
13   Involuntary Treatment?   182
14   Myths, Mental Barriers, and Bad Ideas   196
15   Going to the State Capital   202
16   Public Restrooms (A NIMBY Study)   206
17   Conundra   210

EMPOWERMENT

18	The *Sine Qua Non*: Leadership	223
19	Ethics	233
20	Mobilizing Religious Congregations and Religious People	246
21	Economics . . .	254
22	"How Can I Help?"	269
23	We Can Handle It!	274

APPENDICES

A	Legal Rights of Homeless Americans	281
B	California Homeless Relief Act of 1986	320
C	California Housing and Homeless Bond Act of 1988	329

NOTES   337

Foreword

It was one of those bright, crisp November mornings in Seattle when the presidential motorcade of black limousines, helicopters, and police motorcycles screamed down a cordoned-off and deserted Interstate 5, not more than 100 yards from City Hall.

An impressive show of power, thought the mayor, standing by his office window. I wonder what the president would think, or do, with all that power if he knew that downstairs, in the basement of the government building, nearly two hundred homeless people had stayed through the cold night, sleeping on a bare floor, because all the shelters were full.

What would you do? Not as president, but as citizen. As human being. What would you do about homelessness in America? You know that literally millions of Americans—families, children, the mentally ill, the perfectly okay and the employable, the old and the young, the educated and the uneducated— are without shelter. It is the enduring shame of the nation, and we continue to allow it.

Why? Is it that the problem is just too big? Some say it is. We cannot grasp it. Is it money? Some say the deficit is the problem. We cannot afford it. Or is it will? Is it that this most neighborly of nations, this powerful defender of the American lifestyle, does not have the will to help people on the sharpest edges of life?

In this book, Judge Robert Coates assumes the will is there—in the American people, individually and collectively—to solve the problem. Homelessness is curable. All we need to hear is what good Americans are already doing, to emulate and expand on their achievvements, to proclaim that we are concerned, and to get involved. In other words, we know what to do, and we must act.

Judge Coates's formula is simple. He looks at the sub-populations of the homeless and explains various programs in American cities that have already worked for them. He examines the barriers we place before homeless people—economic, legal, mythic—and shows how they can be struck down. And last, but not least, he shows us how to gain the power to act.

Coates is not new to the work. He has been concerned with homelessness for many years. And he is not politically naive. He knows that there are pitfalls; he meets them head-on and explains how we can overcome them.

Coates is also a realist in that he knows there will always be at least one homeless person in America. But he yearns for the day when that person is so unique that people on the street stop to offer help, and come away feeling good about themselves and their country.

Three years after that presidential motorcade swept unknowing past those homeless people at City Hall, a new president honored Seattle as the U.S. city that has done the most to end homelessness through good ideas carried out by good people.

Those good ideas and others are in this book. The good people are out there in America. If you think it is time to act, here's how.

—Charles Royer
Director, Institute of Politics,
Kennedy School of Government,
and former Mayor of Seattle

Acknowledgments

If people did not wish American homelessness to be seen clearly and handled responsibly, this book never could have been written. Hundreds of people helped, freely giving of their time, thoughts, work and substance, because they believed that the story needed telling, because they wanted to help get the word out that, counter to chic myth systems in vogue with some, solutions to various aspects of homelessness *do* exist. Heroic people are working in thousands of practical efforts, doing their level best to handle this scandalous American condition. They are working, at the very least, to deliver some kindness and contact, some obvious risking-of-oneself for the American human beings who are homeless. And for the health of our cities, our neighborhoods, and of our *children's minds*!

But I digress. And my friends are correct. I do wax "too preachy" about this on occasion (Jeremiah's friends said that to him, did they not?). Here I am acknowledging and expressing my deepest gratitude to those many, many people who participated in the creation of this book. Many are closest friends; some are near-strangers who passed on information, insight, or an important word of encouragement.

Mimi Coates has steadfastly supported the effort from start to finish. Five years ago, she said to me, "Bob, if you don't finish this book you'll never forgive yourself. I'll handle the kids every Saturday morning and you go to the law library and work on it." I did, she did, and she kept just helping, always supporting. It would not have happened without her. Thank you, dear lady.

Our wonderful children, Whitney, who is eight, and Cameron, seven, have been terrific. They have lived with this book all their lives. They have been interested; they've understood my absences, and sometimes they'd spend afternoons at the law library or law school while their dad sat around discussing, editing, writing. They visited food lines and shelters, served dinners, lunches, and breakfasts to stubbly, grateful people, people happy to have a smiling kid bring up a plate of food, look into their eyes, say "hello" and "you're welcome" and treat them like people who mattered. These champions have been troupers; and they deserve to have their dad back.

My mother and father, H Crawford, Jr., and Genevieve T. Coates, were, as always, enormously supportive. I'll not forget Dad sitting and talking over this book's issues. He died at age eighty-three, two days after Christmas, 1989. Born a Philadelphia gentleman and great-grandson of a founder of the Republican Party, Dad was an invalid the last two years of his life, having suffered a broken hip. But he nevertheless looked up many things for me, even finding a two-hundred-year-old account of Elizabethan policies toward England's post–Industrial Revolution homeless (which were considered quite progressive, since, for the first time in Europe, they embodied a distinction between able-bodied poor, who went to working "poor houses," and the disabled poor). "Good King Wenceslas" was Padre's favorite carol, and, though he was very weak on Christmas Day before he died, he managed to sing out its strident verses joyfully, ending: "They who yet may bless the poor, shall themselves find blessing!"

My mother, a brave, clear-eyed soul whose great-grandfather and his brothers drove a head of horses from Missouri to Colorado in 1842, was born on a ranch on the western flank of the Colorado Rockies, near Silverton. Her family raised horses and her mother's maiden name was Taft, coming from the president's family. The past year, particularly, over meals, she helpfully read chapters. Her view of the poor is rural and concrete, and as a former teacher she instinctively looks for crisp prose, behavior to correct, strengths on which to build, and humor.

Three close friends have heroically worked with me through this effort almost from its inception. Rebecca Heldt and Mark Regalbuti were bright, serious law students five years ago when I first met them. They volunteered to assist. Each then took on project after project, in libraries and out, with seemingly endless devotion. They want to see American homelessness handled. They are both, now, well-seasoned attorneys, and Rebecca also teaches law at Western State School of Law. Their lives' service has only begun.

The central, utterly indispensable man helping in this work has been my close pal, Charles R. Dyer, director of San Diego County's law library system and the main local editor of this work. Night after night, month after month, for much of three years, Charley and I have had much fun laboring together on this, usually at the library. One Saturday, close to "manuscript day," we had four word processors at work simultaneously, in different parts of the city, as Charley and I worked with a law clerk. Charley's sheer willingness to work has been astonishing. And, like me, he loves the back-and-forth, the debate over ideas, the avenues to follow up. He also loves (how lovely!) exactitude, so he was wonderful, vigilantly overseeing the final editing.

Charley believes libraries ought to be useful, that the law must be made easily accessible to all in order for a democracy to function. He is strikingly resourceful and organized in this pursuit. He also wants to see our legal systems remain (and be seen as) problem-solving. These are among Charley's altruistic motives for laboring on this book. He has also been helping a friend. Thank you, dear Charley.

Some especially close friends' lives are interwoven with mine and they have always been ready to debate a point, help look up something, respond to an idea, or go hike a beach or leap into a pool to help keep the author on track. Some of these, like Dan Hartl, Cathy Coates and Berneal Cole, sometimes watched Whitney and Cameron, or helped on personal projects, while I wrote. These friends include former law partners Jim Miller, Mike Kaplan, Matt Lees, and Mahmoud Abouzeid, Jr. (and Connie, Joy, Shiela, and Margaret), and Chuck Buck, Larry Beyersdorf, Nancy Carol Carter, Marge Cray, Bill Elliott, Tom Emery, Rodger Farr, Donald Fredkin, and his wife Martha, who, a few decades ago, was the first credible person to encourage me to write, Mary Ann Froley, Hasan and Jan Gumrukcu, Jack Hession, Ken Jones, M. Larry and Shalea Lawrence, Walt and Kit Ladwig, Tom and Ellen Lambert, Bishop George D. McKinney, Jim and Helen Mellos, Bert Monroe, Miller and Kathi Nickel, Suzanne Pertle, Don and Catalina Reeves, Ray Scaramella, Hedy St. John, Frederick Sauls, Dick Shanor, and Richard and Catherine Shouse. Camping and mining partners Don Albright and Ken, Don, and Herb Cilch, with Mark Shrader, put up with my writing by flashlight around campfires.

For general research duties, Anne Schupack and Jim Mellos III were always cheerfully available. And my own extra-competent court staff, Joan Cooper and Marshall Joe Elliott, helped smooth every working assignment. Four good friends, my presiding judges from 1983 to the present, encouraged me and have supported this effort. My profound thanks to Joe O. Littlejohn, Frederick L. Link, Ron Domnitz, and E. Mac Amos.

My agents Linda Chester and Elizabeth Zongker of La Jolla have been wonderful. Believing in the book from the first and never wavering, they "found" the right publisher, Prometheus Books, and steered me to the late S. Arthur "Red" Dembner, a former president of Newsweek Books. Red, in turn, aimed us at an important $100,000 grant, which we secured fast. Elizabeth and Linda injected civilization and professionalism into every stage of the process, and we have become fast friends. Thanks also to Alison Da Rosa of the *San Diego Tribune*, who introduced me to them. Barbara Burke of Burke Secretarial Services cheerily typed draft after draft, often at unbelievable hours, and we were aided by two fine editor/managers, Marybeth Mellin and Laurie Fox, whose indispensable help came in the final months.

We did our research at the downtown main library of the San Diego County Law Library and at the Western State School of Law Library (where I held Saturday morning law clerk meetings for several years). The staffs of these two facilities were ever-helpful. Thanks to them all!

Endless interviews over breakfast and lunch took place at area restaurants, including China Camp, City Deli, the Del Coronado Hotel, El Fandango, Hob Nob Hill, the Broken Yolk, and the San Diego Federal Courthouse Cafeteria.

I wish to offer my sincere appreciation for the efforts of the staff and donors of the San Diego Community Foundation, which contributed $100,000 to help assure speedy production of this book and its delivery, as gifts, to some nine thousand of our nation's leaders. In particular, I wish to thank Helen Munroe and Jeffrey Hale of its professional staff. I also wish to thank the San Diego County Law Library Justice Foundation and its trustees, particularly its chair, Murry Luftig, for providing legal vehicles for this effort.

I cannot bestow enough praise on my publisher, Prometheus Books, and particularly Bob Basil, Lorraine Baranski, Mike Powers, Deborah Thiel, Dan Wasinger, Paul Kurtz, and particularly my final text editor, Reg Gilbert, who streamlined the work and clarified ideas.

Others who helped include:

1. *Judges and Lawyers*: Judge Rafael A. Arreola, Gary L. Blasi, Mark Brown, Justice Edward T. Butler, Brian Cochran, Michael H. Crosby, Karen Di Donna, Judge Norbert Ehrenfreund, Judge Richard Haden, Robert Hayes, J.W. Herrott, David B. Himelstein, Judge Napoleon A. Jones, Conrad Joyner, Judge Manual Kugler (retired), Marianne Lachman, Judge Lillian Lim, Judge Bill Mallin of San Francisco, Judge Robert P. McDonald, Judge James Milliken, Nancy Mintie, Justice Stanley Mosk, James Preis, Helen Rowe, Michael C. Spata, Judge Larry Stirling, Russell D. Ward, J. Carlton Wentz, and Vincent E. Whelan.

2. *Professors*: Baylor Brooks, Karla Castetter, Nancy Crabtree, Michael Dessent, Phil Gay, Tom Golden, Dipak Gupta, Rebecca Heldt, Issa J.J. Khalil, H. Richard Lamb, Judith Lui, David Neptune, Martin Ridge, Paul D. Saltman, Allen Snyder, Aubrey Wendling, Richard J. "Corky" Wharton, and Deans Hadley Batchelder of the Western State University School of Law, Dean Michael Dessent of the California Western School of Law, Dean Sheldon Krantz of the University of San Diego School of Law, Ross Lipsker, dean emeritus of the Western State University School of Law, and Dean Howard Orenstein of the National University School of Law.

3. *Government Officials*: David Alsbrook, Evan Becker, Aretha Crowell, John Dunchak, Norman Hickey, Patrick Kruer, Janay Kruger, David McWhirter, Henry Tarke, and Jan Lee Wong.

4. *Legislators*: U.S. Senator Alan Cranston, U.S. Congressmen Jim Bates and Henry Waxman, California State Senators John Garamendi and Wadie P. Deddeh, and California State Assemblymen Peter Chacon and Phillip Isenberg.

5. *Press*: Alan Abrahamson, *Los Angeles Times*, San Diego edition, Joe Cantlupe, *San Diego Union*, Alison Da Rosa, *San Diego Tribune*, Marty Emerald, KGTV, Tom Gatley, *Los Angeles Times*, John Gilmore, *San Diego Tribune*, Roger Hedgecock, KSDO Radio, Joe Holly, *San Diego Tribune*, Woody Lockwood, *San Diego Daily Transcript*, Neil Morgan, *San Diego Tribune*, and Harry Reasoner, CBS's "60 Minutes."

6. *Fellow Rotarians*: Pam Addison, Russell Boucher, Terry and Brian Caster, Samir Faragallah, Nels Fuller, George Carter Jessop, Ken Jones, Frank Kleber, David Lowenstein, Joseph Lozano, Tom MacDowell, and Larry and Mike Mascari.

7. *Other Business People*: Renis Baak, Howard Gong, Ernest Hahn, Troy Hardin, Stanley Hartman, Fielder Lutes, Scott Lynch, Walter Moore, Chris Mortenson, Allen Perry, Raymond Scaramella, Lee Stein, John Tucker, and Walter Turner.

8. *Institutions*: Alpha Project for the Homeless, Catholic Charities, Episcopal Community Services, God's Extended Hand Mission, Lutheran Social Services, METRO, Presbyterian Crisis Center, Salvation Army, San Diego Central City Development Corporation, Office of the San Diego City Manager, San Diego Office of the Mayor, San Diego Public Library, the Office of the San Diego County Chief Administrative Officer, the Office of the County Counsel, the San Diego Department of Health Services, St. Vincent de Paul/Joan Kroc Center for the Homeless, Youth and Community Services, Inc., YMCA of San Diego County, and the following law libraries: the California Western University School of Law Library, the National University School of Law Library, and the University of San Diego School of Law Library (and one other library: the Baseball Hall of Fame Library, located in Cooperstown, New York). Of course, the many national and local agencies and information sources regarding the homeless aided in every way they could. Many of their names will appear in their stories in this book.

Friends who wielded "laboring oars" in research on particular chapters were:

Chapter 2. Planning Help
David Allsbrook, John Fowler, Larry Johnson, and Dick Shanor.

Chapter 3. The Mayor's Task Force in the Streets
Douglas Regin, Dick Shanor, and Don Reeves.

Chapter 4. An Easy Early Step: Public Drunks
Claude Gray, Larry Wharton, and Barbara Wolfinbarger.

Chapter 5. Women and Children
Jeannie Dorsey, Joan Morton, and Cathy Spearnack. Also assisting were Sasha Gershen, Christine Jiordano, Linda Lutz, Joan Morton, Martha Ranson, and Dick Shanor.

Chapter 6. The Elderly Homeless
Joe Plount, whom I met in a dinner line at the Rescue Mission, and Chris Wagner.

Chapter 7. Homeless Veterans
Robert Van Keuren, Bill Mahedy, Shad Meshad, and John Nachison.

Chapter 8. Runaway and Throwaway Kids
Marybeth Mellin, Linda Newell, and Liz Shearer.

Chapter 9. Cycling Able-Bodied Homeless into Jobs
Steve Baker, Bruce Harris, Rev. Jonathan Hunter, Patricia Leslie, and Stan Shroeder.

Chapter 10. Model Homeless Shelters
Glen Allison, Mary Case, Joe Carroll, Phil Gay, Jonathan Hunter, Maria Valentine, Frank Landerville, and Anne Schupack.

Chapter 11. Affordable Housing
Janay Kruger. Also assisting were Judge Rafael Arreola, Mark Brown, Justin Casady, Brian Caster, Joan Dahlin, Jeffrey Hale, Robert Hayes, J.W. Herrott, Patrick Kruer, Ross Lipsker, Chris Mortenson, Timothy O'Connell, James Rouse, Karen Souza, and Peter Werwath.

Chapter 12. The Homeless Mentally Ill
Roger Farr and Rebecca Heldt. Also assisting were Beth Biddle, John Brophy, Margaret L. Coates, Robert Crossen, Aretha Crowell, Mark DeModena, H. Richard Lamb, Irene S. Levine, Adelle Lynch, Reid Malloy, Allen Moltzen, Cheryl Noncarrow, Tom Rodgers, Henry Tarke, Jacqueline Walus-Wiegle, Michael Weisman, and Jeffrey Wynn.

Chapter 13. Involuntary Treatment?
Rebecca Heldt. Also assisting were Conrad Joyner, David McWhirter, Reid Malloy, Mark Regalbuti, and Jan Lee Wong.

Chapter 14. Myths, Mental Barriers, and Bad Ideas
Ed Cray, Frank Landerville, and Nancy Mintie. Also assisting was Anne Shupack.

Chapter 16. Public Restrooms (A NIMBY Study)
Jon Dunchak and John Fowler.

Chapter 19. Ethics
Gregory Fletcher.

Chapter 20. Mobilizing Religious Congregations and Religious People
Jonathan Hunter, Jack Linquist, Bishop George D. McKinney, Tom Owen-Towle, Doug Regan, Dick Shanor, and Vincent E. Whelan.

Chapter 21. Economics . . .
Rebecca Heldt.

Chapter 22. "How Can I Help?"
Sarah Luth and Pamela Slick.

Appendices

Legal Rights of Homeless Americans
Rebecca Heldt and Mark Regalbuti.

Additional individuals whose assistance was indispensable included Margaret Avery, Dominick Addario, James Battenfield, Jimmie Carter, Irma Castro, Coleman Coates, Dennis C. Coates, Mary Colacicco, Marge Cray, Kent B. Dau, Terence De Guelder, Beverly Di Gregorio, Tom Heitz, Joe Dolphin, Donald F. Duff, Raymonda Duvall, Tom Emery, Tom Fat, Mary Ann Froley, Mike Hart, Nita Jenné, Michael Kaye, Jack Lindquist, Vicky Markey, Mewail Mebrahtu, Dot Migdal, James Mulvaney, Cheryl Noncarrow, Bert Monroe, Elaine Peabody, Mary Phillips, Judith Pruett, Barbara and William Reedhead, Annette Rogers, Hester Rogers, Charles T. Royer, Sharon Sage, Chuck Smith, Dottie Stanislaw, Melissa Steinberg, Lillis Stephens, James Stouder, Kay Stovall, Leonard Swanson, Helen Teisher, Loli Villaoicencio, Eduardo B. White, and Barbara Wolfinbarger.

Special thanks are due to my close friends Larry and Shalea Lawrence, who are hosting a lavish author's party at their historic Hotel del Coronado, and to another close friend, "Sister Winnie" Smith, and all of her co-workers at the sixty-four-year-old God's Extended Hand Mission. Sister Winnies' equally generous and remarkable "street party" (for this book) will precede Larry and Shalea's soirée, aiming at a wide participation, including many homeless individuals.

Finally, I must thank the hundreds of homeless Americans whom it has been my privilege to meet and, sometimes, get to know. I'll name only three. They are friends and they told me it is all right to let them represent all homeless Americans here: Sylvester "Sly" Thomas, Joe Plount, and Richard Spurgeon, whose books of poetry, written on the streets, are an inspiration.

This book is entirely my own, and for all the inevitable errors of fact and judgment I take responsibility and heartily apologize, and for every helpful idea, I confess that it was surely given to me by somebody else.

Introduction

Our doubts are traitors,
And make us lose the good we oft might win
By fearing the attempt.
—Shakespeare, *Measure for Measure*

They stumble past us on every downtown American street, raving, mumbling, or silent. They are begging or earnestly seeking work. They may be in rags, or wearing war medals, or both.

They are America's homeless people, at least a million of them, perhaps three million of them, a growing tide of humanity composed of most anybody. "There but for the grace of God go I," each of us may think, *if* we let ourselves think.

They scare us. They are, say the Jungians, the "shadow," the darker, harsher side of life and of humanity. The great sociologist Max Weber replies that this interpretation is simply an example of the Western world's profound evil, stemming from its ignorance, from its insistence on not being shown tragedy, pain, illness, death. What a culture resists seeing is what it gets shoved before its eyes. So these ghostly homeless have come to haunt us.

Their numbers are expanding, but the problems they pose are solvable—if we can bear to look long enough to see the reality of the homeless, if we can bestir ourselves long enough to implement the solutions already tested throughout this country, if we can muster the courage to act in America's pragmatic, frontier tradition of staring harsh realities calmly in the face. We will do it if we really want to teach our children that they belong to a competent species. This book is about *solutions* available to all great American cities for use in resolving the dilemma each faces *vis-à-vis* America's new homeless.

For pragmatic Americans, the existence of a problem implies the existence of a solution, or, possibly, twenty solutions. We learned this as children. This is also what developmental psychologists call the "single dominant belief of mentally healthy, intelligent children." It is also a central belief of engineers, scientists, managers of all types, and people of the outdoors.

It is striking, however, that with respect to homelessness this belief is either absent or under assault. Some have even treated certain homeless problem-solving as dangerous, since it could deflect efforts from doing the "possible," and even (usually more subconsciously) preserving the need for social service jobs.

To one trained in engineering, science, management, the outdoors, and the law (with an emphasis on mental disabilities), these views became "curiouser and curiouser." For a while, I viewed them simply as enemies. I still do, but I also appreciate that the only effective weapons against them are to

1. Examine them publicly—"surface" them—to enable people to see their attitudes as based in prejudice, in politics, in conditioning, in fear and,
2. Disprove their contentions by presenting examples of people who have produced solutions.

Early 1983 was a time when my life contained a heady and joy-filled mix of satisfactions—a new family, a bright, marvelous wife energetically pursuing law studies, the myriad challenges of my recent judgeship, chances at community leadership in arenas in which I had always been interested. Into this exciting, upbeat scene fell a dull, odoriferous and mysterious package: the homeless.

Without warning, I found myself assigned to a court where my duties included sentencing hundreds of these puzzling, stark, astonishing human beings. My job was straightforward. Follow the law and be ethical. The law required that misdemeanants, once found guilty, be placed on probation, with a judge-devised plan individually tailored to prevent the defendant's return to court. I had to succeed.

The ethical canons allow no slack. Lord Coke expressed it long ago: "A court must never engage in a vain act." No problem. I'll just *succeed* with each . . . but how?

The idea for a book that would present evolving solutions to homelessness came to me in May 1983. I had decided somebody ought to do something about the problem of homelessness. I called a meeting of a group of leaders of social service agencies and was, frankly, nonplussed at the enthusiastic response to my suggestion that we plan a fact-studded, solutions-oriented, citywide convocation, perhaps involving academe, some nine or ten months thence to allow for good preparation. At this, a chubby, earnest man in the front row spoke. "No," he said. "We need this meeting within weeks! We can get it organized, even bringing in people from good programs in Los Angeles, Denver, San Francisco. I think it could be done six weeks from now!"

"Who would organize it?" I asked.

"I will," he replied.

Thus I met a man who was to become a mentor and close friend, great-hearted Rev. Dick Shanor, director of the Methodist Social Service Agency (METRO) and the organizing president, four years before, of an umbrella group of agencies, the Downtown Coordinating Council, which was already dealing with the increasing populations of "street people."

Dick was true to his word and the "Convocation on the Homeless: Our Opportunity" was a success. At it we asked the mayor to establish a task force. He did, and I had a tiger by the tail. It was soon clear to me that somebody in America ought to chronicle "the best solutions" to the problems of the homeless as they appeared around the country. Perhaps consensus could build around some of them. Perhaps a quilt of solutions could be sewn together, one for each city in America, each with solutions born of local experience, but all supplemented by various of the solutions found to work well somewhere else in America. The key also may not always be so much in the good programs themselves, but rather in the processes by which they have been put in place, often against some odds.

Possibly the nation could become inspired, and come to view our visitation by the ghostly homeless as a profound, God-given opportunity for America to do something brilliant. Maybe we would solve the problem of the homeless like a community barnraising. Possibly we would see it as a chance to rise to the occasion, as Americans always have before, thrilling our children, and letting them know in the marrow of their bones that they belong to a competent race, and that life is for living, in curiosity and in service to one another.

This book, therefore, aims to contain the best solution for the discrete pieces of the homeless dilemma. They are not secrets. They simply need to be made widely known, and widely known in one central reference, so people will be able to see that nearly the whole of the phenomenon of homelessness can be responsibly and effectively handled.

National polls show a near-irresistible demand, today, for solution to this blight on our national character.

The existence of homeless populations presents, primarily, a *moral issue* to the country. Leaders must present it this way, and use the arsenal of moral perceptions that are part of our national heritage to broaden the team necessary to create and implement solutions.

This book had to be written in everyday English as much as was possible. Thus, much of it became a translation from the specialized languages—of medicine, social work, religion, law. The book also had to have some limits, and I wish to apologize for its failure to cover some American groups who surely are "homeless," but whom we have come to exclude from consideration under that term. Illegal aliens, for instance, especially migrant farm workers, constitute a problem so significant as to demand its own treatment.

The major solutions are here: job programs that work, model shelter systems that really cycle people off the streets, and the local means to solve the low-income housing crisis and the equally horrendous crisis in mental health treatment, as well as specialized ways to deal responsibly with subgroups of homeless Americans.

This book aims at empowering *you*, the reader, encouraging you to get intelligently involved in one of the great adventures available to our generation: the solving of America's homeless dilemma.

ROBERT C. COATES, Judge
San Diego Municpal Court
September 5, 1990

I
Planning

1

The New Homeless

Christ appears to us in the most appalling disguises.

—Mother Theresa

Homeless people in America today differ greatly from the country's "down and out" populations of the past. Some facts:

- At the height of the Great Depression the destitute made up a third of the nation's workforce. Most homeless adults were employable then. In contrast, only a sixth of today's homeless are employable by "normal" standards (excluding sheltered workshops and the like), with possibly another sixth employable "soon" (with secure shelter and some literacy and job skills courses).
- Single women with children have never before been on the streets in such large numbers.
- Severely mentally ill people have never before been permitted to roam the nation's streets unassisted, bringing their private (treatable) hells out in the open to haunt us and our cities.
- Throughout the nation's history great waves of often-destitute immigrants have entered the country, particularly after the Civil War and in the first decade of this century. Traditionally, however, the frontier absorbed many of these people. Their integration into the American mainstream was also eased by the assistance of humane Americans of longer standing. President Theodore Roosevelt's father is credited with setting up an adoption system for homeless, immigrant children which, in time, placed some one hundred thousand of them in family homes on the frontier. New York's population of homeless children in 1888 was estimated at a number identical to the 1988 figure: twenty thousand.
- Rescue missions today report the average age of their visitors to be twenty-six. Just twenty-five years ago the average age was fifty-seven.

We are said to live in an information age, yet a number of social problems are strikingly understudied. Local researchers have plunged in to study the homeless, but the accuracy of their conclusions are often clouded by the financial limitations of their efforts. America still lacks a definitive study, one that is national in scope.

So how many homeless are there? Absent definitive studies, we might turn to the national census. Unfortunately, while it is to be commended for a well-intended if not terribly comprehensive effort, the census has not delivered us a reliable count of the homeless. Thus, we are left with estimates. Frankly, I trust those made by people who live where "the rubber meets the road" (mayors, city managers, United Way organizers, homeless advocates) rather more than the bright theorists tucked away in ivory towers. In 1987, the theorists at the Department of Housing and Urban Development and at the Office of Management and Budget estimated America's homeless population at 250,000. Simultaneously, the National Coalition on the Homeless was reporting three million American homeless.

I accept the latter figure as the most informed, best-educated guess available of the number of total Americans who experience homelessness in a given year. There is general agreement that a little more than a third of that total (more than a million!) are homeless at any particular moment.

This figure is roughly consistent with fairly definitive numbers one gets using the estimates of individual cities and projecting nationwide. In April 1990, for example, San Diego estimated its homeless at about seven thousand at any given moment; its shelter managers said the number was higher, perhaps up to ten thousand. San Diego's population is roughly 0.5 percent that of the nation, so the national projection from San Diego's figures would come to about two million. Playing with figures from other cities yields similar results. The conservative figure offered by the National Academy of Sciences is 750,000 homeless at any given moment. We also have further disquieting local figures. For example, the *Los Angeles Times* recently estimated that 45,000 people were sleeping in cars in Los Angeles on any given night.

What do we know about those who are homeless? Here are some rough, overlapping percentages of the homeless population:

1. Profoundly mentally ill		33%
2. Looking for work		33%
Half are job-ready, half need some help		
3. Women		15–20%
4. Substance abusers: Drugs, alcohol		33%
(Half overlap with mentally ill)		
5. Veterans (33% of the men)		25%
6. Teen runaways		10%

7. Hobos (healthy, preferring homelessness)	5%
8. "Young louts"	5%
9. Former convicts	10%
10. Elderly	6%
11. Developmentally delayed, borderline retarded	<5%
12. Illiterates, dyslexics	?

The estimates of homeless women are the most questionable of the figures, because homeless women are almost universally shy, uncommunicative, and fearful, that is, not very "countable." A determined, sensitive and in-depth ·count of the homeless is needed, but solutions cannot wait and existing data are useful for now.

Recent city-by-city studies by the National Institute of Mental Health yielded a number of insights. More than half the homeless have never married. Half have serious physical health problems and two-thirds have noticeable dental problems. Half are high school graduates, and one-third are receiving public income benefits (welfare, Supplemental Security Income (SSI), Social Security) but are still homeless. Only one-fourth of those who need glasses have them. The average age hovers between the mid-twenties and the mid-thirties.[1]

Why are we being visited by the homeless? "The poor ye have with you always," Jesus is often quoted as saying (out of context) by non-sympathizers. American cities have traditionally featured "Skid Rows," inner-city neighborhoods where a largely alcoholic population of rather elderly, mission-attending flotsam and jetsam of society was to be found. These manifestations of what Jefferson considered "the European evil" (the cities themselves!) stood as sort of living museums, testimonials to the wages of sin.

In the 1970s, subtle changes were taking place in the composition of groups found on American Skid Rows. By the end of the decade, the trickle of severely mentally ill had become a deluge. Perceptive social service, church, and mission managers began to form coordinating councils to share observations, create plans, and cooperate in meeting the changing needs of the homeless. It was premature to sound much of a clarion call, however, and certainly too early to get anybody to listen. It was the dawn of the selfish 1980s and Jesus' qualified observation was being blared as dogma. (So, relax.)

For half a century America had created a structure incoming president Ronald Reagan called a "safety net," but he vigorously dismantled it in his first term. Reagan's most vulnerable target, as it turned out, was federal support for building low-income housing.

By 1983 I found myself suddenly required to sentence hundreds of homeless people for trespassing-related offenses, like sleeping in parks and under church overhangs. The New American Homeless were upon us. They had fallen upon the nation's cities like winter's first snow, unexpectedly, silently. We rubbed our collective eyes. Our communities went through convulsions of rationalization as we struggled to think about these new ghosts haunting our consciences. We trudged through a sequence of predictable behaviors—denial, hostility (police and zoning measures), and, finally, in most locales, problem-solving.

> We've got to understand the present catastrophe of our cities, or we'll never be able to see the vibrant opportunities for greatness that lie before us.
> —James Rouse (founder of the Enterprise Foundation and developer of the "new town," Columbia, Maryland)

SUGGESTED READING

"The Urban Homeless: Estimating Composition and Size," Peter H. Rossi, Jean A. Fisher, James D. Wright, and Georgiana Willis, *Science*, vol. 235, March 13, 1987, pp. 1336–1341.

Down and Out in America: The Origins of Homelessness, Peter H. Rossi, University of Chicago Press, 1989.

Homelessness and Health, James D. Wright and Eleanor Weber, McGraw-Hill, 1987.

2

Planning Help

If we don't change our direction, we'll wind up where we're headed!
                                                    —Sachel Paige

In April 1990, the report of the Massachusetts Institute of Technology's Commission on Technology and Competitiveness listed as one of the causes of America's losses to Japan in manufacturing the fact that Japan devotes two-thirds of its design energies to manufacturing processes and one-third to the products themselves, while in the United States the figures are reversed.

There is an American tendency to eschew planning, a variety of hubris wherein we descendants of frontiersmen presume that we can, easily, quickly assess the reality of a situation and then, with equal speed and lack of error, know what to do. This is a refreshing feature in a John Wayne western but, alas, it is seldom a good strategy in today's complex, real world, particularly in situations that are maddeningly novel.

The purpose of this chapter is to examine the processes by which a city or community might assess its homeless situation, and how it might go about creating a blueprint for action that is something more than a gut response to somebody else's distress.

ESTABLISH LOCAL HISTORY

The first step is to gather a spectrum of local "grey heads" in the social services fields, and some observers and critics of these people, to create a local history of the delivery of social services, including evaluation of strengths, potential strengths, weaknesses, potential weaknesses, and recent mistakes. This usually-skipped-over phase is all-important, and is usually astonishingly educational. It can lay the groundwork for and make the difference between an excellent integrated and adult response to homelessness . . . and a (frankly, quite stupid) "more of the same" approach.

KNOW WHO YOUR HOMELESS ARE

Hire some "down and dirty" urban anthropology or other research team to do an assessment of the numbers of the homeless, divided into subgroups. An alternate, quicker source is "key informants" working in human service agencies. Most major cities have already taken this step, but the population components of the homeless continue to change, so data can never be too current. Comparison and synthesis of both kinds of estimates can be useful.

KNOW EXISTING PROCESSES FOR DEALING WITH THE HOMELESS

Assess present institutions dealing with the homeless, their missions, what they are doing and what they could do.

CREATE A PERSONAL BASE OF KNOWLEDGE ABOUT THE HOMELESS

All people recommending and/or making policy relative to the homeless need to personally meet and get to know the homeless and the various agencies dealing with them. They must personally be in food lines, eat at soup kitchens, stay in shelters, drop in on agencies. This is all-important. Leaders who find themselves suddenly carrying responsibility for dealing with homelessness need to approach the subject with humility. A distant approach is foredoomed to error.

CREATE A GROUP TO HAMMER OUT A PLAN

It should be composed of thirds—policymakers, business people and service providers. Plans recommended by such a group have the best chance of containing the three elements of success—political feasibility, financial support, and practical effectiveness. Particular attention needs to be given to including representatives of groups whose objective interests will be served by handling the homeless dilemma, but who, if not in on the planning throughout, might end up in opposition to whatever plan has been formulated. Healthy critics are a needed leaven.

CREATE A GROUP TO SELL THE PLAN

This second body needs to be composed of a majority of the most persuasive and committed members of the first group, plus some equally civic-minded "movers and shakers" whose explicit job will be to reach out to sources of greater power—foundations, the media, "big givers," national sources, business and industry—to recruit both assent and enthusiasm and the "clout" to put solutions in place. The group as a whole will explain the details of the plan to the public and simultaneously gracefully gain the needed okays from the leadership of the bureaucracies involved.

ESTABLISH INTERNAL CORRECTION MECHANISMS

While you are carrying out your plan new phenomena will doubtless come on the scene. The demographics of a locale's homeless may change, subtly or dramatically. State or federal legislation may become law, or foundation grants may become available. New leaders may appear at the top, bottom, or in the middle. Public opinion may shift, or particular institutions may decide to participate, or to drop out. Somebody may come up with a better idea!

CAST THE NET WIDELY FOR PLAYERS

The definition of "social service provider" is not written in stone, and it is inevitable that many people and groups who are delivering great and valuable human services may not be noticeable from a United Way–type vantage point. Groups like this might include non-mainline churches, new or very specialized non-profit organizations, business or labor associations, and service clubs.

PLAN FOR THE MENTALLY ILL HOMELESS

The mentally ill are often a great puzzlement for agency staffs, who, accordingly, need help dealing with them. Each community's city or county mental health staff members need to be enlisted as "ground floor" partners, as givers of technical counsel and mini-seminars to shelter directors, developers of mobile "response teams" capable of both outreach and crisis management, including handling threatened suicide cases and psychotic phenomena, and fosterers of grant-patching partnerships with local and state departments of mental health. Begin the reaching out and lobbying for greater resources (from foundations, state government) that will surely be needed.

DON'T LET THE SOLUTION
BECOME PART OF THE PROBLEM

Life is "fired at us point blank," and action generally cannot wait until science has all the answers. No homeless task force should allow itself to become an excuse for delay in taking obviously needed actions. In San Diego, because of a near-frenzy to appear to be "absolutely correct," the momentum that had begun slowed, and some initiatives (the jobs program, a homeless speakers' bureau, needed expansion of women's shelters) were halted for a time. In this period, from the San Diego public's point of view, not a peep was being heard about the city's attempts to reduce homelessness. Momentum means a lot. Keep it moving.

USE CRITICAL PATH ANALYSIS

In any complex business or governmental process, managers have for years used a technique called "critical path analysis." This is just a fancy term for plotting out, on paper, all of the steps that will be required to get from situation "A" to situation "B" (for example, from a vacant lot to a skyscraper).

This will of necessity require consideration of all the predictable (and many contingent) barriers, an assessment of costs, time lines, allotting of responsibility, key permits and governmental decisions, etc. The critical paths mapped for a recent Rocky Mountain mining project, for example, included steps to obtain 450 separate permits. This work can be complex—but it forces good planning.

Use of this and other tools from the arsenal of modern management are "musts" for those who would create realistic, adult, and salable city plans to address the several aspects of homelessness, on the scale needed. No homeless plan is worth doing if it is to be a mere gesture. To participate in such a plan would be immoral. What is called for is the *solving* of aspects of homelessness.

FUNDAMENTALS OF A PLAN

Actions to take inevitably include:

- Expanding and improving shelter systems and seeing that they serve all subpopulations.
- Getting churches directly involved. A church shelter program is a good project to start with.

- Linking jobs programs and case management to existing shelters.
- Getting mental health care actually delivered to the entire population of chronically, deeply mentally ill.
- Expanding the availability of low-income housing.
- Critical path analysis.

Make no little plans; they have no magic to stir men's blood.
                                              —Daniel H. Burnham

The moments in a building's life—conception, designing, construction, and its life as shelter—should each be aesthetic and rewarding. A building or a work of art should never be thought of as something on a pedestal; something precious. If it is not a part of a process of life, it is only a curiosity.
                —James Hubbell, *From the Earth Up,* by Otto B. Rigan

Planning is like housekeeping. Nobody notices it until you stop doing it.
                —Jim Goff (planning director, City of San Diego, 1978–88)

SUGGESTED READING

Learning to Plan and Planning to Learn, Donald N. Michael, Jossey-Bass Publisher, 1973.

Critical Paths: An Essay on the Social Context of Literary Criticism, Northrop Frye, Indiana University Press, 1971.

Thinking in Time: Uses of History for Decision Makers, Richard Neustadt and Richard May, Free Press, 1986.

"Homelessness: A General Information Packet," Homeless Information Exchange, February 1988.

"A Briefing Paper for Presidential Candidates: Homelessness in the United States: Background and Federal Response," National Coalition for the Homeless, May 1987.

"Homelessness: Additional Information on the Interagency Council on the Homeless," U.S. Government Accounting Office, Resource Community and Economic Development Division, September 1989.

"Comprehensive Planning to Address Homelessness: City Initiatives," Kris Zawisza, Homeless Information Exchange, 1987.

3

The Mayor's Task Force in the Streets

I think it is required of a man that he should share the passions of his time at the peril of being judged not to have lived.
—Oliver Wendell Holmes

I felt unease cloud the surface of my excitement. What the hell, we'd have fun at the very least. "It's my last chance to be a boy," Teddy Roosevelt said before the Amazon adventure that cost him his health.

My pal Joe wasn't ready. He hadn't even thought about it. He stood there in his golf pants and his dumb, amiable grin, looking to me for all the world like Prince Bolkonski's nephew in *War and Peace*, an innocent teen enthused about being slaughtered.

"Damn it, Joe, you're going to need to blend in and this won't do it," I said.

We were two of a dozen from the Mayor's Task Force on the Homeless off to join the homeless for a weekend. Joe had fitted the excursion into his schedule like another board meeting or Salvation Army strategy session. His supreme self-confidence got on my nerves and reassured me at the same time. He was a smart businessman and an athlete, used to being both physical and realistic. And ruthless. But how did he think he knew what we'd face? And why wasn't he ruthlessly ready?

I stood there in my studied costume. My eight days' stubble was not bad. Ancient, regrettable shoes covered two pairs of socks (nights are cold under the bridge). I wore old, holey corduroys. My good, blue Hussong's Cantina t-shirt underlay a rotting, stringy one with a bold, circled insignia, "Save Mono Lake." The whole outfit was filthy. My wife, Mimi, and I had spent the previous Sunday ripping out the front lawn of our half-acre suburban home, and these were the clothes I'd worn. An artistic touch was Scotch tape at the corner of my horn-rimmed glasses, which gave me a disoriented, financially embarrassed, Mr. Peepers aspect.

Joe was in this thing because he couldn't stand it, although he made less of it than me. Later, we were to reflect that this time on the streets changed each of our lives and, wondering, we noticed that we had kept active, hung in there through political pressure and criticism, sleepless nights and not knowing what to do, not quite all the way to Shakespeare's "edge of doom," but it sometimes felt like it.

It started in the judges' parking lot at dusk in the confusion of Joe and me so ridiculously dressed, stumbling through clusters of alarmed colleagues, only to be met on the sidewalk (to our great chagrin—our cover was blown!) by a gaggle of television interviewers. Somebody had found out and leaked our going to the *Los Angeles Times*. The paper had promised not to run the story until the next day, but it looked like they'd told others. So we'd be on everybody's evening news tonight.

Hell, God works in wondrous ways. Who am I to question the situations he throws me? It was all to be owned by the public: the planning, the blunders, the peculiar reasons we might give for this grandstand play (as some had called it), as well a any dénouement. We got photograped and interviewed and then we escaped, relieved, into the dark streets, across C Street, heading across town for the mission.

We went down Broadway, winding happily among shoppers and people just off work, those waiting for buses and dates meeting dates, the knots of shabby, grey-bearded types, knitted up in layers of clothing, mostly standing, occasionally shambling along, infrequently panhandling. Our eyes gravitated to these now, because we were with them. We noticed for the first time a remarkable freedom from self-consciousness attendant on being on the street. None of the straights would look at us directly.

South on Fifth. This city is beautiful at dusk! I guess all cities are, but the sunsets here are peculiarly lovely in the spring. And the swirl of human faces is what every city is all about, a love affair with a kaleidoscope, a moving feast of brothers and sisters, bursting with juxtaposed tragedy and joy, contact and indifference, ill health and vibrancy. This is the Washington Walt Whitman loved, the London that terrified Jefferson and other pastoral founders. We skipped down the street, devouring the milieu with the boldness of boys.

We passed the sidewalk café where I'd lunched today with a parole officer. A bum had sat down beside me and I'd turned around, rather charmed —and discovered Dan, one of the twelve who had (I had forgotten) started his time on the streets the day before. He looked grim and I chuckled at him. "What's the big deal?" I had thought. He complained of loneliness, that nobody would look at him. There's a yuppie aspect to Dan, a thoughtful property manager and Kiwanis president. He was too serious about all this, I thought, but I respected the dignity he brought to the issue and recalled Abe Lincoln's defenses against the horrors of his war, the telling of ridiculous jokes that had almost ruled him out as a speaker at Gettysburg.

We were under the spacious awning of a hardware store, and a slim, young, black man spoke before we'd noticed him. "Hi! I saw you!" he said. His piercing eyes combined intelligence, good will, and madness. He stepped up and shook my hand in a rather threatening manner.

"Hi," I said, smiling broadly, grasping his arm lovingly with my left hand, hoping he'd warm up.

"It's good, what you're doing. The Kingdom will be preached, and the least of these little ones shall be beside the Most High." He'd seen us on television. "You should have declared the Savior's Name. Do nothing but what you do in the Savior's Name!" Who could argue with this? I tried to ask about him, but he was into admonition. "Repent, and seek the Savior," he loudly declaimed, clapping me on the shoulder. His eyes were wild but I trusted his warmth. He did seem heaven-sent. Just then, a gentle patrolman glided between us, and Joe motioned me to come on. We would miss the dinner line at the mission.

It was darker and the street glittered with neon. Four blocks south was Market Street. The retail stores and restaurants of the upper Gaslamp Quarter were yielding to tattoo and skin shops, XXX-rated movie houses and seedy bars. The pedestrians were becoming more unseemly. We were approaching the Rescue Mission. A cop winked at us as we passed him at F Street. Insurance.

We saw a hooker on a bench with a one-year-old in her arms. Fast-talking night guys scuttled purposefully past, followed by clutches of sailors. The skin flicks were open for business. The huge underworld of illicit sex yawned temporarily at us, then was gone. Chinese merchants looked at each other seriously. The new Iranian owners of the corner drugstore were benefiting in burgeoning business for being friendly and well-stocked with an astonishing variety of sundries.

Market Street was, as always, serious. It is a broad street that ends at the harbor with the old police station and a pretty clutter of shops and restaurants, including the inveterate Sun Cafe, well known for both its excellent, inexpensive cuisine (full lunch specials are $2.10) and for its loud and fascinating Chinese proprietress, who handles the more affluent, Social Security–provided contingent of the street population with finesse.

Neon flashing on and off, demanding. Flashily dressed prostitutes (the first few, it was very early yet) strutted proudly, eyes bold, wares displayed as at a supermarket. Strip joints and pawn shops and skin flicks were lined up side by side and blared their versions of "Hey, meester! Show time!"

We glided through the crowd, all of it a show, all of it something to fall in love with, if you're Walt Whitman. One part of the brain categorizes and tucks away the hundreds of snapshots, another passes judgments, and yet another analyzes these judgments. "What was my agenda in coming out here, anyway? Oh yes, simply to see and to feel."

Another cop winked. They were quietly out in force, covering their rears if something went wrong. I did feel reassured, but also interfered with. Responsible society is startlingly meddlesome, and, through the penal code, it commands me to be the same.

We skipped off the curb, around some old-timers on canes, and across Market toward the line in front of the Rescue Mission. It may be full for the service. If you miss that, it's no dinner! There was a small mob scene in front of the mission, and a few local business people passed by, frowning at this flotsam that so harms their pocketbooks. The doorway was a crude filter, and some of the weirder specimens were being kept out, having committed some infraction or other in the recent past, thus gaining a listing on the "not okay" list. But they hung around anyway, maybe hoping some pal would exit with a sandwich, or just for socializing, accosting people, raving a bit. One pair tossed a frisbee. The lights were on and the sunset was almost complete. We shivered for the first time and slithered in unobtrusively as our minds kept up their continual snap, snap, snap, gathering pictures, snippets of emotion, the makings of love.

Inside sat three hundred nearly silent men. They were shocking: gaunt, tired, unhealthy as a group (with strapping exceptions sitting about), solemn. What did men look like after Bull Run? Were none as hopeless, none as addled as some of these looked? We walked forward toward two of the few remaining seats, and I picked the craziest-looking young man to sit next to. I sat quietly, watching (wishing for the Tom Mix look-behind-you ring I once owned). I leaned over confidentially to the young fellow and whispered something ("Where you from?" I think). He stared ahead without a blink. A bit later, I tried again. Again I got no rise from him. Was he catatonic? Distrustful? If the latter, he was a bright and able actor. I met a dozen like him, at least, that weekend—they'd be hard to reach with any program (or poll, for that matter). Yet he was there, at a "service provider." Praise God.

Suddenly, a disconcerted group from one of the supporting Baptist churches entered the room and began preparing for the service. I guess this happens every night, and, most likely, every night, one or more of them gasp as they confront the battle-weary crowd. Is this America? San Diego? God's world? Is it really their fault they're like this? Sin and its wages are terrible. Thanks be to God I've not sinned *that* much!

The song books were passed out, and the practiced evangelist cheerfully began with that wonderful, winsome charm Baptists carry with them, not knowing, yet showing their moving, rural, democratic heritage. Songs were sung without any enthusiasm, yet some of the men were visibly moved. (Where are the women?) Docilely, we all rose, row by row, after the sermon (not memorable, yet sweet, on forgiveness), and headed left into the dining hall.

The place was built for basics. The staff was cheerful, inured to the stench and the pain. Most were on the street once, too. The guys were polite. Eating was the thing, and there was plenty. Stew, bread, milk, salad, huge chunks of white cake (I suspected they were showing off for us, but maybe not). Grace was said and we struck up conversations. We were at a remarkably "together" table and the talk was of jobs, interspersed with jokes. Strapping, bearded Little John, across from me, shyly boomed out fragments of his story: Seattle, divorce, a job prospect tomorrow. He felt great, had a roof tonight, likely a job, and a big, fine dinner. Things were looking up! Others were lost in thought.

We bussed our trays and went out into the black night. No sooner did we swing right and have a chance to mentally gasp at our aloneness and the prospect of a night's adventure than a figure fell in beside us and whispered, "Judge Coates? I'm from the Transient Center. They thought you'd like a guided tour."

Well, why not? He was a resourceful-looking chap, almost six feet tall, healthy as a rail-splitter, with black hair, Levis, sneakers, almost the sort you'd like your daughter to date. He started a discrete patter, quickly telling his story and how he'd made it off the street. It had been peculiarly tough working *and* eating. The first two weeks he'd landed a job cooking at Bob's Big Boy. He didn't get a paycheck for two weeks and couldn't stand in lines to eat because he was working. So, absent friends who'd smuggled some food to him, he'd have gone without food for those first two weeks, to say nothing of the companion problems of where to stay, how to remain presentable, keeping the spirit alive. On Broadway, we startled a television camera crew lurking in a doorway, trying to get footage of us. We ignored them, strode on, and quickly lost them in the darkness.

"This is a good bar when you don't have much money," Ted said, and we headed in. It was early and there were only a dozen people scattered around a surprisingly large, Irish-style place. Pool tables stood silent and we took a back booth, ordered a pitcher and talked. It didn't seem very on-target to me, but if the beer would loosen Ted up a bit, why not? He wove the web of the street dilemma: work versus food, five days limit at the mission and back to the canyons, couples splitting up to get benefits (especially shelter), drugs and alcohol, violence, and the "weirdos" to be politely ignored.

"They're starting to ticket people for anything and everything. I guess the heat's on, but I don't know why."

We told him of the $250 million recently committed to redevelop San Diego's downtown, the sort of investment a city would do well to cunningly protect. How cunning is it to throw a few courteous and constitutionally aware police at the street population while allowing the willy-nilly destruction of half the city's low-income housing without providing replacements and permitting the county mental health department to systematically exclude the thousands of mentally ill homeless—to name but two examples of present blindness.

We chatted until the pitcher was empty, and, thus fortified, hied out to the streets again. Where were the homeless after dinner? We came up blank on that one, and Ted wasn't much help either. I was not eager to check out the bridge abutments in the dark, and the police had essentially issued a disclaimer of responsibility for our safety if any of us ventured there at night. We later learned that one of our dozen, Troy Hardin, had slept there, but he was too tough to count as a normal person.

We headed south again. Ted tugged us toward another bar, the Tiki Club. It looked misplaced. Located on a dark, deserted street lined with wrecking yards, it stood out like a lantern in a Somerset Maugham short story. Inside the door sat "Red," sloshing one down. Red had his motor-cycle helmet on the bar and he sat alone, peering straight ahead through dark, dark glasses. He spoke not a word, but after I'd sat next to him for awhile, he shifted his bulk and silently poured my glass full from his pitcher. I glanced over, but he was staring dourly straight ahead. My "Thanks, pal" went unanswered.

Thoughts of our mission circled in my mind. Each of the twelve of us on the Mayor's Task Force on the Homeless had our own agenda, both in general and in coming out this weekend. We all wanted to combine "making a statement" with contributing to the creation of a truly historic report on the city's homeless. Staffless (except for a fine fellow assigned by United Way, Larry Johnson) and powerless (goodness, how subpoena power would have helped!), the task force had proceeded at a painfully tedious pace, on its structured time line, using its expert models, utterly serene in its bureau-cratic ignorance.

We had become frustrated. The phenomenon of homelessness deserved the dignity of a close look. Those in power, on social service agency com-mittees, those elected to solve our problems, or sitting behind paper-laden county desks, were repulsive to us, quite willing, it seemed, to make life-and-death decisions about the homeless on the basis of almost no data and with absolutely no contact with those they purported to be helping. To act with power in utter ignorance is one definition of tyranny. It was the great conservative Edmund Burke's fundamental complaint. It was ours.

We left the Tiki Club, looked up and down Market Street, alternately reassured by the sweet peace of nobody being there, and on alert, since this far-southern stretch was known for cruising predators. We walked west, headed up a less-exciting Fifth Avenue, then decided to find our flophouse and turn in.

Our host for the night, Stan Adams, was a not-so-ordinary recovering alcoholic. Both his arms and one of his legs are crippled, but he gets around quite well. He had fallen off the curb and under a car while drunk, ten years before. He tells the story of Judge Buttermore threatening a long term in jail for repeated public drunkenness, then offering probation with a couple of days in jail plus biweekly Alcoholics Anonymous meetings. Stan had a constitutional aversion to jail, so he opted for AA and has been sober ever since. His cheer is infectious, and you can tell he has a deep, insoluble loneliness that makes him really need to be with you. He's an interesting specimen, running a flophouse for alcoholics like himself, by his wits and on a shoestring.

He took us into his disheveled office, talking up a storm, enjoying our company, and showing off. He ran through the Lysol and blankets and his troubles with the Zoning Administration. His hole-in-the-wall storefront masks a single room, eighteen feet wide and very deep, packed with bunk beds built four high. That night they were to contain Stan, Joe and me, and twenty-eight other men. Stan careened along his (wink, wink) ultra-wise methods. Items:

"Lots of these guys can't read. I send 'em over to Project Jove, where there's a three-week reading course. Then they can at least read a bus schedule or fill out a job application." Makes sense, when one remembers that many on the streets suffer dyslexia and other learning disorders. In every arena, there are great initial answers—but they may only apply to certain subsegments of the homeless. The answers may be harder and more expensive for the others. Triage. Where are the battlefield geniuses applying the triage method? Stan is one, from the school of hard knocks.

"Guys here need little goals. They need to set them, and meet them. You match a guy here with some great big, enthusiastic goal and he'll fall flat on his face—and not feel like trying again. So I get 'em sold on little dreams, dreams a guy can handle today. We'll find another dream tomorrow, and sort of work upwards, follow me? Like getting I.D. That's a manageable dream. Maybe after enough of these successful days, a guy is ready for a reach back to his family. But we've got to build him back, step by step, little victory by little victory. Smells pretty good in here, doesn't it?"

Actually, the smell was quite tolerable.

"I can run a place like this self-supporting on general relief, vets benefits or whatever, but I need some help with the authorities. They treat you like you're some kind of scum. They don't think I'm helping with *their* problem. But it sure is their problem! I could handle maybe a fourth of it for them if I got some support. It makes sense economically, but they're too into bureaucracy."

I had first-hand knowledge of that phenomenon.

"Those volunteer ladies at Christian Community Services are so beautiful. These guys build up venom with the giant, frustrating runaround they get, whether it's welfare, the Veterans' Administration, the Division of Motor Vehicles, the employment offices, whatever. A few days of that and anybody'd be a raving, slobbering maniac. So I have 'em take a day off, go see those ladies. The ladies are nice! They just draw the venom out. And they give guys some listening, some mothering! It's really important. So you tell 'em thanks a lot."

Pretty soon we tired. We figured maybe we should check out our bunk-mates before they're all in the sack. We exited Stan's packing box–stacked, bulletin-board–adorned office, alert to the troops in the big room. Most were occupied, writing, cleaning clothes, getting a shower, preparing for the morrow and engrossed. Some watched a television perched on a shelf ten feet off the floor. Three or four turned and stared at us full-face. A couple of them blurted out, quiet and friendly-like, "Hey, you guys were just on T.V." One said, "Thanks for coming out."

They were a bit distant and I cozied up to one of them. "How long have you been staying here?" I started, as ordinarily as possible, while thinking, "What a klutz I am!" The fellow said something like a couple of weeks, and thanked me for a nice sentence I gave him in court. He did look familiar. I surveyed the faces. Two others stared knowingly—yes, I'd sentenced them too. The small, white one smiled, a good sport. The huge, black fellow glared, all smoldering silence. I banked on his dignity and brains. He had contempt for me, but felt me beneath him and looked like he knew the consequences of public revenge. I stared, eyelids low. confident and regular, doing my best to penetrate a zero-fear stare into him, then turned to my blankets and the lowest bunk by the door.

Like the others, we prepared. My favorite uncle's ancient brown jacket was my pillow. I jotted some notes in the tiny spiral pad I had brought along. I was glad of the double socks and the t-shirts under my long-sleeve flannel shirt, deeply grateful to be indoors, in a bunk, with sheets and a clean blanket. And the smell of Lysol. Dan and Troy and Doug and Neil and the others were all out there someplace. Thank God for the alcoholics in the house. It was warm to be around them. They served as buffers, in other environs, between the straights and innocents on the one hand and the violent and the evil on the other.

I thanked God, and collapsed into fervent prayer. ("Help me see. Help us and all these, and keep us safe. Let this be worthy and productive. Hold Your Hand on me this night. Let us emerge with wisdom and vision and clarity. Help us tell the truths found here. Help us lead the widest spectrum of people to see and become curious. Hold my family always. Just hold us in Your Hand.") I opened my eyes to see a cockroach walk down the two-by-four a foot in front of me, then fell asleep.

I woke up grateful and refreshed. A good night's sleep, and the sun was coming up. Men were moving deliberately, individually, quitetly. I lay there savoring it, meditating, setting gyroscopes, reflecting and reviewing. All was well! I exited very quietly, left Stan the jacket, the outer shirt, and my five-dollar bill. We'd agreed to take five dollars each. It felt more legitimate to be broke. With daybreak, our only real danger was past. I hoped the others were okay, figured we'd count noses at the breakfast line at St. Vincent de Paul.

Outside, six or eight guys stood on the sidewalk. Ordinary fellows, a bit shy, they were full of humble optimism. Two hoped for jobs today. Two others had itineraries—one on the I.D. trek, one to reading school. Stan kept each on a mutually designed program. How the heck could he do that with a fourth of the homeless? That's 750 downtown alone! Were there other Stans available?

Joe emerged looking as happy as me. We kicked it around with the group (the bus was coming and they had passes, thanks to the Transient Center), waved goodbyes, and trudged down several blocks to St. Vincent de Paul. Most of the crew was there, with 250 or so others. It was more of a cross section of the homeless. There were women and a few people with kids. We fell in at the end of the line and eagerly gossiped with each other as our hungry eyes roamed. The women in the doorway looked pretty bad. Vets and others showed up in wheelchairs, some with crutches. Some of the ghostly, gauze-wrapped types looked like they concealed months of filth, perhaps typhoid or diphtheria. What were those wild statistics put out by the Los Angeles County Health Department? Strains of dysentery that killed 10 percent of the children who got them. Two cases of bubonic plague. Who, here, looked deeply sick? How did you tell? Where were the doctors? Where were the shrinks, the psychiatric social workers, the psychologists? As citizens, where were they?

Our psychiatric social worker, Mark de Modena, showed up, ashen-faced from a tour of the faces in line. He'd been counting people who were hearing voices, talking to themselves, or catatonic. He was a street-wise fellow and downtown had been his beat for several years. He stood, shocked. He had seen several very ill, former clients of his.

Me, I was just in line for breakfast. The day before it had rained, said Dan, who was into his third day. The doors hadn't been opened and everybody had had to stand outside for peanut butter sandwiches. Dan told us of two little kids with their mom, standing in the rain, eating the peanut butter sandwiches. Dan also mentioned some young guys helping some older fellows with their coats, with surviving in the rain. Kindness. Compassion for the sick old men.

The ex–street guys on the loading dock had their white aprons on. They handed us each a hot dog. We trudged westward, slightly proud of our slight hunger. Don Reeves and Doug Regin stood north of Market Street; we embraced them like kids. They were quite excited and reported what they saw as they walked all night, pressing it at us in bursts. They stood outside the symphony as it let out and the patrons flowed around them and their rags. Good friends had passed as closely as two feet away without a flicker of recognition. They'd gone to the detoxification center next, where the cops brought the drunks. They'd watched an amazingly efficient process that handled nearly one hundred people per night, half from downtown. The "chronics" or violent among these were taken to jail. We saw ten to twenty a day in court, a few days after they'd been picked up. Thence, they'd roamed the downtown, from the Embarcadero to First Lutheran (no rain, so the usual ninety to a hundred people sleeping under the overhang were absent). Under the Community Concourse Parking Structure, several groups of three or four were camping on the ramp. A guard at the Greyhound depot was ejecting people who couldn't produce tickets. The depot is warm and it has padded chairs. At 3:00 a.m. the Carl's Jr. manager was hassling the remaining people in the dining room. He wanted to close and they wanted to stay inside. There were still a great many individuals and small groups walking the streets. There were no vacancies at the Golden West, a cheap hotel. At the run-down William Penn down the street, a room could be had for $23 and a $3 deposit. By four o'clock, the foot traffic on Fifth Avenue was higher than ever that night. Hookers, alone and in pairs, were on every block. Pimpmobiles were parked on every corner, but no police were visible. A mile north a bus bench was a welcome vantage point. As dawn broke at 5:20 a.m. they'd seen great numbers of people leaving the park. A circuitous route across town brought them to the hot dogs (with dill pickle, plus coffee).

They had some change left so we all hit the Sun Cafe for coffee and toast. We were cheered and headed for the nearby plaza, soon to be remodelled with shiny, no-bums-need-apply accoutrements, to lay on the grass for a snooze. How nice to luxuriate as all the workaholics march past so purposefully! Grass smells so nice! It's sweet to lie on, and evokes such dreams of lazing country days, of childhood on hillsides, of baseball!

We rose to go, winding through bunches of people at this central bus stop, and I found myself face to face with my former law clerk and then junior partner, Bill Grant. Profoundly tactful, Bill suppressed the gaze of alarm to a flicker, and then offered, not too tentatively, "Hi, Bob. On a vacation?" Down the street, feeling the gentle breeze in the cool morning, the simple joy of life invaded us. Each person was an adventure, each encounter brimming with possibilities. The "bumming life," so vaunted by some in the Depression, had its appeal. Discipline and integrity are gorgeous—but only when informed by the spirit, possessed by alive human beings. To flush the spirit clear by the application of a stint of zero responsibility, the freedom of a poetic morning like this one, suddenly seemed a necessity. What is morality but ashes, without such reality? This was real.

Thus singing inside, we moved on past Rachel's Women's Center. No, we couldn't go in, but we did peek and see the stolid dozens filling the couches. We went north to Catholic Community Services (nobody about) and the Balboa Park. Here was a poem worth exploring. The 1979 federal census counted forty-three permanent residents of Balboa Park. Now there were hundreds. They slept under bridges (where the rich have an equal right to sleep, as Victor Hugo observed), in canyons, in every least-expected spot. People got robbed here, raped here, mugged here. The horse patrols crashed through on occasion, spurred by who-knows-what whimsical political or strategic directives. They had tromped through less frequently lately. Whatever the experiment was, it had failed.

The crime rate in Balboa Park has skyrocketed. Families fear to go to parts of this magnificent jewel of a park anymore. They have been evicted by the homeless. But this has yet to be recognized as one of the community's costs of homelessness. The highly organized, very powerful "Committee of One Hundred" and the dozens of other park use groups have yet to join our efforts to solve homelessness here. Curious. One day they will. Our job is to keep up gentle communication, to press hard where the real opportunities and needs exist (each *today*), and to remain sensitive to the right timing for each real interest group, like the lovers of Balboa Park. Our job is to continue the process of analyzing these people's belief systems, including the ones that keep them inactive and the problems static or worsening.

We looked around a bit, didn't see much, and decided that it wasn't the day to go crashing about in the underbrush to conduct interviews. Besides, we had no clipboards or white smocks to complete the ridiculous image. And we were hungry. Where was lunch happening? At the Catholic Worker! Our pace quickened. On the way we sidled into Chuck Valverde's wonderful bookstore on Broadway. Nobody was surprised. Street types entered here all the time. Accordingly, the staff is expert.

"How's it going, Chuck?"

"Well, I'll be darned!" Chuck responded, grinning. "What's this about?" He was pleased and intrigued. We briefly told him what was up and he related a few experiences with street types. Chuck ran this great store with his loving, straightforward enthusiasm. He was a "called man," and he loved the details of all books, and of his downtown. Like many retail merchants downtown, he was so engrossed in his work that he hadn't the time to be involved with the Lions, Kiwanis, or Rotary. He was certainly not to be found in the Chamber of Commerce, or the other political business groups, like the Central City Association. As a result, the damage the homeless did to his balance sheet was not registered as a complaint. He is almost Buddhist in his sweet acceptance of this factor of market adversity.

We carried Chuck's presence with us all the way to the Catholic Worker, and a good thing, too, because we came up short against a television crew. What a pain! I grabbed all the appropriateness I could (fueled by whatever I still held of Chuck's benevolence), jacked up my honesty, gathered my thoughts, and felt very silly. Stupid, really. Here, partly to publicize the situation, I nevertheless thought, "Why ask me? Why not ask those people across the street, in the lunch line? How embarrassing, how humiliating, to speak for these so-easily-available people!"

I gave an interview. Homelessness was peanuts as a problem, compared to others that we had addressed seriously, sometimes even solved. Why the inaction, then? We had slept at a flophouse named America's Last Fandango, Inc. I'd been checking out the mentally ill and the women and children. They should look at the line across the street. "Swing the camera around and show them," I advised.

The cracked, concrete steps of the Catholic Worker were clean and at the top, arms akimbo, stood an enthusiastic, well-scrubbed, Li'l Abner type. Catholic Worker volunteers are truly a type. Fresh from prayer, healthy and hard-working, they seem a lot like Mormon missionaries, but their practicality is startling. They are there to serve, period. There is no looking down; and there are no blank, innocent stares. These people have been trained to love God's reality.

The food was okay, too. It was not too organized, although everybody was trying. It was kind of like scout camp, except that the deep, simple love and respect was pervasive. For our learning purposes, however, it was a bit inconvenient. Only loudmouths felt much like talking. Families wouldn't talk with us at all. Sunburned types with plastered, dirty hair seemed basically okay (one, out of the Marine Corps eight months with hopes for a job, just seemed cheerfully into something beyond his understanding, but he wasn't complaining), while others gazed out of bloodshot, ill eyes and faces racked by inestimable tragedy, deepest grief, and profound alienation. My brothers and sisters, you terrify me! You shake my soul because who (in America) can be ready for the reality that you are?

Some people left. The Boy Scout–types stayed and helped sweep the floors, fold the tables, put out the garbage, dry the silverware. We felt productive. Close to 100 percent of the homeless, in every poll I've ever seen and for every segment—mentally ill, physically disabled, whichever— want to work.

As we cleaned the place, we realized how distant the Catholic Worker staff seemed. Perhaps they were just very shy. Seekers are often inarticulate. We shook a few hands and plunged down the steps into the sunlight, picking our way through stragglers lounging on the steps. Joe wanted to hike on with Don and I wanted to go my own way. Stan voted to come along with me. Off we went toward 16th Street. We soaked in the scene. Wrecked yards. Houses from a cheery, bygone residential era (generally painted green) with oddly disjointed sidewalks and driveways, forgotten in the rush of progress and the street's new elevation. Windows were lost, but clothes hung on clotheslines and junk was everywhere. Land uses mixed in a crazy quilt of transition: industrial, commercial, residential; bars, social agencies and restaurants. Uses struggling against other uses, tides flowing against each other.

Stumbling a bit, we sighted the green front of the mission and the barroom front of Sister Winnie's building. A crowd was gathered. Two men on ladders and one hanging out an upstairs window assisted several on the ground pulling ropes to bring down an unembarrassed sign: "Tug's Neighborhood Tavern." Brute force was winning over sin. Everybody was sweating through a pause as Sister Winnie hollered, "Judge Coates. Praise God. We've been trying to take over this place next door for years and today's the day!"

The hand-picked crew continued their struggle as we followed Sister Winnie upstairs for a Pepsi. It was cool and she was motherly, reassuring to the little boy needing rest in all of us. She reminded me of several wonderful aunts I had, women with cool, green kitchens and bucolic scenes on the walls.

Why was homelessness here? The deinstitutionalization of the profoundly mentally ill is the cause most spoken of. Partisans whisper about two hundred thousand mentally disabled Social Security recipients slashed from the rolls between 1980 and 1982. But the story of the explosion of homelessness can be validly analyzed from many points of view. One may look for origins in the breakdown of American families, in the breakup of industries and the flight of jobs (so-called deindustrialization), in the slashing of benefit networks in general, in the destruction of low-income housing units (and, more importantly, the lack of a national housing policy), as well as in the deinstitutionalization of millions of the deeply mentally ill.

But the viewpoint I've found myself pressed against most often, the one that vies among these as a leading cause of homelessness, is the evil one finds within the very agencies whose declared mission it is to responsibly, humanely help the homeless. In government agencies one finds this expressed most directly in flat disregard for the law, but in governmental, social service, and religious agencies alike one finds a simpler evil: not keeping one's word and not being true to the institution's declared mission.

The afternoon was warm as we passed disheveled business relics, hiking up quiet streets. A fly-buzzing afternoon, lazy. There was something reassuring in the weatherbeaten faces of the old men (are they forty? fifty? thirty?)

coming back to the line by the mission even as cows return to a barn. We fell in with them, feeling good with them, bantering sweetly, gazing openly eye upon eye, hiking around corners toward the mission. "City Rescue Mission" it still said boldly above the door on Fifth Avenue. A crowd had formed even though we were an hour and a half early.

A couple angry wackos were arguing up the street. People kept their distance and the sounds soon subsided. This seemed to be the rule on the streets, except when drugs were involved. Who has the energy to fight, with high priorities elsewhere? I sat against the building with a handsome young black man from Houston. One year out of the Marines, he'd lost a job there and taken a bus here because he liked the San Diego boot camp. It had been a month since then, and he was out of cash and here for dinner. "Wish I'd bought a round trip," he offered. A nice kid, a potential asset to his country, his community. We gabbed on, friendly. He asked about me. I told him and his surprise was gratifying. Stan had said that I looked awful, but I needed reassurance. We shook hands, wished each other luck, and entered the moving line.

Old training surfaced and the ragtag cluster of men outside the door became an orderly file as the time to eat drew near—unpresentable people can be excluded. Inside we were whisked past the large sanctuary and to the back of the big dining hall itself. Friendliness surrounded us. We were there to honor them and they honored us and we grabbed coffee and donuts and sat down. For an hour we talked, shared, questioned, blurted things out between us. We hardly noticed the reporters who drifted in, one by one. After a while they were joining in with questions and then with microphones.

Somebody pulled me off to a side room for a radio interview. I found my voice cracking and was as surprised as the interviewer at the force of my expressions. She gave me respect and time, and as I returned to the great hall, it was nice to see the place full of fellows eating and equally happy reporters having a field day with us. The television crews were setting up a joint camera for all stations and I was asked to step forward.

I felt the way I did at bat in key games. I pulled no punches. The bottom line was that this problem could be solved. Our experience bore out the studies on the numbers of homeless and the subgroupings among them. There were helpless women and children out here. These people were not statistics, they were *people*. Many of them were employable and only needed to be linked with jobs. Many were so pathetically, helplessly mentally ill as to be utterly unable to help themselves. This community needed an aggressive, affirmative program like other cities had—Los Angeles was the best example— to gather these helpless, terrified people in, and gently guide them to SSI disability, medical care, a spot in board-and-care homes. Taken together, these moves would humanely and responsibly cycle these benighted people off of our streets. My key conclusion was that the situation was manageable. In absolute numbers, each segment was a pittance, and the overall numbers (three thousand downtown, another three thousand county-wide) was tiny, too, in a county of two and one-half million. All we needed was the *will,* the community decision. This would obviously be good for business downtown and ultimately save county government a great deal of money in otherwise-rendered general relief, occasional health care, jail, and court costs.

Finally, I asked people to think of the lesson we were giving our kids by letting this situation fester. I did not want my children growing up thinking their community or species was so heartless or incompetent that it couldn't organize itself to handle so serious a problem that was at the same time of such relatively small dimensions.

Don suggested a beer at Morgans, next door, and we embraced and hung onto Doc, Doug, Dick, and Neil, who could not stay. Don said Christine Reeves would pick us up. We piled through the mahogany door at Morgans and pressed up to the bar.

The Gaslamp Quarter of San Diego is lovely in its juxtapositions. The City Rescue Mission is at once a source of moral pride and fervent disaffection. It is widely known, intensely practical, and overused, attracting hundreds of seedy characters to the neighborhood. Next door, Morgans is all brass, white linen, civilized, human solicitation, and dark wood. We didn't exactly fit, except for our triumphant attitudes and talkativeness. We'd done good.

Somebody produced a credit card and ordered a round of drinks. Almost immediately Christine swept in, bubbling. She'd seen the interviews and thought all was "great, grand . . . you were all terrific!" We figured we'd made a breakthrough and had to wait until tomorrow to assess the its extent. Christine brought her big Mercedes Benz around and Joe and I piled in the back seat, collapsing into luxury for the ride to the parking lot. The sign Joe found tacked on his front door when he arrived home read, "Bums Need Not Apply!"

Pickwick goes through life with that godlike gullibility which is the key to all adventures. The greenhorn is the ultimate victor in everything. It is he that gets the most out of life . . . his soul will never starve for exploits or excitements who is wise enough to have been made a fool of. He will make himself happy in the traps that have been laid open to him who has a mildness more defiant than mere courage. The whole is unerringly expressed in one fortunate phrase—he will be always "taken in." To be taken in everywhere is to see the inside of everything. It is the hospitality of circumstance. With torches and trumpets, like a guest, the greenhorn is taken in by life and the skeptic is cast out by it.

—G. K. Chesterton

II

Subpopulations of Homeless, Special Solutions

4

An Easy Early Step: Public Drunks

A man's got to believe in something. I believe I'll have a drink.
                                                        —W. C. Fields

Alcoholics are different. They suffer, the experts tell us, from a hereditary metabolic disorder not unlike diabetes. This disorder means that they metabolize alcohol differently from the rest of us. Their brain tissue, over the years, is changed. There is a substance in a biological alcoholic's brain that helps determine that when the brain is soaked in the tiniest amount of alcohol, it craves more. Hence, alcoholics are not easily able to stop drinking once they start.

Research and books on alcoholism and its progeny abound. One current rage in psychotherapy is investigation and treatment of the psychological damage done to the millions of children of alcoholics—and the psychological damage these children then pass on.

As with most staring-us-in-the-face problems of our modern society, scientific knowledge has not become common knowledge. One great foolishness still believed by most Americans is: "You can't get a drunk to quit until he wants to." But the courts can in fact start alcoholics on the road to recovery. It's done every day. The constructive, everyday work that our courts do is, however, without the lovely, public flair of Judge Joe Wapner. It is not hot news. It is ignored.

When someone drinks six to twenty ounces of booze per day, as most non-recovering alcoholics do, several things happen. One is that every single day, that kind of drinking blasts away about a hundred thousand irreplaceable brain cells. After decades of this, even the Galileos of our population begin to exhibit signs of brain damage. A more significant result of long-term heavy drinking is that the brain, as one of the body's organs, yields to toxic shock. It cannot function in this condition—its owner cannot make decisions or keep his or her word. The first step in an alcoholic's recovery, therefore, is to get him or her off the sauce long enough to get the brain functional. We must also recognize that today's alcoholic has often been consuming many other drugs in addition to alcohol. His or her withdrawal may therefore be a compound one, and therefore longer. For long-addicted and cross-addicted alcoholics, as much as four months may be needed to dry out.

Enter the justice system. It can send an alcoholic away to a nice, locked facility somewhere (San Diego's is in the nearby mountains, amidst oaks and pines) with other gentle alcoholics, at a place where one can do physical work (trail building, fire fighting, and the like), and where Alcoholics Anonymous–type meetings take place daily. This is compassionate treatment. It is the first step to recovery, for tens of thousands annually, in America. Many more ideal settings are usefully employed across the nation, including small group homes, halfway houses, drug and alcohol residential treatment centers (including expensive in-patient hospital settings). The elements common to these facilities are the absence of alcohol or drugs and attendance at AA-type meetings. These start the addict on the road to spiritual and emotional recovery. Such care actually costs the public less than leaving chronic alcoholics on the streets, where the police will arrest them many times each month, transporting them over and over and over to a short-term detoxification center or to jail.

Many Americans need to update their sociological stereotypes of who inhabits our nation's Skid Rows. The missions now report an average age of twenty-seven for homeless adults, as opposed to an average age of fifty-six twenty years ago, and the reason for this shift—destruction of low-cost housing, increasing numbers of single-parent families with no reserve resources, drugs—are many. But the bottomed-out drunks are still there.

In 1985, chronic alcoholics numbered ninety in San Diego, or just 1.5 percent of the homeless population. Although they are a tiny percentage of the homeless, alcoholics remain a very important pain in the collective rears of other downtown residents, visitors (including San Diego's precious tourists, who spend millions annually), the business community, and, of course, the police.

San Diego has over a million residents, but only ninety public alcoholics. They are individually well known to the city's finest, for they must pick up each of them on the average of seven times per month. They account for seven hundred of the city's arrests for drunkenness every month. To be drunk in the sense used in the California Penal Code (which uses a typical definition), a person must be "so inebriated as to be unable to care for his/her safety." The common description for it is "falling down drunk." The jail, being overcrowded (and under Superior Court supervision to become less so), now disgorges alcoholics almost as quickly as the police can unload them from their squad cars. They are typically held in the drunk tanks for just a few hours.

Officers getting off shift late at night have even been mugged by some of these public inebriates, which stiffened the sheriff's resolve to help slow the revolving door, but, ultimately, to no avail. So far it has proved too difficult for the city to secure teamwork between the several governmental agencies that could hold these fellows (only three are women) until they see a judge. The present system, not being pressed by demands for solutions, resists even modest attempts at reducing the problem of homelessness in San Diego.

Like most major cities, ours has an excellent partnership that successfully handles most public alcoholics for the short term. The police are linked with a competent, volunteer alcohol treatment agency (in San Diego, the Volunteers of America), which kindly and with astounding patience and tough love receives its daily and nightly crop of drunk human beings at its Inebriate Reception Center (universally known as the Detox Center). Partly funded via a county contract, this excellent agency offers coffee and cots to sleep it off, as well as street-wise counselors who offer each entrant the chance to start in a program. These programs range from referrals to Alcoholics Anonymous meetings to insurance-paid stays in three-week hospital detox programs to the free, seven-day residential program located right in the center.

In San Diego each month, the Detox Center handles some twenty-four hundred people brought by the police to its downtown, warehouse-like, well-lighted building. The offenses range from mere "falling down public drunkenness" to incidents of drunken domestic violence. Just over half of the arrests take place downtown, the rest from the far reaches of the city. It is a great institution, quietly rendering its services month in, month out, year in, year out to one of the least attractive populations of our society. It succeeds with a huge percentage of the people referred to it—and it is an utter failure with those we are dealing with here, the eighty-seven men and three women who comprise San Diego's chronic public alcoholics.

These are the measures of the Detox Center's success: over 95 percent of those San Diegans brought to the program once are never seen there again. Four years ago, the police were taking thirty thousand people to the Detox Center and seven thousand to the county jail every year—thirty-seven thousand public drunk "events" per year in a city of just over one million population. Only two things make the police bring an alcoholic to the jail rather than the Detox Center—commission of a crime while drunk, or five appearances at the center in a single month. Basically, for the chronic public alcoholic to show up in front of a judge is extremely unusual. The San Diego Police Department says it spends nearly $3 million a year arresting the homeless. About $300,000 of that is spent just on the ninety chronic alcoholics among them, arresting each, on the average, seven times each month. To what purpose? None, that anyone can detect. The alcoholics are not really helped. The public is not protected. The business community is understandably livid (yet strangely absent from organized advocacy). Nonetheless, the pointless, revolving-door process continues.

Here is three-point plan to eliminate alcoholics from the ranks of any city's homeless population: 1) chronic alcoholics must be held in jail long enough to come before a judge and be tried; 2) at sentencing (assuming guilt, and usually there is a plea of guilty in these cases), the prosecutor must be prepared to reveal the defendant's history of convictions to the sentencing judge and ask him or her to sentence the alcoholic to the maximum custody: six months, recovery camp recommended—most judges will comply; and 3) the creation of a mechanism, such as a task force that meets monthly, that will ensure that public alcoholics are in fact being processed in this way.

Some judges will also revoke the defendant's probation on existing cases— holding another six months over the defendant's head on condition he or she agrees to move directly from jail/honor camp into one of the county group alcohol recovery homes. These homes are partially county/state funded, with the rest of the funding coming from the residents. A year or so in the intense and intensely supportive environment of one of these therapeutic homes (with jail hanging over one's head for three years per case) can work wonders with even the most deeply dedicated alcoholic. At the very least, it saves a life for a time.

It actually is this simple. There may be a few local wrinkles depending on the locality. Voter approval of a bond issue for increased jail space may be required. Some mechanism for dealing with the severe health problems found in up to a third of chronic public alcoholics may need to be established (this could be solved by putting the drunk tanks near a hospital). Given the return on the investment, these are mere details.

The initial diagnosis of the situation in San Diego came from a thoughtful city police lieutenant, one of the department's deputy chiefs. Claude Gray is nearing retirement and considered a dependable intellectual within the department. He is tapped for sensitive assignments. He respects constitutional rights and wants to be both compassionate and problem-solving. Gray and I met one fall day in 1985 and soon were talking about downtown problems. "The Detox Center has a physical list," he said of downtown's ninety public alcoholics. "They're the 'chronics.' "

"What are they like?" I asked.

"Well, they're always drunk. They fall in front of cars. They stumble along business-district sidewalks at noontime looking disgusting. They vomit. They shout and rave. They rummage in garbage cans. They lie down in doorways. They pee in the alley. Sometimes they punch somebody (occasionally a cop) or heave a brick through a window. They are *always* a pain in the fanny."

"Why don't the courts handle them?"

"You can't tell these chronics from eighty other stubbly guys, and they're being moved along fast, you know, on the video screen at video arraignment, among the 150 defendants arraigned per morning."

It was true. Twenty years ago, when I started my law practice, I got onto the list of court-appointed attorneys and spent many days monthly, for eight years in the wondrous court where the hookers, alcoholics, brain-damaged veterans, druggies, go-go dancers and all the rest of Nelson Algren's big-city flotsam wind up at one time or another, democratically mixed in with a sprinkling of middle-class matrons whose dogs were off their leashes and hikers who took shellfish out of season at low tide.

Among these, every day, came two or three or four of the chronics. Nobody ever noticed them. The chronics surely don't leap up to label themselves: "Hey, judge, remember me? I was here last week. You warned me, remember? Boy, do I hate jail. There's no booze there!" No, these fellows hunker down. They seek invisibility. They present only the tops of their heads as they pretend to be signing the change of plea form.

"Credit for time served," recommends the prosecutor, whose job it is to press through with the calendar. And the judge, as likely as not a newcomer (this court is an inevitable stop on the court's training program for new judges), almost inevitably can be heard to intone wisely, "Credit for time served." Sometimes she adds, "You'll be released today. Have a good day, sir."

If the judge happens to ride along with the cops some night and talk with Claude Gray, as I luckily did, he or she would squirm with embarrassment, with the realization that each such chronic drunk actually brought to court embodies a cry, a professional message from some very competent police trying to get someone (ultimately, the judge) to hear, "Please, do the responsible thing with this poor bugger. It's a matter of life and death." But the message is seldom heard.

Gray suggested the forming of a Public Inebriate Task Force, made up of all the agencies that deal with public alcoholics on a regular basis. He suggested a schedule of monthly meetings to figure out what to do about the problem. It turned out that judges and others in the system could remember two previous such task forces, assembled at about ten-year intervals. Each was remarkably effective. Each was disbanded after a year or two. This was to be our fate, too. We put a program in place, but then we got tired. We hit a barrier on one recommendation (the creation of a downtown "Urban Honor Camp" to help alcoholics recover). The process of handling the chronics, week upon week, was, I guess, just too mundane to hold our interest.

The member agencies included:

The City Attorney's Criminal Division. Its chief was Ted Bromfield. He was responsible for the prosecutor's files, which were thus indispensable to our meetings. We had been law school classmates and communicated well.

Volunteers of America (the "Detox Center"). The director is Tim Huddleston, a recovering alcoholic. Tim is like a religious figure. His life is a Twelve-Step meditation. Savvy, he is deliberately not political.

The West Fork Honor Camp at Palomar Mountain. Alan Bingham, its director, faithfully drove the 120-mile round trip to San Diego for every meeting.

The County Probation Department, which runs the honor camps. Vicky Markey, the Probation Department's honor camp supervisor and a superb administrator, suggested the joint operation of our proposed urban, alcohol-related honor camp by the Probation Department and the County Alcohol Division.

The County Alcohol Program. Director Bob Reynolds is intense, slightly chubby, and constructive. He could reel off research data at the drop of a hat, and he was aware of political currents and funding sources.

The County Jail. Commander Jim Roache had the biggest stake in altering the revolving-door nature of the institution he ran.

The County Jail Alcohol Program. Director Barbara Wolfenbarger was the task force's in-custody client advocate.

Municipal Court Judge. I am under an ethical commandment never to engage in a vain act, which means that my court's sentencing of these people must hold out hope of preventing them from returning to the court.

Police Department, Downtown Division. This was Claude Gray's turf. Claude reliably kept our statistics, planned, followed through, and kept his department true to his word.

We knew one another. Many of us had some contact with each other through our work. We lasted together for a year and a half, and we managed to accomplish two things: 1) the creation of the Public Inebriate Program, which, first, identified the chronic public inebriates so they could be held in custody long enough to face an informed sentencing judge, and second, armed prosecutors with a full file on these alcoholics when they came to court; and 2) the submission of a well-researched recommendation for a low-cost, low-security downtown "Urban Honor Camp for Alcoholics" complete with thorough economic, correctional, and recidivism-prevention rationales.

Simple, eh? The system for dealing with the "chronics" worked very well. The downtown honor camp was never created. A number of factors, including a jail space crunch and a resulting Superior Court lawsuit, a county government budget crisis, and certain peculiar political currents, have made it impossible to reassemble the task force. We never should have disbanded.

I am convinced that if we hadn't, we would still be operating, and probably on the verge of gaining the Urban Honor Camp.

How could activists in other cities avoid our mistakes and successfully establish a public inebriate program? Most importantly, I would suggest starting at the top and getting the police chief and/or city prosecutor to take the initiative personally. Let them recruit the mayor, the jail alcohol program director, the county probation director, and any other pertinent players. Members of the task force should be selected to combine expertise and the desire to make the program succeed with the power to see that it does. The task of chairperson should be institutionalized in some manner, perhaps by the establishment of a permanent position, for example, via an amendment to the formal rules of the local municipal court.

It did seem that my invitations, presumably because they carried the aura of the court, were more faithfully responded to than those emanating from the police department, the city attorney's office, and others. A judge may be the best overall choice to be the chair and moving spirit, although there are drawbacks to this. I was ethically required to recuse myself from all public drunk cases during my chairmanship. I also had to shield my colleagues from the task force's proceedings in order to avoid any thought that there might be a proscribed "collusion in sentencing" regarding public inebriates rather than the exercise of individual discretion required by state law.

Finally, appropriate, dignified media coverage of the task force and its recommendations is important. It reinforces public commitment to the continuity of this important program.

Gray has estimated that the annual cost to the San Diego Police Department of repeatedly arresting, transporting, jailing, and filling out paperwork about the city's ninety downtown public alcoholics is just under $200,000. Departmental cost estimates—say, of the SWAT team—routinely add 60 percent for "overhead," bringing the total to $320,000. Naturally, this is just a fraction of the cost to city government as a whole, which also has to pay for public defenders, prosecutors, and court time. Private-sector costs (particularly "lost business") add another huge dimension to the social cost of inept handling of public inebriates.

Placing San Diego's ninety people in recovery camp for six-month sentences (with "good behavior" credits, only four months' time actually in the program) would cost about the same as the police costs alone—$320,000.

There are no impregnable fortresses, only those ineptly attacked.

—Napoleon

SUGGESTED READING

"Multiple Diagnosis: Aspects and Issues in Substance Abuse Treatment," Leslie
    Cooper, Vivian B. Brown, and M. Douglas Anglin, Drug Abuse Information
    and Monitoring Project for the State of California Department of Alcohol and
    Drug Program, February 1989.

5

Women and Children

A mother is the holiest thing alive.
—Emerson

When I was first required to sentence the homeless people showing up in court, in 1983, and thus obliged to assess community resources for purposes of probation and "preventing recidivism" as required by law, there were no agencies helping homeless women in San Diego. Today there are the Salvation Army's Family Emergency Lodge (50 beds), the new St. Vincent De Paul/ Joan Kroc Center (330 beds), the Episcopal Community Center's Julian's Anchorage (20 beds), the House of Rachel (14 beds), the YWCA-started Women's Shelter, now operated by Catholic Charities (70 beds), and the large Rachel's Women's Day Center. The community now has substantial assets serving homeless women, but they are not enough. Shelter managers say we need four times the shelter beds for homeless women.

Since 1984 the number of homeless women and families on America's streets has risen dramatically—by at least 180 percent (that is, almost triple) according to the 1988 National Survey of Shelters for the Homeless produced by the U.S. Department of Housing and Urban Development (HUD). It has become accepted that women are the fastest-growing subgroup among the homeless.[2] Despite their rising number on the streets, women are still estimated officially to constitute only 14 percent of the nation's overall homeless population. This estimate is doubtless very low. Women form a much larger part of the homeless than they used to. With their overall presence on the street increasing dramatically, special services to meet the unique needs of women are in high demand.

Studies sponsored by the National Institute for Mental Health (NIMH) have shown that, "homeless women living with their young children present fewer psychiatric symptoms compared to homeless women without children, [yet] the level of impairment may increase dramatically over time unless a quick exodus from homelessness is found. Psychiatric impairment may have an impact on young children whether or not they are in the company of their mother, as many apparently 'single' homeless women have chosen to leave their children behind with relatives and friends while maintaining contact with them."[3]

Unlike their male counterparts, most homeless women are confronting problems related to their sex or role in society in addition to the problems that are part of the debilitating loss of home and job and possible drug and alcohol addiction. These special problems include the increased health care problems commonly experienced on the streets by women, former or ongoing abuse by male partners, inability to support children adequately, and possible loss of children to public agencies or foster care.

Many homeless people—some of the deeply mentally ill, the veterans, the inveterately independent—won't come to the present shelter systems. But for those who will, it is families today, mostly headed by women, that are taking up more space in shelters. Families have nearly doubled their proportional represenation in shelters since 1984. Women now account for two out of every five people in homeless shelters. Three out of four homeless families have a single parent as the head of the household, according to the Washington, D.C., Homelessness Information Exchange. Family members now outnumber unaccompanied men as the major client type in large shelters: 52 percent versus 36 percent.

Is there a "typical homeless woman"? Yes. She is likely to be of two types, according to Eugenie Birch's *The Unsheltered Woman*: 1) A young mother not yet thirty-five with minor children, formerly living in rental housing; or 2) an elderly woman formerly alone in a rented unit, often subsidized. Above all she is poor, having an income below 80 percent of the nation's median wage. In fact, one in two female housholders earns less than 50 percent of the median.

Birch categorizes these women as among what she has termed (borrowing from FDR) the "ill-housed one-third of the nation." She notes, "Females head about 27 percent of all American households today: yet they are disproportionately represented among those experiencing housing problems. In fact, numerically they are the largest subgroup of the poorly sheltered population. . . . Only thirty years ago, the female householder comprised 15 percent of the total households in the United States—today she is approaching one-third. Her needs, particularly for low-cost, decent shelter, cannot be ignored."

Women—women whom we men in the chivalrous world have been taught to revere, and to tenderly care for, to protect and to fight wars for. Women who are vulnerable, who ought not be abandoned. Women who may be very sick, in the agony of depression and madness, in cold and in want. Women being robbed, beaten, raped with impunity. Women living in barbarism. If men love not women, whom will they love?

Possibly children. Suffering. Terrified. Walking all day beside the giants. Humiliated. Hungry and dirty. In real danger. Being abused. Skipping developmental stages. Losing the power to learn, losing pieces of the power to be human. Future voters. Future wards of society. The nation's hope: its very meaning being degraded, soiled beyond belief and, perhaps, beyond recognition by negligent leaders filled with rhetoric and tenderness for flags, but not for the children being taken apart piece by piece, alive.

An Orange County woman communicated this idea, aimed at assisting homeless families by concentrating help on the children, via expansion of existing (temporary) foster parent systems, which exist in every state. Orange County, nestled between Los Angeles and San Diego, is one of Southern California's more affluent areas. In Orange County there are more than ten thousand homeless people. Despite the big numbers of the homeless, this county has provided only eighteen shelters with a total of just six hundred beds. This means that on any given night, and the temperatures often go down into the low forties, there are ninety-four hundred people with no place to stay; no bed, no food, no warmth and no bathroom. Tragically, the most startling statistic of all is that of the ten thousand homeless in this very wealthy county, *four thousand are children*, and half of those, two thousand children, are under six years old.

One Orange County resident recently wrote to me about two homeless children that she cared for. The family was originally from northern Michigan. The children, a ten-year-old boy and an eleven-year-old girl, both quite attractive, came to California with their twenty-nine-year-old mother three years ago. Their mother, being untrained for the job market, tried looking for work as a maid. What she found was the brutal reality of being jobless in southern California. She soon fell into a dark hole of survival. She has yet to climb out of it.

A man almost twenty years her senior whom she met along the way to California turned her onto marijuana and crack cocaine. She soon started prostituting for him and for the drugs. Her children at first begged their mother to get off drugs and leave the man, but they soon fell silent. Their efforts were hopeless. A short time later, the mother's pimp boyfriend decided to use them too. The little boy was his first victim. The little girl had had to fight him off for the last year, "ever since she turned ten."

We already have a system in this nation set up to help, to protect, and to care for our endangered children. It is called the Foster Parenting Social Services Agency. And, every county in this nation can provide the temporary needs of homeless children. People just have to care enough to set the program up, and to act on laws already on the books. This system exists to take a child into protective custody when a parent is unable to feed, shelter, or clothe his or her child. Every homeless child falls into this category of neglect.

Good, caring, parents would never want to drag their children "through the gutter" during bad times. They would, instead, ask for temporary help from their families and friends in order to protect their children . . . if they had any family or friends. Temporary help with the children, coupled with shelter and case management for the parent(s) can be an answer.

Many of these families are dysfunctional to begin with. It is seldom possible for a functional parent to apply for work, save for and find new housing, and care for children while living at nightly shelters, in a car, in a van, in a park, or on the streets. When the families do stay in "transient" motels, the children are at tremendous risk of being harmed, used, abused, or even raped, sodomized, or otherwise molested. The problem as it stands today will, in one decade, be doubled, tripled, or worse, depending on how many children each of these homeless people has brought into the world. Unassisted, these children will become the dysfunctional adults of tomorrow.

There are very few programs at the nation's shelters to help a family on a long-term basis. Where they do exist, there is a long waiting list. The foster parenting network, through a "Respite Care Program," could care for these children. Parent(s) can make a contract with foster families for one, two, or three months to care for their children while they look for work, enter drug or alcohol treatment programs, and/or save for housing.

This "contract" could be renewed, if needed. The social services agency can act as liaison between the homeless parents and the foster parents, but it would be best if no courts or social workers were specifically assigned—unless abuse (physical or sexual) has been reported by the foster parents. In that case, the appropriate agencies should step in.

The parents, together with their children, should first meet the foster family so that they can see where their children would be staying, and see how their children would be cared for. This would take a great deal of anxiety away on everyone's part, in that if it does not appear to be a good match, either party can withdraw after the initial meeting. Ideally, the parents of the children should be able to call their children during the week to check up on them, and visit or take the children out on weekends.

Public-information articles and radio and television spots can be produced and potential foster families can be found through the print media, on television, and on radio, to bring more foster parents into the system. This program could be entitled, "Help the Homeless Children." There are plenty of empty nesters and retirees out there in this country of ours, good, caring, compassionate people who have an extra bedroom or two in their homes. Many of these people have wanted to do something to help the homeless. They would probably apply to be foster parents, if it were only for short-term "respite" care.

This program could be completely set up in a three-to-six-month period, three months being the approximate time needed for individuals to apply for foster parenting licensing and take the appropriate initial classes. Without exception, the care givers should all go through appropriate licensing and foster parenting classes, so that the families are checked out, and the special needs of the children are understood.

The use of the foster care systems in these circumstances would seldom be necessary if good shelters for women, featuring a range of supportive services, are locally available.

Meanwhile, the need is for shelters that meet the special needs of women and children. The first element needed is emergency housing with security and kindliness, assistance in quickly applying for welfare and other benefits, child care, schooling, health care, and efficiently moving to the next, appropriate step of low-income housing. This arena—of the needs of the expanding stream of homeless women and children—is one arena of the homeless with an irresistible emotional and moral appeal. Yet so far the clear trumpet has not been blown. Boy, will it sound one day!

A far larger percentage of homeless women are deeply mentally ill than are homeless men (90 percent vs. 30 percent, in one Los Angeles study), and huge numbers of homeless women stay away from shelters—places where one must acknowledge one's "outcast state" (Shakespeare's phrase) and be with one's main fear: people. So, tender outreach services need to go out where women are, and relate with them. Just be with them. Weep with them. Love them. Perhaps, then, help them.

The women who seek help at the nation's homeless shelters are not the classic "bag ladies" first stereotyped when homelessness worsened in the early 1980s. Martha Ranson, director of Rachel's Women's Day Center, a day shelter in downtown San Diego, says, "The older women who carry their bags everywhere, they don't come to our center. I think one of the reasons they don't is that they are so chronically mentally ill. They don't like the parameters we set forth."

Unfortunately, many readily available research sources echo this dreary view of the life faced by women on America's streets. In a report to the U.S. House Subcommittee on Human Resources, Dr. Ellen Bassuk of Harvard University presented the results of a team study of homeless Boston families, including unaccompanied women and children. Bassuk testified that, "Without an external support network and an adequate, reliable source of income, it is virtually impossible for many families to avoid homelessness, even with governmental or social aid."

One of Bassuk's cases studied was typical.

Linda was born in Tennessee. Her mother, a chronic alcoholic with manic depressive illness, worked intermittently as a maid. As a result, Linda was cared for by an elderly woman who frequently left her alone. At age four, her mother reclaimed her and moved the entire family to Boston. Linda remembers her mother calling her names, beating her with sticks, and locking her in the closet. Unable to tolerate the continuous abuse, Linda became a runaway at age eight. During the next three years, she wandered the streets and was temporarily placed in department of youth services facilities, but always returned to her mother, who beat her severely.

Since that time, she has never lived anywhere for longer than two years. At the age of eleven, she was sent to the New England Home for Little Wanderers for two years. By then she no longer cared about anything and felt nothing. At thirteen she was placed with a foster family where the father sexually abused her.

Feeling hopeless and helpless, she made a serious suicide attempt at fifteen. An older sister took her in, but when she became pregnant and refused to have an abortion, her sister threw her out. Desperate and frightened and with nowhere to go, she lived on the streets in abandoned, rat-infested buildings.

She gave birth to Tommy three years ago. Since that time, they have lived in twelve different places—in the apartments of several sisters, her mother, friends, and a boyfriend in Florida, in abandoned buildings, and in three family shelters. Until recently, Linda disciplined her son by beating him, but stopped when he seemed frightened most of the time. On evaluation, Tommy manifested major problems in every area of development, including language, fine and gross motor skills, and social relationships. He has a developmental age of approximately two years and is already a full year behind.

Without work skills or a high school education, Linda's future is bleak. She currently receives $328 per month from Aid to Families with Dependent Children, has Medicaid, food stamps, and other benefits.

Despite her son's urgent needs and the intensive help she has received from the shelter staff, she has not found stable housing or a day care program for him. With the exception of the department of public welfare, which gives her a check, she has no contact with any social service agency.

The Harvard study found that 54 percent of the preschoolers in shelters suffered severe developmental impairments. These children had difficulty with language, motor, social, and personal development skills. Fifty-four percent of school-age children studied were clinically depressed. Most had suicidal thoughts and suffered from severe anxiety.

What is needed to responsibly confront this reality? Findings in the congressional report stated that government-sponsored programs are unable to adequately address the problem of homeless women and families. In California, for example, most federal emergency assistance funds intended for children are used to help runaway and abused children. Destitute families in need of assistance, whose children are not abused nor runaways, do not yet qualify for aid. The report recommended that, using emergency assistance funds, the Health and Human Services Department ought to develop a model shelter program for homeless families. Such a shelter system could then be used as a model or as models for all state and local governments trying to combat the homeless crisis (see the chapter on shelter models).

Emergency housing has to provide much more than just bed space, the congressional report concluded. Any good temporary dwelling for families ought to feature security and kindliness, help for residents applying for welfare and other aid, plus child care, schooling, health care, and help in moving to the next, appropriate level of permanent, low-income housing. The shelter should also offer "human support" so the family does not slide back onto the streets due to depression, confusion, loneliness, low self esteem, alcohol or drug abuse, or other problems that are likely to be associated with the family's situation.

These needs were realized early on by administrators of San Diego's shelters for homeless women. Sister Linda Lutz, a Catholic nun who works with homeless women and children via the United Way, explains that many women on the streets have never lived independently before arriving on the streets. Many have a history of codependency with not very "together" males, perhaps ones who beat them, had a drinking problem, and/or could not hold a job. These women need counseling and plenty of one-on-one attention to change the patterns that have forced them to rely on people who cannot help them. "Our society often inculcates the feeling women are not successful without a man, and I think many women have bought into that. So a lot of times you'll hear women say, 'Well, any man is better than no man.' "

Many homeless women need help breaking substance abuse habits, while others need emotional support while holding down a new job—often a stress they cannot endure without compassionate backup. Without addressing these needs, a shelter provides nothing more than a temporary stop on the way back to the streets. And that experience underlines for the woman messages of unworthiness and failure.

One poignant example cited by Lutz involves a homeless San Diego woman, now in her fifties, who could not have gotten off the streets and reentered society without the help of an intense, caring program like the Catholic Service's House of Rachel. Like many homeless women, Judy was raised in a dysfunctional, alcoholic family. When she got married, she and her husband recreated the situation. It was psychodrama she had lived with as a child and with which she felt perversely comfortable as an adult. Her daughter in turn repeated this unhappy scenario, and when *her* marriage failed, Judy got the granddaughter to raise. This infused Judy's life with meaning, until a day came, two years later, when Judy's daughter decided to take the child back to live with her. This completely disrupted Judy's life and broke her heart. She plunged into depression, but she decided to try and find her granddaughter in San Diego, whither mother and child had moved.

Judy arrived in San Diego with no money, nowhere to live, and no plan beyond finding her granddaughter. She ended up on the streets and eventually began visiting Rachel's Women's Day Center. "At the time she came to the center she was just emotionally distraught," Lutz remembers. "So the psychologist who visits the center, Dr. Ryan, talked with her, and I talked with her, and she was referred to downtown mental health to get some assistance as an outpatient. I didn't hear from her for a while. She was staying at the Salvation Army's Emergency Lodge."

Judy eventually transferred to another shelter, where she failed to make any headway with her situation due to her internal conflicts and low self-esteem. Eventually she applied to stay at House of Rachel, a place considered to be the cream of the crop of housing for homeless women in San Diego. This comfortable house has fourteen beds for selected women deemed ready to make a real effort to hold down a job and return to society's mainstream. They can stay in the house for up to a year, as long as they keep progressing in their efforts to turn their lives around. They get extensive, sensitive, one-on-one attention, building confidence and self-esteem, and help with what are termed "life skills."

"Judy moved in October and I'd say for a couple of months her progress was just kind of sporadic. She was still emotionally churned up and somewhat impulsive," Lutz says. Like many homeless women, Judy continued for months to struggle with severe depression. She lost her first job as a receptionist after one day. "I should just go get a live-in job and work in somebody's home. This is all I'm good for." Eventually Lutz and Judy's job counselor were able to convince Judy that improper training and impatience on the part of the former receptionist were factors in contributing to her inability to perform at the first try. She took heart. Judy was soon hired for another receptionist position and worked at it for four months—until the job was terminated for reasons unconnected to her performance. Judy's boss was extremely pleased with her work and offered to give her a glowing recommendation. Judy became so confident during the course of her first job outside the home that she decided she wanted to seek a job that offered even more opportunity than clerical work.

"Who knows over the next twenty years if she's going to 'make it,' but she's learned to take small steps with a lot of support. And I think a lot of support was a key to her survival," Lutz concludes.

The Seattle Emergency Housing Service offers sixteen single-family apartments to homeless families involved in its Interim Program. Each family is counseled weekly in the areas of employment, public benefits, finances, and housing. Medical and mental health care are also provided. Families can stay from one to four months while securing permanent housing. During their stay, these families partially support the program by paying $100 to $150 per month to cover utilities and maintenance.

The YWCA in St. Paul, Minnesota, has established a four-stage program for homeless single women and women with children. It focuses on personal and career development and achievement of self-sufficiency. The first stage focuses on immediate security needs of the women. After thirty days or less, the individuals or families begin the second stage, signing an agreement to focus on their work. In the third stage clients move into transitional housing and are attending school full time or are working. By the fourth stage most have moved into permanent housing and arc working full time. They are allowed to take advantage of all services for up to one year. Women are encouraged to pursue professional careers such as banking, transportation, health care, veterinary science, and computers.

In Oklahoma City, Oklahoma, individuals and churches worked together to establish the Ark Interfaith Family Shelter, which serves 102 families a year. Two rehabilitated buildings leased from the county government provide seventy-five beds a night to couples and families on a first-come, first-served basis. The program offers individual and family counseling, drug and alcohol addiction counseling, assistance with job searches, goal setting, and instruction in daily living skills. Families were once admitted for only sixty days, but a 1987 study by Ark administrators showed that families needed more time to stabilize before entering permanent housing. Families are now encouraged to stay for a month after they have secured employment.

A mayor's staffer made a fascinating, simple, "modest suggestion." Set up a new federal government procedure to issue ATM cards to all welfare recipients via a new national program through which people could obtain their monthly Aid to Families with Dependent Children (AFDC) or other relief payments in a timely manner. The staffer went on to suggest that rent or housing payments could be paid directly to the landlord or lender, helping assure that the people being assisted did not lose their housing. The staffer pointed out that the present system, which delegates these functions to the states and local governments, hinders exercise of the constitutionally protected right to travel. Now, movement is hindered, whereas under this proposed system, welfare mothers (in New York City, for example) could conceivably move to areas (such as western Pennsylvania or Houston) where there are housing surpluses. The city involved might have its low-income housing crisis eased somewhat and would be excused from maintaining some welfare hotels, which are costly indeed. New York City reportedly pays some $3,300 per month to house a woman and two small children in unenviable conditions.[4]

A very interesting, but ultimately flawed, experiment was launched in San Diego in 1987, which then failed due to, well, lack of sophistication and the grit to see something past the first series of barriers. It shouldn't have been abandoned, and had it continued it would clearly have helped take care of the problem of homeless women and children in this city.

One of San Diego County's fifty-three Rotary clubs decided to fund a call for a citywide "Service Club Consortium" to aid the homeless. This effort was to be called "Community Celebration." Some wealthy fellows put up some seed money and assembled a broad-based group of leaders from many service clubs including Rotary, Lions, Kiwanis, and Soroptomists. One initial, publicized goal of the group was to devise a concrete plan to expand existing temporary shelters serving women specifically and simultaneously to beef up case management and aftercare capacities at these shelters. The leader of this group suggested that an appropriate goal would be to "flatten" the problem of inadequate resources for the city's female homeless, with or without children in tow, to handle it, once and for all, and to keep handling it "so this barbarism does not recur here."

This goal required creating a "consensus plan" for paying for the improvements and renovations. The consortium had planned to unveil its plan at a highly visible press event, hoping to sell the entire city on the idea, with the help of the several directors of women's and children's agencies. Professional fundraisers were hired—but ultimately never used. Had they been loosed on the service clubbers alone they would have more than met their goals. Fundraising was planned, including foundation grant applications and approaches to big givers. It would have featured a flurry of community events. Strangely, this bright vision, linked to one of America's traditional but untapped sources of energy with respect to problems such as homelessness—the nation's service clubs—failed for lack of leadership. These clubs are out there in every American city and town, always seeking projects. Why don't they tackle a large, deeply moving one, like fully meeting the interim shelter needs of all the homeless women of the area?

Housing, both in the form of supportive, caring shelters, and in the form of the city's lowest- and low-income housing stock, remains the central need in addressing the plight of women and women with families on America's streets.

Where there is no vision, the people perish.

Proverbs 29:18

Women dream till they have no longer the strength to dream; those dreams against which they so struggle, so honestly, vigorously, and conscientiously, and so in vain, yet which are their life, without which they could not have lived; those dreams go at last. All their plans and visions seem vanished, and they know not where; gone, and they cannot recall them. They do not even remember them. And they are left without the food of reality or of hope.

—Florence Nightingale

SUGGESTED READING

Child and Youth Services—Homeless Children, the Watchers and the Waiters, Vol. 14, No. 1, Haworth Press, 1990.

Rachel and Her Children: Homeless Families in America, Jonathan Kozol, Crown, 1988.

The Unsheltered Woman: Women and Housing in the '80s, edited by Eugenie Ladner Birch, Center for Urban Policy Research, Rutgers University.

Emergency Aid to Families Program: Hearing Before the U.S. Congress House Committee on Government Operations: Subcommittee on Intergovernmental Relations and Human Resources, 99th Cong., 2nd Sess. 77-84 (March 19, 1986) (Statement of Dr. Ellen Bassuk).

Home is Where the Heart Is: The Crisis of Homeless Children and Families In New York City: A Report to the Edna McConnel Clark Foundation, Janice Molnar, Bank Street College of Education, 1988.

Homeless Children and Families In New York City, Janice Molnar.

The Tragedy of Homeless Children and Their Families in Massachusetts, Ellen Gallagher, Massachusetts Committee for Children and Youth.

"The Homeless and Their Children," Jonathan Kozol, *The New Yorker,* January 1988.

"Psychological Functioning of Children in a Battered Women's Shelter," Honore M. Hughes and Susan J. Barad, *American Journal of Orthopsychiatry,* July 1983.

"Redefining Transitional Housing for Homeless Families," Dr. Ellen L. Bassuk, *Yale Law & Policy Review,* vol. 6, pp. 309–330, 1988.

Housing the Single Parent Family: A Resource & Action Guidebook, Dept. of Community Affairs, Trenton, New Jersey, 1987.

Welfare Hotels: Uses, Costs and Alternatives, U.S. General Accounting Office, 1989.

Taking Action: A Comprehensive Approach to Housing Women and Children in Massachusetts, Joan Forrester Sprague, Women's Institute for Housing and Economic Development, 1988.

Women, Poverty and Progress in the Third World, M. Buvinic and S.W. Yudelman, Foreign Policy Association, 729 Seventh Avenue, New York, NY, 10019, 1989.

A Status Report on Homeless Families in American Cities, Laura Dekovan Waxman and Lilia M. Reyes, U.S. Conference of Mayors, May 1987.

Family and Nation, Daniel Patrick Moynihan, Harcourt, Brace, Javanovich Publishers, 1987.

Welfare: Income and Relative Poverty Status of AFDC Families, Human Resource Division, U.S. Government Accounting Office, November 1987 (pamphlet).

Family and Child Homelessness, Homeless Information Exchange, May 1989.

No Place Like Home: A Report on the Tragedy of Homeless Children and Their Families in Massachusetts, Ellen Gallagher, Massachusetts Committee for Children and Youth, Inc., September 1986.

The National Resource Center Bibliographic Database Search: Families and Children,
    Policy Research Associates, Inc., National Resource Center of Homelessness
    and Mental Illness, January 1990.
*Inventing a Non-Homeless Future: A Public Policy Agenda for Preventing Home-
    lessness,* Madeline R. Stoner, Peter Lang Publishing, Inc., 1989.

The Robert Wood Johnson Foundation at Princeton, New Jersey, launched a nationwide study of homeless families in August of 1990. Publications emanating from
this are expected to be definitive.

6

The Elderly Homeless

Honor thy father and thy mother that thy days may be long upon the
land which the Lord thy God giveth thee.

—Exodus 20:12

Rents are rising downtown! This is a dreaded specter to the thousands of
Americans who have inhabited the older, single-room-occupancy hotel rooms,
or SROs, the traditional "cheap rent" spots. Many of these inhabitants are
among the nation's elderly poor who live on fixed incomes, often limited
to a single person's Social Security pension. The SROs are being torn down
at a rapid rate nationwide, and the numbers of SRO rooms lost, between
1978 and 1988, city by American city, bear an unsettling resemblance to
the absolute numbers of homeless individuals in those respective cities. As
supplies shrink, prices rise. Rents in America's downtown SROs have more
than doubled over the last decade. The elderly poor with incomes who planned
to live their retirement in relative comfort are being squeezed out onto the
streets. About 5 percent of the homeless are elderly. Take this story from
the *San Diego Union* of March 29, 1990:

> When aging ex-pilot Hamilton Jackson hit town three years ago, the cleanest
> and cheapest place to live was the William Penn, a downtown hotel that
> was once very much uptown. But now the hotel's owners have big plans
> for Jackson's little room, uptown plans that clearly do not involve down-
> on-their luck guys like him who pay by the week. "Everybody's scared
> to death," Jackson said, sitting in the worn-out sofas in the dingy lobby.
> "We've got no place to go but the streets." Because private developers will
> be doing the ambitious $2 million renovation themselves, there will be no
> government money to relocate Jackson or any of the other twenty-five
> hotel residents. Raymond Ellis spent twenty years living in the stately red-
> brick hotel on a corner of Fifth Avenue and F Street. Now, old age and
> a reliance on crutches restrict his world to the two block area between
> his hotel room and the Star Club bar.

Some thirty million senior citizens live in America's urban areas today—more than three-fourths of our seniors, with over half of them living in the central cores of our cities. Having lost roommates or spouses, a majority of these elderly people live alone, and, until recently, their living circumstances, while lonely, were civilized. These people often suffer disabilities and they try to find neighborhoods where low-income housing combines with ease of walking access to the full range of services they need.

Recent "street surveys" of the homeless elderly, which have oddly dropped the bottom age of "elderly" to fifty-five years old (life on the street does increase a person's "mileage"), placed the percentage of the elderly at between 12 percent and 19 percent of the general homeless population. In cities like Chicago, which has a system of senior service centers, more than one-third of the "contacts for help" by the elderly have to do with housing problems.

However, according to a recent United Way study, the rising cost of health care threatens to erode the economic gains made by the elderly in the last two decades. Additionally, rents have climbed an average of 71 percent since 1981, with Social Security benefits increasing only 43 percent. Locally it can be much worse. A 1989 Chicago study showed a 60-percent average rent rise in just three years, with some residents paying 75 percent of their income for rent.

With these economic factors, the number of homeless elderly is on the increase. The San Diego Regional Task Force on the Homeless estimates that individuals over age sixty account for approximately 5 percent of the county's homeless population. According to a 1987 survey conducted by Senior Community Centers of San Diego (an agency that serves approximately three hundred meals per day to San Diego's downtown elderly), as many as 8 percent of its clients are homeless. An estimated additional 6 percent are "episodically homeless," a euphemism used to describe a person forced into homelessness every month when government and pension benefits cannot carry him or her through.

Affordable housing is increasingly hard to find. In line with the national trend, more than fifteen hundred older residential hotel rooms (often called SROs—single room occupancy hotels) were lost by the late 1980s in San Diego because of aggressive downtown redevelopment. As a result, there has been a dramatic increase in SRO rents with an accompanying rise in the number of older people who are on the streets. Approximately 30 percent of SRO housing provided shelter to seniors. Those seniors lucky enough to find an SRO typically spend 65 percent of their income on rent for these spartan rooms.

Shep, a downtown resident for twelve years, lamented the current housing situation:

I've lived in the same hotel for the last ten years. I used to pay $105 for a room ten by twelve feet, with a bed, dresser and chair. I could eat pretty well, although even then I had to eat at the local senior center at the end of the month. My rent is now $325 a month—same room, same damn bed I've been sleeping in for the last ten years. The difference is, now I sleep in that bed for three weeks, and live with friends or on the street the last week of the month. It's not right! But what can I do?

Many elderly like the SROs because they can be rented by the week or the month, making it easier to manage on a minimal income. In addition, there is a built-in network of hotel managers, desk clerks, storekeepers, and other residents who can keep an eye on older residents, screen visitors, offer credit, make loans, and give advice. Seniors often choose to live downtown because of the easy access to the services they need, as well as the companionship of other elderly people. For those elderly who have physical disabilities that prevent them from using public transportation, easy access becomes even more critical. Because of the condensed urban environment, downtown dwellers are also able to set up a social network of shopkeepers, waitresses, post office clerks, and police. All of these networks make up the glue that enables a continued independent existence for many older city dwellers.

For the older people who face the streets (many for the first time), existing shelters and programs do not meet their needs. Shelters provide for short-term stays (often five days), sometimes based on the assumption that job-training programs and other types of assistance will enable clients to move out and up into a better situation. Many older people are unable to work because of physical problems and must rely on a fixed income for the balance of their lives. Those 2 percent who are able and wish to work must face the stereotypical attitude of most employers, who see them as unemployable. When able to get work, many older people contend with dead-end jobs or low-wage positions.

Attitudes are beginning to change, however, as employers realize that older workers are often more reliable than young workers; and as fewer young workers are entering the workforce, some employers are starting to explore hiring older workers. In fact, many fast-food companies actively recruit the elderly, who are sometimes able to work up to high-paying restaurant management jobs within the company. Some seniors are able to stretch their marginal incomes by purchasing low-cost showers and meals, and then living in shelters a few days each month. Some have part-time or casual labor jobs to supplement Social Security benefits. One seventy-four-year-old woman living on the streets in Escondido, California, works twenty hours a week at a fast-food restaurant. She pays for showers at the

YWCA, keeps her clothes and belongings in a locker at the bus station and sleeps on park benches at night. She says things are working out for her and she doesn't feel threatened by others who live on the streets.

Roland is an amazingly fit sixty-four-year-old man who says that because of his bad experiences in flophouses he has opted for homelessness. He lives in a cardboard box behind a shrub on a tiny street near Greenwich Village in New York City. In his element on the streets, Roland is a successful entrepreneur who provides useful services to more needy Bowery-area men. He is a "runner," someone who does errands for cash. Roland is such a fine runner that he has graduated from the "get a bottle and keep the change" level to working only for social workers, priests, and nuns. He does not drink, use other drugs, or panhandle. Roland presents a rare type, but he is not unique. He may be homeless, but he is not a bum. Roland is a survivor, and knows how to make the best of his situation.

Many local community agencies provide food and shelter during the day, a place to socialize with others, clothing, and a place to receive mail. In the evening, though, homeless people are on their own. The older and more fragile homeless are at the mercy of those who are younger, stronger, or meaner.

Who are these elderly homeless? To many Americans, they are winos, Skid Row bums, or unwise people who haven't planned for their old age. In fact, they may be all or none of these things. Although the plight of the homeless has received greater visibility in the last few years, most of the extra attention has focused on the younger homeless individuals and families affected. These are perceived as victims of a changing and often unforgiving society. Homeless seniors, however, are often seen as responsible for their own situation. Ironically, with the tremendous growth of the older population in this country, the group being given the short end of society's concern is this subpopulation, which, along with families with children, will swell the ranks of the homeless to proportions never anticipated, if rents continue to rise or other factors dislodge them from their perches within civilization.

Of course, there are many elderly homeless who are alcoholics or mentally ill. Some have incomes that would allow them to rent lodgings, but they choose not to rent so they can spend more money on alcohol. For those who want to change, it is virtually no problem to get into a detoxification program. For many, though, the habit runs so deep that detoxification is never really an option.

For many elderly, a lack of willingness to accept services may be the most difficult dilemma. It implies a loss of that treasured American trait of independence. Many seniors will actually turn down services or beautiful lodgings because of their refusal to become more dependent on others.

Sometimes even the social agencies prefer to help the younger homeless, who are seen as "salvageable," able to be recycled back into the workforce. These are seen as having a future, or being worth the effort to mainstream back into society.

Phil is a sixty-seven-year-old man who has been evicted from two hotels because they were converted to upscale living quarters. He had been working at a local gas station in the evenings, a job he had held for four years, but the manager didn't want a homeless person working for him, so Phil was fired. Phil went to a downtown agency that provided job placement, but was told that he was too old to work. "Too old—damn!—I've been supporting myself since I was seven years old. How can I be too old to work? Am I too old to eat?" Adding insult to injury, Phil was told by the worker to go down to the Social Security office for help. "That seems to be their answer to seniors who are homeless—go to Social Security."

Federally funded services for the homeless do not specifically exclude older homeless people, but (as with the homeless mentally ill) the elderly have trouble using these services. Most programs are designed for the young, facilities are not handicapped-accessible, locations are often geographically spread out, and staff, while aware of the needs of a younger homeless population, are often utterly ignorant of the unique problems facing older people who are homeless. The handicaps that accompany old age (hearing loss, chronic health problems, etc.) are too often brushed off as those of a difficult client.

Charles, a seventy-seven-year-old retired college professor, first moved into an SRO to maintain his independence—it took too much effort to maintain his apartment. The combination of a rent increase and some expensive medical bills once almost forced him onto the street. Recent rent increases have made him cut back on his food budget. He talks of his experience at a food assistance center run by a church-affiliated agency. "I'm a pretty well-spoken person, and I think that the worker felt I was conning her. She questioned my income and made me walk back to my room to retrieve some receipts. It took me nearly an hour and a half, and when I got back, she told me that she was too busy to see me. When I protested, she said I was an old man and was probably ripping off Social Security anyway. Don't I deserve the same respectful treatment as someone younger?"

In some regions Americans are waking up to the plight of the homeless in general, and to that of the elderly homeless in particular. As the baby boomers age, interest is growing in things like dependent care for aging parents, and careful scrutiny of how and where elderly Americans live— whether it be in board-and-care facilities, in convalescent homes, or on the streets. In some states legislation is helping the elderly who want to sell their homes to move closer to their children without taxing their capital gains. Prosecutors are looking into insurance scams that falsely convince elderly people that they will have full medical coverage for services not covered by Medicare.

Good work on behalf of the elderly homeless is being done. There are many interesting studies available. Survival strategies are discussed by Carl I. Cohen, a professor of psychiatry at the State University of New York Health Science Center at Brooklyn, and Jay Sokolovsky in *Old Men of the Bowery: Survival Strategies of the Homeless* published in 1988. Sharon M. Keigher, Ph.D., has written *Relocation, Residence & Risk: A Study of Housing Risks and the Causes of Homelessness Among the Urban Elderly*, 1989, available through the Metropolitan Chicago Coalition on Aging.

Innovative day shelters are also being established. In Boston, the Kit Clark Senior House offers a day program devoted exclusively to participation by homeless seniors. The house serves multiple duty as one of Boston's nutrition sites, a home health agency providing adult day care, a community mental health clinic (with a large alcoholism unit), and a transportation program. All are funded under Title III of the Older Americans Act. Another Boston agency, Home Medical Services, has a program for temporary shelter of seniors in collaboration with the Boston Housing Authority. This program sets aside six rent-free units as temporary shelter solely for the homeless elderly. Eligible elderly can stay in one of the rooms for up to forty-five days, with an allowance for three fifteen-day extensions.

In Pennsylvania, all state lottery money goes to senior citizen programs. Elderly there can ride all public transportation for free, for example. They also get prescription assistance and many other benefits. Harrisburg is advertised as the best place in the United States in which to retire.

Progress is slow in this arena, however. Few voices are being raised (and Claude Pepper is, alas, gone!). As long as economic conditions continue their squeeze, we can expect the homeless elderly population to grow. Concerned citizens can advocate the care and compassion these people deserve as parents, friends, and fellow human beings. They are our heritage and they once cared for us. Soon, we shall be old, too.

Men are like grass, which rises up in the morning, and by afternoon it is gone.

—Isaiah 40:6–8

Let everyone witness how many different cards fortune has up her sleeve when she wants to ruin somebody.

—Benvenuto Cellini

SUGGESTED READING

The Unseen Elderly, J. Eckert, Campanile Press, San Diego State University, 1980.
Relocation, Residence and Risk: A Study of Housing Risks and the Causes of Homelessness Among the Urban Elderly, S. Keigher, R. Berman and S. Greenblatt, Metropolitan Chicago Coalition on Aging, 1989.

7

Homeless Veterans

A body at rest tends to remain at rest; a body in motion tends to remain in motion unless acted on by some outside force.
—Sir Isaac Newton (Law of Inertia)

When somebody says "homeless," what are the first images that come to mind? Often it is that of the shiftless drunks who chose their fate, the modern version of John Calvin's "undeserving poor." But add the word "kids," or "women," or "mentally ill," or "veteran" to the word "homeless" and sympathy flows.

"Homeless veterans" evokes shame (among other emotions) in Americans. And anger, that the nation we love would so let down those who have served it. We shudder at the cold, short memories, the injustice, the inequality of treatment of veterans of Vietnam with those of other wars. In America today, no segment of the homeless—save perhaps homeless women with children—evokes such strong, positive emotion, or can claim such a fierce band of supporters within the regular population.

Veterans share a history and common scars. They have very special gifts to give, now maturing gifts. And, by God, they're boot-camp trained and chastened by fire. They all know (as the rest of America will be learning, in the years ahead) that, "There, but for the grace of God, go I."

The Vietnam veterans movement is coming of age in America. Vets in their late thirties on up into their fifties are running companies and otherwise are in positions of power, but many broken comrades remain on the streets. They haunt all of us, but especially other vets. "There, but for the grace of God, go I."

After World War I, we called them "shell shocked." After World War II and Korea, they suffered from "battle fatigue." After Vietnam, they had "post–traumatic stress syndrome." As the words get longer and more jargonized, we leave our concerns for war-torn veterans in the hands of "the professionals." And because the Vietnam War was politically unpopular, we severely limited the funding for veteran "reentry support" programs compared to previous wars. It is as if we blame the shell-shocked infantry soldier for our embarrassing political mistakes. Many such soldiers came home traumatized, possibly blasted apart, and found themselves unloved and usually shunned.

Bless the Vietnam veterans movement. This band of heroes just may be forging a viable, moving example for the nation to see by building community out of chaos, reaching out and solving problems, creating coalitions, tramping the legislative halls, and pencilling out the grant proposals. Being a team. Building teams. Being humble. Reaching down for all sorts of frightening, repulsive, ill, possibly undeserving, surely wretched . . . comrades. Because there, but for the grace of God, each and all of us go.

One out of three of the males on America's streets is a veteran.

The general American public is becoming ready to consider the historical realities of the Vietnam War, as perspective improves with distance. This is evidenced by the popularity of films on Vietnam subjects, such as *Platoon* and *Born on the Fourth of July*, and of songs such as Billy Joel's 1989 "We Didn't Start the Fire," which speaks movingly of "homeless vets." More auspiciously, the veterans themselves are bestirred. The taboos are lifting, possibly clearing the way for realism and problem-solving.

THE STAND-DOWN

In 1986 veterans groups in San Diego banded together, formed their own non-profit outfit, Vietnam Veterans of San Diego (VVSD), and got the county government to establish the Office of Veterans Affairs. With this beachhead, they organized a remarkable weekend event, the "Stand-Down." In military parlance a stand-down is a respite after a battle or series of battles when troops are congratulated, rested, and helped. They get every type of attention they need, from medical care to new equipment to morale boosts. San Diego's first Stand Down was held in 1988. It was not merely a success—it moved the city and made history as a compelling model of veteran's outreach. Efforts are now afoot to see that Stand Down is replicated in dozens of American cities as a dramatic way to "call in" the homeless veterans who now dwell under bridges, in encampments among bushes, in canyons and parks, in doorways, and on grates. Veterans' leaders from eighteen cities visited San Diego for its third Stand Down, in 1990, to take blueprints for the event back to their home towns. In 1991 a *national* Stand Down is planned. Stand Down's organizers have inspired, and given assistance to, a pair of ambitious, Stand Down–like outreach efforts, "Home for a Day for Homeless Youth" and the "Women's Resource Fair" for homeless and battered women.

Before the Stand Down the word is sent out, carried to homeless veterans by veterans, person to person, buddy to buddy, calling out into the canyons and parks and dumpsters. "Come on in! Get a hand here, pal! There'll be food. Dignity. Help. Jobs. Clean up those bench warrants. And *we're* running it. You'll be *somebody* with us, and we'll be honest with you. We've been there. We'll help find a lot of the things you need. And, by golly, we'll see that you get those things if you're willing to help yourself today. Come as you are!" About half of San Diego's estimated fifteen hundred homeless veterans attended the 1990 Stand Down.

The 1988 Stand Down took place in the city's huge, central Balboa Park. With green tents, signs, flags, and tables, it looked for all the world like a street fair mated with a MASH unit. It had sign-up spots for:

- Jobs
- Shelter
- Veterans benefits (with all the computer backups to get all needed answers instantly.)
- Social Security, welfare
- Medical care
- Voter registration
- Meals
- Mental health help and counseling
- Clothing—for warmth, and for job interviews
- Hair cuts, showers
- Even an on-site municipal court, replete with volunteer judges, lawyers, clerks, computers, everything needed to carry on official business. Nearly five hundred arrest warrants were cleared, mainly with orders of "volunteer work" at veterans or job agencies.

The event's volunteers included doctors, lawyers, judges, clerks, social workers, and others, most veterans themselves. Buy the end of Stand Down, they looked a little like the homeless, and some of the homeless a little like the volunteers.

The brigades of vets were thus enticed in and treated well. They were given a strong blast of community, a shot of genuine buddy-bond. It was a form of love that was longed for, understood, and deeply refreshing. From this success, the team of organizing groups has launched into a raft of ambitious projects. They are out after grants.

HOW TO ASSIST HOMELESS VETERANS

Homeless veterans, very unfortunately but very understandably, are not exactly flocking into shelters and veterans centers for comprehensive aid. This is because the proper specialized aid, which might keep the individual homeless veteran psychologically tied to a veterans organization, is generally unavailable. It is also because most homeless veterans, not unlike many female homeless and certain individuals among the deeply mentally ill (catatonic people, for example), tend to profoundly distrust everybody. Unless approached in very special ways, they just won't come in to take advantage of services designed for them, no matter how effective they may be. We also need to recall, of course, that we are speaking of people who are combat-trained as well as combat-damaged. They know how to forage; they know how to defend themselves. In the case of many Vietnam veterans, they are often convinced that mainstream society, by rejecting their war, has rejected them. Why would these warriors, still proud in some recesses of their battered souls, wish to get "captured" into the bosom (or maw) of a network labelled "assistance" by a people known to be both hostile and untrustworthy?

The outreach teams have to be veterans, and they cannot do their work in button-down collars and dark suits. Psychologists among the veterans say that short- and long-term treatment programs for veterans must deal with certain "victim-type," neurotic (and psychotic) belief systems. Confronted gently, such problems can be dealt with, and the veterans they afflict enabled to heal. Asked what messages he would wish given to veterans considering participation in the Stand Down, John Nachison, a psychologist and a founder of VVSD, offered,

> "If you've ever thought there'd be a time in your life when you'd have to make some changes, make it this weekend. Take a stand. You can't go on blaming. We're in this [veterans] community together. It's *your* responsibility to decide to get your life started. Only when you do that can you make a move." When you talk to homeless, that's what you hear: "This agency did this to me. That one rejected me. Somebody treated me badly." There's a lot of denial out there. People can't begin to get better till they get "psyched up," motivated. Otherwise, Stand Down is just enabling people to stay stuck in addiction. The idea is not to get them all dressed up with nowhere to go. As is said, "with half a tank of gas and you can't get there from here."

The major failing of Stand Down, added Nachison, is that, "We have no funds to follow up, and that's a tragedy, because the homeless leave no return address."

BRIEF HISTORY

During the Nixon and Carter administrations, the perception grew that not only did the nation owe a shamefully unacknowledged debt to its veterans but that large numbers of Vietnam veterans were unserved via ordinary, Veterans' Administration channels. Efforts to address the situation culminated in the Vietnam Veterans Readjustment Act of 1979, which established local veterans centers throughout the country. There are now almost two hundred of these centers nationwide. Their purpose is to heal the "psychological wounds of war."

In 1981, however, the enthusiasts of the incoming Reagan administration attacked the nascent outreach efforts, preferring instead an approach they called the Vietnam Veterans Leadership Program, which built on the fact that all those who served in Vietnam seemed to share a fierce bond, and the reality that some veterans were doing well in society. Good people were recruited to run this effort, but it didn't work; cynics felt that in some locales the new units acted more like Young Republican Clubs, tending to look haughtily down on the vets for whom they supposedly existed to help. Fortunately, Congress prevented the dismantling of the veterans centers.

With the toehold of the underfunded veterans centers, some remarkable local work has been done. In San Diego, for example, the local center is run by the VVSD. The group has set up three charmingly named programs. Perhaps most important for the long term is the "Landing Zone," an alcohol recovery house for forty-six homeless veterans. Second is the "Dust Off House," for eighteen homeless Vietnam veterans as they phase into work. These houses are safe, sane, sober places to live, with medical and jobs help built in. The vets are required to save at least 70 percent of what they earn toward getting an apartment. Average stay: five months. VVSD Executive Director Robert Van Keuren says of it, "This has gotten the whole community working together for these veterans. This embodies the way to get Vietnam vets off the streets." Third is the Homeless Veterans Re-entry Project, which serves as a screening and referral jobs program. And fourth, Stand Down.

The "storefront-type" veterans centers program is an excellent one, but Congress should strengthen it. Van Keuren, the full-time executive director of this hard-hitting local program in San Diego, was paid only $18,000 per year. With a family, small children and the prodigious energy he lavishes on his work night and day, this was laughable. The local accomplishments in San Diego are significant, but such work product cannot be expected of center directors nationwide if they are offered such picayune salaries.

CONCLUSIONS

1. Congress needs to fiercely maintain support for service-connected disabilities and expand support for the local Vietnam Veterans Outreach Program (the veterans center program). Congress could also use the Veterans' Administration to set up a pilot program of shelter specifically for homeless vets, using many local (presently all locally funded) models, like the ones in San Diego. Congress could also amend Title 38 of the U.S. Code to make explicit that veterans suffering from service-connected disability, including Vietnam post–traumatic stress disorders, would be entitled to help at such shelters.

2. The McKinney Act of 1988 now funds $750 million in aid for homeless programs each year nationally, but only $1.5 million of this is available for veterans efforts. The most frequently heard general complaint about the administration of the McKinney Act is that there is no requirement that grants in any given local area be integrated. A veterans jobs grant, for example, might be released in April and a veterans housing grant released in October. The two would be used to immeasurably greater effect if planned and spent together, to create a comprehensive support program. The grants are also too small, often only $150,000, to really accomplish much.

Homeless veterans are not now being served under the McKinney Act. President Bush has praised the act and claimed it as his own vehicle to aid the homeless. It needs tending by his administration. Its work needs to be fully funded to help the one-third of America's homeless men who are veterans.

3. Without local low-income housing into which rehabilitated veterans might relocate after their stint in a shelter, there can be no ultimate success. A legislated linkage between HUD housing rehabilitation programs and veterans programs is needed, with veterans doing the rehabilitation labor and provided Habitat-style (more on this later) opportunities to work their way to home ownership.

4. The unique need of the homeless Vietnam veterans, beyond housing and outreach, is for a nationwide system to provide adequate inpatient mental health treatment. "The need is for treatment milieu," says Nachison. "Psychiatrists and other mental health professionals at the veterans hospitals are well-qualified and excellent at dealing with the commonplace psychoses, depression, stresses, neuroses, but they likely know nothing about *combat*. Vietnam Vets have tried for years to get such a 'combat unit,' in southern California with no success." The combat center in Palo Alto is one of the few in the nation, with barely enough beds for its own locale. Tools need to be selected to fit problems, not the other way around.

5. The "storefront-style" veterans centers need to become more "veteran-

driven" entities that meet the homeless and near-homeless veterans where they *are*. Veterans of all eras go to these centers, and they need to feature many more services and linkages with other community services. These centers could be expanded to incorporate the aggressive features of private veterans entities, such as VVSD. Shelters where veterans can live together are a first step off the streets, and these must include entry mechanisms to inpatient treatment centers, to handle the now-familiar combat disability called "post-traumatic stress disorder."

6. The Job Training and Partnership Act allocates too little money for veterans. Veterans as a group are able-bodied. They suffer much less frequently from the "gross psychoses" that beset so many other homeless people, probably because of armed services entrance requirements and the fact that mental illness is typically manifested in some form before the usual military entrance age (eighteen to twenty-two). Veterans want to work. And with some trust-building and some "sprucing up," most will be able to work. Will America be able to face up to the justice of her debt to these warriors? At the barest minimum, will we help them to get a job?

7. Veterans services must be made accessible. Veterans leaders liken accessing the present Veterans' Administration programs (which they praise as high quality) to going to a huge, modern supermarket, along with hundreds of other neighbors, loading up a shopping cart, and then being required to stand in a single check-out line for weeks, while the food rots and most comers get discouraged and give up.

Properly assisted, homeless veterans might be able to supply a leaven to the effort to find solutions for the general problem of homelessness, by providing highly visible models of success. Federal monies matched with local funds could create several dramatic local victories like Stand Down. This in turn could dispel the greatest underlying cause of American home-lessness: the persistence of the lie that the problem is hopeless and unsolvable.

> It is rather for us to be here dedicated to the great task remaining before us—that from these honored dead we take increased devotion to that cause for which they gave the last full measure of devotion—that we here highly resolve that these dead shall not have died in vain—that this nation, under God, shall have a new birth of freedom—and that the government of the people, by the people, for the people, shall not perish from the earth.
> —Abraham Lincoln (Gettysburg Address)

SUGGESTED READING

A Bright Shining Lie: John Paul and America in Vietnam, Neal Sheehan, Random House, 1989.

Out of the Night: The Spiritual Journey of the Vietnam Veterans, Rev. William Mahedy, Ballantine Books, 1986.

Home From the War; Vietnam Veterans: Neither Victims Nor Executioners, Robert J. Lipton, Simon & Schuster, 1973.

Stress Disorders Among Vietnam Veterans, Charles R. Figley, Brunner-Mazel, 1978.

Defending the Vietnam Combat Veteran, Barry Levin, J.D., and David Ferrier, Vietnam Veterans Legal Assistance Project, 1989.

8

Runaway and Throwaway Kids

Hold fast to dreams, for if dreams die,
Life is a broken-winged bird that cannot fly.

—Langston Hughes

I dream of a place where everyone is nice. There's rows and rows of clean white houses.

—A homeless child, 1989

America has created a sad new subculture in our society, a roving band of adolescents with no place to call home. Street kids. They sleep in cardboard boxes in the parks, or on deserted downtown roofs. They eat what they can beg or steal. They band together for protection. Systems designed to take care of kids have no room for these semi-adults, and real adults are their biggest enemies.

The National Network of Runaway and Youth Services generously estimated in 1987 that one to three million teenagers were wandering the streets in U.S. cities, searching for a safe place to spend the night. Most estimations place the maximum figure at eight hundred thousand. Some are runaways. Many will return home, at least for a while. Some are throwaways, told by their parents to get out and stay out. Some are victims of the systems designed to care for them, kids who have grown up in hospitals and treatment centers and foster homes, kids without even a concept of home. Those trying to work with them say that many of the kids on the street will stay there indefinitely, becoming addicted to street life. Many, ultimately, will die there.

The common misconception is that these kids could go home, if only they would. This is not true. A report by the 1989 House Select Committee on Children says nearly half a million children are in foster homes, detention facilities or mental health institutions. There are no reports on what happens to these children once they turn eighteen. More and more of the kids on the street are there because they have been discarded. Their parents, for myriad reasons, have turned them away and said, much as an angry teenager might, "Leave us alone." On the street kids talk of being locked out of the house, sent away to a nonexistent relative, or abandoned on the road. Some come from homeless families—up to 30 percent of our homeless population may comprise families with children. Others have families so abusive and cruel that the street seems a relative haven to them. They are homeless in the strictest sense of the word. They never had homes.

Liz Shear is the executive director of San Diego Youth and Community Services, one of the nation's earliest agencies to recognize and help homeless teenagers. When Shear wants to pull a listener's heart strings, she talks about the movie *ET.* "When people remember that film they remember how enchanted we all were with ET. We all cheered for him and wanted him to be able to go home. We kept saying 'ET, phone home.' Well, these kids are just as engaging, but they have no home to go to."

They have no recognized rights. Teens are too old to get help from the overtaxed child protection agencies, and too young to get legal identification. To be on their own officially they must be emancipated by the courts. This is not the first thing on a hungry kid's mind. They don't qualify for welfare—it is parents who receive Aid for Dependent Children benefits, not their kids. The average education level for kids on the street is eighth grade; many are illiterate. They are incredibly resourceful, imaginative and brave, but unemployable. All their talents are used up by basic survival.

"The image people have of these kids is that they are the slime of the earth," says Shear. "They may behave like the slime of the earth after a while, but they are bright. They behave in street-wise ways." Studies show that up to 90 percent of the kids on the street were sexually or physically abused before they became homeless. All will endure further abuses on the street. More than half will turn to prostitution for money; more than a third will become intravenous drug users. Some get pregnant; at least then they are eligible for medical and financial aid. Most are at high risk of contracting AIDS. Thousands of teenagers die anonymously, without families to grieve their loss, and are buried in unmarked graves. Street kids are sophisticated and uneducated, filled with bravado and terror, emotionally crippled and developmentally arrested in a state of enhanced adolescent angst. They have been robbed of their childhoods, and their futures are grim. And, thus far in this wide land of ours, they have been offered little hope.

The pioneers who work with these kids see two approaches to dealing with teenage homelessness. The first is to work with the kids on the street, in outreach programs and runaway shelters like San Diego's Storefront Shelter, described below. The second is to begin to convince our society that we must begin really caring for kids again. "Start liking children again!" Does that sound hard? Today's wounded teens are tomorrow's troubled adults. The increasing numbers of kids on the street will have a hard time contributing to a society that has deserted them.

San Diego's Storefront Shelter for homeless teens opened its doors in 1986. By 1989, more than a thousand kids were getting help there each year. The shelter has been kept open through the wits and persistence of its parent agency, San Diego Youth and Community Services, which operates the shelter in collaboration with Catholic Charities and METRO (a Methodist agency). Like most shelters for kids, the Storefront Shelter uses a multi-pronged, subtly persuasive system for helping kids get off the streets.

According to Shear, the first job for any agency working with street kids is to create an effective outreach program. "The kids will not come to you," Shear says. "They have been abused by most adults they've known and exploited by every adult system—the police, the care givers, the johns." More than half of homeless youth (58 percent) have never been inside a shelter. The Storefront's outreach workers hang out on the street, in the fast-food restaurants and the all-night markets, handing out condoms and bleach, talking with kids about AIDS, helping with advice and referrals, developing a rapport with the kids and a reputation among them as people who can be counted on for something. Gradually, a few decide to spend a night at the Storefront. They tell their friends.

The shelter is in a warehouse district dotted with soup kitchens and rescue missions. Up to twenty kids can spend the night there, sleeping in a dormitory-style room. They get plenty of food and attention, clean clothes, and medical care. The rules are simple and absolute—no drugs, alcohol, sex, violence, or weapons. The first time a kid appears he or she gets a caseworker. Over time, a plan for the future emerges. The workers are realistic and practical. They know it may take months for a kid to establish enough trust to even want to keep coming back for more; and trust is the only tool the shelter workers have, since no legal way exists (or is proposed) to compel compliance.

Shear says certain basic approaches are essential in helping kids progress from the street. First and most important, these kids must be helped to regain, or to gain for the first time, a sense of self-esteem and self-respect. This is no mean task; it is also thrilling when it succeeds. Caseworkers have to empower the kids, help them learn how to solve their own problems.

At the Storefront kids have access to medical treatment and referrals to dentists and other health-care professionals. Self-help groups like Alcoholics Anonymous and Narcotics Anonymous meet regularly at the shelter. Kids can get legal services, from learning how to become emancipated to finding out what their warrants and arrest records really mean.

The Storefront's twenty beds are completely insufficient for the four hundred or so kids on San Diego's streets each night. Other programs in the city offer a total of about fifty beds for teens, still far from enough. Shear realizes the need for more beds, but resists any suggestion of creating more massive shelters for kids. Shelters don't work unless they serve twenty kids or less, Shear insists. If you warehouse teens, you lose them. The energy level is so high, the individual crises so intense, that the shelter would become much like the street—confusing, hostile, and inhospitable. Institutionalization, Shear says, does not work.

The Storefront Shelter offers the first stage in helping kids off the street, but Shear and others realize it is only a Band-Aid. After spending some time off the street making plans for the future, kids need transitional housing, a place to live while they gather the resources to move on. In social services terms, they need to learn independent living skills. Most street kids, Shear says, are not ready to live on their own. Even if they had money and an apartment they would still bomb out. They need time in group homes, or shared apartments, or a special kind of foster home capable of handling troubled kids in a caring way. Kids instinctively create what Shear calls second-chance families, by banding together on the street and forming mini-communities. The most mature kids, the natural leaders, become parents in a sense, looking out for the welfare of the weaker ones. But they still don't have adult helpers, role models who can serve as examples of healthy adult living. They need substitute moms and dads who can offer mature advice and helpful hints. These kids need the basics—how to pay bills, divide up chores, handle household emergencies—in learning how to create and maintain homes. Many have never been exposed to sane and healthy daily life. "If we can train them in the practical skills of living together and the softer skills of interrelating, we have a real good shot at success," Shear says.

Ideally, a homeless teenager would go from the shelter to transitional housing to affordable independent housing. Programs around the country are providing bits and pieces of this overall approach, but as yet none has been able to put it all together. Most use what Shear calls the "step back and punt" approach, mixing and matching whatever happens to work for each child.

Hand in hand with the housing issue is the challenge of making street kids employable. For the most part they have no work skills, and no ability to delay gratification long enough to wait for a paycheck. The Storefront workers have come up with many creative ways to help kids make money, concentrating on small jobs that offer immediate payment, like passing out leaflets in the street.

The real solution for homeless kids is prevention—keeping them at home or in a safe environment with a competent guardian. In 1974, leaders of programs for homeless youth formed the National Network of Runaway and Youth Services. Runaways were being seen in large numbers for the first time. They were not all ultra-resourceful Huckleberry Finns. Also in 1974, Congress enacted and President Ford signed the Juvenile Justice and Delinquency Prevention Act and the Runaway Youth Act. In 1977, this act was amended as the Runaway and Homeless Youth Act. In 1982, journalist Dotson Rader graphically described the lives of street kids in a *Parade* magazine article that brought an outpouring of concern and donations. The response formed the basis of the National Fund for Runaway Children. Rader continued portraying the plight of kids without homes. His ongoing work will soon be published in a book on America's homeless youth.

The network has grown to include over five hundred agencies and shelters dealing with homeless kids. Nonetheless, thousands of kids get turned away every year for lack of space and staff. And homeless kids are still vastly ignored. On a societal, governmental level, Shear says, we need the Younger Americans Act. The United States has no unified youth and family policy. We need a national statement of principle on what kids are worth to us. The National Network of Runaway and Youth Services is mounting a major push to bring about passage of this act. Such a bill has been bounced about on the federal level, as originally sponsored by the late Rep. Claude Pepper (D-Florida), champion of the elderly. Sen. Christopher Dodd (D-Connecticut), who worked on the original bill with Pepper, has carried on the cause. The act declares our nation's "most valuable resource" to be our children. It takes powerful steps toward providing "national systems for shelter, mental and physical health care, top-quality educational opportunities, training and job readiness help." Among the steps called for are "(5) the widest range of civic, cultural, and recreational activities which promote self-esteem and a sense of community; (6) comprehensive community services which are efficient, coordinated, and readily available; (7) genuine participation in decisions concerning the planning and managing of their lives."

The price tag: a tiny $29 million. The 1990 appropriation for the Runaway and Homeless Youth Act ought to be doubled to $50 million, as proposed by Rep. Tom Tauke (R-Iowa). This would double the number of children who could be served to over a hundred thousand. If enough pressure were applied by everyone who cares about kids, this could happen in 1991.

What damaged kids need, Shear says, is the chance to learn what home means. A study of foster kids says the things that made a major difference for them were loving compassion; honesty; listening; and consistency. According to Shear and most advocates for children, every kid needs, very fundamentally, to establish a strong sense of self-worth. This is a hard trait to learn if you don't see it in others! The second critical ingredient is positive adult role models. Even the most damaged kids, the ones who have been battered and belittled into oblivion, can benefit from being around stable, secure adults. Kids, particularly teenagers, need to develop the ability to think critically and discover solutions. And they need to have access to the decisions that affect their lives.

> But a bold peasantry, their country's pride,
> When once destroy'd, can never be supplied.
>
> —Oliver Goldsmith

SUGGESTED READING

"To Whom Do They Belong? A Profile of America's Runaway and Homeless Youth and the Programs that Help Them." National Network of Runaways and Youth Services, Inc., 905 6th Street SW, Suite 411, Washington, D.C., 20024, 202-488-0739, 1985.

"Runaway and Homeless Youth and the Programs That Help Them," Runaway and Homeless Youth, Office of Inspector General, Department of Health & Human Services, Region X, October 1983.

"Runaway/Homeless Youth in San Diego County," San Diego Youth and Community Services, 3878 Old Town Avenue, Suite 200B, San Diego, CA, 92110, 619-297-9310.

"Homeless and Runaway Youth Receiving Services at Federally Funded Shelters," GAO Report to the U.S. Senate, H.R.D. 90-45, U.S. General Accounting Office, Washington, D.C., 20548, December 1989.

"Homeless Children: A Neglected Population," E. Bassuk, M.D., and Lenore Rubin, Ph.D., *American Journal of Orthopsychiatry*, April 1987, 57(2): 279–86.

Coming to Our Senses, Morris Berman, Simon & Schuster, 1989.

III

The Major Solutions

9

Cycling Able-Bodied Homeless into Jobs

To be able to work, to be useful and to love.
                    —Sigmund Freud's definition of mental health

Without work all life goes rotten.

                                        —Albert Camus

Freud's declaration is a remarkable one, but even the most afflicted of the homeless, those severely disabled by mental illness (a third) or substance abuse (up to a third), overwhelmingly declare that they want to work. Loss of a job is among the personal disasters most frequently cited as the single event that pitched an individual or a family into homelessness. Low-skilled jobs that pay adequate wages are being phased out in the United States. A 1989 projection about the U.S. economy by the Labor Department, in an issue of its magazine *Labor* devoted to changes in the 1990s, made these conclusions:

1. Women will fill half our jobs and the number of minorities in the workforce will rise to one-quarter.
2. Education will increasingly be the factor that distinguishes "haves" from "have nots."
3. The labor force will be 70 percent larger by the year 2000, but growth is decelerating. The high-technology retail and service industries are projected to grow, while manufacturing and mining, for example, will fall off, as they have been for two decades. Thus, many previously highly paid, low-education, union-wage jobs are simply vanishing. Growth will be in areas involving computers, health, and management—all areas requiring education. Similar growth will occur in low-paying service and retail jobs, but pay will be at or near minimum wage.[5]

The American income curve will no longer be bell-shaped, with the huge middle we have always presumed to be the bastion of American democracy. Instead, our economy is creating a "two-bump" curve of educated "haves" and uneducated and disabled "have not" populations. If this ominous gap widens, it will spell explosive politics for America, to say nothing of industrial dysfunction and a staggering public burden of prison and social service costs. The best anti-welfare program is a job. Some attention by the administration and the Congress to the subject of whether America ought to have some sort of an "industrial policy" (as do Germany and Japan) is called for. If we don't change our direction, we will wind up where we're headed.

Professional surveys undertaken in various cities by job specialists have concluded that nearly one-sixth of any city's homeless are actively looking for work and are "job ready"; another sixth are looking for work, but their skills, self-esteem and appearance need sprucing up before they can be successful.

Jobs programs for America's homeless are facilitated in conjunction with shelters, and they roughly resemble the two approaches presented here, which can dovetail.

THE INSTITUTIONAL APPROACH

San Diego Episcopal Community Services operates a typical job program for homeless people. In 1988 this work program established a modest, supervised center serving homeless people, building on a 1984 effort that had been originally paid for by city government. Today, the center operates by contracting with local businesses for various types of work projects that homeless people can do. ECS's success, however, can be largely attributed to its belief that these efforts must include more for a person than just a day's work. By helping the homeless improve their skills, ECS hopes it will help many down-and-outers return to the mainstream of society, that is, a stable living situation, steady employment, and a manageable life. "Teach a person to fish and you feed him for life."

Among the most successful components of ECS's casual labor program is its low-cost crash reading and writing course, which teaches non-readers and functional illiterates how to use a bus schedule or fill out a job application. Indeed, such basic skills constitute major steps forward for those who are willing to help themselves. The program's first reading class consisted of six homeless "clients" who studied each morning from 9:00 a.m. to noon, then worked in the ECS center from 1:00 p.m. to 4:00 p.m. Instruction included reading and basic math presented at the individual client's level.

Through the years, ECS has refined its overall program, increasing the services it offers its job-hunting clientele:

- Stable, temporary housing equipped with showers (so job seekers arrive for work or interviews both rested and clean).
- Lunch (one cannot stand in a food line and work at the same time).
- Job-placement counseling, personal counseling, and assistance in rudimentary life planning.
- A living arrangement that is safe, warm, supportive, and conducive to good mental health (so that job applicants arrive at an interview with a smile and pleasant attitude—two things required on most jobs).

Homeless clients begin their work experience after ten to fifteen hours of assessment work time, to permit evaluation of each client's employable skills. Those with good social skills and work habits get part- and full-time employment, not just day-to-day assignments. Clients considered "unemployable" are assessed more deeply to determine whether or not their dysfunction is temporary or chronic. In either case, proper follow-up is insisted on (and made possible) with referral to the appropriate rehabilitation program or programs.

The ECS Downtown Work Center is now almost completely self-supporting. Beginning in 1988 with eight to twelve clients a day in a three-hundred-square-foot room, it now operates out of an eighteen-hundred-square-foot building on the same downtown block with the other ECS downtown programs. This proximity prevents the severe dropout rate built into so many other programs, whose homeless are expected to keep appointments punctually, trudging around a big city.

During its first year, the ECS "job shop" was run by one heroic volunteer. Today, three people—a program manager, an office assistant/bookkeeper and a floor supervisor—run the shop. Operating on a $120,000 budget for the 1989-90 fiscal year, the center employs twenty to twenty-five clients daily. Clients earn $4.25 per hour. They get worker's compensation benefits, but little else in the way of insurance.

IMPLICATIONS FOR AMERICAN CITIES

With the right help at least one-third of the homeless might be cost-effectively cycled off the streets and into a more normal existence. Agencies in Denver, San Diego, and Seattle that have been offering work to the homeless for several years conclude that once a city sets up a homeless jobs program, the cost per permanent placement is about $2,000. This figure is deceptively low, however, reflecting only costs to the cities, since refinements in initial programs inevitably include formal partnerships with state and federally funded job-placement programs, and sometimes with local private industry councils. In 1988, ECS spent a total of $203,000 (including the $120,000 for the ECS Work Center) to serve 450 clients, 65 of whom garnered full-time jobs or on-the-job training.

The federal government has several programs in place that can provide money for local job training and job placement. But first, one has to ask for the help! Two U.S. Department of Labor programs, both authorized under the 1988 McKinney Act, are targeted specifically at helping the homeless, but these are, alas, drops in a large bucket. They provide only small grants and these grants are not necessarily integrated with grants for other programs. The larger of these two federal efforts is called the Job Training for the Homeless Demonstration Project. In fiscal year 1989–90, the Labor Department allocated a mere $11.3 million to a score of public and private groups throughout America to carry out a variety of initiatives that help homeless people become productive members of society. This pittance was and is a scandal, especially in view of the Reagan/Bush declarations about the importance of jobs for the homeless. The second initiative taken under the McKinney Act is the Labor Department's Homeless Veterans Reintegration Project. This serves homeless veterans and, in theory, offers a range of services: job counseling, résumé preparation, job-search assistance, remedial and vocational education, job placement, long-term job-retention programs, and on-the-job training. In addition, assistance with job-related transportation, clothes, tools, alcohol and drug counseling, and counseling for post–traumatic stress disorder are available from the project sponsors or through referral to other sources. However, the sad truth, again, is that an integrated program for veterans actually providing these services is very rare in America.

A separate program, also under the jurisdiction of the Labor Department, is the 1983 Job Training Partnership Act. JTPA provides job-training and employment services for economically disadvantaged adults and youth, dislocated workers, Native Americans, migrant and seasonal farm workers, veterans, and older workers. The cost of this program is $3.4 billion a year, including the Job Corps. The state block grant portion totals $2.8 billion annually, with the major goal to move jobless adults and older youth into permanent, unsubsidized, self-sustaining employment. However, like many legislative schemes in this era of meaningful gestures, this act sets up an intelligent framework with woefully inadequate funding. Under it, state and local governments have primary responsibility for the management and administration of job-training programs. Governors approve locally developed plans and are responsible for monitoring compliance with the provisions of the act. JTPA contains five titles, but Titles I and II are the most germane to the homeless problem.

Title I, "Job Training Partnership," sets up an administrative structure for the delivery of job-training services and the drawing up of local job-training plans. It sets performance standards and mandates: 1) state job-training coordinating councils formed by governors to provide advice and counsel on training components of the act, as well as to play a critical role in planning employment services; 2) service delivery areas designated by governors to receive federal job-training funds—automatically eligible are units of local government with jurisdiction over a population of two hundred thousand or more; 3) the use of private industry councils to plan job-training and employment services at the local level. This part of the act—working with private-sector business leaders to provide workers trained for actually available jobs—is vital.

Title II-A, "Training Services for the Disadvantaged," provides for a system of block grants to states to support local training and employment programs. Funding is based on relative unemployment levels and the number of disadvantaged people in a state. Services are targeted to the poor, but 10 percent of any city's participants can be non-disadvantaged individuals who face other employment barriers. Programs aim to train people for productive, unsubsidized work. Information on these programs can be obtained from JTPA offices through local elected officials such as mayors or county boards of supervisors.

The Interagency Council on the Homeless is a Washington, D.C.-based coalition of all federal departments that administer McKinney Act funding. Its publications announce all McKinney funding and list non-federal programs that also assist the homeless. Another organization of interest, also located in Washington, is the National Alliance to End Homelessness.

Administrators of San Diego's ECS jobs program describe it as a "perfor-mance-based" contract with the city. A three-track program, it is administered through the Private Industry Council/Regional Employment and Training Consortium at a cost of $203,000 per year. Of the total, $130,000 comes from city funds. Track One is casual labor that takes place both in a supervised workshop and in the community as day labor. Track Two is permanent, full-time work with a minimum of twenty days employment. Track Three is permanent, full-time work with on-the-job training of at least sixty days. Funding for Tracks Two and Three comes from JTPA and from the city through a federal community development block grant. The contract itself is administered through the San Diego Private Industry Council. Track One is funded through a San Diego development block grant.

In 1987 ECS contracted with the city for a program that mixed the three tracks. Each casual-labor placement cost $300, with a total of 385 individuals working at least ten hours a week through this phase. Forty-five people were placed in Tracks Two and Three. Track Two, the shorter-term, full-time program, cost $800 per placement, while each Track Three-trained placement cost $2,000. ECS met Track One goals in 1988–89, but fell short in Tracks Two and Three. The year's total dollar contract total ended up at $190,000—a trivial amount for a county of 2.3 million people with an estimated seven thousand to ten thousand homeless at any given moment!

MORE POSSIBLE PLAYERS

State employment development programs exist in all states. These are typically designed to dovetail with, and generally to administer, the federal job-placement and -training programs. In California, New York, New Jersey, and Colorado, for example, these programs create councils of local employers. Employers gratefully use such "funnels" of screened and often newly trained personnel. Employing this specialized population greatly reduces their personnel and training costs. Local community colleges are also enthusiastic players in this scenario, since they already have technical and employment-oriented training facilities. Because these schools are usually funded by the state, the cost to the homeless jobs program can be negligible.

PLANNING AND STARTUP

The initial questions for the government planners and other agencies dealing with the homeless are: 1) who is already working in this area?; 2) whose legal responsibility is it to work in this area (that is, to interview, screen and test, train, and place people needing work)?; 3) what mechanisms of teamwork and/or competition already exist (and who manages this network)?; and 4) what improvements are needed, at what cost, and from which resource pocket?

Cities often will match local funds with those of regional employment and training councils. Typically, the startup funding for a homeless jobs program will not be a matching situation, but rather a single grant from the first outfit that recognizes its own interests in creating such a program. Usually this is a municipal government. As the program gathers the base data necessary to help managers evaluate and design programs, the city should be able to recruit other agencies as active partners. Such partnerships can have many aspects—from designing contracts to sharing existing services offered by social service agencies.

In San Diego, for example, the first contractor with the city was a not-for-profit group headed by an urban anthropology professor from the University of California at San Diego working with two other professionals.

Now, six years later, it is run by the more established entity, Episcopal Community Services. In the late 1970s, ECS's downtown services organization operated from a one-room office. Today it consumes a whole block of clinics and offices and integrates a range of services such as emergency assistance, therapy, and alcohol- and drug-dependency counseling. ECS's network of services for street people includes:

Episcopal Downtown Services—Emergency assistance with food, clothing, shelter, transportation, crisis intervention and case management is provided for homeless and near-homeless adults and children. Special services for homeless veterans are offered. One of the county's most comprehensive employment programs for homeless people operates at this location.

Friend to Friend Clubhouse—Matches are arranged between homeless and near-homeless mentally ill adults and volunteers for friendship, support, education and recreational activities. This support is often the only positive, esteem-building contact the mentally ill members have. It is of enormous importance to them because it can prevent rehospitalization. Field trips, special activities, skill-building classes, help with daily personal chores, and experience at self-governance round out the clubhouse program.

Downtown Health Services—A state-licensed facility for primary medical care, its medical team provides service for all ages. Student interns, doctors, nurses, and community supporters with clerical skills all volunteer their time.

Ex-Offender Re-Entry Program—The oldest program in the downtown cluster, the program offers immediate employment for ex-offenders via the employer members of the Private Industry Council. This includes shelter, transportation to and from the job, counseling, information, and referral. It works.

Counseling—Professionals offer educational and healing counseling to groups, individuals, families, and clients of other ECS programs. Specialized groups meet to discuss grief and loss problems (for example, Parents of Murdered Children). This branch offers workshop courses in parenting, self-esteem, and addictive behaviors.

Chaplaincy—Traditional chaplaincy services are provided at two San Diego hospitals and to people in nursing homes, prisons, jails, and other institutions.

Julian's Anchorage—This boarding home for women and their children provides long-term shelter, a safe and caring environment, and supportive services for young women who want to become self-sufficient. Volunteers abound.

Project P.A.R.A.—The Program for At-Risk Addicts seeks to promote behavior change among intravenous drug users in hopes of slowing the spread of AIDS.

These programs have won their spurs. They comprise a substantial resource base for San Diego and represent all the Episcopal churches in the county, including a powerful body of lay members backing up the efforts.

THE COOPERATIVE, MULTI-AGENCY PATTERN

We are beginning to see a pattern emerge. In time, existing social service agencies are consistently given the authority and the resources to do their jobs *vis-à-vis* the homeless by segments of the community, both private and public, whose moral, political, or legal duty it has been to engineer such solutions. Using what already exists in one's community (even if in only rudimentary form), one need not reinvent any wheels. The primary job of the local mayor, task force on the homeless, mental health director, health director, United Way manager, church or synagogue leader, or other individual who takes the local lead consists of putting together existing pieces with a few newly tooled parts. Here, the simple power to convene can prove to be very effective.

Some of the new pieces (such as housing and mental health care initiatives) may be expensive, but can be started, and assembled bit by bit. As we shall see, local leaders are not without alternatives; many of the options currently available will produce significant governmental cost savings, thereby partly paying for the new initiatives. One important part of community efforts is that they be integrated and comprehensive. San Diego is one city with a painstakingly prepared, comprehensive plan to address homeless issues. Information about this may be obtained from the city's Regional Task Force on the Homeless. Information on another good example of a comprehensive approach can be obtained from the Seattle–King County Private Industry Council, located in Seattle, Washington.

WHAT KIND OF JOBS?

There is a big need on the streets for the revival of the "day-labor job"— work similar to the assignments doled out during the Depression at hiring halls. Homeless people (even with shelter housing) need money to eat, to buy bus tokens, and to purchase personal items such as toothpaste. They need to make phone calls—about 35 percent of the homeless can identify family members somewhere—and to buy clothes or a good meal on occasion. Of course, some want money for alcohol and drugs.

Day labor can also be a stepping stone to a better job, a place to live, and, ultimately, a better life. "Keep your dreams accomplishable," reads a motto in a flophouse for alcoholics. This is a crucial concept for those who have hit bottom, for those who are no longer sure if they can accomplish anything. For such people, the distance out of the deep hole looks to be miles. Huge dreams can stifle and discourage. People "just off the streets" need to plan one thing at a time.

Retraining is the most expensive way to help the homeless and the least widely applicable solution, but it also can be the most rewarding and inspiring when it works. Some government funds are available for this. Of the five hundred homeless people placed in jobs by San Diego's Episcopal Community Services' 1987 contract, only fourteen were retrained for their jobs. These jobs ranged from salesperson and heavy equipment operator to word processor and food services manager.

Many managers drive home at night thinking of the homeless. "How can I help?" often turns into, "Who among the homeless might I employ?" One person who asked such a question is Charles Dyer, director of San Diego County's Law Library System. Dyer unburdened himself to me this way:

> Will the homeless work out for what we need done? Here in the law library, even for a simple shelver's job, a person has to be able to read numbers and to report on time. He/she should be presentable, not offensive in appearance or smell. Yet, I would guess that we're more flexible than many employers. It would, I think, be the rare homeless person who could work out here.

In construction work, for example, where foremen might be tolerant of appearance, absenteeism is unforgivable. A portion of the overall job must be completed by a certain time so that the entire sequence of work can proceed. Much manual labor is finished before the trade workers arrive. Some people work along with the trades; others work elegantly, fitting their time in before, between, and after others. Even the lowest guy on the totem pole has to be there on time!

TYPICAL JOB BARRIERS

What barriers face a homeless person who hopes to get and keep a job? Below are some possibilities:

- No shower. Arrives smelling poorly.
- No sleep. Exhausted, so cannot perform.
- Depressed; feeling low about self and life.

- Can't read or write. Dyslexic?
- Alcoholic and/or substance abuser.
- Separated from family; no support systems.
- Chronic, untreated mental illness.
- Misdemeanor record. Arrests for sleeping in the park. Fears contact with authorities because of an outstanding court warrant.
- "Bad paper," that is, administrative or other less-than-acceptable military discharge, or no high school diploma.
- Over- or under-medication for physical or mental illness.
- No hope.

Dyer continued,

> When I think about employing the homeless, I realize how bad our present situation is at the law library. We have had upper class college students assigned here on college work-study programs at well above the minimum wage. And often even they don't work out. Frankly, the majority of them are more trouble than they're worth. And these are college students.
>
> Any homeless person we could hire at the law library would be able to get a job anywhere, because to do even our simplest work, he'd have to be smart, nice, clean, and be a team member who is pliable and pleasant. The homeless are, by definition, chasing the basics of life. Such an existence strips away the veneers of civilization that are actually the first requirements of such jobs as we have here.
>
> Yet the law library can't afford to train or make work for those with the problems I mentioned. And we get all the qualified applicants we need for the work we do. I guess institutions like us won't be of much help as employers of the homeless.

Not right away, anyhow.

GETTING READY

Considering the many stumbling blocks, it may seem that the homeless have little chance of landing any type of satisfying, permanent employment. But while the obstacles are great, the jobless have a better chance of succeeding if they are well prepared to enter the workforce. Beyond providing the basics of survival, several other services are required to help the homeless succeed at work.

Friends, Support Systems. Defusing the anger that naturally builds up in people who live on the streets can be a difficult task. The homeless have usually butted their heads against one seemingly insensitive bureaucracy after another. One San Diego flophouse manager found a solution. "We send them to Christian Community Services," says the manager of this home for male, dry alcoholics. "Those ladies over there are wonderful. They're the kindly, gentle moms or aunts these guys had or always wished they'd had. They drain off our fellows' venom. They soften them and help solve some problems. After a day or two of this, the guys are ready to go back and throw themselves against the cold bureaucracies again."

Literacy. Episcopal Community Services has demonstrated that ordinary folk of ordinary intelligence can be given a three-week course in reading and writing that enables them, at the very least, to fill out a job application. It can be a breakthrough for these individuals. Basic reading skills can open life-changing doors to opportunity.

Counseling. A little bit of help can go a long way. One female client in a downtown San Diego work center was physically abused by her former spouse. When she arrived at the center, she was unable to separate the effect of this abusive relationship from her personal self-worth. Without the necessary self-esteem, several attempts at full-time employment had only ended in failure. She had been living "down" to her own expectations. However, after two discussions with the work center manager, she was able to understand the importance of separating her past abuse and her present value as a productive human being. She soon found full-time employment as an airport security guard and was able to make a success of it.

These intimate, one-on-one encounters with homeless clients demonstrate that many steps can be skipped in the job-preparation cycle. For some people, it may be merely a matter of obtaining the proper shoes before they can begin a job promised to them. Sometimes a client may be temporarily dysfunctional because he or she lacks the right medication. Not having a simple mailing address or message phone number has kept many qualified homeless people from being hired. Clients in job development are, for the most part, cooperative and willing to participate. A triage approach, like that of a MASH unit, is used. The clients who are not willing quickly weed themselves out. Although the homeless population as a whole is not lazy, there are always a few lazy people in any group. Still, every client must be approached as willing to participate and to work through the cycle to success. People tend to hire up or down according to others' expectations of them. Accordingly, it is vital to these efforts that people doing the hiring expect the best from their clients and lay out a positive plan for success at the beginning of each relationship.

A NON-AGENCY JOBS MODEL

Be ye doers of the word, and not hearers only.

—I James 1:22

Five years ago, Bob McElroy decided to become a doer. A native of San Diego, McElroy had spent two seasons with the New York Giants football team, retired therefrom and had a religious experience. Like many others in the 1980s, he became a "born-again" Christian. Every day on his way to teach classes at San Diego City College, he saw homeless people. This handsome, charismatic man was moved ("called," he said) to help them— but how?

McElroy began by feeding a few homeless people. Every evening he drove a truck full of meals to Balboa Park, a huge, green oasis near downtown San Diego where many of the city's homeless had taken up residence. McElroy began learning the truth behind the old cliché, "If you give a man a fish, you feed him for a day. But if you teach him to fish, he can feed himself for life." McElroy found that his hungry patrons, mostly men, didn't use his sustenance to help find a way to get off the streets. Instead, they filled their bellies and went off to find the nearest drug dealer or liquor store.

It wasn't exactly the kind of help McElroy had been hoping to provide. After two months of evening feedings, McElroy decided to change tactics. The solution to homelessness, he decided, was first to get the homeless part-time jobs and eventually to land them full-time jobs. This would put them back into society's mainstream. He rented a tiny office in the Gaslamp Quarter and started what would become the Alpha Project for the Homeless.

Today, when job seekers arrive at McElroy's office, he screens them personally, to determine how serious they are about finding work. "If the first question out of their mouths is 'How much does it pay?' and they cringe when I say '$5 or $6,' then I know they're not hungry enough yet. But if a guy says, 'I'll clean toilets. I just gotta have some work,' then I know he's ready." They must also be alcohol- and drug-free, he stresses. McElroy devotes most of his time to clients who faithfully return to his office each day in hopes of securing a job. As in football, desire is all.

Once McElroy has sent a client out on a job, he can assess his or her (about 10 percent of the Alpha Project's clients are women) job skills, dependability, and attitudes. When he gets a request for a permanent employee, McElroy can give an accurate idea of the job-seeker's capabilities to the potential employer. With the help of other agencies, McElroy's workers get the essentials they need to maintain their job—food, clothing, shelter, medical care, and a stable address. The program's success has been built upon in-dispensable agency teamwork developed over the years.

During the past four years, according to Alpha Project figures, the program has placed almost fifteen hundred homeless people in full-time employment. "We have an obligation to provide an opportunity for those who want to become independent and self-supporting once again," McElroy declares. *Want* is the key word. Those who succeed with the help of the Alpha Project are people who are motivated to get off the streets and back to a normal way of life. Still, McElroy estimates only 20 percent of the homeless are ready to take advantage of what the Alpha Project offers. Others, he feels, are more inclined to stay in the "dead-end cycle" that is offered by government and private agencies.

McElroy accuses most agencies of merely "warehousing" the homeless. They provide food and shelter, but no incentive or hands-on help to find a job, he maintains. Too many of the homeless take advantage of this situation. On a typical day, many of them visit a mission to eat dinner, stay out all night drinking or using drugs, then return to the mission in the morning for breakfast. They sleep during the day, then repeat the cycle. To be fair, agencies do offer homeless clients bus fare to other parts of the country on the premise that they are returning to see family or start a job. On the streets, McElroy says, the ploy is known as "seeing the U.S.A. the homeless way." Thus, agencies actually help perpetuate the homeless problem. "It irritates me to see money pouring into the problem with little or no direction. We're creating jobs for social workers," he says. McElroy should know, but traditional jobs professionals wonder about McElroy's statistics and point out that his clients do not get literacy or other training and are paid less than union scale. They have to be pretty job-ready and healthy to fit into McElroy's system.

McElroy spent fifty days on the streets of San Diego learning about the homeless way of life before deciding to open the Alpha Project. On the streets he concluded that "everything" was available, everything but a job above minimum wage. Food, shelter, even legal help were there for the asking, but other than day-long dishwashing jobs that paid minimum wage, McElroy couldn't find a job! He also concluded that some enterprising homeless men and women have become professional panhandlers. In some cities, he says, they earn up to $80 a day—tax free—by begging on the streets, and often end up using this money for drink or drugs—the very thing that often caused them to become homeless in the first place. Understandably, such panhandlers are unwilling to give up their new-found profession in exchange for a legitimate job at $5 an hour—less than half the daily return from panhandling.

But for those who are tired of the streets, McElroy stands ready to help. Like many who have found a technique that helps homeless people, he is obsessive about his quest. He believes the only way to break the cycle of homelessness is to find people jobs. Even his extensive entry interviews with those who come to the Alpha Project for help are legendary. Says McElroy, "We're a get down, get dirty, gnarly kind of group that doesn't take any b.s. We take the guys who really want to work and focus all of our attention on them."

McElroy's hard line works with many. He maintains that in 1989 he placed some six hundred homeless clients in full-time jobs, more than twice the number placed in 1988, most in the construction industry. Many of his clients already were skilled in carpentry, plumbing and other trades, but others were not. McElroy trained those without skills by finding contractors willing to hire his men at $6 to $10 per hour for larger projects. The Alpha Project built the Kansas City Steakhouse & Nightclub, located in the Gaslamp Quarter. For this, the project trained and employed 120 homeless people. Of those, McElroy says 87 went on to gain full-time employment. Extra revenues generated from the work went back into the organization's payroll or were used to buy new tools and equipment for work on future projects. About thirty Alpha Project clients helped renovate the Gatehouse, a home for runaways. Today, all thirty are employed, McElroy gloats.

McElroy is particularly proud of the fact that, unlike the agencies he ardently criticizes, Alpha Project uses no government subsidies to pay its bills or help its clients. Most of the money clients earn on the projects— 88 percent—goes back to them as salary. The remainder helps pay for equipment, tools, trucks, and insurance. In his fourth year of operation last year, McElroy says he drew an annual salary of $8,600. His 1988 operating budget totaled only $56,491—equivalent to what many in McElroy's position at similar agencies might earn just to run such a program. With that modest amount, the Alpha Project was able to place three hundred homeless clients in full-time jobs and secure low-cost housing for them. McElroy estimates that his men's work saved taxpayers $140,000 in welfare payments alone. "It doesn't take millions of dollars to solve the problem. It takes desire and motivation," he says. "Agencies only look for handouts from the government." To stay afloat, the Alpha Project depends almost solely on volunteer efforts, and that's the way McElroy wants to keep it.

With the work-placement component of Alpha Project well-established, McElroy has raised his sights. He now hopes to find a place to house many of the homeless who come to him or are referred to him by other San Diego agencies. Ideally, he would like to offer clients long-term housing of three to six months. "Our idea is to locate a facility outside of the inner city in order to escape the negative influences that that environment creates," he says. Many clients need to remove themselves from the pressure and the availability of drugs and drink. Therefore, McElroy aims to locate his housing project in a rural town called Campo, located an hour east of downtown San Diego. Workers would be bused from the shelter facility to the city for work.

Though he could still be teaching at City College or expanding the personalized fitness business he started five years ago, McElroy chose a different path. His efforts to help the homeless turn their lives around are now the theme of his life. McElroy likes to remind people that, "Jesus was a homeless guy" who earned his living as a carpenter. McElroy himself tries to emulate a down-to-earth way of living. Like the men and women he trains, McElroy is ready to work hard. "I was meant to get down and work with homeless people. That's *it*."

Twenty or thirty years ago, when an unemployed people finally landed a minimum-wage job, they would have little problem finding housing they could afford. This is no longer the case. In California, for example, the 1990 minimum hourly wage is $4.25, or $736 a month before taxes. Rarely can decent housing be rented for less than $500 monthly, so it is clear that such an person cannot survive alone. He or she must double up on roommates or work two jobs. Because of hard, cold facts like these, jobs experts are calling the 1990s "the decade of the working poor." More and more people will be living the way college students have—with unrelated individuals, or even in a living facilities seldom seen anymore in cities: boarding houses. Most cities still permit this type of zoning.

Clearly, to have a sizeable segment of the U.S. labor force experiencing such unsettling living conditions will not help business, particularly the service businesses, which so frequently employ people at or near minimum wage. As the existence of low-income housing near job sites has proven indispensable to create a strong business climate, it follows that a healthy and happy, *housed* workforce is essential to good business. But business is in a bind, because an entire economy has been built on the foundation of low-paying jobs. The business community has to notice that payment of such low wages will have intolerable consequences for it in the long term, but because no easy, competitive option appears to exist, it now turns a blind eye.

The other big employment theme for the 1990s will be *partnership*. Jobs programs—both from the standpoint of community job training, placement, and education, and from the employer's vantage point—will need to be integrated with other programs (housing, mental health and other health services, day care, etc.). Depression-era Civilian Conservation Corps camps had this feature, too. These services can no longer afford to be independent. Increasingly, education will be brought to the workplace, aided by the astonishing ease and effectiveness of videotape technology. Video cassette packages are both fascinating for the learner and extremely effective at teaching. The Ford Foundation is experimenting with "new milieu" ideas matching peak-hour staffing (for example, breakfast, lunch, and dinner hours in restaurants) with education during break times at the employee's own pace. For employees who wish to climb the career ladder, education is always the answer. At the turn of the last century, Alfred North Whitehead declared, "There will in the future be no appeal from the judgments pronounced on the uneducated."

The third key factor as America moves into the 1990s is that at any given moment, some regions in the country will be experiencing labor shortages. Today, for example, the industrial-park–dotted San Bernadino area east of Los Angeles urgently needs workers, and its private industry council is taking vigorous steps to bring in and train needed workers. Linkages need to be created to match qualified, previously homeless people, identified somewhere else, with the jobs in such locales. The fourth key to cooperative solutions to the employment dilemma is low-income housing with "case management." The Labor Department has studied the model jobs program for the homeless being administered by Episcopal Community Services and augmented by resources from six other agencies using the case management method. Using case management, it usually takes six to nine months for an individual to make the change from living on the streets to living independently. It is a process in which more and more decision-making is transferred to the client.

The cases that will need managing will become increasingly structural. We'll be seeing more and more ex-offenders as our country's stance toward law and order becomes more strident. Ex-convicts "are basically coming out homeless," says San Diego Private Industry Council executive Stan Schroeder. "They often don't want to see their families, or their families them. And this is not just recent offenders. We see them homeless ten to twenty years out of prison. They're locked out of lots of jobs; it's a long road back."

Likewise we are now seeing the first of a flood of brain-damaged and mentally retarded babies, the result of drug use by parents. Schroeder notices more and more young children with poor job skills, a condition he attributes to disrupted family life, use of chemicals, poor modelling, etc. He suggests that we will be making more use of the "small group home," a concept now in wide use with retarded people, and possibly return to previously familiar institutions, such as the work farms, long thought of as a humane venture, where partially disabled people could live, relatively near families and friends, with work and dignity. One of these is still in operation in Roanoke County, Virginia.

An *unemployed* existence is a worse negation of life than death itself. Because to live means to have something definite to do—a mission to fulfill—and in the measure in which we avoid setting our life to something, we make

it empty. . . . Human life, by its very nature, has to be dedicated to something.
—José Ortega y Gasset

SUGGESTED READINGS

Helping the Homeless Be Choosers—The Role of J.T.P.A. in Improving Job Prospects, National Commission for Employment Policy, Washington, D.C., 1990.

Training in America, Anthony Carnevale, Leila Gainer and Janice Villet, American Society for Training and Development, Alexandria, Va., 1990.

10

Model Homeless Shelters

> She wrapped him in swaddling clothes and laid him in a manger, because there was no room for them in the inn.
>
> —Luke 2:7

Since the homeless are a new phenomenon and cities' responses have varied greatly across the country, the systems of shelters that have appeared have varied widely in quality. Further, many homeless people stay away because of their distrust or their mental illness, because they dislike being manipulated and "case-fodder," or because of pride. The following excerpt from Portland, Oregon's *Homeless Times* newspaper gives some of the flavor of this.

> The thought of shelters sends shivers down poor people's spines because they're afraid they'll end up at one. They fear the humiliation. They can't bear the stench of air staled by sweat and vomit. Or the crowded mass of humanity punctuated with anonymous carriers of lice, tuberculosis, hepatitis, and pneumonia. They are frightened by the mad ravings of the mentally ill. And the angry outbursts of haunted veterans. And the sound of elderly men weeping in their sleep, mourning for places, times and people now gone. If you've ever been to a shelter, you know it's true. This country's current methods of sheltering are shamefully inadequate. Because the prevailing attitude is not to deal with the problem as best we can. Only as little as we can.

These thoughts are not atypical. Neal Cohen, head of Project HELP, an outreach program, says three-fourths of the mentally ill homeless claim they are victimized in shelters, which they believe to be unsafe. Further, most shelters in America permit someone to stay only a short time; and the systems permitting longer stays generally do so only with the most stable, those with jobs, or receiving public assistance.

For the homeless, there is a stark, national need for longer term, gentle, and sensitive shelter systems. One formerly homeless woman, a Navy veteran, described her recovery from living on the street as comparable to what a Vietnam veteran or an ex-POW experiences. The lack of a safe haven is such an anomalous situation for a "normal" person that to be exposed to street life for any amount of time forces one to succumb or adjust: to become, for awhile, unbalanced, or to seek solace in drugs or alcohol. Recovery is a long-term process that long-term shelters can address.

City governments (for example, New York's) have responded, but the most promising shelter systems to evolve thus far are those run by church-based groups, generally fueled via aggressive, ecumenical fundraising efforts that embrace government monies as they become available for shelter elements that may be exempt from church/state restrictions. Such entities are able to carve out some "creative running room" not available within the bureaucracy of government, and to remain strikingly agile, adjusting week by week to changes in street needs as well as the shifting winds of government and foundation funding.

To be homeless means, simply, to not have a roof. The most obvious way of addressing homelessness is to provide the needed roofs. The experts who have done this for decades in our country's Skid Rows have been the people who run the rescue missions. These buildings have been around since before Gen. William Booth founded the Salvation Army in 1865.

As we have seen, the homeless of America in the 1980s and 1990s, however, are a vastly different human mix than the traditional Skid Row populace whose average age stood steadily above fifty until the beginning of the 1980s. By 1983 the average age had plummeted to the mid-twenties. The homeless population now includes high and expanding numbers of severely mentally ill people (upwards of 33 percent), the physically disabled, veterans (up to 35 percent in some cities), women (14 percent and rising), and whole family units. Helping these people accordingly requires shelters and their staffs to meet vastly different requirements than in the past, and, ideally, in vastly different facilities. America needs a radically new Skid Row shelter design, new model shelter systems for the 1990s.

While our images of homeless shelters had become quite stereotyped, across America the realities had changed drastically. A wide spectrum of approaches to "temporarily" housing the homeless now exists, each with its own merits and drawbacks. Here we present two examples of shelter systems that are in place and working in San Diego. Both are proven and effective; both could work almost anywhere. One is a "Taj Mahal" of shelters, large, centralized, extremely comprehensive and sophisticated, the other a network of small, specialized group homes dotting the city. The two systems have many features in common: professional, modern management, strong reliance on volunteers, and effective case management in assisting the homeless in obtaining health care, welfare, Social Security disability benefits, veterans benefits, and all the other services typically bound in red tape. Both programs assist people through the daunting process of obtaining housing that will sustain them in their desired reentry into society.

THE TAJ MAHAL

The brand-new, $11.6 million St. Vincent De Paul/Joan Kroc Center of San Diego opened in August 1987. It houses 350 people, serves 1,350 meals daily to resident and non-resident homeless people, offers a full-service medical clinic, and has a huge, underground parking garage for the safety and convenience of staff and volunteers. The center's founder, Msgr. Joe Carroll, refers to himself as a "simple priest from the Bronx." This is true and is humbly said, with more than a bit of jocularity. Such a master communicator is Father Joe that, while raising the $11.6 million needed to build the center, he successfully touched Protestants, Jews, and Catholics alike, raiding service clubs, neighborhood gatherings, bean feeds, and upscale receptions—often a dozen a day, all over the city. To explain his enthusiasm, Carroll would say, "God has given me a simple direction. 'Joe,' God has said, 'Raise ten grand a day.' "

Open less than two years, the center enjoys national and international recognition. It has been featured in articles in *Newsweek, Reader's Digest,* and *Architectural Record,* as well as on "60 Minutes." The center's honors include the premier international award from the 1987 United Nations' International Year of Shelter for the Homeless, presented by the London-based Building and Social Housing Foundation, which is an independent, non-political housing research and education institute. This award was physically presented to Father Joe in London by the archbishop of Canterbury.

Twenty-five years ago, Carroll came to California as a young man trying to escape the crippling effects of New York winters on his arthritic knees. Like the people now pouring into the St. Vincent De Paul Center, Carroll was homeless when he arrived. He had only $50 in his pocket. A priest at a parish in Carpinteria, California, near Santa Barbara, took him in. After five years, Carroll had himself become a priest, and he had dedicated himself to helping the poor.

In 1950, the Catholic Diocese of San Diego created the St. Vincent De Paul Center as a semi-autonomous agency to serve "unsheltered people" in San Diego. In 1982, San Diego Bishop Leo T. Maher appointed Carroll to be president of the center, giving him specific instructions to create larger programs to help the increasing numbers of homeless in San Diego. Carroll's vision to help the homeless was revealed. It was not penny ante. As the Carpinteria priest and his parish had done for him a quarter century before,

Father Carroll was determined to do for San Diego's homeless.

Things looked bleak in 1982. It seemed that the government couldn't kick in funds toward the proposed facility because of the constitutional "wall" between church and state. In addition, parishes were unused to supporting efforts on such a scale. This is when Carroll earned his unofficial seven-letter nickname, "The Hustler." He cajoled San Diego's wealthy and not-so-wealthy into opening their wallets to help finance an ambitious, spanking new ("I have to work there, you know") Taj Mahal for the homeless.

Soon a downtown city block was purchased and a creative architectural design developed by San Diego architect Fred De Santo. During these planning stages, the St. Vincent De Paul Center was providing temporary shelter in an old hotel, housing two hundred homeless people each night, turning away many.

The new center is located in a beautiful, three-story building at 15th and Imperial Avenues in eastern downtown San Diego. The place is unlike any other homeless shelter in America. Inside the 350-bed center are high ceilings, top-of-the-line furnishings, a medical clinic, dozens of offices, a chapel, a children's day care center, a permanent elementary school of the San Diego Unified School District, computers, a huge dining room that converts to a basketball court, a kitchen that serves 1,350 meals each day, the aforementioned underground parking garage, and a fifteen-thousand-square-foot courtyard with benches, landscaping, pillars, and a fountain.

The center was not converted from some other use as are most warehouse-type homeless centers. It was designed to house a hard-working population of previously homeless people as they make the steps toward permanent life off of the streets. That is the aim. Schlage electronic locks on resident rooms increase security and save money on lost door keys. A new code is placed in the door lock and a replacement credit-card key is made for about twenty-five cents. For safety, approximately forty hidden security cameras survey the common areas: hallways, TV rooms, the underground garage and the courtyard. Two security guards are on duty day and night. People feel safe (except for the paranoids, who stay away). The building employs a cost-cutting energy system, using the building's distinct, twin air-intake towers, a cogeneration power system, skylights, and an interior courtyard. These were, of course, carefully designed for the center and are linked to a computerized energy management system to keep utility bills low.

Case management is the method used by the center to help its clients. Homeless people don't just wander up to the door of the center and gain entrance. Instead, they are referred to the center by other agencies about the city—the County Welfare Department, the courts, or church agencies. Appointments are made, and the homeless person (hopefully of a rather organized sort, possessing both watch and calendar) appears at the center's front desk.

Two types of case management are used at St. Vincent De Paul, depending on whether the client is a short-term or long-term resident. All short-term residents have their affairs managed by the agency that referred them to St. Vincent De Paul, explained Mary Case, the organization's executive director. The center provides food and shelter for these homeless clients, while the referring agency handles all other aspects of helping the client get back onto his or her feet.

The center's residential area is of two kinds: emergency, for those staying one to thirty days, and transitional, for those staying six to eighteen months. The second and third floors serve as housing units and are sectionalized for families and single men.

Long-term residents at the center, those staying up to eighteen months, receive their case management services from licensed counselors at St. Vincent De Paul. All case managers hold either a bachelor's or master's degree in social work. The thrust of case management is simple—the counselor and the client come up with a detailed plan to get the homeless person back on track. Then they meet regularly to discern that steady progress is being made toward meeting those goals. Whether clients need a job, permanent housing, psychological or emotional counseling, help with financial problems, or all of the above, the counselors at the center can make arrangements for the appropriate aid.

The social workers' goal is to stabilize their clients' lives by helping them set attainable goals, then showing them how to reach them. This process begins soon after the homeless client arrives at the center for "intake." This rather institutional word is the center's term for learning about its new residents' situations. Case says three different case management workers assess each long-term client staying on the center's third floor. This alleviates bias, says Case, as well as allowing a broader perception of the client through three sets of eyes rather than one. Homeless clients are asked how they got into their current situation, how long they have been on the streets, and how they would like to change their lives. This so-called "workability study" helps the counselor assigned to the case set reasonable goals with the client.

To make any real progress, the homeless person must be highly motivated to change his or her situation, Case stressed. While the case workers monitor their clients' progress, they meet with them just once a week. Accomplishing goals, whether it be applying for jobs, seeking needed medical attention, or simply enrolling in a seminar, is strictly up to the client. Clients in the center's long-term residency program stay an average of about six months before "graduating" from the program. The center's staff members each handle about fifteen cases at any given time.

Although short-term residents at the center are monitored by the agency that referred them to St. Vincent De Paul, they can take advantage of some of the center's internal programs, such as school for their children. The referring agencies complete the workability study on the clients and are in charge of counseling them and providing other services such as help with health, legal, and financial planning. Public school classes for up to fifty children are held in a large main floor room. There is also child care and after-school care available. Various support services run by the county and private groups operate from the center. According to Carroll, "The center is designed to literally break the cycle of poverty. So, rather than referring people to some other places in the city for assistance, we can do it all here." The center thus provides offices for a county welfare worker, a consumer credit counselor, and other agents of social service agencies, so these people's agencies can team up to help the residents, "break the cycle of homelessness."

A year after its doors opened, the St. Vincent De Paul Center was operating at capacity. Nearly a thousand men, women, and children receive some services there each day. The center has made a particular difference with those residents remaining for more than thirty days. Of such graduates in 1988, 83 percent were successful in maintaining a stable income and finding permanent housing. The success rate for the thirty-day program is 78 percent. Carroll expects an even greater success rate as time goes on.

Funds for the St. Vincent De Paul Center are raised through a constantly changing, kaleidoscopic array of donors and events. The primary source of funding is from individual donors, who provide 50 percent of the budget. Fifteen percent of the financial resources come from a variety of fund-raising events, such as benefit dinners, auctions, an annual triathalon, church collections, mailings, barbecues, roasts of Father Joe, walk-a-thons, and parties. To give a feel for the ecumenical breadth of support, San Diego Rotary Clubs and the San Diego Trial Lawyers each kick in over $50,000 a year. Another 15 percent comes from corporations and private foundations. The remaining 20 percent of funds is provided by government sources, pinpointed to particular work.

The two main government grants the center receives are a transitional housing grant and a health care grant. The transitional housing grant is a result of the Stewart B. McKinney Act of 1987. This grant provides the center with $1.7 million over a five-year period, $340,000 per year. The health care grant provides direct support to the medical clinic on a dollar-per-patient basis. The average annual amount of this support is $150,000. Other governmental support comes from grants through the Federal Emergency Management Administration (FEMA), which supplies a per-bed reimbursement, San Diego's Emergency Shelter Program, and the San Diego City Housing Commission. Volunteers are an essential resource as well, dozens of whom act as support to the paid staff. At present, the center utilizes the services of 350 volunteers.

Since the shelter can only accommodate 350 people, it accepts families and individuals on a qualification basis. Present qualifications are:

- Families with children receive priority, although single people are accepted.
- Applicants must be physically and mentally stable and able to work toward their goals.
- Applicants must agree to abstain from drug and alcohol use and must do so.
- Applicants must be capable of living in a group setting. They should be earning an income or have an immediate potential to earn one or to receive one via a government entitlement, like Social Security, SSI, welfare, veterans benefits, etc.

Statistics regarding the resident population at the center change daily, but the center estimates that roughly 33 percent of the residents are children, 22 percent are single parents, 20 percent are single males, 15 percent are parents in two-parent families, 9 percent single females, and 1 percent single-parent males. When the center is full, the ratio of children to adults is 1:2.

Within St. Vincent de Paul/Joan Kroc Center there are a raft of inter-related programs. These include:

Sheltering Programs. These form the beginning of help for most homeless assisted at the center. The emergency program embodies a plan to help people who show up expressing a need for shelter during the late evening and on weekends and holidays. Those who obtain a referral through the San Diego Police Department, the Battered Women's Hotline, Infoline, or any local church or synagogue are allowed to stay for the night or throughout the weekend. When it comes time to leave they can speak with a staff member about additional shelter time.

The Short-Term Voucher Program shelters the homeless for up to fourteen days. Case management is provided during this time by the referring agency. During their stay, residents set goals, agree to work towards them, and are responsible for their own progress. The program is referred to as a "voucher" program because vouchers for extended shelter time are given out at week's end, according to the residents' success in accomplishing their tasks.

The Extended Housing Program provides shelter for the homeless person for a maximum of thirty days. This program is designed in the same pattern as the short-term voucher. Every week, the vouchers are given out in accordance with the residents' progress towards their goals. Case management continues to be the responsibility of the referring agency, and case workers must have received special training designed to teach the making of a "client workability assessment."

The Transitional/Independent Living Program is designed to provide shelter for a longer term. Here, the residents are welcome to stay for six to eighteen months. The applicants chosen for this program are those who have been recognized by the staff as being highly motivated, capable, and open to change. Case managers here are provided by the center, to teach clients money management. Goals of this program include learning how to establish a bank account, saving enough money for a security deposit and first and last month's rent, and purchasing essential furnishings and supplies.

Lastly, the center's Housing Program exists to provide some shelter residents with resources and information that will assist them in finding permanent housing on leaving the shelter. The housing program is designed to interview and refer shelter residents to rental housing, shared housing, or other housing agencies in the San Diego area. This program sponsors weekly workshops on budgeting, building confidence and self-esteem, apartment search techniques, information on area rentals, tenant/landlord responsibilities, and goal setting and attainment. The workshops are given by volunteers who have experience in communicating with people in crisis situations and have the knowledge to assist the residents in their search for housing. The housing program has a staff specialist who assists the residents with counseling and aids them in accessing help from such otherwise mysterious resources as HUD and FEMA. A Rotary revolving fund has been an important element here, supplying, after one has income, the security deposit and last month's rent, which often stand as insurmountable barriers to housing.

Employment Preparation and Placement Program. Many homeless want to work, but just aren't ready. This "getting them ready" program is co-ordinated by a specialist in training residents for work. Topics covered in the training sessions include job outlook in San Diego's major employment markets, financial assistance information, and learning about job markets, employment applications, interviewing, résumé techniques, job skills assessment, and keeping a job. A valuable asset that the employment program shares with the housing program is the Resource Center, with all the materials and personnel available to assist the homeless in changing their situation. The Resource Center contains phones, typewriters, a computer, a photocopier, area resource information, and an answering machine that bypasses the main switchboard for employment/housing calls, so callers can't tell they are calling a homeless person.

Children's Educational Program. This program gives homeless kids the chance to learn, while at the same time giving their parents time to look for employment. All school-age children at the center are required to attend school. The shelter's school, offered through the San Diego County Office of Education's Summit Schools program, is in one room. Classes are taught by three certified public school teachers, three teacher's aides, and many volunteers.

Every child is evaluated upon entrance and is allowed to progress at his or her own pace. The shelter assists the children with its highly positive environment, promoting self-esteem building, and helping them prepare for an easier transition to a permanent school situation. After school, these children attend an activity program staffed by three full-time workers who are experienced with children in recreation, teaching, and athletics. Every week, the staff chooses a theme and plans activities and lessons around the theme. The program averages about thirty children a day and often has a waiting list. Children of working parents receive priority.

The children's education program incorporates children's play therapy, a children's study group, and a tot playroom. The children's play therapy is similar to a stress management session for the adult residents. The therapy includes between eighty and a hundred children every evening, and centers around making friends and getting along with siblings and parents. The children's study group meets weekly to reinforce educational skills in ways that are fun. Young adults from local parishes work with the children in a variety of educational games emphasizing reading, English, and math.

The purpose of the tot playroom is to provide parents of toddlers some free time so that they can concentrate on finding a job, while knowing the kids are surrounded with love and security. Social workers point out that the tot playroom also serves as a child-abuse preventative in a high-risk environment.

Medical Clinic. This unique clinic provides care not only for the residents of the shelter but for any homeless person in the San Diego area. People can simply walk into the clinic from off the street. Fifty percent of the patients are residents from other sheltering programs in San Diego. In its first year, the clinic had seven thousand patient visits. The medical clinic is staffed by volunteers and paid employees. The volunteer staff consists of doctors, lab technicians, nurses, and secretarial help. The clinic has a modest paid staff that includes a director, a nurse manager, a social worker, a pharmaceutical technician, a receptionist, and an office manager. Eight to ten staff members work in the clinic on any given day.

The clinic provides primary medical care, tending to the basic needs of the homeless rather than providing ongoing care. Studies have shown that homeless people are sick much more often than the average person and have more complicated medical problems because of prolonged overexposure to the elements and lack of sustained care. Also, many homeless people walk the streets for days and months without shoes. Because of these factors, homeless people are susceptible to many types of medical problems, including serious respiratory ailments, skin infections, and foot problems. The center's clinic sees an average of seven thousand patients per year.

Day Center. There are many homeless people who cannot meet the criteria for the center's sheltering programs. The Day Center tends to some basic needs of those individuals by providing daytime bathrooms, lockers, showers, soap and grooming supplies, haircuts, and clean clothing. The unsheltered can get mail and register to vote at this address, as well. Other services available to the chronically homeless include a daily lunch program serving 650 street people a day, a medical clinic, and emergency housing when the weather turns bad.

Support Services. A variety of secondary programs offer special services and training in specific areas. Positive Parenting class is offered to help adult residents in their roles as parents. The general stress and the crisis nature of homelessness often act against positive interaction between parents and children. Directed by the county mental health department, this program helps parents cope with specific problems and suggests ways of disciplining children without resorting to abuse. Image Consultation is a volunteer barber who gives center residents haircuts. Shaving supplies are also available. Chore Responsibility is a residential requirement to do six hours of work per week around the center. This aims to motivate residents and help foster a sense of community. The Homeless Outreach Team is a collection of specialists who provide assessment services for individuals referred to the center. The Literacy Program teaches the adult residents how to read. The Alcohol Education Program tries to help resident families affected by alcohol abuse.

Men's Night Shelter Program. This program provides sleeping space for about 150 homeless men in a building attached to St. Vincent De Paul's main quarters. There are no qualifications to stays from one to thirty nights except that clients obey these simple rules: no violence and no alcohol or drugs on the premises. Rather than providing a complete, monitored rehabilitation program, the night shelter is instead aimed simply at giving some people on the street a safe, comfortable place to stay and maybe the beginnings of a fresh start.

Opened in November 1989, this shelter has less stringent rules than the center's regular housing. Unlike the families, women, and children housed in the main quarters, men staying at the night shelter do not have to be referred by an agency, explained Ron Mathieu, the Men's Shelter program manager. To gain admittance, the men merely call the shelter any day between 8:00 a.m. and 10:00 a.m. The men must adhere strictly to hours set for coming and going. During the first seven days of their stay, they must be out of the shelter by 6:00 a.m. and in at 7:00 p.m. After the first week, they can return as late as 10:00 p.m., and do not have to leave until 7:00 a.m.

The shelter accepts men who may be using drugs or alcohol, or are severely mentally ill. As long as they do not abuse substances on the premises, the men are welcome to stay and to use the other center services. The night shelter has its own counselor and Mathieu hopes to offer health seminars once or twice a week. Because of the restrictive hours, regular meals are not served, although soup and snacks are available. Those who work receive a sack lunch each day.

During the day, anyone off the streets—men and women—can visit the shelter to shower and clean up. "We don't assume anything," Mathieu says. "Maybe they live together with several people and they come here for their showers. We don't ask questions." Each person receives a kit with shampoo, a toothbrush, and a razor. On Tuesdays and Thursdays, the visitors can discard their old and often dirty clothes for new ones they choose from those donated to the center. The housing at the night shelter is less private than the quarters in the main center, where rooms have locked doors. Night shelter residents stay in cubicles and each person has a locker for possessions. "We don't want to make it so comfortable here that people stay forever," said Mathieu, "but if they want to change and make a difference, they can." St. Vincent De Paul hopes to construct a similar shelter for women and children.

The Job Training Center. The center hopes to build this facility across the street from the existing shelter. Plans for it are being drawn up and will include two large classrooms and additional emergency shelter for two hundred men, women, and children. The job training center will provide job training opportunities. Able and motivated people can participate in the program, to be sponsored by major corporations. The job training program will make use of the two large classrooms and a computer lab.

The proposed job training center and the night shelter program mark a significant change in the portion of the homeless population that the St. Vincent De Paul Center will serve. In these programs, the center will begin aiding those more disabled people who do not meet today's entry qualifications. The St. Vincent De Paul Center is one of the most dynamic, creative and flexible institutions on the American scene today. In keeping with its progressive style, the center's planners have several new programs under consideration, including:

- The reopening of a batch of suburban trailer parks, via the Bankruptcy Court and/or creditor banks, using tax provisions creatively.
- AMA- and San Diego County Medical Society–sanctioned broad appeals for volunteer doctors with emphasis on pediatrics, psychiatry, and podiatry.
- Broad solicitation of foundations, locally and nationwide, for research grants, capital, and program funding.
- Linkage with large food businesses, from big farming concerns to supermarkets to government surplus food. These organized linkages have been so successful that a food distribution system run by the

center serves twenty thousand San Diego families each month and has been expanded in six short years to serve half a million people throughout the United States, Mexico, and Guatemala. This element of St. Vincent De Paul's efforts is called the SHARE program (Self-Help and Resource Exchange).

Center managers are brainstorming, too, about leasing large hotels, or obtaining rural land by gift for an adjunct "farm facility," or using excess federal facilities, including moth-balled warships. Around every city there are always vacant structures. Creative and vigilant non-profits can often find a way to create irresistible "offers that can't be refused."

THE DECENTRALIZED APPROACH

With cat-like upon our prey we steal; In silence dread, our cautious way we feel. No sound at all! We never speak a word; A fly's footfall would be distinctly heard.

—Gilbert & Sullivan, *Pirates of Penzance*

While Carroll and his center are housing and helping hundreds of homeless people a day, another group is performing similar miracles with similar numbers of people in a much quieter way. In a sense, it aims at the "bottom half" of the homeless, while Father Joe's efforts aim at the "most able half."

The Transitional Housing Demonstration Program developed by San Diego's Episcopal Community Services houses only fourteen single men at a time, in seven, one-bedroom cottages built in an older residential section of San Diego near downtown. "Locating that kind of program in that particular area of the city, we really had to deal head on with the NIMBY ('not in my backyard') problem," explained Jonathan Hunter, director of transitional programs for Episcopal Community Services. "In terms of the number of people that have been served, basically about forty-five to fifty people per year go through our transitional housing program. Of those fifty people served in the first year, about 75 percent were asked to leave before they completed the program. If you look at just that figure, the success rate was only 25 percent. However, when we did follow up on those people that we had asked to leave, we found 75 percent of them were still employed and in stable housing six months later. They didn't go back to homelessness."

The residents can stay as long as they need to, and are closely assisted by case managers who are intimately involved in their progress. The program is small, the involvement intense. And fourteen men who have been rejected by all available services are given long-term shelter in a place they can call home. Hunter says the program's objective, or ministry, is "to give leadership in social outreach, and unconditionally provide services without regard to race, religion, ethnic or national origin" in the geographic boundaries of the Episcopal Diocese of San Diego.

Transitional housing for the homeless is only one of *twenty-five* ECS social service programs, which employ over two hundred people and had a budget of $6 million for fiscal year 1989. The ECS philosophy differs radically from those of its peers. In fact, ECS aims to help those who cannot be helped by other social service agencies. According to Hunter, ECS has three unique purposes: 1) regard for the needs of the whole person; 2) primary emphasis on service to those not included in existing efforts; and 3) advocacy for changes in public policy that will free the most vulnerable among us from dependence on the shifting winds of political will.

What Makes ECS Different?

"One of our guiding principles is to work with those who are most difficult to serve and those who are most often rejected by other programs in the community," Hunter said. "ECS has accepted as part of its mission a willingness to work with those who are truly at or below the bottom rung of the ladder and for whom there is no such thing as a safety net. We are not interested in creating large institutions which must inevitably begin to focus on their own needs for survival."

It takes more than a program philosophy to make a difference in the lives of those who have been turned away from every possible form of assistance. The ECS workers can do what others cannot because of their deeply ingrained belief in commitment to working with the whole person. "It is our conviction that homelessness and dysfunction are symptoms of underlying social problems which can only be addressed by first creating a broad base of stability in a person's life," Hunter explained. And ECS, perhaps uniquely among street agencies, believes in examining and correcting its own behaviors, often with new programs discovered to be needed.

"When it comes to problems with behavior," Hunter said, "smaller programs can ask the central question, 'Whose problem is this?' In an institution the problem is the institution's need for control. Once you leave the institution, there's no longer a motivation for managing your behavior. Independence, which is the basic lifestyle we all work toward, can only be learned by doing. Independence cannot be taught or mandated through institutional control. When someone comes to our emergency assistance office and reports that they are hungry, there may be as many as ten or twelve factors underlying that hunger. Simply giving them a bag of food does not address that hunger."

But trying to address the myriad problems these people have could seem quite overwhelming. Experience shows that people in crisis will rarely follow through on more than one referral and certainly not on two or three.

"So, if we identify that the hungry person needs medical care for sore feet, as well as employment, shelter, spiritual counseling, and alcohol recovery services, we must be prepared to meet as many of those needs as possible, and the programs addressing those needs must be within short walking distance from each other."

ECS now has a cluster of services along a block of Broadway in downtown San Diego. In that block it has a residential, case management, and employment program for ex-offenders, a full-service family health clinic, emergency assistance, crisis counseling, a chapel, an employment program, a work center, Twelve-Step alcohol recovery groups, and an AIDS prevention and education program for intravenous drug users. Within three blocks there is a clubhouse for homeless people with chronic mental illness. The long-term transitional program is located ten blocks away.

Intentionally Mixed-Population Transitional Housing

One very promising approach is the mixing of subpopulations of homeless into a single transitional housing situation. Taking over a former apartment complex, the Youth and Community Services Organization of San Diego, which had previously emphasized work with runaways, mixed young homeless families with children (ten with two parents, ten with a single parent) with ten elderly homeless, plus another "leaven" of a dozen of what are called "low-income anchor people" (college students, interns, foreign students, and staff). These are supposed to be stabilizing factors. The intent is to deliberately create a symbiotic mix—disparate people able and wanting to help each other. The result, hopefully, is a mini-community or even a very large family.

THE NEED FOR MULTIPLE APPROACHES

The St. Vincent De Paul Center now houses some five hundred people in a relatively confined space, making the existence of institutionalized rules and regulations a necessity. As the center grows and changes, the numbers will increase and so must the bureaucratic structure. Dealing with the "top groups" of the homeless thus far, the center has demonstrated impressive rates of success. Housing officials at the center say that during the past four years, 78 percent of the clients served in the transitional housing programs had a steady cash flow and the same residence a year after they left the program.

The dozens of small, social model programs used by ECS could conceivably wind up serving more homeless people than St. Vincent De Paul Center, if ECS had a financial wizard like Joe Carroll to support them and a better way to convince homeowners throughout the county that they could live with small transitional housing residences in their neighborhoods. Placement efforts are now costly.

Remarkably, Hunter believes the ECS model could eventually enjoy the same success rate as that of St. Vincent De Paul. Its current statistics are already admirable, with a 50 percent success rate reported. Hunter and ECS have found that 25 percent of the clients who go through its program establish solid lives, acquiring jobs and stable living quarters, and *also* dealing with many of their emotional issues, such as drinking and family problems. On the next rung, 25 percent find steady employment and housing, but may not eradicate their drug or drinking problems, nor deal successfully with relationship issues. Another 25 percent make some progress in both areas, but it is not sustained, while the remaining clients make no progress at all. "If we can achieve a 20 to 25 percent success rate, we see that as a good program, especially assuming another 20 to 25 percent make good progress although they do not achieve all their goals," Hunter said.

Hunter believes the ECS social model programs have more enduring effectiveness than the larger institutional models, because big institutions tend to take over and control people, while small programs stimulate self-control and community involvement. The decentralized approach used by ECS is far more flexible and able to dig deeper into the homeless subpopulations, to assist the less attractive, more helpless, more disabled, less motivated segments. A visualization of the centralized approach would be a homeless village dominating a section of a city. While some homeless might like the village concept, many others may either reject it or be objectively unfit for such a setting. Regimenting and organizing many of the homeless may truly be like organizing anarchists—a slippery task at best and often impossible. The decentralized approach, deftly and quietly handled, may be the more politically palatable approach to solving the problems of homelessness in many cities. It relies on the ability of professionals to quickly obtain small shelter units throughout the city, so that no one neighborhood reacts with alarm. Staying within existing zoning laws, ECS manages to obtain houses and small clumps of apartments without creating a stir and gives its clients the opportunity to integrate themselves with mainstream society.

The St. Vincent De Paul Center and ECS are meeting the same basic needs in distinctly different populations of the homeless community. Both offer homeless people a refuge, a variety of health, employment, and social services, and an opportunity to shift into a different gear, toward a more stable, secure lifestyle. There are arguments for and against each approach, but the ability of both programs to serve and survive demonstrates a critical point in providing shelter for the homeless: one solution will not work for all.

> There is no limit to what we can accomplish if we do not care who gets the credit.
>
> —Winston Churchill

SUGGESTED READING

Homelessness: HUD's and FEMA's Progress in Implementing the McKinney Act, U.S. Government Accounting Office, Comptroller General of the United States, May 1989.

Homelessness: Implementation of Food and Shelter Programs Under the McKinney Act, U.S. Government Accounting Office, Comptroller General of the United States, December 1987.

"Homelessness: Critical Issues for Policy and Practice," The Boston Foundation, 1987.

"Pushed Out: America's Homeless," National Coalition for the Homeless, Thanksgiving Day, 1987.

11

Affordable Housing

There are three root causes of homelessness in America: lack of housing, lack of housing, and lack of housing.
            —Robert Hayes, founder, National Coalition for the Homeless

To provide a decent home and a suitable living environment for every American family.
            —Federal Housing Act of 1949

America's housing crisis is solvable, beginning at the local level. It is particularly so if HUD should bestir itself to immediate actions. The great myth about American homelessness is that it is not solvable. The great myth about our housing crisis is that funding for the housing that is needed cannot be found. However, for a half century, America had a federal low-income housing program that worked: this program built houses. The near-elimination of that program beginning in 1981 has been a major cause of homelessness, and the resumption of some federal support would greatly help us now. Federal help for new, low-income housing is not, however, on the immediate horizon, but even if the federal government should begin to contribute some funding, we will have to look to local areas for the working mechanisms, the real solutions.

A cautioning word here. What follows is the description of a discouraging set of realities that have gotten us into the mess we face, acknowledged to be a "national affordable housing crisis" by everyone who has cared to look. But the situation need not be the way it is. This crisis is people-made, and it can be solved by people. HUD Secretary Jack Kemp, along with President Bush and the Congress, of course, is in the best position to lead us in taking the steps of highest leverage in any solution. On the local level, however, there are dozens of homely strategies that have proven successful. For the local mayor, city manager, housing, United Way or other leader, there exists an immediate need to know the options, and to act. This chapter presents thirty such strategies in hopes that local constituents will press for simultaneous and vigorous action using many techniques at once, and that leaders will lead.

First, some history. Until World War II, most Americans still lived on farms and ranches and they built their own homes. Old-timers still recall starting out with a single-room cabin that they'd built by hand at the end of a harvest season, gradually adding on rooms, year by year. No more! We moderns have gone from the agricultural age (farm houses) to the industrial age (city homes), and are now moving on to the communication age—with politics and economics combining to cause profound problems for housing all the people. Today, we are fat cats—houses average five rooms. In the early 1900s houses had one to three rooms. While five people shared a house then, today there is an average of 2.75 people per dwelling unit.

We are demanding more in our housing, but we can afford less. The Affordable Housing Committee of the National Association of Homebuilders provided the following information:

> For millions of Americans, the search for affordable housing represents an ever-growing challenge. During the past decade or so, housing cost increases have outpaced income gains, making it more difficult for households to purchase a home. Between 1971 and 1987, while median family income increased 183 percent, median home prices rose 249 percent. During the Bush administration, 58.7 million Americans will fall within the prime homebuying age group of twenty-five to thirty-four. Of that number, fewer than one-half will be able to own a home. Just within the past eight years, home ownership rates among the twenty-five-to-thirty-four age group have fallen about 8 percent. In addition, at the same time that home ownership opportunities have decreased, tax law changes have reduced incentives for owning a home.
>
> Rents also have increased dramatically as a percentage of income, leaving many households at risk of joining the homeless. Any sudden or unexpected setback, like illness or loss of a job can easily lead to the forfeiture of a rental unit. *Six million* low-income American renters must now allocate more than 50 percent of their income to rent. Among young, single-parent families, rents average 58 percent of income. The demand for low-cost rental housing is increasing, but supply is shrinking as low-cost rental units are lost or in danger of being lost through the upgrading or abandonment of units and the expiration of use restrictions. Moreover, the rental affordability problem has been further exacerbated by the Tax Reform Act of 1986, which almost wiped out incentives for investors in multifamily projects. [Emphasis original.]

Oddly, HUD is not the definitive source for solid data on the state of the nation's low-income housing. The acknowledged best source thus far is a thirty-one-page 1989 publication of the Joint Center for Housing Studies at Harvard University, *The State of the Nation's Housing*. Among the seven key findings of this study: 1) rents have risen dramatically since 1980, up to 30 percent in the West and the Northeast; 2) the percentage of the average renter's income devoted to paying rent has increased dramatically—some pay 75 percent of their income in rent, and 6.6 million poverty-level households are paying more than 50 percent. The problem is acute for young families with children: 70 percent use more than half of their income for housing. According to the study,

> Record-level rents block households from progressing up the economic ladder. Low-income renters must compete for the shrinking supply of low-cost housing, a situation that is likely to worsen. Federal budget cutbacks and expiring use restrictions threaten the subsidized housing stock, while upgrading and abandonment put much of the unsubsidized, low-cost stock at risk of loss.

It has been estimated that the United States has experienced a net loss of 1.2 million low-income housing units since 1980, and that the annual loss now approaches three hundred thousand: the curve is beginning to plunge downward. This is occurring at a time when the number of poverty-level renters living in unsubsidized housing units and paying more than $300 per month for rent (1988 dollars), had more than doubled between 1979 and 1985.

THE FEDS HAVE RETREATED

America's funding commitment to providing housing assistance for new low-income housing declined 82 percent between 1980 and 1988. In fiscal year 1981, federal funds assisted 217,000 new households through federal Section 8 and public housing while in fiscal year 1989 fewer than 85,000 received assistance. Affordable rental housing is vanishing throughout the country. According to *The State of the Nation's Housing*, the failure to produce additional low-cost units between 1980 and 1988 has helped contribute to a total loss since 1974 of over a million units with rents below $300 per month. States have also reduced their financial commitments to low-income housing, according to the National Low Income Housing Coalition.

In most American cities, an adult working full time at a minimum-wage job earns $609 a month (4.3 weeks of forty hours at $4.25 an hour, minus taxes). He or she, young or old, is obviously not able, alone, to rent a one-bedroom flat or apartment for $500 per month. When housing is in short supply, rents rise. Today one-third of U.S. families have annual household incomes under $15,000, and one in seven Americans (over thirty-two million people) live below the poverty line (defined in 1990 as $11,203 annually for a family of four; $5,572 for an individual).

Thus, the honest, working poor, our nation's traditional backbone, are increasingly being found in shelters and in food lines, about to be joined by thousands more, the experts tell us, projecting present trends. Why? What follows are some chilling trends that affect low-income people:

- Middle America's salaries aren't keeping up with inflation of housing prices and rents.
- Real income is dropping for the poor in a low-paying service economy.
- Social problems, racism, and other features of indigestion in the "melting pot" are increasing.
- Families are increasingly broken and dysfunctional.
- Drug and alcohol dependency are widespread.
- Poor schools and education standards are proving inadequate for a high-technology economy.
- Stern enforcement of housing codes is breaking up the one-house extended families that once were the rule in America, and that still are in many "ethnic" neighborhoods.[6]

THE FEDERAL GOVERNMENT
MUST GET ITSELF ORGANIZED

HUD has also become a disorganized, disgraceful bureaucracy. According to a recent Ford Foundation report:

> HUD's role as the key agency responsible for implementing federal housing programs has not been a strong one. Its activities during the 1960s and 1970s left a legacy of mismanagement and an inability to meet consumer needs that persist today. Based on a case study of HUD's property disposition policies in the 1980s, it is clear that the agency is committed neither to maintaining a high-quality stock of subsidized housing nor to protecting the low-income tenants in these buildings. These shortcomings cast considerable doubt on the advisability and, indeed, the capability of HUD, in its present form, to administer low-income housing programs.[7]

Certainly HUD Secretary Jack Kemp needs to clean up his department's Augian Stables, but he must simultaneously challenge the American private sector to produce affordable housing as its response to the great national housing crisis. Kemp is reported to be addressing many building-industry conventions each month, attended largely by developers. Here, he has an opportunity to raise the public interest, and to ask for help. He needs to encourage these leaders to defer any "instant profit" instincts, and to take on, as part of their workload, low-income housing projects. Kemp will accomplish little regarding his low-income duties until he is personally willing to make a significant minority of these developers irritated with him. He must challenge them.

Kemp is experienced at staring over a line, into eyes of powerful, respectable people who wish him some harm and bravely calling a needed play. "To honor, as you strike him down, the foe who comes with fearless eyes," runs an Edwardian poem. Kemp must lead and if he does not, history will relegate him to oblivion. He knows how, but will he? In his contemplation of the matter, Kemp might consider a passage from Henry Pringle's classic 1931 *Theodore Roosevelt*.

> One day, in 1895, at Police Headquarters, Jacob Riis came to [Roosevelt's] office with Lincoln Steffens. They asked whether he was a possible candidate for President of the United States, and Roosevelt leaped to his feet, red with rage. "Don't you dare ask me that!" he almost screamed. "Don't you put such ideas into my head. No friend of mine would say a thing like that. Never, never must either of you remind a man on a political job that he may be President. It almost always kills him politically. He loses his nerve; he can't do his work; he gives up the very traits that are making him a possibility!"[8]

The key, highest-leverage moves available regarding low-income housing in America are in the hands of HUD Secretary Jack Kemp. With great respect, here is what I think Kemp needs to do:

- Act forcefully to preserve the existing, federally supported housing stock by renegotiating the contracts with those unit owners whose units are about to come to the end of their "low-income life"—480,000 are expiring in the next five years. This is the nation's number one housing priority, and one of the most important of any of the nation's priorities.
- Obtain an amendment to the savings and loan bailout legislation that will eliminate the present prejudice against multi-family units (in the "risk-based capital" provisions). This one change will create an incentive for good financing packages for low-income projects. There should be no penalty for funding low-income projects. They should be placed on a par with single-family residences.
- Use the HUD secretaryship as a bully pulpit from which to jawbone private-sector leaders into playing an urgently needed role in solutions.

- Rehabilitate the nation's thousands of dilapidated and largely abandoned urban housing units into decent, low-income housing.
- Real incentives must be built into all systems that could deliver low-income housing. The secretary should search continually for these, and maximize them. Too often federal programs become mired in local politics. This must be stopped.

FACTORS PRICING LOW-INCOME HOUSING UPWARD

Housing prices are rising in urban areas. Several factors lead to higher housing costs. Reduction in densities, changes in zoning patterns, speculation, development fees, managed-growth programs, and environmental mitigation are all causing problems in supply and demand.

The "haves" see real estate as a safe investment. Those who have discretionary income move up and often keep the old house as a rental. Many invest in real estate on the side, while holding other jobs. They buy, fix up, and sell houses for profit. A number of factors are driving housing and land costs up. Among them are speculative churning of land and property, gentrification of old neighborhoods, and redevelopment of the inner cities with a net loss of housing supply.

Local codes should be revised to accommodate affordable housing. Strict state building codes and local ordinances are a major problem. These aim at worthy goals—saving energy, upholding civilized light and air standards, caring for the handicapped, and keeping things fire-safe—but collectively they cost a lot of money. Relaxing these codes has been a consistent demand of the builders and operators of new lowest- and low-income housing, including those of homeless shelters. Examples of standards that could be relaxed include requirements for off-street parking (many people who pay $200 to $300 a month for SRO housing don't have cars, nor do they attract many driving visitors), landscape standards (extra set-backs, more trees, more lawns) that cost more to maintain, and micro-design standards such as requirements for, say, red tile roofs. San Diego has *114* sign ordinances. Are they really all needed? Examples of requirements that might be relaxed to enhance low-income housing are:

1. Restricted housing starts.
2. Environmental mitigation—preserving wetlands, etc.
3. Development fees levied per dwelling unit, including water-hookup, traffic, park, and open-space fees.
4. Managed-growth ordinances and zoning designed to reduce the

amount of land available for housing and to restrict the number of building permits available each year.

Other factors that diminish the low-income housing stock include:

1. Double-digit interest rates. The cost of financing housing is high. The annual interest rate for housing loans is usually between 9 and 12 percent. With a thirty-year mortgage, a $100,000 house paid for with a 9-percent loan ends up costing $292,000; two-thirds of the cost winds up being interest. With a 12-percent loan the cost ends up being $373,000—almost three-quarters interest! A 6-percent loan, on the other hand, still more than most of our parents had to pay, would end up costing only $218,000, a little more than half interest.
2. Financing laws and loan qualifications are usually stricter relative to low-income housing projects. Savings and loans cannot redline, but they are not required to grant every loan request. Because banks naturally like projects with higher profit margins, they like to finance higher-priced housing.
3. Bureaucracy is omnipresent. From HUD to state agencies such as the California Housing Finance Agency, agency bureaucracy is so cumbersome that red tape alone can prevent production of real, low-income housing units within a reasonable time frame. The longer the time it takes to get a project approved, the higher its ultimate cost. Few builders have the staff and the time to go through a lengthy process. Bureaucracies surely need to streamline review procedures, giving priority to low-income projects.
4. The state and federal governments have opted out of the low-income construction game and have abandoned support for existing housing stock.
5. Every year, tens of thousands of low-income units built in the 1950s and 1960s are being relieved of their federal deed-restriction obligations. As loans of thirty years ago are being paid off, these units are becoming middle-income (gentrified) housing, or they are torn down for new development. Half a million units will be lost in the next few years, unless action is taken by HUD and Congress.

Demand is then driving American housing costs up. Low-income housing is drying up. People like choices, yet our choice of housing types is rapidly fading. To make matters worse, the supply of appropriately zoned city land is decreasing, causing further escalation of land values. In twelve major metropolitan areas, the average annual increase of the median price of a home has been between 5.3 percent and 11 percent. The U.S. average is

8 percent. Nationwide, the average home in 1969 cost around $19,900. Today it costs $93,100. One of the most extreme examples is provided by San Francisco, where in 1969 the median price for a home was $31,200 and in 1989 the median price had leapt eight times, to $259,700!

The national need today is vast: 1.5 million low-income homes are needed now and that number is steadily growing. It is no coincidence that the numbers of homeless people has an eerie correspondence to that number. A report by the U.S. Conference of Mayors showed that the numbers of lowest-income SRO hotel rooms lost over the past decade in each city was uncannily close to the official estimation of the number of homeless people in that city.[9] About half of the low-income, SRO hotel rooms had been "taken out" by redevelopment projects. The rents in the remaining units had more than doubled, forcing many residents (often elderly people on pensions, including Social Security) into the streets, at least for part of each month.

During my weekend on the streets in 1984 I met Joe Plount, age sixty-seven, in the Rescue Mission food line. A healthy and cheerful former merchant seaman, he had a pension plus Social Security retirement, but could only afford a hotel room seventeen days each month—he was forced to live on the streets the other thirteen days of the month. He thought this was odd, and humorous, since he had two pensions!

TYPES OF LOW-INCOME HOUSING

The following is a list of types of affordable housing, including a description of each and a short explanation of some of the kinds of financing that have enabled their construction.

Rescue Missions (shelters, three hundred to five hundred beds). Facilities and programs include emergency care up to thirty days, counseling, maybe child care, feeding, and health care. Rescue missions are usually operated by a church or social service agency. *Method*: find a leader; find a site; find funding and an operator; professional fundraising; government funding; free land; sponsorship by a charity; beneficial loans.

Transitional Housing (one hundred to two hundred units). Facilities and programs include a counselor for every twenty families, job training (both mother and father), child care, health care, an apartment for eighteen to twenty-four months, adoption by a family to help bridge to society and normal living patterns, some rent, the starting of a savings account, pleasant common areas, children's lunches. Usually operated by a church or social service group. *Method*: professional fundraising; government funding; free land; sponsorship by a charity; beneficial loans.

SROs (two hundred to three hundred units). Small studios (mini-kitchens or no kitchens), some bathroom facilities or bathroom facilities down the hall, old-hotel style, some common area, security, limited parking, .3 to .5 spaces per dwelling unit, privately operated. *Method*: old renovated hotels; new construction needs HUD money or government subsidy such as redevelopment funds (see example for funding of such a project later in this chapter.)

Federally Assisted Housing ("Section 8" Housing). Rent subsidized apartments or SROs. *Method*: Section 8 rental certificates; moderate-rehabilitation Section 8 certificates remain with the dwelling units for fifteen years; rental rehabilitation apartment tenants get certificates or vouchers and the owner of the project receives low-interest, second-trust deeds for remodeling.

Public Housing. Usually built and owned by government, usually apartments. *Method*: housing authorities; local, state or federal governments build and operate with government funding.

Low-Income Apartments. Usually older units and older neighborhoods, not as many amenities. Sometimes deferred maintenance. *Method*: buyers assume financing; usually smaller projects; low overhead; owner-operated.

Student Housing. Dormitories, cooperatives, apartments, sorority/fraternity houses. *Method*: financed and owned by colleges, universities, national fraternal organizations, cities.

Military Housing. No zoning problem here because of the Supremacy Clause, two hundred to three hundred per project, or twelve to fifteen townhouses per acre (twenty-two to an acre!). *Method*: financed by the U.S. government; doesn't need zoning; doesn't pay fees.

Seniors Housing. Condominiums or apartments (all sizes). *Method*: density bonuses; lower parking requirements.

Special Programs. Runaway teenagers' shelters, halfway houses, Narcotics Anonymous and Alcoholics Anonymous facilities, abused women shelters, YMCAs, YWCAs, veteran programs, church-subsidized housing, immigration housing, farm workers' facilities in agricultural areas, AIDS shelters. *Method*: need charitable fundraising and sponsorship.

Houses for rent. Usually older houses, small, older neighborhoods. *Method*: build new housing; rehab rundown units.

Stripped-down small houses, small lots for sale. Higher density lots of three hundred to four thousand square feet, no fencing, some design for future improvements. *Method*: density; less frills; owners do extra improvements.

Mobile Home Parks. Seniors, families. *Method*: density; low cost.

Habitat for Humanity. Method: lower costs through sweat equity and volunteer expertise.

Lease-Option Houses with liberal terms so tenant can own. *Method*: bad markets; helps builders make payments.

State and Federal First-Time Buyers Programs. Method: Low-interest loans to buyers for the down payment so they can own, not rent; need legislation to expand programs.

Unusual Sites. For example, housing built on steep slopes. Cave-like dwellings are being explored by low-income housing innovators in San Diego. The great advantage is low land costs (often on city or other publicly owned land).

NIMBY

As covered in the appendix on legal rights, and in the model shelters and public restrooms chapters, the typical American cry of, "Not in my back yard!" is a form of selfishness found in all cities. Unchallenged, NIMBY can prevent the solving of homelessness since lowincome housing, shelters, clinics, runaway centers, and other facilities must be located *somewhere*.

Relative to low-income housing, the NIMBY attitude is especially mindless because, with careful architecture and social services planning, it has been proven over and over (as in Seattle, for example—see the chapter on leadership) that the creation of new, low-income housing can greatly enhance the live-ability of neighborhoods, even upscale neighborhoods.

The respected Urban Land Institute recently completed a study of government-owned lands that shows that government owns nearly 25 percent of most "infill" land parcels within most cities. These parcels could be used for low-income housing if the governments had the courage to brave the howls from some in local neighborhoods and the intelligence to ward off such protests using good amenity planning, early communication with and involvement by local residents, and use of local moral leaders, such as church and synagogue leaders.

In a residential area, NIMBY concerns need to be met head on, and *solved*. "When local governments put out the word that they are going to create both needed facilities dotting the city (such as low-income housing) and work to answer residents' legitimate concerns, solutions always emerge," said Walt Ladwig, former planning director for the County of San Diego. "If, on the other hand, local governments knuckle under, instantly, to every apprehensive voice, there can be no solution." The leading citizen concern is for lack of street parking as higher densities are permitted. In Evergreen Park, a suburb of Chicago, these real concerns were answered with a mix of parking answers: blocked-off streets forming large parking areas, alleys wherein access could be had to on-lot parking, and even a bond assessment. Parking is the biggest problem with density and the better use of existing housing. "But all that's needed is imagination and a commitment to solutions," Ladwig said. "Isn't it fundamental that problems exist to be solved?"

Ladwig admitted that density can be overdone, recalling the sixty-five people once discovered in a four-bedroom home in Santa Ana, California. To address this, he suggested permitting second units on lots and (with essentially all experts) scattering low-income housing all over the city." He advocated a position against segregation. "Let a variety of people live together. It's healthy," he concluded.

Politicians and government need to take bold steps and stand up for unpopular housing projects. The private sector must be willing to take less profit, wait longer for profit, become more creative, and, particularly, bond together with neighborhoods and community groups to overcome objections. Oftentimes community resistance to change can be answered by high-quality designs that match the community aesthetic, and with *their* goals being met. It also helps enormously if the project appears to "come up from the bottom." This process requires education of the neighborhood or community, and may double the time it takes to complete a housing project.

Given the history of housing in America, the types of low-income housing it is now possible to construct, and the various private and local, state, and federal government sources of money available to fund housing programs, there are a number of strategies that local leaders can use to solve the problem of homelessness in their areas. The following are thirty such strategies.

THE TEN MOST POTENTIALLY EFFECTIVE LOCAL STRATEGIES

It is true that the biggest immediate "bang for the buck" strategies are those that HUD Secretary Kemp could employ at the federal level, but a number of efficient local strategies can be pursued. Incentives need to be thought through and built into each step of the process, and refined as the process unfolds.

1. *Find and mobilize local housing leaders.* Everyone involved in housing and in neighborhood development must make affordable housing a number-one priority. Once this platitude is uttered, a local cadre of housing experts needs to be purposefully developed. Knowledge is power. This country and its local leaders cannot rest until the 1949 Housing Act's goal of affordable housing for all is a reality. Local politicians should not be afraid to stand up for what is right for the people and the people then need to stand up for those politicians.

2. *Challenge the private sector.* Let the housing industry provide housing. Analyze its actions and offer endless incentives. Support public-private ventures. Encourage developers to get involved, very creatively. Have them produce programs and zoning recommendations. Have them set numerical

goals. Offer them bonuses and incentives. Point up the dependence of all local industry on low-income housing for workers, and of the urgent need for *regional* business planning. When planning is regional, housing needs pop into bold relief—they cannot be ignored.

3. *Implement inclusionary zoning ("sprinkled") citywide.* Each new construction project should have a portion of it allocated to new, low-income housing, especially projects over a hundred units. Normally, inclusionary zoning requires that each project have a percentage of 10 to 20 percent of low-income housing. If this proves impossible in a particular project, have the contractor/developer contribute to a citywide low-income housing fund. This has worked magnificently in Montgomery County, Maryland, and in several New Jersey counties that have simply required that a flat percentage (often 15 percent) of all housing be low-income housing.

4. *Give density bonuses for affordable housing.* A city can increase zoning densities (dwelling units per acre) to achieve affordable housing goals. This is incentive-building at its most productive. Planning directors should be directed to review community plans to see where increasing housing density will work. Then programs should be designed to allow for the production of affordable housing there. This helps reduce land costs and some of the fixed costs of any construction project, whether it has twenty units or two hundred units. Higher densities can help bring the cost per dwelling unit down. This will require changes in local codes.

5. *Encourage non-profits, joint ventures, and foundations to produce affordable housing.* An organization called The Bridge in San Francisco and an organization called HAUS, Inc., in San Diego are already active. The sole mission of these non-profit groups is to produce quality, affordable housing. Business and community leaders make up the organizations' boards and do the fundraising. (See the end of this chapter for further information.) This strategy is a "wave of the future," and can have the enormous advantage of a grassroots, neighborhood momentum and energy. The non-profit status of a group expedites projects, because it carries the glow of the public interest. As a result, project time can sometimes be cut by up to a year.

6. *Encourage churches, foundations, social service clubs and community development corporations to be catalysts.* Several projects have been built, funded, and operated by religious congregations, foundations, social service clubs, and community development corporations. These organizations are usually broad-based groups close to the need. They are good operators and have broad fundraising capabilities.

7. *The tax credit engine.* State and federal tax credits can create the great incentive of giving investments a yield of up to 18 percent, with the added advantage of good public relations. The 1986 Tax Reform Act created the low-income housing tax credit (Section 42, I.R. Code). The legislative

authority for this credit expired at the end of 1989, but it was extended to the end of 1990 (lobbying, yes, is needed here!). Owners are required to keep housing built by taking advantage of this tax credit low-income for up to thirty years.

Tax credits reduce taxes dollar for dollar, and are accordingly greatly valued by builders. Congress was attempting to stimulate low-income housing production. The calculation of the credit basis is complex, not including land, but approximates the cost of construction. A "credit rate" of 70 percent of net present value of the basis over ten years is then figured. It sounds complicated, but it boils down to about 9 percent of the cost of construction each year for ten years. Obviously, this can recoup almost all of the construction cost. The section gives a little less credit if the developer uses tax-exempt bonds or federal housing money for construction. But the credit is transferrable as a security, via partnerships. This sets up a fine tax shelter for people making less than $200,000. There is a limitation on passive losses for individuals ($250,000 per year), but corporations can buy all the tax credits they may need on the open market. The actual value to a developer initially is about half what the credits are. So, for a $1 million development, the value to the developer at the inception is thought to be just under 50 percent of the construction costs.

The reason this, alone, cannot fill our entire low-income housing needs, is that public dollars must be added to make projects economical. Usually 70 percent of the financing must be equity (25 to 55 percent of the cost, the higher figure if, as in California, there is a companion state tax credit). The problem is, where is the other 20 to 50 percent coming from? The usual answer is a public agency buying the land (or perhaps it already owns the land) and kicking in some mortgage money. The real need here, clearly, is for *local government commitment* (see the chapter on leadership). There are state-by-state caps on the gross tax credit, so this is a competitive game, by categories of low-income housing. The more social services that are built into a project, however, the more likely that it will be approved. These caps ought to be removed by the Congress—as should the "sunset date" of the tax credit itself. A new SRO constructed by this method on donated San Diego city land will have rents ranging from $199 to $257 per month.

8. *Take maximum benefit of the savings and loan bailout,* into which Congress inserted three incentives to aid low-income housing: a) a right of first refusal by non-profits to purchase foreclosed properties—what an advantage!; b) a requirement that the S&Ls create a pool of funds estimated to generate at least $50 million per year, perhaps as much as $100 million per year for low-income housing; and c) a new, rigorous reporting system for S&Ls to prove that their lending policies include low-income housing, and that they do not discriminate. Community groups are now trooping

to the S&Ls to help them do their duty.

9. *Maximize the use of redevelopment funds for housing.* Many redevelopment agencies are legally required to produce some low-income housing. In many cities, huge pools of money are involved. Many don't meet their goals. Monitor these funds carefully—make this a priority in any redevelopment area. Your local mayor, legal aid society, university urban studies department, and media ought to serve as watch dogs.

10. *Maximize the use of HUD Section 8 rental rehabilitation money.* This program allows tenants to receive new Section 8 certificates certifying that they are part of a federal program to subsidize rents—a significant help for apartment owners and tenants alike. The idea is for older neighborhoods to get their status and their apartments upgraded, for the owners to get low-interest, second-trust deeds while poor tenants get subsidies. Normally, this program involves projects in targeted census tracts that are under twenty units in size. The problem with this is gentrification—use of these federal funds intended to spruce up low-income housing to turn that very same housing into higher-income units. This must not be permitted, and Congress should act with an amendment to keep rents reasonable, but low, as a condition of receipt of these federal funds.

A converse grave danger is that, absent aggressive municipal efforts to foster housing rehabilitation, low-income housing (often owner-occupied) will be lost simply because it is not maintained. Foster maintenance! The Enterprise Foundation estimates that we are adding forty thousand lowest-income housing units per year, while physically losing three hundred thousand units per year, of which at least a hundred thousand are lost due to fire, urban renewal, or abandonment.

While all federal housing development programs together create only forty thousand new affordable units per year, over three times that number are repaired with federal community development block grants, city aid, rental or farmers' programs, and nearly another two hundred thousand poor homeowners are helped with emergency home repair and weatherization via federal and state programs. These save houses with bad roofs and failed heating rather cheaply. Weatherization and home repair programs spend $500 to $4,000 per unit while block grant rehabilitation programs average $10,000 to $15,000 per unit, and new construction costs $40,000 to $80,000 per unit or more.

OTHER PRACTICAL STRATEGIES

11. *Institute linkage fees.* Linkage fees are fees paid by commercial and industrial developers to provide low-income housing. They can range from

$2 per square foot to $14 per square foot. These fees are normally paid at the issuance of the building permit or at certificate of occupancy. When linkage fees are charged, they increase rents for business. Think long and hard before doing this. Meet with business leaders, who argue that this strategy hurts consumers and slows growth.

12. *Don't create ghettos by putting all the affordable housing in one neighborhood.* Encourage grassroots action so that all neighborhoods feel a responsibility to create housing for all economic levels. Don't impact only one community; sprinkle efforts throughout many cities and neighborhoods. High-quality design will help with this goal. People like good design because it is functional, aesthetic and respectful. It makes people feel good! Zone for low-income housing "up front": require it of every developer, in every section of town. With no discrimination and clear rules applicable to all, it will be hard for anybody to complain, harder yet to block valuable projects. Zoning changes allowing "infill" via "grannie houses" and guest houses are a civilized way to buttress extended families and simultaneously serve low-income housing needs.

13. *Fight to decrease the erosion of existing affordable housing units.* This is the national housing priority of most immediate importance. A 1988 report by the National Low-Income Housing Preservation Commission predicts that some 523,000 units subsidized by HUD are at risk of being lost over the next fifteen years, most in the next five years! Several hundred thousand units have already been lost, and the moratorium on changes runs out September 30, 1990. We all need to urge Congress and HUD to offer low-interest refinancing plans to owners of these existing low-income housing units. Local governments could, of course, purchase and operate these units. Local governments could also require written proof of financing for new projects before issuing demolition permits for old ones, and/or require demolition bonds for housing units. (Some great developments get demolished, and then financing falls through, leaving only a vacant lots, often for years.) Local government can also require, by ordinance, that every new project everywhere include some low-income housing units.

14. *The Habitat Concept.* Start programs wherein low-income people help build their own housing with neighbors helping. Sweat equity helps reduce the cost of housing. Habitat for Humanity, whose most famous volunteer is former president Jimmy Carter, is an excellent program and should be investigated and invited to your city. This modern barn-raising technique can really take off if it uses low-cost, government land (see the end of this chapter). The habitat concept has not yet been applied to urban homesteading (see number 28 below), but that match should be made. In Baltimore, a neighborhood non-profit organization, People's Homesteading Group, builds three to five houses at a time under the habitat model. Members

are primarily female heads of household, and the average rehabilitation cost per house is $11,000. This is for home ownership!

15. *Work with local media to alter the image of public housing*, which has undeservingly been given a bad name. The history of American public housing is generally the history of excellent housing (I grew up in an excellent federal housing project next door to one dedicated by President Franklin D. Roosevelt). The public housing projects that have failed are the tall, stark ones that look like prisons. Nobody likes to think he or she lives in a prison. Give respect, get respect. Attention to design and thoughtful selection of social amenities can make public housing work. Invite the media to projects; let them interview tenants. Make the places great. Change the image.

16. *Apply for HUD money and lobby Congress for an increase in housing-related appropriations.* One of the keys to affordable housing is financing. Unfortunately, the federal government did not do a commendable job in the 1970s and 1980s of administering and funding needed projects. Sadly, the dollar commitment to housing has decreased markedly since 1980. America needs to make housing a national priority again. There are other fourteen federal programs to investigate:

  a. Comprehensive Homeless Assistance Plan
  b. Emergency Shelter Grants Program
  c. Supportive Housing Demonstration Program—Transitional Housing
  d. Supportive Housing Demonstration Program—Permanent Housing for Handicapped Homeless People
  e. Supplemental Assistance for Facilities to Assist the Homeless
  f. Section 8 Assistance for Single-Room-Occupancy Dwellings
  g. The Stewart B. McKinney Homeless Assistance Act.[10] It mandates identification and use of surplus federal buildings for the homeless. The courts will enforce it.[11]
  h. Property Disposition Program (federal property for sale)
  i. Community Development Block Grant Program
  j. Emergency Community Services Homeless Grants
  k. Emergency Food and Shelter Program
  l. Homeless Children and Youth Education Grants
  m. Additional Domiciliary Beds (Veterans' Administration)
  n. Tax credits

17. *Promote shared housing programs.* Help people find roommates to help reduce housing costs. A program in Atlanta, Georgia, has been very successful in placing students with seniors. In this case, seniors must be over sixty years old and the students must be over eighteen years old.

18. *Institute a "3R program" (remove, refurbish, resell).* In Orlando, Florida, there is a program whereby, rather than tear down old housing,

the city takes a house, finds a lot for it, refurbishes it, and then sells it to a low-income person. (For further information, contact the HANDS organization in Orlando.)

19. *Give tax incentives.* If your city has an income tax, property tax, utility tax, special taxes, or high fees, give credits or reduced taxes to those who will provide affordable housing. New York is an example of a city that has used this method well. (Further information, contact the New York Housing Authority in Manhattan.)

California Revenue and Taxation Code section 214(g)(i), for example, allows an owner of rental property having 20 percent or more units as low rentals to receive a rebate of local property taxes for the purpose, that year, of lowering rents further, or of improving habitability (including amenities like playgrounds, child care, etc.) Non-profit corporations are being organized to assume the role of general partner and consultant to help decide how to spend the money and to handle the heavy load of paperwork.

20. *Contact the Federal Housing Finance Board.* The savings and loan industry has a new program: it will pay the federal government a special tax to be used to subsidize financing for an estimated twenty thousand new affordable housing units. This year, the program will dispense $78.8 million worth of long-term, interest-rate subsidies to qualified home buyers and low-income developers of rental and for-sale properties.

21. *Encourage infill development.* Infill sites are sites that have been overlooked during development booms. Rather than have developers build on only the fringes of the city and in suburban areas, they should be encouraged to develop "infill" sites in the existing communities. The following are six strategies for cities, architects, developer groups, and redevelopment authorites to use to motivate interest in infill development, according to the Urban Land Institute:

a. Stimulate developer interest via publicity campaigns, meetings with real estate interests and design competitions.
b. Remove obstacles created by government. Reduce delays in project review and study possible code revisions.
c. Create neighborhood support for infilling. Establish review meetings, enact special procedures and provide area targeting.
d. Show that there is lower risk and advantageous financing. Do demonstration projects, encourage maintenance and rehabilitation, institute service upgrading, and study interim uses.
e. Address site-specific problems. Increase land availability, reduce the high cost of land and improvements, and correct infrastructure problems.
f. Increase land availability by eminent domain, encourage land swapping, tax vacant land at higher rates, and penalize land banking.

22. *Investigate selling municipal bonds for low-income housing.* This strategy has twice been proven successful (for $50 million each time) in Seattle. Units built this way need not compete for the above-mentioned tax credit. The projects can get an additional subsidy that, with the low interest from the bond-financed mortgage, should substantially reduce rents. (For further information, contact the Seattle Housing Authority.)

23. *Contact national foundations that help fund housing programs.* Try local foundations, of course, but also larger, national foundations which, by charter or policy, are interested in funding housing initiatives. For further information, contact the Neighborhood Funder's Group Membership Directory in Westport, Connecticut. The following are thirty-two of the most active foundation-related sources of housing funding:

Amoco Foundation
ARCO Foundation
BP America
Center for Community Change
Cleveland Foundation
Connecticut Mutual Life Insurance
Discount Foundation
Fannie Mae Foundation
Ford Foundation
Fund for the City of New York
George Gund Foundation
The Harris Bank Foundation
Hartford Foundation for Public
    Giving
Heinz Endowments
Hudson-Webber Foundation
Hyams Foundation
James Irvine Foundation

Local Initiative Support Corporation
Manufacturers Hanover Trust
Marianist Sharing Fund
Eugene and Agnes Meyer Foundation
The Milwaukee Foundation
Morgan Guaranty Trust
National Trust for Historic
    Preservation
NCB Development
New Haven Foundation
New Prospect Foundation
New York Community Trust
New York Foundation
David and Lucile Packard
    Foundation
James C. Penney Foundation
Pew Charitable Trusts

24. *Create affordable housing design competitions for city-owned or other suitable, available sites.* Encourage design teams that have expertise in housing to compete in competitions. Competitions like these help local firms gain experience and notoriety. They also show communities a variety of concepts for housing and create public interest in affordable housing. A successful demonstration project was recently done in the state of New Jersey.

25. *Create neighborhood support.* Politicians, developers, and neighborhoods should all learn to work together so that affordable housing projects are acceptable and commonplace in each neighborhood. (Projects noted by the Urban Land Institute to have succeeded in this neighborhood support

exist in Minneapolis, Baltimore, and Phoenix.)

26. *Create housing trust funds.* Cities should consider creating housing trust funds to provide affordable housing. Taxes—general fund monies, fees, bonds and several other finance vehicles could be used to create a fund to construct housing projects. There are now twelve cities with housing trust funds. Seventeen states have such funds and nine more are in various stages of forming them. The San Diego Housing Commission is willing to provide further information about creating a housing trust fund.

27. *Study the need for floor area ratio (FAR) bonuses.* These are incentives for building affordable housing. Many downtowns give FAR bonuses to developers who will create affordable housing units. As an example, an average block has between 60,000 and 120,000 square feet. With a FAR of 6 on a 60,000-square-foot block, a developer would be allowed to build 360,000 square feet of building (6 × 60,000). Cities could give bonuses of approximately 2 FAR for building affordable housing, and require that a project be at least 75 to 80 percent residential. In return, the developer would be allowed to build an additional 120,000 square feet (2 × 60,000 square feet) on the block in question.

28. *Reactivate the Urban Homestead Program.*[12] This program allows qualified poor people to "claim for residence" abandoned buildings on which no taxes are being paid. This technique has been applied with most success in Eastern cities, such as New York, where a neighborhood has become so run down and crime-ridden that the federal government would not be much criticized for "giving away" government assets. It also works well in cities where land values are generally low, like in the Midwest, particularly in ghetto areas. This program works best using a non-profit neighborhood group (possibly partly funded by the municipal government, to encourage grassroots initiative and other advantages) that might go after and obtain a number of housing units on which HUD has foreclosed. This HUD program has been referred to as "ossified, a fossil," because of its terrible red tape, and also because its "giveaway appearance" does not go down well with habitual penny pinchers. On the other hand, the program could provide a massive vehicle, in the hands of a determined city council or housing commission, for the kind of initiatives needed to solve the housing crisis.

29. *Lobby the state and federal governments.* They must do their shares. Team up with other locales. Housing loans should target certain segments of the market and link them with housing programs on both the federal and state levels. A word needs to be said for the lobbying efforts already doing a good job on the federal level. Support them. Join their cause and influence their policies. Stick your neck out! We all need to handle this thing together. Contact the National Low-Income Housing Coalition in Washington, D.C., and the National Coalition for the Homeless in New York City.

Analogous coalitions exist on the state level. In California, for example, the California Right to Housing Campaign can now command an "alert letter" from nearly thirty thousand Californians. Political professionals opine that when a California group can do that, via direct mail, in numbers upwards of fifty thousand, that group has clout. The nurses have it, and the teachers, the truckers, the doctors, the chambers of commerce and the Sierra Club, to give some examples. Why not advocate for the homeless? The state level, in California, is where great action is. California's voters are expected to approve a second low-income housing bond issue ($450 million total) in 1992.

Remember, when the U.S. Constitution was ratified, America contained 1.7 million politicians. Everyone was a politician. It was expected. The price of liberty is vigilance, and participation. Wade in—you'll enjoy it!

30. *Lobby Congress about the S&Ls.* Congress needs to amend the massive savings and loan bailout legislation to put multi-unit, low-income housing projects on an equal footing (within the S&L "reserve requirements") with single-family residences. This one incentive could lock in the savings and loans, and possibly a huge swath of developers, as active allies. Surely other incentives for financing low-income housing could also be built into this massive reform.

A second point regarding the S&L scandal is that there is a reservoir of foreclosed and in-construction housing available for low-income purchase. Apartments may be bought in Dallas, it is said, for as little as $5,000. This presents a conundrum—an apparent large opportunity connected to the tough problem of the lack of federal, state, local, and even private cash to subsidize the purchase or completion of units. Nevertheless, a national S&L affordable housing inventory is needed, and an assessment of the scope of both the opportunities and the costs that it represents.

IS THERE MONEY AVAILABLE
FOR THESE APPROACHES?

Surely. If an individual project's numbers work, it can easily be financed. If the project is right but the numbers are marginal, then creativity and teamwork involving the private sector, government, and lenders is needed to make these projects a reality. Prime sources to finance projects are commercial banks, savings and loan banks, foundations that make grants, state government, HUD, private wealthy donors, local housing authorities, churches, service clubs, community leaders, redevelopment agencies, and community development corporations. As the sample housing project that closes this chapter shows, low-income housing packages are created by piecing together funding from several sources to finance a single project.

DISCOVER A NEW SAVINGS AND LOAN PROGRAM

In the summer of 1990, low-income housing will receive a shot in the arm from a seemingly unlikely source—the beleaguered savings and loan industry. Although the number of S&Ls is down nearly two-fifths from a decade ago, the survivors, roughly three thousand of them, are paying a special tax to subsidize financing for an estimated twenty thousand new units of affordable housing. In exchange for bailing out the savings and loan industry last August, Congress decided that the federally chartered regional banks that make money on S&L banking transactions should divert some of their profits into affordable housing. This year the resulting Affordable Housing Program will dispense $78.8 million worth of longterm interest-rate subsidies to qualified home buyers and low-income developers of rental and for-sale properties. This cash infusion should help create twenty thousand units of housing, valued at up to $1 billion, according to the Federal Housing Finance Board (FHFB), which is in charge of the program. The actual number of units funded, however, depends on the terms of the proposals submitted by individual financial institutions competing to dispense the subsidies.

The FHFB estimated that the cut-rate funds would lower the interest rate to low-income buyers or developers of low-income property by an average of 1.5 percentage points. Funding for the new program is coming from the country's twelve regional home-loan banks, which act as "bankers' banks" by extending the cash advances (including mortgages) used by financial institutions to fund their activities. In turn, the banks book profits from the interest earned on those advances. The thrift bailout law establishing the program calls for the regional banks to redirect a portion of their previous year's profits earned in this way, starting at 5 percent this year and increasing to 10 percent in later years, into affordable housing. Lenders in California, Arizona, and Nevada, for example, will vie for pieces of the San Francisco-area regional bank's $20 million in earnings earmarked for the affordable housing program. The first installment of the subsidy money became available in July 1990, when the FHFB announced the projects it had chosen to fund, based on recommendations from the twelve regional banks. New applications should be made every year. The decision-making board will eventually consist of four members nominated by the White House and approved by the Senate, plus the secretary of HUD.

Most of the regional banks have elected to reserve some of their affordable housing funds and conduct a second round of financing that would free up remaining subsidy money in mid-November, according to Stephen Johnson, an FHFB legal advisor. Under the scoring system, according to rules announced by the board, lender applications receiving the highest priority must do at least three of the following:

- Create low-income home ownership or rental opportunities and permanent housing for the homeless.
- Convert foreclosed properties held by the federal government into low-income housing.
- Incorporate participation by non-profit and community groups.
- Use resident management and homesteading techniques to empower the poor.

Although the twelve regional banks can devise customized subsidy programs within the framework set forth by the FHFB, most of them have indicated they will forego that option in order to give lenders the maximum flexibility to fashion their proposals, according to Frank Willis, executive director of the Housing Opportunities Foundation of the U.S. League of Savings Institutions. In many instances, non-profit housing developers, community groups, and local housing finance authorities are expected to put together projects for consideration and then seek a lender as a sponsor to enter the proposals in funding competitions.

STATE GOVERNMENT'S INFLUENCE ON LOCAL COMMUNITIES

California law requires that local communities meet low-income housing needs, but because there are no "teeth" in the law and because of a lack of executive leadership, California's cities and counties have not yet had to comply with its provisions. According to the *San Diego Union*,

> A startling new housing report shows that California cities are doing a lousy job of producing low-cost housing units—despite a 1980 state law that says they must do much more. Prepared by the California Coalition for Rural Housing, the report is a stinging indictment of the state's housing strategy, which for ten years has relied on local government to implement statewide housing goals. Experts predict that the findings may inspire the Legislature to reconsider how California tries to dig itself out of the current housing affordability mess. Scheduled to be released next week, the report surveyed housing activity in cities throughout the state.
>
> Five years ago, state officials working with local jurisdictions determined that six hundred thousand new low-cost homes needed to be built by 1990 to meet the state's housing need. Every city in the state agreed to build a "fair share" of the total housing need. Communities subsequently submitted local plans to the state Department of Housing and Community Development for approval. However, only 16 percent, or 97,424, of the needed units have actually been built, according to the twenty-page study, called "Local

Progress in Meeting the Low-Income Housing Challenge."
The new report paints a dire picture of local inaction.

- Despite the requirement that every municipality do its part, 24 percent of all California communities haven't produced even a single unit of affordable housing. Cities in this category include Emeryville, Cerritos, El Monte, Hermosa Beach, ·Rosemead, South Pasadena and Fountain Valley.
- Only 11 percent of those surveyed met 100 percent of their local share. This list includes the cities of South Gate, Inglewood, and Costa Mesa.
- Sixty-six percent of California municipalities haven't met half of their fair share goal.

No matter how the numbers are examined, "low-income housing production is critically lagging behind the need," the report concludes.[13]

VISIONARY IDEAS FOR HOUSING TODAY

1. Vacant housing—old hotels
2. Mobile homes—temporary housing
3. Tube sleeping quarters—Japanese-style
4. Tents—pavilions
5. Navy ships—moth-balled vessels
6. Military barracks
7. Camps in mountains and desert expanses
8. Houses in depressed towns—use vacant structures (give welfare recipients a choice?)
9. Under-used, government-owned facilities
10. Private sector—adopt-a-homeless-person programs
11. Architects' publications regarding new or old materials, cheap techniques
12. Pre-fabricated or manufactured housing
13. Churches—cracker boxes
14. $2,000 houses—cement blown over chicken wire with frame over slab

Choices set people free. Americans, their planners, and their builders need to change our dated image of a dream house in the suburbs for everyone. We need to re-learn what makes different people comfortable in a home: space, security, privacy, affordability, and a variety of other needs. We need to change today's housing myths, based so heavily on the "Leave It To Beaver," post–World War II images of the 1950s. Then we need to organize to provide housing in a spectrum of new ways, not expecting each person to live in the same kind of housing. Choices, choices, and more choices must be our creed.

A 1990 SRO[14]

This San Diego project comprised 221 dwelling units and 88 parking spaces. Rents for studios ranged from $232 per month to $335 per month, with appliances. For such a unit with no kitchenette in the room, and with either no bath or a half bath (communal bath available) rent could be as little as $207 per month.

Costs

Direct Costs

Land	$1,125,000
Construction	3,790,000
Off-site improvements	42,000
Contingency (3%)	113,700
Contractor overhead (3%)	118,371
Contractor fee (5%)	197,285
Fees, building	20,000
Fees, water & sewer	165,750
Architect and supervision	120,000

"Soft" Costs (fees)

Construction interest	225,000
(6 months, 10% of 4,500,000)	
Construction loan fee (1%)	67,500
Permanent loan fee (1%)	67,500
Taxes during construction	30,000
Insurance	20,000
Legal	10,000
Marketing	-0-
Furniture, liners, appliances	281,000
Floor & window coverings	125,000
Developers fee & overhead (5%)	260,655

Total Costs	$6,787,761

Funding

Redevelopment agency	$ 850,000
(Grant 20%: 1/3 of that year's low-income allocation of	
$3 million, or 2% of the overall $40 million annual budget)	
Loan amount	4,500,000
(from the developer's banker)	
Developer cash/equity	1,437,761
(mom, savings, and partners)	
Total Financing	$6,787,761

Annual Operating Budget

Income	
Rents	$1,057,841
Expenses	
Operation & maintenance	469,704
Debt service on loan	473,892
(10% on $4,500,000)	
Return on developer's equity (10%)	114,245
Total Operating Budget	$1,057,841

This SRO won a national award in 1990. The builder says it could not now be replicated in San Diego because of a clever move of NIMBY origins by the City Council that wiped out the building and zoning breaks necessary for such a project's success. This formula works in a financial and political environment that meets four conditions: 1) strong local government support clearing the way with zoning variances (such as easing off-street parking requirements); 2) a grant from the local redevelopment agency or HUD; 3) a minimum of neighborhood opposition; and 4) an experienced builder with some capital and a good banker. There has been a national focus on this formula for the construction of new SROs by private enterprise (with some government help) in order to generate a profit renting rooms at rents between $207 and $335 per month.

Typical downtown redevelopment plans show a mix of retail shops and medium- to upper-income ("yuppie") housing to make the area "viable," even "vibrant." But the presence of these neighbors may soon reach a political critical mass in which they organize to act as modern suburbanites to exclude further intrusions of SROs and other low-income housing. For this reason, efforts should be made to spend the maximum share of redevelopment funds on lowest-income, downtown housing *first*. A redevelopment agency could

PHOTO BY DAVE GATLEY

PHOTO BY DAVE GATLEY

PHOTO BY DAVE GATLEY

spend all its budget for three or four years on new SROs, until the units lost to redevelopment (private and public) over the last decade have been replaced. Then it could develop its traditional retail space and upscale housing.

This bright idea is apparently unthinkable. The presence of thriving retail areas populated by big spenders can mean happy bankers and city treasurers, so, naturally, such plans get priority. The urban planners say one should "go for a healthy mix," but the idea of replacing the lost SRO rooms quickly and early on in the process remains a worthy one—quite possibly a *sine qua non* of successfully preserving and replacing low-income housing in the downtowns of America's cities.

> For it is often necessary to walk backwards, as a man on the wrong road goes back to a signpost to find the right road. The modern man is more like a traveller who has forgotten the name of his destination, and has to go back whence he came, even to find out where he is going.
> —G.K. Chesterton

SUGGESTED READING

Corrective Capitalism: The Rise of America's Community Development Corporations, Pierce & Steinbach, Ford Foundation, 1987.

A Decent Place to Live, Enterprise Foundation, 1625 Eye Street, Suite 1015, Washington, D.C., 20006, 1988.

Affordable Housing: The Years Ahead, Louis Winnick and Nancy Andrews, Ford Foundation, 1989.

Affordable Housing in Older Neighborhoods, National Trust for Historic Preservation, 1989.

Community-Based Development: Investing in Renewal, Lance C. Buhl, National Congress for Community Economic Development, 1612 K Street N.W., Suite 510, Washington, D.C. 20006, 1987.

Principles and Practices of Community Development Lending: A Five-Step Investment Model to Strengthen Bank Community Development Lending Programs, Charles E. Riesenberg and Carolyn P. Line, Federal Reserve Bank of Minneapolis, 1989 (great, useful flow charts).

Affordable Housing in Older Neighborhoods: Multiple Strategies, Byrd Wood, ed., Preservation Forum, National Trust for Historic Preservation, 1989.

Homelessness in the States, Lee Walker, The Council of State Governments, Division of Policy Analysis Services, Iron Works Pike, P.O. Box 11910, Lexington, KY, 40578-9989, 1989.

Housing America in the 1980s, John S. Adams, Russell Sage Foundation, New York, 1987.

Making Infill Projects Work, Eric Smart, The Urban Land Institute, 1985.

Rental Housing, W. Paul O'Mara and Cecil E. Sears, The Urban Land Institute, 1090 Vermont Avenue NW, Washington, D.C., 20005, 1984.

"The Price of Regulation," Peter Werwath, which can be obtained from the Enterprise Foundation, Columbia, MD, 301-964-1230, 1990.

Inventing a Non-Homeless Future: A Public Policy Agenda for Preventing Homelessness, Madeline R. Stoner, Peter Lang Publishing, 1989.

The Right to Housing: A Blueprint for Housing the Nation, Dick Cluster, 1989. Available from: Community Economics, Inc., 1904 Franklin St., #900, Oakland, CA, 94612.

The Excitement of Building, Millard and Linda Fuller, Word Publishing, 1990.

Infill Development Strategies, Real Estate Research Corporation, Urban Land Institute and American Planning Association, 1982.

The State of the Nation's Housing, William Apgar, Dennis Di Pasquale, Nancy McArdle, and Jennifer Olson, Harvard University Joint Center for Housing Studies, CIS Graphics Communication, Inc., 1989.

The famous James W. Rouse's Enterprise Foundation of Columbia, Maryland, 505 American City Building, Columbia, MD 21044, 301-964-1230, P.O. Box 1490, Alexandria, VA 22313, exists to foster meeting America's housing needs. Its publications are useful and timely. Recent ones include:

City Homes: Unique Rehab Effort Stems Loss of Marginal Rental Housing, Peter Werwath and Nadine Post, 1990.

Lease-Purchase: One Road to Homeownership, Cecilia Cassidy, 1988.

Cost Cuts, a monthly series on housing rehabilitation issues and ideas. Typical topics: "Creating Accessory (Granny Flat) Apartments," "Risk Control in Low-Cost Construction Management," "Software for Housing Accounting."

12

The Homeless Mentally Ill

Every institution is the lengthening shadow of a single significant person.
—Ralph Waldo Emerson

Meet Roger Farr, Utah farm boy and Mormon elder turned public health doctor. As senior consulting psychiatrist for the Los Angeles County Department of Mental Health, Farr was sent on a "quite normal" assignment in January 1981. He was told to go to the office of the Los Angeles Department of Public Social Services (DPSS—the welfare department) in the Skid Row area, find out why 60 percent of the welfare workers were exhibiting symptoms of severe stress, and tell the county how to "fix" the problem.

Farr discovered that the workers were dealing with a new social phenomenon, the appearance of hundreds of people of a type not noted before on the streets. The new homeless had arrived, and welfare workers were experiencing them first. A significant number of these homeless (nearly 40 percent, it later turned out) were deeply mentally ill. This is the story of what grew, via Farr and his associates' labors, into the nationally acclaimed "Skid Row Mental Health Project."

In 1985, an unpublished statistical report from the Survey and Report Branch, Division of Biometry and Applied Sciences of the National Institute for Mental Health, estimated that on any given day in 1985, about 125,000-250,000 individuals are considered severely disabled mentally ill out of an estimated 2.8 million individuals who are homeless. Local studies, however, have shown this segment to be doubling every four years; and Dr. Ronald W. Manderscheid of the National Institute for Mental Health said of this: "That makes sense."[15] Thus it may be that half a million deeply mentally ill Americans are homeless at any given moment in 1990. "In a great and rich country like America," *Newsweek* recently asked, "how can this be so?"

Until about twenty-five years ago, large mental hospitals cared for the severely mentally ill who, by the way, comprise relatively constant percentages of every population in every culture in the world. In the late 1950s, atrocious conditions were exposed in many state mental hospital systems across America, and the resulting drumbeat for reform coincided with the creation of a new class of drugs—"psychotropic drugs," also called "phenothiozenes." In controlled, supportive, hospital research settings, a great majority of the most severely mentally ill saw their gravest symptoms diminish. If these patients did not become fully functional, at least they appeared not to be dangerous, either to themselves or others. They were able to interact with others and, in some cases, improved greatly in insight and ability. The thought dawned on Americans that perhaps the great, expensive (and maybe evil) hospital edifices could be torn down.

The most popular idea or solution linked theoretically with use of the new medicines became "community care." Its delivery was envisioned by the responsible and compassionate as a less expensive, supportive "board and care" facility. It all sounded wonderful, and an amazing coalition of advocates participated in the transition from state hospital care to community care, including such diverse players as President John F. Kennedy and California governors Ronald Reagan and Jerry Brown. Reagan is most frequently blamed for the actual implementation of 1960s deinstitutionalization in California, but it was during Brown's tenure that the deepest cuts in California's mental health budget occurred. State officials of both political parties carved away at mental health programs and blocked efforts to provide the crucial, continuing "community care" without which the great experiment in liberty and decency for the mentally ill called "deinstitutionalization" was doomed to failure.

A calculation is helpful to understand the range of changes wrought through deinstitutionalization caused by this twenty-five-year-old system. If California had maintained the old system, there would be some eighty thousand chronically disabled mental patients in its state hospitals; instead, there is a mere forty-two hundred such patients today, half of whom are the criminally insane. The cost of this hypothetical eighty-thousand-patient system in today's dollars would be $4.2 billion; the present California mental health budget, including outlays by both the state and all fifty-eight California counties, is only a little more than $1 billion. In real terms, mental health care in California is receiving less than one-fourth the funds it did in 1963. Other leading areas of governmental expenditure, such as education, highways, water supply, and law enforcement have, by contrast, kept pace with 1963 levels or exceeded them, in real terms.

As though this loss of funding were not enough, between 1980 and 1982 the new federal administration slashed nearly 350,000 Americans from the rolls of the Social Security program for the permanently, totally disabled—SSI—under the theory that these were among the "welfare chiselers" who needed to be booted off the government dole. Two hundred and fifty thousand of these people were chronically mentally ill. Those with a family or other support system to sustain them for the three to five months required to demand and receive a hearing, got back onto SSI. For those living alone in a cheap hotel or in a board-and-care home, the $520 checks just stopped one day. There was nowhere to go but the streets.

Today, California has between twenty thousand and sixty thousand homeless mentally ill haunting its cities. California contains roughly one-tenth of all Americans, so by this calculation America must have two hundred thousand to six hundred thousand deeply mentally ill people on its streets.

EVOLUTION OF AMERICA'S MODEL MENTAL-HEALTH PROJECT SERVING THE HOMELESS

The initial mission of Farr's project was to improve the relationship between the staff of DPSS and their clients, which had deteriorated throughout the 1970s. Large numbers of young, chronically mentally ill men and women had flocked to the area during that period, in the wake of deinstitutionalization. They were attracted to the decaying Skid Row area because it tolerated bizarre behavior and abounded with drugs, alcohol, and missions. It was cheap to live there.

A preliminary survey conducted by Farr in 1982 revealed that between 30 and 50 percent of the approximately ten thousand homeless people then in the Skid Row area (about 40 percent of the men and 80 percent of the women) were suffering from a chronic, incapacitating mental illness. The closest mental health facility then was three miles away, and most Skid Row residents refused to go there. At any given time, about a quarter of all of the homeless in Los Angeles County were in the Skid Row area.

In Farr's estimation, by January 1981 about half of the staff of the DPSS office had requested transfer or filed a grievance for stress. Interviews with DPSS clients were being conducted through a half-inch-thick glass partition wrapped in wire mesh. A sign posted near the door directed clients to check their weapons before passing through a metal detector.

The staff of Farr's Skid Row Mental Health Project began to provide mental health consultation and education for the DPSS staff. It gave classes in emergency crisis management and evaluation, and in how to refer the most difficult clients. The programs had almost immediate success in helping the DPSS staff cope with their chronically mentally ill clients.

One of the greatest lessons of the Skid Row Mental Health Project is that hands-on treatment for the homeless chronically mentally ill must be provided *on their own turf*. Most mentally ill people living in Skid Row are highly independent individuals who would rather suffer homelessness, dehumanization, and starvation than lose their freedom. They are unwilling to leave Skid Row, even briefly, because they are afraid of a confrontation with the police that might lead to jail. Many Skid Row residents are too impaired to deal with the harshness of traditional mental health systems; they are frightened and skeptical of traditional mental health services and professionals. For those reasons, the project staff's early efforts to link DPSS clients with treatment services outside the Skid Row area were a failure. It was only when the project began to piggyback mental health services onto the existing services of the many missions and agencies in the Skid Row area that it was able to reach and help the homeless mentally ill. Some of the charitable organizations in the area have been providing food and shelter to the homeless for more than fifty years. These groups serve tens of thousands of meals each day and provide more than eighteen hundred shelter beds. Like the staff of the DPSS, however, the staffs of these facilities have had very little formal mental health training and, by the early 1980s, felt increasingly overwhelmed by the avalanche of mentally ill people into Skid Row.

In the winter of 1981–82, the Skid Row project began to provide regular mental health consultation, case management, education, emergency crisis management, and other direct clinical interventions at the missions and other agencies. The "team" arrangement was synergistic. Today, Farr praises the agencies for providing the solid foundation on which the mental health project could build. "They were the bricks," he said, "and the project was the mortar. We built together." Farr believes that piggybacking services was a critical step in gaining the trust of the Skid Row homeless community. Before the partnership began, the project staff were distrusted by the denizens of Skid Row. Only after the project had gained the trust of the community on its own turf could it successfully begin to provide treatment in its own facilities. The presence of the Skid Row project staff working inside the missions convinced the people of Skid Row of their support and concern for them. Until the fall of 1983, the project's services were provided only at the DPSS office or inside missions and agencies.

Most mission volunteers are "graduates of the streets," people known and trusted by the residents of Skid Row. These staffers have also proven to be talented lay psychotherapists, often the only people able to communicate with the highly reticent and frequently agitated members of the homeless mentally ill population. With a little professional training, these dedicated people have become invaluable as mental health links and care providers.[16]

One successful "mental health patch" developed by the project is weekly drop-in rap sessions held at local shelters. The goals of the rap sessions are to help higher-functioning individuals with serious mental health problems to understand their mental illness and to encourage them to seek treatment. The groups also provide practical instruction on living around Skid Row, and they help alleviate loneliness. The key to the success of these rap sessions has been their informality. Anyone can belong to a group and may come as often as he or she likes. Participants are often known only by their first names. The groups are led by a project staff member, but mission staffers function as co-therapists. Farr believes that mental health professionals must learn to cheerfully embrace this kind of loose therapeutic relationship and limited goal-setting if they are to help the homeless.

An important component of the project is its attempts to bring new arrivals to Skid Row into treatment *before* their condition severely deteriorates. The staff of the service know that the longer a chronically mentally ill person remains homeless, the more resistant to treatment he or she becomes. It is therefore seen as the staff's continuous duty to be alert and opportunistic in their work. In turn, the days staff members spend on the streets themselves help build the project's trustworthy image and create a street-educated staff.

As an outreach initiative, the project enlists the help of staff of Traveler's Aid, whose main office is located in the Los Angeles Greyhound bus terminal in Skid Row. Homeless mentally ill people often arrive by bus, the victims of so-called "Greyhound therapy," the callous practice employed by some communities around the country of giving mentally ill individuals one-way tickets out of town. Other homeless people arrive in Skid Row after leaving home communities on their own, hoping for a better life in "sunny California." However, the great majority (about 70 percent) are "home grown" Angelinos, and research has shown that, despite "Greyhound therapy," the mentally ill homeless are seldom transients. As a group, this population is too fearful and too disorganized to move.

The project nevertheless now has a contract with Traveler's Aid whereby a staff member regularly meets buses and escorts anyone who appears to have a serious mental disability to the drop-in "outpost." Begun as an informal arrangement between Traveler's Aid and the Skid Row project, this part of the outreach program was recently formalized. The program has similar but more casual arrangements with the many local missions and agencies that regularly refer patients to the Skid Row Mental Health Project. Referrals began slowly at first, but as trust and relationships have built up, they have grown into a steady, substantial flow.

Despite their proximity to one another, the many missions and agencies providing shelter, meals, counseling, and other services to the homeless of Skid Row were rarely in contact when the Skid Row Mental Health Project was launched in 1981. They were working too hard at a steadily expanding task. In 1981, Farr, Lee Hopson, assistant director of the Midnight Mission, and two other area service providers formed the Concerned Agencies of

Metropolitan Los Angeles, known to everyone today as CAMLA. Fifty-five agencies and groups now belong to CAMLA, which became a private, non-profit corporation in 1983. CAMLA has served as the prototype of the Countywide Coalition for the Homeless in Los Angeles and other homeless coalitions around the country. One of CAMLA's achievements has been to improve the relationships between the agencies, the homeless people of Skid Row, and the city police, who are all represented on CAMLA. Farr notes that the police have gained a far better understanding of the residents of Skid Row since they joined the organization. Today Los Angeles police are likely to bring a homeless mentally ill person in crisis to the project's drop-in area rather than take him or her to jail, as they would have before the formation of CAMLA. Teamwork in this arena must continually attempt to include everyone working here.

One of CAMLA's most significant early projects was the joint development, with the Department of Mental Health, of a directory of services to be found in the Skid Row area. The 100-page directory, completed in April 1982, lists every private and public agency providing services in the Skid Row area, the types of services offered, and the names and telephone numbers of contact people at the agencies. A local business contributed the money to print four hundred copies of the directory. CAMLA and the county mental health department also prepared a shorter "street" version of the directory for distribution directly to Skid Row residents. A refinement of this project under development in San Diego is computerization of a similar directory with daily updating. Such a linkage could allow a worker at any agency searching for a bed for a homeless person or family to "search" by computer rather than by making dozens of phone calls.

Since the Skid Row program was begun in 1981, Los Angeles County has established fifty-nine different programs specifically for the homeless mentally ill. Astonishingly, before 1981 there was none. Funding for most of these program elements came via a major funding for continuity of care, under legislation authored by California Assemblyman Bruce Bronzan. It is unlikely that the current explosion of help for the homeless mentally ill and the increased state funding would have occurred but for the well-publicized beacon of the Skid Row program. This pioneering program demonstrated that community mental health *can* and *must* assume a creative, nontraditional role in reaching out to destitute members of the mentally ill population. The project has served as a model for programs in San Diego, St. Louis, Houston, Denver, and Washington, D.C., among many American cities.

The Skid Row program also helped to generate national attention to the problems of the homeless mentally ill. The program captured the interest of America's mental health community in 1982 when it was given an award by the National Association of Counties, which called the program "one of the most innovative mental health programs in the country." That same year, William Mayer, director of the federal Alcohol, Drug Abuse, and Mental Health Administration (ADAMHA), visited the program. The first ADAMHA Roundtable on the Homeless Mentally Ill, held in 1983, was an outgrowth of Mayer's visit.[17]

The Skid Row program has been described in many local and national publications, including *Time, U.S. News & World Report, Psychology Today*, the *L.A. Times*, the *New York Times*, and the *Washington Post*. Farr believes that this media attention has contributed significantly to growing public and legislative support for the homeless mentally ill, and from the beginning, he encouraged his staff to foster it. In 1982, the U.S. League of County Governments, meeting in Baltimore, presented the project with its highest service award, and in 1986, the American Psychiatric Association gave the project its prestigious Gold Award. Farr has been called to testify many times before committees of the Congress since 1982. Additionally, Farr served as consultant to and participant in a television documentary entitled "Bag Ladies," which received the Golden Globe Award in 1982. This documentary has been shown to congressional committees by Farr, and has been used across the country to awaken the public to the plight of the homeless mentally ill.

Reaching out, Farr has recruited volunteer psychiatrists for the care of the homeless mentally ill in his program. With the Southern California Psychiatric Society, Farr initiated a program in which psychiatrists volunteer to spend a minimum of four hours a month for at least six months at a homeless shelter in Los Angeles to monitor medication and conduct SSI evaluations. Farr has christened the effort the "Good Ship L.A." The program is inspired by the *Good Ship Hope*, the seagoing hospital serving the world's poor and needy. Dozens of Los Angeles–area psychiatrists have since volunteered to work in the shelters via the program.

In 1988, the Skid Row project employed thirty staff members and had a budget of more than $800,000. In April 1983 the project moved from its cramped quarters in the DPSS office to the Weingart Center, which houses several programs for the homeless in Skid Row. At the center there is space enough (more than 4,250 square feet) to provide a comprehensive range of county and other services to clients *in one place*. In 1984, after receiving substantial state mental health funding for the first time, the project's name was changed to the Skid Row Mental Health Service, recognizing its permanence.

The philosophy of the Skid Row service is that the homeless mentally ill must have practical assistance before psychiatric treatment can have any impact. Therefore, the program provides not only basic psychiatric care, such as medication management, but also a full range of services that help the homeless mentally ill secure food, shelter, a safe physical environment, medical care, transportation, appropriate social services, and vocational rehabilitation. The clinic also provides medication management and crisis evaluation. Each one of the severely disabled clients of the service requires an enormous amount of individual support. The case management staff— two psychiatric nurses and several psychologists, psychiatric social workers, and paraprofessional community workers—help link clients with the program's many services as well as with services of other agencies. Patients are often offered transportation and helped to negotiate with the sometimes cold bureaucracies.

At the Weingart Center, which is open seven days a week, 8:00 a.m. until 6:00 p.m., a homeless mentally ill person in distress can receive a full psychiatric evaluation without an appointment at the service's cheery drop-in area. Professional staff are always on duty, screening and helping clients and referring them to proper services. If clients need hospitalization, clinical staff can place a seventy-two-hour hold on them so that they can be hospitalized.

Though women constitute only 10 percent of the homeless in Skid Row, they make up 29 percent of the drop-in area's clientele. Their attendance here is even more surprising considering the menacing demeanor of many of the men that loiter around the Weingart Center. Farr noted that whereas only one-third of the homeless men in Los Angeles suffer an incapacitating mental illness, more of the women do. Women on the streets live lives of unspeakable barbarism. "The fifteenth century would not have tolerated this," declared Farr.

Several twenty-four-hour stabilization centers in Skid Row now operate, under guidance from the service, on county contracts. Two of these are located inside missions. The mission staffs have concluded that their jobs can be done more effectively as part of a team effort, and have come to recognize the urgent mental health needs of a huge segment of the Skid Row population. They are also responding to the importuning of the helpful, determined staff of the Skid Row service.

What follows is a point-by-point development of the Skid Row Mental Health Service, for use as a checklist should a locale wish to replicate it:

1. Reaching out, establishing links with mission staffers and others on Skid Row.
2. Reaching out to experts beyond Skid Row: volunteer psychiatrists, business and service club people, foundations.
3. Organizing Skid Row service providers, CAMLA-like, and expanding communication links (directory, computer lash-up).
4. "Patching" services of one agency to those of another, to solve an individual's problem (especially to address medical problems).
5. Unique personnel selection: hiring only people with stamina and

a "can do" attitude.

6. Shifting the program from a referral mode to the direct treatment of the homeless mentally ill.
7. Establishment of in-patient mental hospitals (with four to ten beds, at the end of a hall) inside of missions.
8. Setting up an SSI and veterans' benefits clinic.
9. Keeping the programs and the staff innovative, responsive, "on their toes," and continually open to changing needs and opportunities.
10. Organizing drop-in rap sessions in missions and agencies.
11. Recognizing the vital importance to the homeless of trust and a sense of community. Building a sense of belonging.
12. Playing the "mental health facilitator" role. Therapists act as links between agencies and various departments of mental health treatment systems.
13. Setting up the Greyhound bus depot and other "outposts" for reaching the chronic mentally ill early.
14. Adding staff to pursue funding grants for studies using public health (grid) methods.
15. Designing activities with the knowledge that a county- or region-wide approach is needed for each metropolitan area.
16. Adding a vocational rehabilitation component to direct clients toward eventual work and feelings of usefulness.
17. Teaming up with (and empowering) the police.
18. Catalyzing non-profit groups like the Salvation Army, Catholic Community Services, Alliance for the Mentally Ill, and others, to create and fund neighborhood clubs providing a range of social and support activities for the chronically mentally ill.
19. Involving clients' families (often the longest-lasting and best energy source for continuity of care).
20. Teaching money management (in association with the Social Security Administration), helping with bus passes (transportation clinic), and rendering other practical assistance.
21. Establishing seven-day-a-week drop-in centers, available to anyone who needs help.
22. Targeting priority programs for homeless women, children, and others who are the most vulnerable on the streets.
23. Engaging in and recruiting others to engage in advocacy for the homeless mentally ill before legislative and administrative bodies and in the courts.
24. Assisting patients into placement in long-term care and residential facilities, as appropriate.
25. Going to the private sector for needed support that governments

will not supply (providing donuts, lockers, legal assistance, self-defense instruction, and literacy—and literature—classes, ad infinitum).

26. Develop supported programs to allow the chronically mentally ill to live independently, but with twenty-four-hour support.
27. Develop intensive, case-managed programs with low staff-to-patient ratios (twenty to one at most) and target patients who frequently use emergency rooms and who frequently decompensate (become psychotic again, often because of failing to take medicine).

CASE STUDIES

These four Boston case histories were presented in a pioneering 1984 book, *The Homeless Mentally Ill*, published by the American Psychiatric Association. They show not only the severity of the mental illnesses themselves, but the great difficulty in rendering meaningful mental health care to homeless people in the absence of the program linkages that Farr has pioneered in Los Angeles. These linkages are described later herein.

The Intermittent Shelter User

M is a fifty-four-year-old man with chronic schizophrenia. He first experienced psychotic episodes at age twenty and has been continuously psychotic ever since. Currently he takes antipsychotic medications and attends a community day program for deinstitutionalized patients. He receives Social Security assistance and a Veterans' Administration pension.

M denies that he has any psychiatric disorder. He insists that his problem is only "storms" that occur frequently and interfere with his capacity to think and function. He evidences loose associations, bizarre thoughts, and a shifting delusional picture, with occasional auditory hallucinations and thought blocking. At its best M's behavior is socially inappropriate, agitated, and distant. As his "storms" get worse, he becomes increasingly paranoid, frightened, hallucinatory, agitated, and bizarre. His life plans are unrealistic, and he has little motivation to change.

M's history includes more than forty psychiatric hospitalizations in the Veterans' Administration and community mental health systems. Since his deinstitutionalization into a supervised community living situation, he has never stayed in one place for long. During the past four years, he has lived in two community residences, a board-and-care home, a halfway house, three nursing homes, a veterans' home, one hotel (recurrently), three shelters for the homeless, and the county mental health center inpatient unit. After a brief stay in any of these places, M typically says, "I can't stand this place any longer. The storms are all around me. Can't you get me into something else?" If hospitalization or other housing is not arranged, he leaves. He often requests a return to a previous placement, and he consistently blames the mental health system for not providing adequate housing.

Banned From Shelter

K is a twenty-seven-year-old single man who has been diagnosed as a chronic schizophrenic. He first became psychotic while attending college in Boston, had a brief remission of symptoms, and has been continuously psychotic for the five years since college graduation. Although he has a case manager, he refuses treatment, including medications, with the exception of his demands that forms be filled out for welfare. He receives SSI and spends the money entirely on expensive radio equipment, which he then uses for barter in the streets. For the past five years he has lived almost entirely on the streets of Boston, New York, and San Francisco.

Although continuously paranoid, delusional, and hallucinatory, K does not physically threaten himself or others and is able to care for himself. Hence, he rarely spends time in hospitals. He has had only four brief admissions during several years of illness. He not only denies his mental illness but also insists that he is superior to other patients and staff. He treats all care givers with contempt. K spends most of his time hanging around a local university, with which he has a delusional affiliation. Passing himself off as an academic, he uses his caustic wit to keep people at a distance. During the winter he regularly sleeps in the ducts of the university heating system. Following angry confrontations with university authorities, he turns to shelters for food and a bed.

When he does seek shelter, K clearly finds it a humiliating experience and verbally abuses clients as well as staff. He insists that staff are part of a plot to control him and typically escalates his verbal assaults until he is asked to leave. After a series of such incidents, he is temporarily banned from one shelter after another. He has also been asked to leave two halfway houses for persistent verbal harassment of clients and staff. On the streets K appears much calmer. He takes great pride in his independence and ability to survive without help. He claims to prefer the streets to shelters and other housing.

The Regular Shelter Resident

P is a thirty-eight-year-old single man suffering from chronic schizophrenia and alcoholism. He began to drink heavily in early adolescence. He was first noted to be psychotic after sobering up in detention at age seventeen.

He currently attends a social club for patients, attends Alcoholics Anonymous daily, takes antipsychotic medications, maintains a good alliance with his case manager of three years, and receives SSI. Nevertheless, he continues to drink daily, and, when not in a detoxification center, hospital, or jail, he lives on the streets and sleeps in a shelter for active alcoholics.

P worries about his inability to control his drinking. He spends most of his money on alcohol and is usually a pleasant drinker, but periodically comes to the attention of police because of violent outbursts. At present, P is on probation for charges of drunken and disorderly conduct, destruction of property, assaulting a police officer, and public loitering. When he sobers up in jail, a hospital, or a detoxification center, P experiences frightening hallucinations and believes that his thoughts are broadcast aloud. These symptoms have never been controlled by medications, but they become tolerable if P stays slightly intoxicated.

Thus, for the past ten years, P has not gone for more than three days outside an institution without drinking. Drinking eventually initiates his cycle of violent behavior, arrest, jail, or transfer to a hospital or detoxification unit. Despite more than thirty hospital admissions, several jail terms, and innumerable detoxifications, P has not achieved sobriety outside an institution for nearly twenty years.

P believes that he will be institutionalized permanently when he develops Korsakoff's syndrome, a psychotic disease that sometimes afflicts chronic alcoholics. For now he prefers to live on the streets and sleep in a shelter. He dislikes the confinement of institutions, the homosexual demands in jails, the intolerable psychotic symptoms when sober, and the lack of freedom in detoxification centers. The freedom he values so highly may be only the freedom to drink. No treatment has diminished his thirst for alcohol. Meanwhile P is slowly killing himself.

A Treatment Success

L is a thirty-year-old single woman who carries the diagnosis of chronic schizophrenia. Turning psychotic at age seventeen, she spent ten years on the streets before responding to treatment. She currently lives in a structured halfway house, attends a social club for patients, takes antipsychotic medications, receives SSI, and maintains regular contact with her case manager and her therapist.

In adolescence, L began experiencing auditory hallucinations, paranoia, ideas of reference, and grandiose delusions centering on her identity as a famous rock star. After her initial psychotic break, she lived on the streets or in shelters for almost ten years, interrupted only by brief hospitalizations. She terminated almost thirty hospitalizations after a few days by signing herself out against medical advice. L was never on any medications long enough to determine whether she would respond or not.

During the years of living on the streets and in various shelters, L used illicit drugs and alcohol, was often abused, was occasionally violent toward others, and formed no close relationships. She bore two children, who were given up for adoption. As part of denying her illness, L consistently refused offers of help from care givers in shelters and hospitals. She declined welfare and housing. When her grandiosity or delusions were questioned in any of these settings, she became violent or fled.

This pattern was interrupted two and a half years ago, when, in a violent outburst, L destroyed her parents' home and was court-committed to the state hospital for one year on the grounds of dangerousness. During her first five months of hospitalization, she continued to resist treatment; she was preoccupied with her delusional world. For the first time, however, L did take antipsychotic medications on a regular basis and met consistently with one staff member, whom she began to trust. After six months she began to relate to other staff, including the community case manager with whom she had refused involvement during her years on the streets. Her paranoia, ideas of reference, and auditory hallucinations began to diminish.

At the end of her year's commitment, L elected to stay in the hospital and to plan an appropriate discharge. She was soon transferred to a community hospital. She began working with a new therapist, who followed up regularly after discharge, and continued to meet with her community case manager. L got SSI and was accepted into a halfway house. The main condition for placement was her ability to control her violent outbursts; fortunately, they decreased steadily. Over five months, she slowly made the transition to living at a social club during the day and a halfway house at night. L's emotional equilibrium and ability to control her behavior continued to improve slowly. Discharge from the hospital occurred without problems.

At present, L has lived in the community for more than a year. She continues to make steady progress in developing social skills and control of her behavior, although she remains delusional much of the time. She is forming some friendships, participates regularly in all treatments offered, and feels hopeful about the future.

The 1984 Task Force report commented,

> These four patients in many ways exemplify some of the more difficult problems among the homeless mentally ill in Boston. Their case histories provide a realistic view of the psychopathology, housing problems, and treatment difficulties that caretakers confront. In the first place, they exhibit serious, chronic, and refractory psychopathology. Chronic psychotic illness

and substance abuse produce withdrawn, fearful, and help-rejecting behaviors. These patients typically deny illness, seek interpersonal distance, and retreat into a delusional world of paranoia, grandiosity, or disorganized oblivion. In addition, they often manifest difficult behaviors—violence, substance abuse, or just boisterous unruliness. Life on the streets, with its realistic dangers, reinforces their paranoia and exacerbates their other problems.

These patients spend relatively little time in hospitals. When hospitalized, they behave well enough to exercise their right to refuse treatment and leave after brief admissions. They are either "young chronics" who have never had significant institutionalization and deny their illnesses, or older, chronically hospitalized patients who have now been "deinstitutionalized" but not successfully placed in the community.

As the cases above illustrate, even when low-cost housing is available, these patients often gravitate toward a disorganized, isolated life-style in the streets. Many have been evicted from their own homes, apartments, halfway houses, and rooms because of their difficult and "unacceptable" behavior. They sometimes settle into shelters, but even shelters have limits on behavior so that they often spend time on the streets. Life on the streets and in shelters, while dangerous, affords them freedom, anonymity, and interpersonal distance. In congruence with their paranoid delusions, they often develop a counterculture identity that glorifies the independence of street life.

These people are extremely vulnerable to stress, have a terrible time handling tasks of daily living, cannot negotiate the easiest of bureaucratic systems, and exhibit odd behaviors and episodes of "acting out." They are, therefore, very susceptible to becoming homeless and unresponsive to traditional treatment strategies. The nature of serious mental illness and also the stigma that accompanies it places these individuals in precarious economic circumstances and, without good support systems, excludes them from the life of the community. The cyclic and chronic nature of the illness generally means these people cannot support themselves by working. Without earned income they depend on the now-fragmented patchwork of federal, state, and local government social programs that once supported the disabled. Today, mentally ill individuals experience great difficulty gaining access to and eligibility for even these well-intentioned programs.

There is also a severe shortage of affordable residential housing options for them, such as board and care homes, cheap "SRO" hotels and the like. There are very few treatment beds. The chronically mentally ill are, of course, at a disadvantage in the highly competitive low-cost housing market because they are seen as the least attractive possible tenants by most landlords. Further, elderly and physically disabled persons are preferred over the chronically mentally ill as tenants for *public* housing for the handicapped. "From them that hath not it shall be taken away even that which they have. . . ."

Despite all these factors and obstacles, most seriously mentally ill persons never become homeless. More than 65 percent live with their families. Many others live in residential treatment programs, in group homes, and in independent apartments. A huge minority, however, cycle between homelessness and inadequate housing, jails, and hospitals.

Homeless mentally ill persons need a comprehensive, coordinated, and accessible system of basic and specialized services to establish and maintain themselves in the community. Like all homeless people, they need decent, low-cost housing, a steady source of income, access to medical care, and opportunities for social affiliations. Economic and social policies that meet the needs of homeless people generally will, of course, also help the homeless mentally ill. Any solution, however, that does not include specialized approaches for them will leave most of the homeless mentally ill behind.

MENTAL HEALTH WORKERS REJECTING THEIR PATIENTS?

Farr believes, sadly, that in the mental health field, at least in the early 1980s, when the phenomenon of mass homelessness was new, many workers, directly or indirectly, tended to reject the chronically mentally ill homeless. He thinks that this rejection was most commonly expressed by, first, refusal to accommodate schedules to the actual needs of these individuals, who, for example, may need to be seen daily for the first two weeks of contact. Second, mental health workers often approached such clients coldly and officially. The homeless are highly sensitive to who likes and accepts them and understand such negative messages instantly. They then would not return for more help, to the relief and satisfaction of many of the mental health workers, according to Farr.[18] These observations are included, with great respect, simply to underline the fact that, without great staff sensitivity and rigorous quality control by administrators based on numbers of people *actually helped over time*, the systems now in place in America may continue to spit out the homeless mentally ill as quickly as all the policemen or Farrs or Mother Theresas in the nation can bring them in. Individual heroic acts alone will not result in long-term help for these people. But demand by society and its leaders for long-term *good results* will. These systems are, after all, owned by the American people.

During the past two decades, as state mental health budgets were shrinking, many local elected officials wanted no complaints as they cut mental health programs. Their selections for the director's posts in county mental health departments, accordingly, often reflected this. They hired quiet people and, in some cases, people who knew how to keep others quiet. If the elected board searched, in addition to finding a loyal and silent servant, they might also find one who was so conveniently ignorant of medicine and the ranges of good care that he or she would not even suspect that a hue and cry might be appropriate response as programs were slashed again and again.

Many such individuals did appear in key posts during the 1970s and 1980s, but, fortunately, they are now seemingly being replaced by able, committed, risk-taking administrators who really care about their patients.

One of the regrettable legacies of this recent period has been a supposed measure of program success called "units of service." This term can mean numbers of medicine shots given, numbers of five-minute interviews with a social worker, and so on. Obviously, increasing the numbers per hour of many such items will not necessarily mean better mental health program efficiency, but it can easily mean that patients are being given less attention. It was often presumed, however, that a mental health administrator who increased these "units of service" during his or her tenure had done a fine job. This illogical conclusion took no account of real results. Use of the term "units of service" should be viewed as a red flag to those concerned for patients and the quality of their care. *The measure of success should be the long-term outcome in the lives of patients helped.*

The deterioration of American treatment systems for chronically mentally ill did occur over much of America, but some islands of good care have survived. In Ohio, Gov. Richard F. Celeste took a personal interest in the state's mental health programs. It is no accident that Franklin County, Ohio, has been the seat of several programs chosen as models by the Robert Woods Johnson Foundation. But over America generally, as budget cuts lopped off element after element of long-term care for the most profoundly disabled of our fellow citizens, silence reigned. Some psychiatrists and psychologists protested publicly. But too many mental health professionals remained quiet.[19]

Thankfully, this era has ended, and at the local and the national levels a wind of reform blowing. Lewis L. Judd, director of the National Institute for Mental Health, recently underlined the biochemical basis of most major mental illnesses and predicted that cures for many of them will be discovered during the coming decade.[20] Judd declared that most homeless mentally ill people's problems could be managed with presently available treatment, but getting some of the homeless to agree to treatment may be difficult. "We cannot just willy-nilly pick them off the streets." In an ideal world, he added, mental illness would be treated as a medical condition, "instead of a civil rights and legal issue." Judd pointed out that only 6 percent of medical insurance policies cover mental illness. "That's pretty horrible in light of strong emerging evidence that mental disorders are not unlike other illnesses." Part of the problem is the common perception that mental illness is "hopeless and incurable." This false understanding generates inattention, neglect, and low priority for those with mental illness. Judd wants to reverse those stereotypes. "We have a major public educational task at hand to educate the public and decision makers about the true nature of these disorders," he said. "They are not caused by weakness of the will. They are not a character flaw, and these are not [people who are] morally problematic. These are brain-related disorders that require careful diagnosis and artful treatment. There are things we can do, and a lot more we could do if we could broaden the research effort."

NIMH has made the homeless mentally ill a priority. In fiscal year 1989–90 $4.5 million was allocated to launch a program of research and research demonstration grants focusing on homeless mentally ill adults and homeless families with children at risk for severe mental disturbance. Together with the institute's funding under the McKinney Homeless Assistance Act, these monies nearly doubled NIMH's resources for this initiative over the previous year. Establishing a new office to coordinate this initiative, Judd said, "Improving the care and treatment of severely mentally ill individuals who are homeless or at risk of becoming homeless is among the most pressing public health needs facing this country, and must be one of the most important priorities across all divisions of the Institute."[21]

In a seminal but now largely superseded book, *The Homeless Mentally Ill*,[22] Farr described his method.

Two basic approaches should be considered in planning for mental health care for the homeless mentally ill: the target groups approach and the phased intervention approach.

The Target Groups Approach

Given the present limited resources of the public mental health treatment system and the large numbers of homeless mentally ill, consideration must be given to selecting target groups from within the general homeless population. It is very difficult to be selective, because all of those suffering deserve the opportunity to receive help. However, with current resources so limited and the need so great, if one does not single out target groups, one can soon become overwhelmed, and no one will receive any assistance.

Selection of specific target groups should be made with several principles in mind: which groups are more acutely at risk, which groups are more amenable to treatment, and which groups offer the best long-range opportunity for salvageability.

With this in mind, the following "target groups" may be considered:

1. *The newly arrived, homeless mentally ill.* Our work in the Project has shown that the longer a chronically mentally ill person remains homeless, the more difficult he is to reach and the more resistant he becomes to mental health treatment. At times, the newly arrived mentally ill homeless are still taking antipsychotic medication or have just recently discontinued the medication. They are more in touch with reality, and treatment rapport is more easily established with them. Some still have some fragment of a relationship with their family or previous mental health treatment program.

It is important to capitalize on these remnants of family relationships. At times, contact with the family can be reestablished, and with guidance and support, it may be possible to return these people to their home communities and their families. The Skid Row Project has an excellent working relationship with various agencies who provide free transportation back home.

The newly arrived are also less likely to have been subjected to the alcohol, street drugs, or the violence so prevalent in Skid Row. These factors severely aggravate underlying mental illness and make help much more difficult to provide.

2. *Battered and at-risk children and runaway youths.* Children and runaway youths are sometimes more amenable to treatment and are more salvageable, but only if this is rendered before the youth "accept" street life.

3. *Homeless women.* Recent NIMH studies conclude that the incidence of severe mental illness among homeless women is about that of men: nearly 40 percent. But women's shelter managers opine that there are both more homeless women than are being officially estimated, and that the ones not being counted are likely to be much more mentally ill. They are vulnerable and are often victims of violence. They should be targeted early for outreach and assistance.

4. *Dual diagnosed homeless—mentally ill substance abusers.* Two NIMH-funded studies, those in Los Angeles and Baltimore, yielded almost identical conclusions regarding substance abuse by homeless individuals. About one third qualified as *current* abusers, while 69 percent had abused sometime during their lives. It was clear that, among the homeless, chronic abuse is something quite different from current abuse. In every study reviewed by Tessler and Dennis,[23] nearly half of the mentally ill subgroup were judged to be also abusing alcohol or drugs.

Three quarters of those currently in need were not receiving any mental health care.[24] "Many had received services in the past and were apparently disillusioned by their experiences."[25]

5. *Homeless elderly.* This group is most vulnerable but often more amenable to being helped. They should receive high priority for assistance.

Phased Intervention Approach

In general, traditional mental health treatment approaches do not work for the homeless mentally ill; that is why they are homeless. In planning mental health treatment programs for this population, one must be creative, innovative, and compassionate and assume an advocacy role. Outreach is an essential ingredient to any program that assists these groups.

It is helpful to think of mental health treatment or intervention for the homeless mentally ill in three basic phases when considering the development of programs:

Phase 1, the emergency first-aid phase. This phase is somewhat equivalent to a "battalion aid station" in a battle zone. In this phase of intervention, emergency assistance is given under acute circumstances. Programmatic goals are early identification and outreach, emergency mental health consultation, training for shelter and other agency personnel, and the "patching" of a mental health program onto existing shelter and agency programs. Development of mental health "drop-in centers" in large catchment areas where homeless congregate can provide a temporary "safe haven" and a focal point from which first phase intervention goals and objectives can be accomplished.

Phase 2, the stabilization phase. During the stabilization phase, the homeless mentally ill receive an opportunity to spend anywhere from five to seven days in a "stabilization center." This center should be set up in cooperation with a private shelter or agency that is known and accepted by the homeless mentally ill. At the center they would be given an opportunity to clean up, rest up, and get physical health care as well as intensive mental health care. They would also be provided with linkages to other services, such as social services, vocational rehabilitation, counseling, and so forth. It is anticipated that as many as one-third of the homeless mentally ill could be stabilized in this center to return to their families, communities, and other appropriate mental health care facilities and programs.

Phase 3, the long-range solutions phase. Long-range solutions to the problems of the homeless mentally ill must be found if any of the programmatic planning is to have lasting benefits. It is of very little value to give shelter and intensive emergency mental health treatment to a person unless this is followed up by some long-range solution to the problem. The "stabilization phase" should automatically be followed by long-range programs for those who require continued long-range mental health care. The Social Security Disability Program, vocational rehabilitation, Veterans' Administration benefits, board-and-care facilities, and so forth, should all be a part of the long-range treatment program. Placement in a therapeutic living center may be necessary for those who are unable to cope with life on their own or do not have a family or supportive structure to return to.

WHAT IS TO BE DONE?

> All the king's horses and all the king's men
> Could not put Humpty Dumpty together again.
> —Mother Goose

No one wants to reinstitute the era of the massive "snake pit" insane asylums. But to move, today, to the community-based, highly supportive, case-managed system envisioned when the hospitals were closed two decades ago is now a bit more complicated than it would have been then. First, most state and local mental health budgets are a fraction of what they were a quarter century ago, in real terms, and are competing for their very lives with every other demand on government, from streets, schools, and sewers, to retirement funding and promotion of the arts. Second, the clients of such a tidy system are not all nicely locked up, as they were two decades ago, nor are they in relative health and safety. Instead, many have lived for years under the most brutal conditions. These clients have now been trained to distrust government systems, particularly those labelled "mental health," and most live in jurisdictions where the laws permit involuntary treatment only of the near-catatonic.

According to Farr, in the course of a year, the Skid Row project has contact with forty-five hundred of the ten thousand Skid Row homeless— contact that can be as cursory as a chat on the street or a single visit to the drop-in center. But of these forty-five hundred, perhaps fifteen hundred receive meaningful case management help. Of these, perhaps one-half "take" to the program, and are really assisted, long-term. "It takes time with individuals, eight months, sometimes, of a guy dropping in for coffee and talk, before he really gets with a case plan. So we need to have at least an intermediate plan in mind for each such person." The system is predicated on significantly assisting about one-third of those seen and on another third being unhelpable without a change in the laws relative to involuntary treatment (which can mean, all agree, a wide spectrum of pleasant, caring environments nowadays). As for the final third, Farr said, "We'll lose them. They're so into drugs, so physically lost, so unreachable."

Recent history has shown us that, as all of the other elements of solution in a community—an adequate range of lowest-income housing, case assistance, etc.—have come together to form a cohesive, warm system, the success rates in the mental health sectors have also risen. We can only hope, as doctors using triage analysis always have, that surrounding conditions will improve.

Farr estimates that the Skid Row project serves only one-fifth of the mental health needs of the ten thousand homeless on Los Angeles' Skid Row (and Skid Row is only one of eleven "areas" in Los Angeles County with concentrations of homeless: containing a total homeless population estimated by Mayor Bradley's office at 50,000). Farr said a budget five times the present level of $800,000 would meet present needs. This is $400,000 per thousand homeless individuals per year, but it doesn't really cover long-term community care. Realistically, this figure should be considered the amount needed only to establish an initial treatment and intake entity. Farr likened it to a MASH unit or a battalion aid station in a war zone. Such a unit takes in sick and wounded, does a quick triage analysis to determine whom to treat, with what resources (and, of course, who is to be declared hopeless and to be made comfortable to die), gives emergency treatment, and winds up with a few patients walking away, cured, and the vast majority bandaged up and bundled into ambulances or planes. In the case of our homeless mentally ill MASH unit, most of the "ambulances" never get to a "hospital" of appropriate, continuing care. To continue the analogy, Farr said, "our ambulances run off cliffs." They run in circles for a while. They dump their cargoes. But the next phase is missing.

HOW WILL WE FIND WHAT WE NEED?

What will good, continuing care for these disabled people cost, and whence will the dollars come? This question has only begun to be asked in the United States. Fortunately, it is being addressed in fresh ways, and among the best is a 1987 report from the California Commission for Economic Development, chaired by Lt. Gov. Leo McCarthy. The report, entitled "An Integrated Service System for People with Serious Mental Illness," is twenty-one pages long and presents a practical plan for sustaining all of the needed elements of long-term care for the spectrum of chronically mentally ill, using small community resource agencies (CRAs). These entities would be run only by non-profit organizations with private boards of directors. They would serve up to 150 resident patients with a staff of ten. The plan postulates no new monies, but recommends amendments to existing federal and state laws to permit integration of present "categorical" programs and their funding. Some locales are already experimenting with such "fund-patching."[26]

The estimated annual operating costs of a 150-person CRA is $800,000 to $900,000, and the report estimates that new arrangements can save about $3 million a year that would otherwise have been spent by the government on those same 150 chronic individuals as they cycled through the various county systems. This does not include costs of jails, courts, public defenders and prosecutors, probation departments, sheriffs, police, or welfare. Nor does it include SSI or other public monies, which will remain available directly to members for food, clothing, shelter, and personal allowances. These potential savings, which glitter like Shangri-la at the end of the road to excellent mental health care, were described differently by Farr. About 70 percent of the total mental health budget for the state of California and its constituent counties goes for acute hospitalization of the mentally ill. Farr estimated that at least half of that 70 percent is occasioned by the "failure of the system" or lack of any overall system that addresses the long-term needs of chronic patients. Another way of saying this is that with the present system, few chronic patients are receiving continuity of care, and thus can be expected to have relapses and be expensively rehospitalized every twelve to fifteen months. "You can count on it. Annually. Just like the birds coming back to Capistrano," Farr said.

A new funding source has been created in recognition of this problem, via California's Medi-Cal program, and intensive management programs are being installed using specially trained clinicians with smaller caseloads. The aim is prevent these expensive rehospitalizations.[27] Half of the 70 percent spent on acute care, or about one third of the entire present state and county mental health budget, is now being wasted paying for these needless rehospitalizations. With a solid aftercare system, this one-third of a billion dollars could be saved and reallotted to pay for all or part of the aftercare itself. The California situation is mirrored across the nation.

The key precondition to treatment, of course, is housing and the stability it brings. For the chronically ill and permanently disabled, housing can be supplied by aggressively pressing these people onto the SSI rolls. Once on that program, the disabled person receives $520 per month in federal monies for life. According to Farr, Los Angeles County estimates that for every four hundred people assisted onto SSI, the local government saves $1 million, year after year! This savings is attributed to the fact that these people are no longer moving through the various "revolving doors" of the many county departments.

Los Angeles, San Francisco, Kern, and San Diego Counties (no doubt, among others) now have official programs aimed at these savings, testimonials enough to the dollar incentives involved. The potential savings are so large that, while a single leap to the futuristic system envisioned by California's Economic Development Commission does seem distant, given the time required for enabling legislation, steps toward such systems need to be taken immediately. Surely computer-assisted critical path analyses (the kind used commonly in heavy construction industries to analyze costs and strategies for various construction sequences) could be applied here by local government financial planners. Their incentive would be to create the needed breakthrough models for themselves and for the nation for long-term community care for the chronically incapacitated mentally ill. And in a fiscally rational way—maybe at a savings!

In 1988 the National Conference of State Legislatures published, as part of its "Legislator's Guide" series, a 148-page book entitled *Mental Health Financing and Programming*, by Rebecca T. Craig and Barbara Wright. The book depicts an integrated system aimed at easy access to needed services, reduced bureaucracy, and a cohesive, tightly run system that prevents duplication and unnecessary inpatient care."[28] The book recommends strong *state*-level leadership, and the sections on financing and future challenges are particularly helpful. The exploration of funding sources lists total national expenditures at $11.1 billion (federal 59.5 percent, state 37.8 percent, and local 2.7 percent),[29] with expensive inpatient care absorbing *64 percent* of all state-controlled revenues for the mentally ill.[30] Per-capita state expenditures for mental health care vary widely. New York, for example, is spending substantially more than twice what California is, $67 versus $29 per capita per year.[31]

STRATEGIES TO FINANCE MENTAL HEALTH CARE

The National Conference of State Legislatures' guide describes a number of innovative state funding strategies:[32]

Managing care for the seriously mentally ill. The two most common models for this strategy use health maintenance organizations (HMOs), which are paid per capita by the state, and preferred provider organizations (PPOs), which offer discounts to the state, with the client exercising choice between several such organizations. These choices can be enormously important to treatment outcomes, says Aretha Crowell, San Diego County's mental health director. San Diego County has initiated a "Choice Point Model," which has two goals: to facilitate the seriously disabled's access to all help and benefits to which they are legally and medically entitled, and to make explicit the linkages between public mental health services, private services, a wide range of housing options, and case management.

The starting point for the analysis was, most appropriately, the needs and rights of the people for whom the services exist—the patients. Choice Point recognizes that people with persistent, disabling mental disorders (people likely to be, or become, homeless) tend to be systematically given poorer-quality and less help. Explicit steps are included to rectify this. "The mental health system must be able to adapt to the changing picture of the people it serves," declares the program description. It sets up separate systems to serve disabled people with long-term psychiatric illnesses. Another very refreshing feature of this approach is that it attempts to include the problem of substance abuse, which in the past was often used as an excuse for defining a desperately ill individual's problems as the province of others (non-mental health professionals), especially the substance abuse treatment systems. The result of such thinking had been a quiet subpopulation of the most helplessly ill falling through the system's cracks, very often into homelessness. The National Conference guide explores a number of innovative programs of this kind in New York, Minnesota, and Pennsylvania.

Shifting funds from hospital to community services. Farr has urged this strategy. Realistic local responsibility-taking, as described in the Choice Point model above, is paramount. Major state overhauls with fresh funding may also be called for, but absent such heroics, note the experiences of Vermont, Louisiana, Rhode Island, and Texas in making a transition that supports community care while reducing inpatient hospital costs.

Mandating health insurance coverage. Insurance carriers do not like this strategy, but twenty-seven states employ it. Clearly, people helped in the private care systems are less likely to become a drain on the public care systems, or to become homeless.

Risk-pool coverage of mental health services. This strategy distributes people seen as having high risk of mental disorder evenly among the health insurance carriers, much the same way that high-risk drivers are distributed among auto-insurance programs. Fifteen states have created risk pools, with a wide variance in the mental health coverage offered.

Bonds to finance capital improvements. Why not go to the voters? In many states, the decrepitude of the state hospitals themselves is a serious cost consideration. Faced with three financing choices (pay now, lease, or borrow), Colorado and Massachusetts have gone the bond-financing route. Colorado has pioneered with a creative mechanism whereby provider contracts specify that the State Division of Mental Health receives the provider's "first earnings" to send to a trustee to pay the debt, and the state is not obligated in any way. However, having the bond payments made via the state gave the bond's insurer the confidence necessary to underwrite it.

Reuse of surplus hospital property. This strategy may have sizeable potential in some states, since state hospital populations have declined almost 80 percent in the past twenty-five years, yet only 16 of the 274 state psychiatric hospitals have closed. These properties are, of course, state mental health assets. More than twenty thousand acres of land and 370 buildings were transferred to other owners between 1970 and 1985. This property constituted 11 percent of the land in use at state hospitals in 1985. Another 450 buildings were vacant. Other state government agencies have moved in, mooching off these mental health properties, some of which contain prime real estate. A Massachusetts plan proposes selling such land to developers while extracting a promise to set aside units to house community-care mentally ill clients. Clear controls need to be exercised by legislators, or these precious mental health assets will be frittered away and the potential for solutions they offer will be lost.

Encourage entrepreneurship for community mental health centers. The idea here is to provide some services at a profit in order to subsidize other programs. While this strategy, if successful, can make monies available outside of government funding channels, the state runs the risks of loss of control over the money-making ventures, bad publicity if the efforts fail, and political fallout if there are no clear guidelines on how any profits are to be used. The guide offers suggestions on steps necessary to implement such a program, and describes efforts underway in Colorado and New Hampshire.

Community-based mental health care for the permanently disabled can, of course, only be accomplished if there is an adequate, supply of local low-cost housing, plus sympathetic zoning to surmount the NIMBY problem. Many states, California included (see the California Health & Safety Code, sections 50680 *et seq.*), have enacted such legislation.

One final fact needs stressing. Our systems must be made truly attractive to the chronically mentally ill or they will continue to be rejected by the people they are trying to help. As one patient aptly said, "I may be crazy, but I'm not dumb." Poll after poll of patients, homeless or not, has revealed the three things they want the most: a nice place to live, a job, and a friend. "Offer them those and they'll stay," Farr said. "They do better if you're nice to them, and the mental health systems have been kicking them." Another way of summing up the above wish list: "Beef up the non-mental health things." The research now bears this out.

A number of the most recent NIMH studies agree that, "There is an emerging consensus that mentally ill homeless persons are difficult to engage in services, that they tend to perceive their needs differently from the way mental health providers see them, and that they give basic needs priority over clinical treatment."[33] Nonetheless, they are not rejecting all services. "In this sense they are discriminating," the report continues. "The challenge is to increase the acceptability of services and to determine what works best for whom."[34]

CONCLUSIONS

Los Angeles' Skid Row Mental Health Service has shown America the way relative to the many needed aspects of asked-for and voluntary mental health assistance. But what of those who will not seek help? What of those whom Farr has called the "bridge and bush brigade," the fearful, paranoid, utterly lonely ones who are often the most delusional? If a person is homeless, the police may take him or her to a mental health facility under dramatic circumstances—when the person is perched on the edge of a bridge threatening suicide, for instance. But today's mental health system seldom takes such a person in. Instead, those truly in need are generally coughed right back onto the streets. One San Diego police sergeant, Terrence De Guelder, said that three times he has participated in coaxing a shabby, homeless person, bent on suicide, off of the bridge's lip. In each case, he took the person, with a full report, to the County Mental Heath Department's intake clinic. And in each case, within hours he participated in clean-up efforts for that same homeless person's suicide. The protection supposed to be offered as a matter of *right* to the "gravely disabled," those whose serious mental disorders make them a "danger to themselves or others," has been distorted all out of recognition, in California as in the rest of the nation.

Although the plight of the homeless mentally ill has received much media attention in recent years, and while efforts are being made to begin to meet the needs of this population, those needs still far outstrip the available resources. The homeless mentally ill are seen in ever-increasing numbers in every community across America, and their presence is a testimony to the gigantic failure of our society and its mental health treatment system. The streets have become the asylums of the 1980s. A 1987 Harvard study concludes that the size of this segment of the homeless is increasing at the rate of 18 percent per year, a population "doubling time" of 4.2 years. The nation needs fast, effective action.

The American Psychiatric Association's *The Homeless Mentally Ill* declares:

> Meeting basic needs is essentially a political question, one of social justice, whereas the provision of services commonly becomes a technical or administrative problem. The domain of mental health practice cannot be restricted to the letter: decades of research have demonstrated the intimate relationships between poor social environments and mental instability. Mental health service providers cannot be expected to compensate for elemental scarcities in resources, but they can join a growing constituency in organizing efforts to challenge the official priorities that have created Homelessness and that continue to swell its ranks.[35]

SUGGESTED READING

The first two studies are particularly recommended.

A Synthesis of NIMH-Funded Research Concerning Persons Who Are Homeless and Mentally Ill, Richard C. Tessler, Ph.D., and Deborah L. Dennis, M.A., Office of Programs for the Homeless Mentally Ill, National Institute of Mental Health, 1989.

Down and Out in America: The Origins of Homelessness, Peter H. Rossi, University of Chicago Press, 1989.

"A Study of Homelessness and Mental Illness in the Skid Row Area of Los Angeles," Roger K. Farr, M.D., Paul Koegel, Ph.D., and Audrey Burnam, Ph.D., Los Angeles County Department of Mental Health, March 1986.

Nowhere to Go: The Tragic Odyssey of the Homeless Mentally Ill, E. Fuller Torrey, Harper & Row, 1988.

Molecules of the Mind, Jon Franklin, Laurel, 1987.

Mental Health Financing and Programming: A Legislator's Guide, Rebecca T. Craig and Barbara Wright, National Conference of State Legislatures, May 1988.

Local Responses to the Needs of Homeless Mentally Ill Persons, United States Conference of Mayors, May 1987.

NIMH-Funded Research Concerning Homeless Mentally Ill Persons: Implications for Policy and Practice, Joseph P. Morrissey and Deborah L. Dennis, National Institute of Mental Health, December 1986.

The Homeless Mentally Ill: A Task Force Report of the American Psychiatric Association, H. Richard Lamb, M.D., ed., American Psychiatric Association Press, 1984.

"Community Support Systems for the Homeless Mentally Ill," Irene Shifren Levine,

Anne D. Lezak and Howard H. Goldman, *New Directions for Mental Health Services*, Jossey-Bass, June 1986, pp. 27–42.

Engaging Homeless Persons with Mental Illnesses into Treatment, Debra J. Rog, Ph.D., National Mental Health Association, June 1988.

The Homeless Mentally Ill: No Longer Out of Sight and Out of Mind, Rebecca T. Craig and Andrea Paterson, State Legislative Report, Human Series, National Conferences of State Legislatures, vol. 13, no. 30, September 1988.

Community Care for Persons with Serious Mental Illness: Removing Barriers and Building Supports, Rebecca T. Craig, State Legislative Report, Human Services Series, National Conference of State Legislatures, vol. 13, no. 35, October 1988.

"Update on Programs for the Homeless Mentally Ill," Marilyn Sargent, *Hospital and Community Psychiatry*, vol. 40, no. 10, October 1989.

Helping Mentally Ill Homeless People: A Manual for Shelter Workers, Mary E. Stefl, Ph.D., ed., American Public Association, 1915 Fifteenth St., N.W., Washington, DC 20005, 1989.

Access, a quarterly publication of the National Resource Center on Homelessness and Mental Illness, a division of the National Institute of Mental Health, 262 Delaware Ave., Delmar, NY 12054, 800-444-7415.

Homelessness and Mental Illness: Toward the Next Generation of Research Studies, Deborah L. Dennis, M.A., and Joseph P. Morrissey, Ph.D., eds., Office of Programs for the Homeless Mentally Ill, National Institute of Mental Health, 1990.

"Executive Summary: Chronic Mentally Ill Young Adults with Substance Abuse Problems: A Review of Research, Treatment, and Training Issues," Dr. John A. Talbott, (chairman of the Department of Psychiatry at the University of Maryland School of Medicine), University of Maryland School of Medicine, October 1987.

13

Involuntary Treatment?

> We have these academic debates about the propriety of forced treatment
> and commitment of people, but they mean nothing. The real issue is that
> there are no beds and no dollars. The problem is not an abundance of
> civil liberties for the homeless; it is a scarcity of beds.
> —Robert Hayes (founder, National Coalition for the Homeless)[36]

In the 1960s an enthusiasm for civil rights and liberty swept America. With
it came a passion for careful safeguards to see that people were not arbitrarily
or erroneously swept into existing mental health systems, to languish there,
forgotten. Feeding this passion was the discovery of many inhumane conditions
in the nation's huge mental hospitals employed to house (but, too often,
not to treat, or even to treat kindly) the hundreds of thousands of Americans
suffering from the major, disabling psychoses that have always beset about
2 percent of mankind.

Simultaneously, in the 1960s, medical research hit upon spectacular
chemical breakthroughs in the treatment of the two major families of severe
and disabling mental illnesses—the phenothiazine class of drugs (or anti-
psychotics) for schizophrenia and other "thought disorders," and lithium
carbonate, for the treatment of the manic-depressive "mood disorders." The
public response was enthusiastic and, with the concept that most mental
patients could, henceforth, reside in their home communities, safely and
happily with families, possibly holding down jobs and living very normal
lives, the step to a repair of the involuntary treatment laws was a small,
logical one. Public enthusiasm arose in large part from a belief espoused
by many mental health professionals that once deinstitutionalization took
place, the released inmates would simply be able to function in the community.
Deinstitutionalization came to be viewed as ushering in a new era of unbridled
freedom for a large and previously incarcerated population. The brave new
idea aimed to shift the care of the seriously mentally ill from state mental
institutions to community mental health centers (CMHCs). Nobody corrected

the trajectory when the aim proved a "miss."

In theory CMHCs were to operate as outpatient divisions of mental health hospitals, concentrating on acute mental cases. Thus, from 1955 to 1984 nearly half a million patients at state mental hospitals were released into America's communities. In practice, however, and in historical perspective, deinstitutionalization has proved to be an utter failure. America's large, highly visible homeless mentally ill population is the barbaric, lasting legacy of deinstitutionalization.

Deinstitutionalization failed for several reasons. First and foremost, it was a plan fueled by blind idealism, a reform program based on virtually no empirical track record. There was no solid proof that the release of several hundred thousand seriously mentally ill people from state hospitals would improve their treatment. In a strikingly American, naive way, freedom was equated with improved treatment. This lack of foresight by mental health professionals and politicians alike was accompanied by a lack of legislative regulations to establish firmly a cohesive and comprehensive working relationship between the state hospitals and the CMHCs. Naiveté was also manifested in an ominous (and still growing) "gentrification of care." Thousands of seriously dysfunctional individuals who were released into the community were not offered meaningful treatment. Rather, CHMCs eventually focused on such challenges as couples with marital problems and people experiencing mid-life crises. Many psychiatrists and psychologists, unfortunately, succumbed to their desire to treat attractive, hopeful individuals, rather than the sometimes repulsive, seriously mentally ill people who were most in need of care. Tens of thousands of those most in need of care fell through the cracks of an extremely inadequate mental health care system, and onto the streets.

THE MYTH OF "FREEDOM"

Imposing mental health treatment on somebody conjures up terrible images. We think of pathetic people peeing on themselves, neglected, alone and in pain, in some bleak back ward of an ugly state hospital. We think of scenes from *One Flew Over the Cuckoo's Nest*, of electroshock therapy, or of political dissidents being silenced by tyrannical countries. Too often, the courts have also held this vision of involuntary commitment for mental health treatment. While recognizing that the state has the right under its police powers to commit those people who present a danger to the community, as well as the right (and duty) under its *parens patriae* powers to provide care and treatment for those unable to care for themselves, the courts have recently created a thicket of due process considerations to "protect" the proposed recipients of such care from overzealous state intervention.[37] To justify their position, judges frequently fall back on recitals of the severity and stigma of involuntary confinement. The California Supreme Court stated in a 1979 case:

> This court explicitly recognize[s] that civil commitment to a mental hospital, despite its civil label, threatens a person's liberty and dignity on as massive a scale as that traditionally associated with criminal prosecution. One has only to imagine the horror experienced by a competent person falsely committed as mentally disturbed in order to appreciate that freedom is openly on trial at a civil commitment proceeding.[38]

The court went on to opine about the stigma attached to a person's reputation as a result of such commitment, the resulting difficulty in getting a job or practicing certain professions, and the fact that criminally convicted mentally disordered sex offenders occupied the same state hospitals to which those involuntarily committed were confined. Furthermore, the court pointed out that those involuntarily committed or for whom conservators (more on these shortly) were appointed lost other freedoms, such as the right to manage their financial affairs, not the case even for criminal convicts.

It is this picture of the mental health treatment system that stands in the way of many helpless people receiving the care and treatment they so desperately need. Hand in hand with these concerns is a parallel concern expressed by social commentators, jurists, and legislators that involuntary treatment programs and conservatorships will be discriminatorily applied to the homeless mentally ill as a means of getting them off the streets and out of the public eye, rather than out of a desire to provide much-needed treatment. The U.S. Supreme Court stated this concern in *O'Connor v. Donaldson*:

> May the State confine the mentally ill merely to ensure them a living standard superior to that they enjoy in the private community? That the State has a proper interest in providing care and assistance to the unfortunate goes without saying. . . . Moreover, while the State may arguably confine a person to save him from harm, incarceration is rarely if ever a necessary condition for raising the living standards of those capable of surviving safely in freedom. . . .
> May the State fence in the homeless mentally ill solely to save its citizens from exposure to those whose ways are different? One might as well ask if the State, to avoid public unease, could incarcerate all who are physically unattractive or socially eccentric.[39]

Few of us know very much about aberrant psychology, and we have been easily led by intense rhetoric regarding "liberty" in this area. So we have erred, we say, "on the side of liberty." Unfortunately, we have also erred in that we prefer not to know the facts and, ignorant, we have been able to preserve our clear consciences and to act purely (ruthlessly) from theory.

In most states today, very few mentally ill people are hospitalized for any lengthy period. More common is a check-in for a few weeks of "acute care." Among those found to be chronically, permanently disabled by a grave mental illness, most are voluntarily assisted. For those who refuse help, the help rendered is almost always in the person's home community, on an out-patient basis, with the assistance of a responsible person who may be a family member or, if the family cannot provide the help, a public official called (in California) a "mental health conservator." Appointed by the courts, the conservator makes living arrangements for the patient, or conservatee, including medical care and housing with family, "living independently," or perhaps living in a boarding-house-like facility called a "board-and-care home." These places today leave much to be desired, but they are civilized shelter and, more often than not, are run by caring individuals who are in the business out of a real desire to help people.

Helen Teisher, co-founder of Parents of Adult Schizophrenics (now named the National Alliance for the Mentally Ill), is a brilliant woman whose middle-aged son has long been assisted by a conservator appointed under 1967 California legislation designed to reform the mental health care system. Teisher considers conservatorship process an "institution without walls." She said, "My son has his freedom to live in the community and function there, and to take advantage of the community's many resources. But if he had no conservator, who does represent legal authority and whom he respects, he would fall all the way to the streets." The money issues are handled between the client and the conservator, not the family.

From the conservatorship, the conservatee typically receives the housing, support of his or her relationship with family, medical care, help in gaining government benefits, assistance with finding MediCal doctors, management of money for basic human needs (the rest available for any use by the conservatee), and a stable, often long-term supporter and friend in the person of the conservator.

The ideal conservatorship system would also offer opportunities for recreational activity and appropriate vocational training and job opportunities. Conservatees say they get in trouble because their "days are empty." Good aftercare would fill these days with positive activities, which can help save these people from agony, and also save taxpayers' precious funds. These funds are now being spent lavishly on rehospitalizations when spectacular relapses occur.

Supportive drop-in (or "socialization") centers can also serve a vital need. The National Mental Health Association's local chapters often sponsor these, as do some church welfare agencies, often via contract with public mental health agencies. More sophisticated doctor's care would also help. There is a tendency, presently, for overworked doctors to be unavailable in times of crisis and, more ominously, to over-medicate patients. A well-funded and kind system would be able to minimize these difficulties. Kindness, intelligence, commitment and good relationships pervade good mental health systems. Today, with resources spread scandalously thin, many of our good workers are too often under stress and cannot afford to lavish these human essentials on their troubled clients.

Good programs will attract those who need help. America can afford these programs and can afford to keep them respectful of their clients. We know how. Why not do what we know to be right? A very important word of caution here, however. It would be inhumane and result in a bizarre usurpation of people's rights if we reformed our civil commitment laws without a concomitant influx of adequate funding into community care treatment systems. That must come *first*. This lesson must be underlined. It should have been learned from the poorly planned process of deinstitutionalization itself. The existing system for community treatment of the homeless mentally ill typically applies Band-Aids to gaping wounds.

Currently, because of the lack of available beds, the application process that a mentally ill individual must endure in order to get into treatment is so complex that many of these easily daunted individuals desiring treatment cannot reasonably access it. A related problem is that individuals in most communities do not have a choice as to what kinds of treatments they may receive, i.e., inpatient therapy as opposed to "drop-in centers." Some counties, San Diego County included, are beginning to allow clients a range of choices between types of treatment. The mental health care systems today are just not "user-friendly," at least for the poor who are chronically disabled. They must be made so, and an explicit test of their success needs to be their popularity with all their consumers, especially the most disabled, chronically ill individuals.[40]

Grave disability standards need to focus on the reality of people actually having a history of providing for their own basic needs. At present, laws in most states make it very difficult to hold for evaluation or rehospitalize individuals who need further treatment. When hospitalized for evaluation, it is nearly impossible to place the person, against his or her will, in a "conservatorship status" wherein others decide living location and treatment. For instance, after having received temporary care, seriously mentally ill individuals typically come before our courts and are able to refuse further treatment. As will be discussed, the reason such individuals are released back into the streets is that their competency is evaluated only with respect to their condition *at the moment they appear in court*. The rationale given for releasing such individuals is a tender regard for their freedom of choice; after all, if they "appear" to be able to take care of themselves and look like they can function as outpatients, shouldn't they be released to make room for others? The focus ought to be where the legislatures originally intended: on providing for the basic needs of the disabled mentally ill— but only after the legal burdens are met. Standards of care for the seriously mentally ill should apply equally to inpatients and outpatients. Likewise, funding needs to be increased equally for facilities providing involuntary treatment as well as the augmented board-and-care facilities that would attract those individuals who could be reintegrated into society if presented with more choices about types of treatment and living settings.

MODIFYING COMMITMENT LAWS

Laws concerning involuntary civil commitment need to be amended. The right of seriously mentally ill individuals to refuse treatment must be balanced against the duty of society to help people whose conditions are so grave as to require that help and treatment be imposed. Of course, the person deserves the maximum possible respect. Mandatory outpatient treatment should be considered before involuntary commitment, which could be held as a measure of last resort. But, to reiterate, such proposals for changing the law will do no good (and would likely do harm) unless and until there is a large influx of the funding needed for the community mental health treatment system originally envisioned by the proponents of deinstitution-alization. A street is not a home. By now that much ought to be clear.

Typically, state legislatures did a good job, back in the 1960s, but in many states that work has been eroded in practice and by appellate courts. Typical of state laws enacted then is California's 1967 Lanterman-Petris-Short Act,[41] which provides that only people found "gravely disabled" qualify to have their liberties (to refuse treatment) restricted, that is, to have mental health care given them against their will.[42] The act defines "gravely disabled" as "a condition in which a person, as a result of a mental disorder, is unable to provide for his basic personal needs for food, clothing, or shelter."[43] (Emphasis added.) Many other states have adopted "gravely disabled" statutes in various forms.[44] In some states, such as New York, the "gravely disabled" criterion has been adopted through judicial opinions.

The concept of grave disability makes great good sense, but over the years, the courts have, in a curiously intellectual way, done violence to the statutory intent and to the plain meaning of the statutes' wording. The courts have only been willing to evaluate and consider an individual's mental condition at the moment of the court's hearing. While this clears a court's docket, individuals who appear to be stable, but who may have had a history of years of rooting in garbage pails and of repeated relapses and hospitalizations associated with not taking medicines, are cast onto the streets until their physical condition deteriorates. This revolving-door process can be curtailed only if legislatures direct local officials and trial courts to consider an individual's recent life activities and proven behavior patterns. Critical factors to be evaluated are whether the person has demonstrated that he or she will or will not take prescribed antipsychotic drugs, or will return to alcoholism on top of a grave mental illness, and thus be essentially certain to relapse without the help of a conservator. Under the present state of affairs, the court hearing almost invariably takes place following several days or weeks of observation or hospitalization, during which the person has generally been taking the medicines and/or abstaining from alcohol, and therefore, *voilà*, often appears in very good condition on the day of the hearing.

An example of the charade inherent in such an approach is a California case, *Conservatorship of Murphy*.[45] In *Murphy* the California Court of Appeals reversed the trial court's finding of "grave disability" and simultaneously set a new judicial standard in such cases. The facts were undisputed. Two physicians testified that, although he was apparently not gravely disabled *during* his hearing, Murphy, who was living in a care facility, had not stopped his drinking, and that, if left on his own with no conservator, he would inevitably return to alcoholism and "in all likelihood again become gravely disabled and a threat to himself if not others."[46] The trial judge, who was in pain at his dilemma, declared,

> Well, the problem, of course, is that the present condition of Mr. Murphy is such, as he sits here today, that he does not appear to be gravely disabled, however, the reasonable probabilities are, and I think the great weight of the evidence is, that if he were to be left to his own devices, he would very shortly be back in the realm of those who are greatly disabled because of the intoxication problem and the ingestion of alcohol. It may sound like rampant paternalism, but in my view, that is a characteristic which is currently present in part of his make-up, and has to be taken into account in determining grave disability.[47]

The court reaffirmed Murphy's conservatorship for another year.

This compassionate result was overturned on appeal. The Court of Appeals declared that, "The pivotal issue is whether Murphy was 'presently' gravely disabled, and the evidence demonstrated he was not."[48] The court relied on the fact that both expert witnesses at trial had testified that Murphy was "presently capable of managing his own affairs, i.e., capable of providing for his food, clothing, and shelter." The trial court had impermissibly relied on the "likelihood" that, if released, Murphy would return to alcoholism at some future time.

The illogic followed in *Murphy* was relied on and further expanded in another California appellate case, *Conservatorship of Benvenuto*.[49] In *Benvenuto* the patient was a schizophrenic and, like Murphy, displayed no overt symptoms at the hearing. However, based on the evidence that Benvenuto's apparent sanity was attributable largely to his taking anti-psychotic medications, and that he was unlikely to continue sane if taken off conservatorship, the trial judge granted the county's petition for reappointment of the conservator. Again the appeals court reversed. It held that the only issue for consideration was whether Benvenuto was gravely disabled during the hearing, and that evidence that Benvenuto was unlikely to continue taking his medication and thus inevitably would relapse into psychoses is "no evidence" of grave disability.[50]

Might it be that these trial judges, who are not insulated like their appellate colleagues from the gritty, day-to-day reality of dealing with mentally ill people, were able to form a more accurate picture of the effect that denial of a conservatorship would actually bring? After all, it is the trial judges who will have to see the patients return in a deteriorated condition. And, trial judges are not unfamiliar or inexperienced in predicting human behavior based rationally on proof. Day after day, in every type of civil and criminal context, the trial judge is required by the law to predict human behavior. They do this, if I may say so, rather well.

The result of these two decisions has been dramatic. Its hundreds of human victims may be found in any community in California, in alleys, doorsteps, dumpsters, and gutters. The homeless mentally ill cannot go home. Sometimes the reverse occurs. Perhaps the most notorious case involving involuntary treatment of the homeless mentally ill is that of Joyce Brown, who was removed from the streets of New York as part of Mayor Ed Koch's campaign to provide care and treatment for these least fortunate citizens. She became a *cause célèbre* for the press, which touted her as "fiercely independent." At trial, the judge listened to three expert witnesses state that Brown's physical condition had seriously deteriorated over the year during which social workers had kept her under observation on the street, and that she had recently exhibited aggressive and abusive behavior that they feared would soon result in her being physically assaulted. The state's experts all opined that involuntary commitment was necessary to preserve Brown's health and to save her from harm by others. Brown also presented three experts, each of whom testified that she was not gravely disabled, but, while mentally ill, was capable of providing for her own needs on the streets. The trial judge engaged Brown in a lengthy examination, and concluded that she was lucid, intelligent, even humorous at times, and that she took fierce pride in her ability to care for herself. He theorized that her difficulties arose more from poverty and the lack of adequate, affordable housing than from "grave disability," and stated, "There must be some civilized alternatives other than involuntary hospitalization or the street." In the end, he ordered Brown released.[51] This decision was reversed by the Appellate Division of the New York Supreme Court. Looking not at Brown's appearance and demeanor at trial, but rather at the numerous examples of her physical and mental deterioration over the preceding year, the court ordered that she be retained for involuntary hospitalization.[52]

There is a second legal impediment to a finding of grave disability: the burden of proof. In all other civil matters the standard of proof by which a party may establish a finding (more likely than not) in order to prevail is a mere "preponderance of the evidence." The California Supreme Court, on the other hand, has decreed application of the far more demanding *criminal* standard, i.e., the familiar standard of proof "beyond a reasonable doubt and to a moral certainty." In addition, this must be found by a unanimous jury verdict.[53] The *Conservatorship of Roulet* opinion, which has become a landmark in this field, noted that a finding of grave disability could result in "serious deprivation of personal liberty,"[54] and that the due process clause of the California constitution required such proof by a unanimous jury in conservatorship proceedings. The majority declared that courts "must not be swayed by the fact that appellant's liberty was taken away for her own good."[55]

Roulet sets the standard for California, but the United States Supreme Court, in *Addington v. Texas*,[56] has ruled that "clear and convincing evidence" is the constitutional minimum required for involuntary commitment of an individual for an indefinite period to a state mental hospital. In this 1979 opinion, the court noted that twenty-five states had already adopted this standard, mostly by statute. Another fourteen states (not including California, as *Roulet* had not yet been decided) had adopted the more stringent criminal standard of proof beyond a reasonable doubt. Since the criminal standard exceeds the constitutional minimum, those states need not move to the more relaxed standard.

We take, here, a brief digression into the logic of the *Roulet* opinion. The reason that the demanding standard of proof and jury unanimity exists in criminal cases is to protect a possibly innocent person. The underlying theory has always been that it is better to err on the side of caution, that is, that it is preferable to "let ten guilty people go free than make one innocent person suffer." But in the context of mental health laws, application of the same standard leads to exactly the opposite results—we tend now to err *against* the side of caution. That is, application of the current standards ensures that as long as there is *any* doubt of the mentally ill person's ability to provide for himself or herself (on the day of the trial), the law says society must not intercede. In fact, under the current scheme, society may only intercede and appoint a conservator after the homeless mentally ill person has been proven beyond a reasonable doubt gravely disabled at the time of the hearing. Accordingly, under the current interpretation, the fact that a homeless mentally ill person may well have had only one window of lucidity in an otherwise uniformly gravely disabled existence—at the moment of his or her conservatorship hearing—acts as a nearly absolute bar to the imposition of the conservatorships that many deeply ill people so desperately need.

In response to this miserable state of affairs, the California legislature was prompted in 1986 to enact California Welfare and Institutions Code section 5008.2, which specifically allows admission of evidence concerning the historical course of the person's mental disorder at trial. This statute has apparently been unchallenged for the past three years. It has not been the subject of a single published court opinion. Section 5008.2 is an important step toward legal recognition of the fact that grave disability cannot rationally be found by looking to the proposed conservatee's state at a single court hearing of a few minutes, at which most mentally ill people would be artificially lucid because of medicine. The California courts, mental health officials and lawyers should use this tool, and simultaneously raise their voices to the legislature to call for additional humane and real-world mental health law.

Linked to the standard-of-proof difficulties in obtaining court consent to a conservatorship or to involuntary treatment of the gravely mentally ill is the issue of what type of evidence is needed as the basis of proof. Traditionally, the state has had to prove that the person was dangerous to himself or herself, or dangerous to others. While "dangerousness" still remains an element in the commitment/conservatorship process, the majority of states no longer require that this dangerousness to self involve physical injury. Recognizing that gravely mentally disabled people frequently exhibit an indifference or inability to recognize the need to fulfill basic human wants such as food, shelter, and clothing, the states have adopted differing standards of "dangerousness" for the gravely disabled that reflect this incapacity to care for personal needs. The most often reiterated standard found in both statutory law and court opinions is reference to "recent overt acts." This allows the court to review the subject's conduct in the preceding thirty to ninety days to determine whether the inability to care for basic needs poses the necessary danger to self. Among the states that have adopted this approach are Georgia, Michigan, Nebraska, Oklahoma, and Washington.[57] Among other more relaxed standards, Arizona, Maryland, and Minnesota have adopted an approach allowing commitment upon a finding that failure to immediately hospitalize the individual would pose a "clear and imminent danger" to self or others.[58] Other states, including Kentucky, Missouri, and Ohio, allow commitment if the individual poses a "substantial risk of causing serious harm" to himself or herself or to others.[59] Of course, this usually involves a trade-off in the courts. The broader and more relaxed the type of evidence admissible, the more stringent the burden of proof and procedural requirements (i.e., notice, hearing, confrontation and cross-examination of witnesses, etc.).

To make matters even worse in most California counties, there is a bureaucratic structure that can protect the courts from the possible assaults of hordes of proposed conservatees (whom, we all recognize—wink, wink— would only swell the demand made on a shrinking county budget!). This structure is empowered by the local board of supervisors to interview and investigate and, crucially, *to decide which people will be calendared for court hearings.*[60] Citizens ought to be able to hope, when their legislatures enact laws aimed at helping the most disabled of their fellows, that the help provided will go to all such disabled, equally. Sadly, for the severely mentally disabled in America, this is not so. One county officer in charge of deciding which disabled people to bring to the court's attention has estimated that three to five times the existing number of mental health conservatorships would be needed were he to schedule court hearings for all the people brought to his attention who in fact met the California law's standard of grave disability. He saw it as his sad task to choose between such gravely disabled human beings and to fatefully relegate the vast majority to lives of no care, misery, and the streets. He said that his choices are made largely on the basis of physical health. As the people wear down in that department, year after year, they move forward, in a sort of grisly waiting line.

The problem, of course, is rooted in the budget. Too many people are in need of help. The statutory law, in its present majestic equality, does not flatly declare that all such gravely disabled people have an equal right to the assistance of the state. In various counties of California different agencies have been given the responsibility of conducting conservatorship investigations.[61] This power is often exercised via hearing officers, who are not necessarily legally trained. These people follow orders. I have had occasion, in the sentencing of one homeless mentally ill offender, to make pages of "court's findings" bearing on the issue of grave disability (amassed during a trial), and to obtain an excellent, in-jail staff psychiatrist's report that concluded that the individual was gravely disabled and needed a conservator appointed. These reports were then forwarded to the county mental health office while an attorney was appointed, "effective immediately," for the purposes of representing the person in the conservatorship process and while application was made for a Superior Court conservatorship hearing.

The unraveling by the bureaucracy then began. After a hiatus during which a sensitive appointed attorney might have evaluated the situation and his or her client's interests and communicated with the mental health department to make sure all documents were in place, a person from the department visited me to explain that no attorney was yet on the case since "that is not when we get attorneys into these matters." Next, I was told that the proposed conservatee had been "released." This meant no conservatorship hearing. I asked for the written records to be forwarded to me. Before they arrived, I happened to attend a luncheon meeting of the local Psychology and Law Society and found myself seated beside a woman who, it turned out, was with the mental health department. Her business card read, "Superior Court, Hearing Officer." I mentioned having referred the case and, to my amazement, found out that she was the very person who had signed the order for no hearing. I asked her what she had thought of my three pages of findings. She said she had not seen them. I asked what she had thought of the psychiatrist's report, which had concluded that the gentleman was gravely disabled. She said she had not seen it. So I asked, "How was he? He must have been quite cogent after two weeks of thorazine." She replied that she had never seen the man. Flabbergasted, I asked her the basis for her "no hearing" decision. She said she could only decide things based on "what they give me," and confessed to having had no legal training.

The man in question (I'll call him W) was a profoundly mentally ill homeless person who had been living out of garbage cans for seven years. W's first words to me, in response to the question, "Who is your attorney?" (since he'd told my clerk he had an attorney), were loudly shouted, "Jesus is my attorney!" This undeniably ill man was denied the conservatorship hearing that could have been his access route to the life-saving help California law appears to guarantee those so gravely disabled by a severe mental disorder that they cannot provide for their basic needs for food, clothing or shelter.

Rights? A legal system equally administered? A society of laws, and not of men? A nation honestly attempting to help the many who are poor, and to teach its children the message of the Good Samaritan?

THE KEYS ARE INTEGRITY AND MONEY

If the system provided a full range of mental health treatment alternatives to fit the needs of each individual, with the staff in place to implement them, the courts would be more amenable to ordering involuntary treatment. The key, of course, is *money*—until state and local budgets allocate the funds to create and expand outpatient programs, judges will believe themselves faced with only two alternatives, each equally onerous: commitment to hospitalization or release to the streets. Most states have provisions for involuntary commitment to outpatient programs, and the courts have consistently insisted that involuntary hospitalization be proven to be the least restrictive means available to provide the care and treatment needed. But all too often the outpatient programs don't exist, or exist with too limited a capacity to provide care for even a fraction of those needing it.

In 1986, Georgia's mental health statutes were amended to provide statutory criteria for outpatient commitment.[62] Such commitment requires a two-step process. First, there is an evaluation of 1) whether the person's treatment history or current medical status indicates that his or her condition is likely to deteriorate such that, without intervention, hospitalization will be required, and 2) whether the person is able to voluntarily seek and comply with the requirements of outpatient treatment, based on mental history, nature of the mental illness, and current mental status.

If the evaluation indicates that involuntary outpatient commitment is appropriate, the second step in the process is consideration by both the evaluating physician and the court of whether appropriate outpatient treatment is available and whether the patient is likely to comply with the outpatient treatment well enough to minimize the likelihood of becoming an inpatient.

While this legislation is definitely a step in the right direction, the crux of its success is bound to be the availability of appropriate outpatient programs. All the legislation and good intentions in the world are useless until they are backed up by the funding to put in place a full-service outpatient mental health treatment system, responsive to the widely varied needs of the clients it is intended to serve, and serving each person meeting its criteria. Until this happens, too many courts and mental health administrators will continue to see only two options: full hospitalization or no treatment at all.

The budgetary ax having hacked away all the fat, a lot of the meat, and even some bone from mental health programs—three-fourths of the mental health budget, in real terms, since 1963—little is left of treatment programs for the chronically disabled, deeply mentally ill. So the argument is cogently made by those closest to the problem that to focus on changing commitment laws is to pursue a red herring. "Funds come first!" declares Jim Preis, attorney and executive director of Los Angeles' Mental Health Law Project. I cannot bring myself to accept the present irrational and harmful legal situation, however. America's commitment laws should be reformed, as indicated by Richard Lamb, professor of psychiatry at the University of Southern California and chair of the American Psychiatric Association's standing Task Force on the Homeless Mentally Ill (see appendices). He simply proposes a return (as I see it) to the plain reading and original intent of the 1960 commitment laws.

1. The inquiry into the proposed conservatee's possible grave disability must look to his/her ability to provide for basic human needs for food, clothing and shelter, looking at the *actual life patterns* of the subject person, including

patterns of taking or not taking medicines; and

   2. The court should look not at the proposed conservatee's instantaneously "present" ability to provide for those needs, but ought to look to the person's immediately previous life habit patterns . . . and then *predict* if the person is likely or not likely to be able, absent a conservatorship or other involuntarily imposed, least-restrictive form of treatment, to be able to provide for those basic human needs. If not, the court must order the person to be given the help (including decent housing, and kind human support systems) he/she needs.

Absent good community care systems and such legal changes, large numbers of America's most alienated, utterly mentally ill individuals (perhaps one third of the total of all chronically mentally ill Americans, or up to 750,000 people, and rising) will continue to exist in barbarous conditions, haunting our cities, shuffling and raving, or silent, sad, and terrified, horrifying us with their stark agony, peopling the dreams of our children and our judgments of ourselves. Our commitment laws need to be changed because they solve no problems, and today they command no respect.

   The numbers and the level of barbarism of this very public phenomenon are approaching comparison with the Holocaust . . . right here in America.
   —Jim Preis, chief counsel, Mental Health Associates of Los Angeles

SUGGESTED READING

Nowhere To Go, E. F. Fuller, M.D., Harper & Row, 1988.
"Needed Changes in Law and Procedure for the Chronically Mentally Ill," Richard Lamb, M.D., *Hospital and Community Psychiatry,* May 1986, vol. 37, pp. 475-480.
Madness in the Streets: How Psychiatry and the Law Abandoned the Mentally Ill, Rael Jean Isaac and Virginia C. Armat, Free Press, 1990.

14

Myths, Mental Barriers, and Bad Ideas

It's not what people know that gets them in trouble, it's what they know that ain't so.

—Mark Twain

One of our country's fundamental freedoms is free speech. Anybody can hold any opinion on any subject, even if he or she knows little or nothing about it. Thus, a startling commonplace in our country has become the recklessness with which professional, educated people permit themselves the luxury of unsupported opinions. It follows in regards to America's homeless that most of us hold strong opinions, many of which beget myths that significantly hinder efforts to solve the homeless problem. What I offer in this chapter is a list and an exploration of these myths, in hopes of helping to "beat back the barbarian hoards." These myths need to be confronted head on—in cocktail party chatter, in public forums, and in the legislative halls—in one ignorant mind after another.

The homeless are not an attractive group. Many stink and look terrible, often because they are suffering from physical and mental diseases. They have often been brutalized, and they may be very angry. Some are deeply addicted to drugs and alcohol. Many are crazy. A few may be dangerous. Their presence on a business's doorstep will doubtless hurt that business. Many families no longer picnic in certain parks because of the homeless. Contact with some of these individuals and derived media images can easily lead to the acceptance of damaging myths about the homeless:

The mentally ill were better off in the huge mental hospitals. They should be put back in there; they'll get more help. No expert on the subject recommends this. Most of the nation's chronically mentally ill (comprising at least 30 percent of the nation's homeless, according to the National Institute for Mental Health) can be humanely assisted and medically helped best in their own families' homes, in their own neighborhoods. But resources must be allocated to pay for the necessary community aftercare that will prevent the current agony of needless, enormously expensive rehospitalizations of these people. Currently, hospitalizations are gobbling up to one-third of the state and local governments' total allocations for mental health care. Programs in Los Angeles have shown that when humane, voluntary options are offered to the mentally ill homeless for food, shelter, and treatment (as opposed to the deprivation of the street or the dehumanizing experience of involuntary hospitalization), the vast majority of them do come indoors.

The Greyhound Theory: if we help them too much, the homeless will flock here! The National Coalition for the Homeless has compiled information showing that the mayors of virtually every American city polled have expressed the opinion that the homeless will migrate to their jurisdictions if even the most basic services are provided there. Also known as the Homeless Mecca Theory, the Greyhound Theory has been tested repeatedly and always found to be fallacious. One case in point is San Diego's $12-million "Taj Mahal for the Homeless," otherwise known as the St. Vincent de Paul/Joan Kroc Center for the Homeless, hub of a twelve-hundred-bed "Homeless Village" in San Diego. This effort has been the subject of two "60 Minutes" reports and countless other stories on national television and in the print media. After each broadcast or major report, the center's administrators and others working with homeless concerns in San Diego have been alert for "bumps on the gauges," indicators of a surge in the number of homeless people seeking services in San Diego. None has ever been noted. This stands to reason when one considers that survey after survey in city after city has revealed that two-thirds of any locale's homeless have lived there more than five years, and over 80 percent for over a year.[63] Also, 75 to 80 percent of "homeless" runaway children remain twenty miles or less from home. The vast majority of the homeless are not transient, except some serious job seekers, and families whose last possession is a car.[64]

Nobody cares about them anyway. Americans do care. A *Newsweek* poll published in March 1988 placed solving homelessness among the top three items on the American people's agenda. That neither presidential candidate made much of this speaks more about them personally than it does about the American people. Americans' concerns about the homeless have increased with their consciousness of the issue. A January 1990 *San Francisco Examiner* poll concluded that three-fourths of San Franciscans now rank homelessness as the "top problem" facing that city. Public officials who have not been leaders in this arena will soon be forced to wake up, as an impatient public demonstrates its interest in making changes now.

The homeless do not vote, so they can be ignored with political impunity. Although lacking an address, the homeless now have the legal right to vote. Voter registration efforts are sprouting among them—and, most significantly, the base of advocates sympathetic to homeless concerns is also widening.

Church people, particularly, are a growing yeast in the body politic. Homeless concerns can no longer be ignored with impunity.

The situation is overwhelming, hopeless. As Eleanor Roosevelt once said, "It's better to light one candle than to curse the darkness." Nihilism, while in vogue in some subcultures is, after all, an untenable position for any human being of any culture and education. Supporting the notion that homelessness is hopeless are the tendency to overestimate the numbers of the homeless and the failure to address the problem by breaking it into its component parts. It is vital first to take people's concerns seriously, and then to present a range of rationales for responding to homelessness. One usually starts with the lowest common denominator—economic self-interest. A fact-based discussion can demonstrate that preventive measures and those that address the root causes of homelessness may be more expensive initially but in the long term save societal resources. This argument will never reach the most cynical among the public and politicians who realize that the cheapest way to deal with the homeless problem is to do absolutely nothing and to let the homeless die in the street. But for the majority who are unable to accept the uncivilized prospect of bodies in the street, convincing arguments can be made for the fact that it is economically more advisable to invest in humane social service responses than to let the societal problems accompanying homelessness spiral destructively out of control and then to call upon the very expensive and not very effective resources of the police and the judicial and penal systems. Solving the problem of homelessness is not a hopeless proposition. It is the fragmented, knee-jerk, finger-in-the-dike approaches that are truly hopeless.

The "worthy" versus the "unworthy" poor. Worthy poor are people who don't make trouble, that is, are invisible. They don't bother us with their tragedies or remind us of our responsibilities. The "unworthy" poor? They're bums, alcoholics, drug addicts, criminals. Obviously, this response is ignorance in action. Being treated brutally from infancy, growing up with violence, ignorance, alcohol, drugs, and poverty may make one unpleasant, but not less worthy. Such thinking ignores the humanness of all people, and translates into apathy and abandonment. A typical result of such thinking is the creation of programs for substance abusers that are too short in duration to do any good (thirty days for chronic alcohol and drug abusers, for example). We know that for most substance abusers it takes two to four months to "dry out" the brain from the medical condition of toxic shock. Only after toxic shock has subsided can a person begin to gain insight into his or her condition. We know that substance abusers are expected by all knowledgeable experts to backslide, to "fall off the wagon" at some point. Yet we continue to see creation of programs that are too short, non-empowering, and unforgiving (no second chances).

They chose this life, let them raise themselves out of it. I did it myself; let them do it themselves. This pernicious lie is untrue for at least 95 percent of today's homeless. Every poll of homeless people shows that over 90 percent want to be off the streets and want useful work. Even the more than 30 percent who are deeply mentally disabled list useful work and good mental health care as their two top needs. Certainly, these people may have made some mistakes, even grievous ones, but the consequences they have suffered have been far beyond any "choosing."

Homeless people must be immoral, or else they would not be homeless. Given the mostly irrational fears we have of the homeless as we pass them on the street, it is no wonder that some assume they are bad characters. Some may be, but not because they are homeless. Most are good people, or would like to be. They want to be contributing members of the community. People who believe the homeless to be immoral are buying into the Calvinist doctrine that if one does good works one will prosper without fail, and that not being prosperous is a sign that one is not good. It is the extension in the other direction of the fallacious belief that one is a better person because he or she has a better, or more voguish, automobile. A Mercedes Benz does not a better person make. Lack of a home does not a worse person make. Thoughtful people acknowledge that, "There, but for the grace of God, go I."

The nearly homeless, those who can barely afford rent, are actually more likely to open their homes to homeless people or families than are rich people with many unused spare bedrooms. There is generosity and goodness in many of the poor—and in many of the homeless as well. Each is an individual. Status, or lack of it, does not accord immorality. Actions, or, for those who can give and refuse to, lack of actions—these are the basis for deciding the moral value in us all.

The homeless will vanish if police exert enough pressure. "Vanish" where? Police action has not worked and cannot work, even when (as in San Diego and Santa Monica) it has been vigorously attempted using well-trained volunteer police who are scrupulously respectful of everyone's rights. The homeless are simply the very poor of the community who, in this last decade, lost their access to low-income housing, adequate jobs, and the social services that, before, had kept them off the street in times of hardship. We have seen the pattern repeatedly in Los Angeles: when police pressure is applied downtown, the homeless population swells in the beach communities; when the beach communities attempt to force them out, they return downtown. They never leave the municipal boundaries. Police sweeps of the homeless are simply urban musical chairs.

The homeless are just like you and me, single people and families just like us. This myth is the well-meaning inverse of some of the others, but it is problematic nonetheless. It prevents us from taking the necessary close look at the real problems of the homeless. In a sense, the statement is true. Take a look at your savings account. Most of us are about three months away from homelessness. I have been amused recently to happen upon articles about what middle-class couples experience when remodelling their homes. Apparently, the simple removal of a wall or part of a roof in the home can often cause such stress that the marriage does not survive. If this is the case, it cannot be too difficult for people to imagine the distress and fear of having nowhere at all to go at nightfall.

INTELLECTUAL "HIRED GUNS" FOSTERING MYTHS ABOUT HOMELESSNESS

There are some Americans who think they have an interest in buttressing some of the myths that are helping to keep American homelessness in place. Noticing that the American people are stirring about homelessness and are telling pollsters they want something done, these people are taking action of their own. They are hiring so-called experts to churn out scurrilous articles for the purpose of underlining selected distortions and lies about the homeless. "How about an article showing the homeless to be campers?" (or all crazy, or on the streets by choice, or crooks, or addicts, or few in number, or annoying as they panhandle, or dishonest about themselves, or . . .) In the winter of 1989 and the spring of 1990, opinion editorials appeared in news-papers around America, including the *New York Times* (January 26, January 31, February 2, and February 5, 1990), the *Wall Street Journal* (April 10, 1990), and the *San Diego Union* (February 18, 1990). Most were sponsored by a New York entity called the Manhattan Institute of Policy Research, which boasts a staff of ten. The themes were:

- The rise in homelessness is not the fault of conservatives, but of the liberals who let them out of the nation's loony bins.
- The homeless mentally ill ought to be herded back into big hospitals.
- Since there is no definitive data to prove the case, the lack of facilities and the lack of funding are not factors causing homelessness.
- Huge numbers of homeless people choose homelessness by choosing drugs, so why help at all?
- Homelessness does not present a moral issue; the main thing is that the homeless are unsightly.
- The homeless are different from people who are not homeless.

Robert Lekachman, distinguished professor of economics at Lehman College, considers the institute "an ambitious, far-right outfit" and its president, William M.H. Hammett, a "thrusting yuppie on the make, getting money from the same people as all the other right-wing think tanks," in other words, such entities as the Sarah Scaife Foundation of Pittsburgh, the J. Howard Pew Freedom Trust, the Smith Richardson Foundation, and the John M. Olin Foundation, all conservative foundations. Hammett is a former president of the Center for Libertarian Studies, who, it is fair to say, disdains any social program not privately funded.

But why would a foundation want to support attacks against the homeless? What is the gain? Is it simply misguided? If so, I hope this book helps. But, alas, not all motives are pure. There is money to be made through the manipulation of urban real estate. Property values can be driven down by preventing the spread of good community programs. Buy up small landowners, plow, and rebuild. *Voilà*. A brand new office building, hotel, or shopping center where several SRO hotels once stood. The homeless? Just get the police to push them to another part of the city.

For more details on such matters, see the chapters on housing and the economics of homelessness.

The moral here is that we need to be cautious regarding sources of information that view the homeless contemptuously. As a great French Resistance editor and playwright, Albert Camus, once wrote, "Every gesture of contempt contains the seeds of fascism."

SUGGESTED READING

How to Lie with Statistics, Darrell Huff and Irving Geis, Norton, 1954.

15

Going to the State Capital

Give us the tools, and we will finish the job!
— Winston Churchill (to the U.S. Congress, 1941)

It may now be time for some strong political actions at the state level. A San Diego experience illustrates the mounting of a campaign for state action. The idea turned out to have been before its time in 1986, but it helped pave the way for real progress. The hero of this action is a loyal Republican businessman named Joe Dolphin, owner of a nationwide private ambulance service. His past affiliations included the presidency of the local Republican businessmen's organization and the presidency of the county Salvation Army. A healthy, vigorous, and remarkably ordinary person in other respects, Dolphin also has an ordinary, healthy heart. When he saw San Diego's homeless up close, as my partner for a weekend "on the streets," he became infected with the need to help those who wanted to help themselves off the street.

By its closing of large state mental hospitals, then by slowly dismantling the community mental health treatment system, and finally by enacting through voter initiative a series of severe budget cuts, California by the mid-1980s had severely reduced its role in the arenas having to do with homelessness. Those in charge of the remnant systems were expendable, do-or-die commanders left to offer resistance in outposts and bunkers, as the main army retreated.

Dolphin said, "Let's get the state involved!" After our weekend on the streets Joe huddled with me, Dick Shanor, Police Commander Larry Gore, Salvation Army Commander Bill Lutrell, Travelers Aide's Mary Colecicco, Sister Linda Lutz of Catholic Community Services, Doug Regin and Raymonda Duvall, the irrepressible Father (now Monsignor) Joe Carroll, and the Central City Development Agency's Dave Allsbrook. These brought others in from time to time and, in a series of hard-work meetings over several months, we hammered out a joint plan for "the best state action we believe to be needed at this time."

Dolphin took the proposal to the governor and leading state legislators. We made a number of changes to meet what the governor's people said he wanted and would sign. The proposed legislation went in as Assembly Bill 2839, the Homeless Relief Act of 1986 (its full text is included in the appendices). The bill was introduced by Assemblyman Peter Chacon, who represents a part of San Diego that is one of the poorer districts of the state and who, accordingly, is an expert in low-income housing. Since California then had a Republican governor, a Democratic state assembly and a more statesmanlike, almost equally divided state senate, it made sense to line up the Democrats but concentrate on the Republicans. Dolphin and I did this to start, and as things evolved Gore, legal aide Greg Knoll, Father Joe, and Captain Lutrell joined us to carry the game to Sacramento.

Dolphin paid the bills. He ultimately shelled out more than $30,000 over a one-year period, for advertising expertise, a logo (the forget-me-not flower), mailing lists, a lobbyist, and a key consultant, the highly respected Alan Post, a former state legislative analyst. Post attached his telling endorsement to an suggestion made by Sen. Larry Stirling. Stirling found us a source for the needed $90 million called for in the bill, to be spent over three years to fund a statewide pilot project.

The thrust of the bill was to strengthen the existing street agencies and to allow them, under the concept called "case management," to provide all kinds of assistance services to the homeless, from job placement and counselling to assistance through the bureaucratic mazes to securing housing. It was a super, gleaming plan and it had broad support, some of which was drummed up by our various networks and some by Dolphin's public relations people. At every hearing there was a spectacular array of priests, Salvation Army beneficients, police, judges, poverty and corporate lawyers, ministers, and business leaders. One assemblyman confessed that he couldn't vote against us or his wife would give him hell. "I couldn't live with that." Despite a great deal of skepticism about a humane but untried idea, he hunkered down and voted for the bill.

Bills seldom sail through the California legislature. There is such an army of well-organized, well-informed, computerized, instantaneous-response lobby groups in Sacramento that no proposal can escape debate and dispute. Our bill generated overt opposition from the right wings of both parties and more covert opposition from people who felt that a public acknowledgement of homelessness as a problem to be confronted would necessarily involve an allocation, some day, of blame for the failure to solve it. Others saw the bill as ominous, an opening wedge to fiscal excess once state responsibility was assigned.

The crunch, of course, came over money. We'd found the new money source, but we became weary when the Democrats told us, basically, "Thanks, but we have more traditional constituencies, and their programs can use the bundle you've discovered. They thank you, too." So in Assembly's Ways and Means Committee the bill was pared down to a pittance. It became a $3-million, three-year pilot project affecting San Diego only. Rhetoric echoes hauntingly on the cold streets, where poor people have heard empty promises before. Big talkers slink away, when asked to put up or shut up.

But the substantive provisions of the bill were still good, and they survived. We took the tiny, pilot project bill, with our hopes, back to Gov. George Deukmejian's office after the final votes were recorded (Senate: twenty-eight for, one against; Assembly: forty-nine for, twenty-five against), expecting a signature and maybe, even, some gratitude for our small assistance regarding the state budget. On September 30, 1986, Gov. George Deukmejian signed the Homeless Relief Act of 1986 into law. He then used his line-item veto power and drew his blue pencil through the money provisions. There would be no program.

The homeless were to have no relief, at least in 1987. However, there were a number of classy moments along the way. Dolphin's public relations people made the purple forget-me-not the symbol of the legislation. It was on our letterhead, and, in a fake flower form, they began appearing in (free) vases all about the legislative offices. Who could refuse such a gift, and, once it was displayed, who would dare "forget" by voting "nay" on A.B. 2839?

Father Joe was asked to offer the morning's prayer for the entire legislature one morning. After asking God to assist in the reelections of all the legislature's members, he requested divine intervention to assure a correct vote "for" A.B. 2839.

Positive results of our work were that the team of San Diegans and others across the state had deepened their communication channels and learned that there was active, entrenched opposition to doing the right things for California's homeless. We learned that solving the dilemma of homelessness was not yet an idea whose time had come. We also learned from Joe Dolphin, who taught us something we had forgotten: representative government can never work without brave citizens who are willing to put themselves and their resources on the line for good government. By his example, Dolphin showed us the sort of practical intelligence, courage, and political audacity that citizens in every state must muster, so we can responsibly meet and conquer homelessness. Thank you, Joe.

A man does what he must in spite of personal consequences, in spite of obstacles and dangers and pressures—and that is the basis of all human morality.
—John F. Kennedy, *Profiles in Courage*

SUGGESTED READING

Homelessness in the States, Lee Walker, Council of State Governments, 1990.

16

Public Restrooms (A NIMBY Study)

Thou shalt have a place also without the camp, wither thou shalt go forth abroad; and thou shalt have a paddle upon thy weapon; and it shall be, when thou wilt ease thyself abroad, thou shalt dig therewith, and shalt turn back and cover that which cometh from thee.
—Deuteronomy 23:12–13

Since their beginnings, cities have tried to cope with human excrement. Since the time of Lister and Pasteur we have known that if we don't provide a place for it people will get sick.

America's new homeless are a strikingly unhealthy lot. They suffer, and carry about every known disease of man. Respiratory disorders are particularly rampant. Los Angeles studies conducted at the Robert Woods Johnson Clinics revealed the homeless of Los Angeles to have a higher incidence of tuberculosis than any subpopulation ever reported in American history (50 percent). One public health doctor has called our burgeoning homeless population a "public health time bomb," and called our homeless areas "seething cauldrons of disease."

But locating *one* public restroom in downtown San Diego proved to be such a heroic venture that it consumed some of that city government's leading brains for ten years. For the last four of those years, the San Diego city budget contained all the money needed to provide a public restroom. Finally, the single restroom was opened. But during that "no public restroom" decade, tons of filth dirtied the streets, sidewalks, doorsteps, and parks of San Diego, an otherwise gorgeous, tourist city. "Not In My Back Yard" created this municipal helplessness.

The public restroom minidrama most clearly illustrates the stunning power of small groups of determined citizens to prevent the solution of an obvious public problem, even when virtually everybody has agreed that it must be confronted and solved quickly. Why the paralysis in this case? Because, while everyone acknowledged that public restrooms were urgently needed down-

town, nobody wanted the facility next door. No elected official had the guts
to make a decision and ram it forward. Besides, in the Byzantine alley fight
of modern, interest-group-dominated city politics, this was not a big ticket
item. The politicians applied the most basic of political rules—don't offend
anyone if you can possibly help it.

In 1977, San Diego's cheerful and gutsy Mayor Frank Curran ventured
into the only city-provided, downtown public restroom not inside a building.
Hizzoner was appalled by what he found. Reached via a darkened stairway,
this underground den had been thought progressive when installed in the
1890s. It was then a bright, tiled, modern ornament to a fountain-resplendent
one-block park. By the time Curran was in office, however, it was a dark,
graffiti-covered hideout for muggers and deviants. Curran verified its dangerousness, and demanded action.

The city manager commenced a study, one thing led to another, years
passed, and finally the city's redevelopment arm, called the Center City
Development Corporation, included a plaza restroom in its redevelopment
plans, making a legally binding vow: "We will open a replacement facility
. . . soon." The city's top engineer-administrator, Deputy City Manager John
Fowler, carefully studied the public restroom problem—its geography, politics,
technology, and history. He looked at examples of public restrooms worldwide.
He looked at the range of possible sites: public, quasi-public, and private.

A site had to be found. Biology, retail economics, and legal obligation
dictated speed. The city manager and the City Council budgeted the money
for a public restroom. The city's broad electorate supported the restroom.
None wanted it in their back yard, however. A sea of positives was faced
by one powerful negative. It took five years and five city budgets, each proudly
pregnant with the needed funds, to deliver the single public restroom.

Styles of facilities were studied. The old, Paris pissoirs (where gentlemen
were photographed in the 1920s doffing their bowler hats while relieving themselves) were found to be still in storage, but unsuitable because they were
"pay toilets" and would serve only a small population. New facilities were
required. Letters went out to urban leaders and manufacturers worldwide.
Dozens of ingenious designs were reviewed and tested. Salespeople descended
on the city, touting their wares. Interesting designs included plastic one-person
toilets (common in Paris) that flushed their entire insides and portable, mobile
home-type units. But these all came a cropper a simple modern perception.
It is dangerous to eliminate. An attendant is needed (as the French government long ago concluded: it placed a cheery, red, white and blue–garbed
lady within the Arc de Triomphe, selling toilet paper). Attendants are required
because of the wide range of users: rich and poor, tourist and homeless.
The space needs and costs rose while the most imaginative solutions offered
by the planet's best geniuses were ruled out. Simultaneously, the site survey

team was narrowing the list. Considered first were trolley stops and parking garages. Next, private property owners (the Lions Clubs' senior-citizen highrise, bus stations, AMTRAK). Next, institutions that were quasi-public in nature—parking structures and businesses with long, street-facing walls, such as department stores and shopping centers. Finally, city-owned structures: the proposed new police station, the engineering operations building, the Civic Theatre, and City Hall itself. The answers came in a chorus: "No. No. Not in my back yard!" A responsive city government, courteous, respectfully democratic, small-town timid, backed off. The city manager's brave staffers hunkered down. They explored the possibility of requiring all redevelopment projects to include restrooms on their main floors. They looked to other government-owned land like the Port District and the trolley.

Seasons came and went. Budgets continued to brag. Street people and suburbanites alike continued to pee in alleys. Some miscreants were hauled off to jail. Recidivism was rampant. The U.S. Grant Hotel (an upscale downtown hotel recently renovated at a cost of $82 million) painted the lower eight feet of its building four times in a year. U.S. Attorney General Edwin Meese came to town and called for winning back the city's streets. Nonetheless, the seasons passed, and the budgeted funds were quietly saved or spent elsewhere, year after year.

Fowler and his assistants, however, were not to be denied. They finally hit upon a solution, sold it to the neighbors, and, before anyone could blink, smoked up a good design, sailed it through the City Council and—*voilà!*—in August 1987, a scant decade after the campaign's commencement, victory was announced. Mayor Maureen O'Connor is unreliably rumored to have given this important public facility its ceremonial first use.

The location: a side street, facing away from City Hall and the Civic Theatre, across from a busy, new trolley stop and kittycorner from two of downtown's proudest hotels, both battle-weary for the lack of a public restroom. Other objections were brushed aside in the rush to decision, amid reassurances that staffing of the toilets would solve all imagined problems, keep the peace, and maybe even frighten away unsavory characters.

The city's one downtown restroom now hosts an average of 344 "event-free" uses daily. A sign asks, "No washing." (Not, "*Lavese sus manos.*") The nearby hotels send copies of their "guest comment sheets" to the mayor's office every month, supporting evidence for their estimate of an annual $1 million total expenditure and income loss occasioned by the presence of street people. In fact, however, the restroom has had no impact on either the presence or the activities of homeless people. NIMBY, here, was truly a misguided sentiment.

In retrospect, the city team's members saw the following lessons in their decade-long adventure with a downtown public toilet:

1. Public restrooms are a perennial downtown need (the first Rotary Club project in the United States established a public restroom in downtown Chicago), and each city has to meet that need by way of city policy. The best answer is foresight: requiring developers to provide street-access public restrooms within all buildings or developments above a certain size.
2. "Sprinkling" public restrooms all over downtown would have taken the pressure off a particular site. More restrooms might mitigate the perception of a concentration of the homeless, since alleged adverse effects would be shared and accordingly reduced. No one could complain of being singled out.
3. Persistence pays off, and luck is the intersection between preparation and opportunity.
4. NIMBY is a formidable urban political force and must be acknowledged, outwitted, outargued, or neutralized. When confronted by NIMBY, successful organizers find allies; look for weak, irresolute, slow-moving, politically uninvolved neighbors and they time moves correctly and move swiftly.
5. A redevelopment agency is a good source for architectural and construction funds; occupancy (hotel) taxes are a good source of operational and maintenance funds.
6. A merger of the restroom needs of the homeless and of others, especially transit users, provides substantive rationale for public restrooms, and facilitates to some degree the selection and acquisition of a site.
7. Public property, particularly underutilized street right-of-ways, is probably the optimum location for the restroom.
8. The proper design of a public restroom is vital in advertising the facility for potential users other than the homeless. For safety and sanitation, a full-time attendant who doubles as a cleaner is essential.
9. The facility must open no later than 7:00 a.m. and close no earlier than 10:00 p.m. to meet the needs of the homeless.
10. The location of a public restroom should be in an area of high visibility and pedestrian activity, so that it feels safe and is fully used.
11. The cost of an adequate facility is now running from $100,000 to $200,000, plus architectural expenses. This cost may go down if, as looks possible, mass production begins to play a role in restroom construction.

When I was a teenager, I found myself downtown and I had to relieve myself. There were no facilities available to me, so I got on a bus to go home. I almost made it.
    —U.S. Supreme Court Justice Thurgood Marshall
    (when asked why he got involved in the Civil Rights Movement)

17

Conundra

Half the time, 90 percent of this game is mental.

—Yogi Berra

"When we roll up our sleeves, deciding to handle a problem—watch out, world!"

Even if that mythical American attitude characterized U.S. efforts to diminish homelessness, aspects of the problem would remain deeply puzzling. Many necessary solutions would remain seemingly unknowable.

AN AVALANCHE OF INCOMPETENTS

"The Man with the Hoe"

Bowed by the weight of centuries he leans
Upon his hoe and gazes on the ground,
The emptiness of ages in his face,
And on his back the burden of the world
Who made him dead to rapture and despair,
A thing that grieves not and that never hopes,
Stolid and stunned, a brother to the ox?
Who loosened and let down this brutal jaw?
Whose was the hand that slanted back this brow?
Whose breath blew out the light within this brain?
Is this the Thing the Lord God made and gave
to have dominion over sea and land;
To trace the stars and search the heavens for power;
To feel the passion of Eternity?
Is this the Dream He dreamed who shaped the suns
And marked their ways upon the ancient deep?
Down all the stretch of Hell to its last gulf
There is no shape more terrible than this—

More tongued with censure of the world's blind greed
More filled with signs and portents for the soul—
More fraught with menace to the universe . . .
                                    —Edwin Markham (1852–1940)

Both white and black family structures are today in such disarray that eleven of every twenty white children and nineteen of every twenty black children now alive will spend a significant part of their growing-up years in single-parent households. And for the little boys or girls being raised by a single parent of the opposite sex, the chances are high that the parent will be both highly stressed and angry, specifically, with people of the opposite sex. Children's sense of self-worth can be seriously diminished if they come to think that their parent believes them to be members of an evil group!

And for children unlucky enough to take up alcohol or drug use (or both) at an early age (nine, ten, and eleven in many cases), or to be under the supervision of physically abusive or alcoholic parents (or both)—for these children great landscapes of the usual, necessary developmental stages through which children and teenagers must pass to become adults are obliterated. Like kittens blinded by having their eyes covered up during a critical week for eye development in cats, these people can become permanent children.

These are the nation's growing avalanche of incompetents. Most of them cannot or will not wish to hold a job, to understand life, to have great relationships, or to live lives in normal ecstacy and gratitude toward Creator and existence. Experts expect this growing group to be surly, stunted, almost animal-like, and enormously expensive to society whether we ignore them and pay horrendous public prices in police, prisons, welfare, and in that most terrifying prospect of all, a stupid, ignorant and uneducable electorate, or whether, on the other hand, we laboriously attempt to restore them to semblances of social functioning and dignity.

These broken Humpty Dumptys are among our homeless. What to do? It beats me. After one praises the St. Francis–like compassion and sophistication of some of the religious groups working with these kinds of homeless (I've found these particularly among Catholics, Pentecostals and Episcopalians, and the agencies dealing with runaways), and after having uttered some platitudes about respect, dignity, the brotherhood of mankind, integrity, and the sanctity of the family . . . what else can one say? It does beat me.

FAILING PHILOSOPHY, SOFT RELIGION

Television has blared its mediocre message into the conscious and subconscious minds of Americans since World War II. It has succeeded, in large measure, in replacing religion and its helpmate, philosophy, as the source of national mythologies. With several caveats, readers are referred to the University of Chicago philosophy professor Allan Bloom's 1987 book, *The Closing of the American Mind.* Bloom begins with a personal observation (unsupported by any poll or other empirical data) that, while in the 1940s and 1950s entering college students predictably brought with them a wide cross-section of religions and philosophical points of view and positions, today they are homogenous: they are all nihilists. And unlike previous generations of undergraduates, they are fiercely unwilling to examine the underpinnings of this ancient heresy, nor are they wiling to consider the range of other possible ways of viewing life. They have closed minds and they do not believe in the usefulness of the concept "truth."

In the early days of our republic survival meant action, and religion, de Tocqueville said, animated us. Further, the varieties of religious views were all stamped with the robust virtues of the frontier and its endless opportunities. "When America ceases to be good," de Tocqueville wrote, "she will cease to be great." Historically, America's activist religions have been Judaism and Christianity, but in the words of born-again homeless job expert Bob McElroy, "Most of today's Christians sit on their fannies and act like the hypocrites Jesus couldn't stand. They need to get down and dirty with poor people, like the Lord did." Few Americans today can say with Carl Jung, "I have no need for belief in God. I *know* God."

Bloom has been criticized more for his prescriptions than for his diagnosis, and it would have been helpful had the prescription been described in numbers. The waning of sleeves-rolled-up, get-out-of-the-way-I'm-*solving*-this-problem religiosity is certainly observable, however.

Are there solutions to this? Well . . . there is thoughtfulness. The great psychiatrist Rollo May told us that humility and habitual tentativeness were the "hallmarks of a cultured person." This is a starting point. Perhaps also the presence of God. The great Jesuit philosopher Teilhard de Jardin wrote, "Joy is the most infallible sign of the presence of God."

BUREAUCRATIC AND POLITICAL DEADLOCK

"Paralyzed by special interests and shortsightedness, Washington no longer seems capable of responding to its growing challenges." These are the words of a *Time* cover story from late 1989. Our government has abandoned its orientation toward problem-solving. With our government facing the most massive budget deficit in history, *Time* said, neither the administration nor our legislators are willing to take the steps necessary to reduce the rising level of red ink.

This trend was aptly characterized as the "now-nowism" (of both spoiled voters and government alike) by Bush administration budget director Richard Darman. Conservative analyst Kevin Phillips has called the phenomenon the result of "a frightening inability to define and debate America's emerging problems." As the nation rockets toward the twenty-first century, many wonder how we will pay for the present and the past at the same time. More importantly, can we regain political realism?

Another expression of "can't-do-ism" has been the taxpayer revolts in various states. The anti-tax revolt began in 1978 in California with Proposition 13. Many states followed, limiting and hobbling their local governments. Since, voters have gone initiative-wild, looking for ways to fund special interests and needs, because government now has less money to use to respond to them. Last year, California presented its voters with twenty-nine ballot initiatives.

Young people see the effects and control of money on our public life, and they shy away from politics and public service, both once considered everyone's duty. Those brave souls who do seek public office will find their constituents and the media delighting in making their lives miserable, a far cry from the respect for bravery that might help attract talented leaders.

WHERE ARE THE HEROES?

One of America's scientific giants, Roger Revelle of the University of California at San Diego, asserted that, "Forty percent of the homo sapiens who have ever been alive are alive on the planet today." He then asked, "Where are the geniuses? Where are the giants like Galileo, the Buddha, Beethoven, Goethe, Lincoln, Newton, Theodore Roosevelt, Elizabeth I, Shakespeare, Thucidides, Marie Curie, and Socrates: the hundreds of towering minds and spirits which, statistically, one would predict would be visible among us today and available to lead us out of the dilemmas which beset us?" Geniuses are needed, and heroes. With such people focused on and engaged in the solutions to the homeless dilemma, America would of course be a lot more likely to get the situation resolved, speedily. We need to identify these folk among us, to welcome them in and honor them, and to select them as our leaders.

In *The Culture of Narcissism*, cultural anthropologist Christopher Lasch stated that, largely as a result of the skill of America's advertising executives, our nation has been transformed into a narcissistic nation. Narcissism does not lead to heroism. To the contrary, the narcissist perceives all surroundings in terms of how they affect him or her. Here we think of "trophy wives" and "trophy husbands" and of economist Thorstein Veblen's theories of conspicuous consumption. Narcissists are small.

Heroes live at the opposite end of the human spectrum. Heroes are not the Ollie Norths of life. They are those whose lives embody human models. They are leaders by the power of their own integrity, and not because of position, force, wealth, or greed. Narcissists are corruptly selfish. Heroes spend their lives devoted to causes larger than their own lives. Because of their commitment, they discard the disabling neurosis that bogs down others. Heroes take personal responsibility in all things and grow by continually inquiring, "What did *I* do to contribute to that result? How can I make a contribution?" Narcissists find others to blame. Heroes, since they learn to live in integrity, continually grow in life and are, by definition, on a self-refining, spiritual path. They deepen themselves quite naturally, because they are seeking truth—in order to live by it, and to usefully use it. "What else is there to do?" one might ask. Well, look around you. You'll see people engaged in plenty else! Heroes know the difference between anarchy and freedom, since they habitually take personal responsibility and are devoted to being useful.

"Why do we see few heroes today?" I asked biologist/philosopher Paul Saltman. His answer: "There's no perceived percentage in it today." Heroism is not exactly applauded or rewarded in America these days. But it is practiced. Stories of heroes and heroines dot this book and heroes and heroines are all around us. They are, in modern America, not generally found "out in front," however, being vaunted in the media. The media is too interested in peddling its messages of mediocrity, too busy eroding our brain power with inane, irrelevant messages antithetical to heroism. The media is too courteous to offend the mediocre with the inconvenient news that their lives are hollow. The media is, also, occupied. It is selling soap.

DRUGS AND ALCOHOL

While drug use in the nation has skyrocketed since the 1960s, per-capita alcohol consumption, oddly enough, has remained fairly stable for the past thirty years. But soaring drug use is a growing blight. Cocaine continues to be the drug of main concern throughout most of America's major cities. In 1988, increases in cocaine-related deaths were reported in Atlanta, Dallas, Denver, Detroit, Miami, New York, Philadelphia, Phoenix, San Francisco, and Seattle. A decline was reported in some cities like San Diego, but the equally cheap drug, methamphetamine, presents an exploding problem, with 48-percent increases in overdose deaths in 1988 in four major cities. Cocaine ranked as the highest cause among emergency room fatalities in every major city in the United States in 1987 and 1988, except in San Diego. Cocaine prices have stayed low and stable and supplies (largely from Latin America) are plentiful. With this, heroin use has plunged. Heroin was long the nation's number-one fatal drug, but some cities such as Atlanta, Denver, New York, Philadelphia, and Phoenix had increases in heroin deaths in 1988, while declines have been noted in Detroit, San Diego, San Francisco, and Washington, D.C. By contrast, deaths due to heroin-cocaine combinations (speedballs) increased in Washington, D.C.

Recent research has shown that very heavy use of marijuana kills five times the brain cells (half a million per day of heavy use) as heavy boozing. More ominously, it often serves as the sociological door to other illegal drug use. It is often cited as a secondary drug problem in treatment admissions throughout the nation, and most drug users use several drugs, often together, with alcohol. The mixes are deadly.

Deaths related to the hallucinogen PCP show a declining trend in Los Angeles and many other large cities recently, including Chicago, St. Louis, San Francisco, and Washington, D.C. Both San Francisco and San Diego report upward trends in stimulant-related deaths in 1988. Methamphetamine crises rank first among drug-related emergency-room visits in San Diego, second in Phoenix, and third in Dallas. In 1988 such visits increased by over 47 percent in Atlanta, Phoenix, San Diego, and Seattle. Stimulant abuse remains at low levels in Boston, Detroit, Miami, and Philadelphia. Use of barbiturates and sedatives/hypnotics is reported, but declining in most cities. However, barbiturates rank third among illicit drugs detected in Chicago.

I recommend to all Jon Franklin's *Molecules of the Mind*, the dramatic story of the last decade's research into the chemistry of the brain and its meaning relative to "the mind" and to various addictions to chemicals (as opposed to "natural highs" from aerobics, etc.). The book helps explain how troubled people slip easily away from reality into addiction.

Illicit use of prescribed mind- and mood-altering drugs has also grown explosively during this period. It drives a vicious cycle in which it is in the economic interest of our huge chemical and drug industries (to name only two of many affected industries) to perpetuate, to heighten, and certainly *not* to resist the increase of drug abuse. So this process expands itself by circular causation. Our national resolve is steadily being weakened because of the growing numbers of addicted citizens. At least one-third of America's homeless are drug and/or alcohol dependent.

What to do about this? Well, Twelve-Step self-help groups (Alcoholics Anonymous and its progeny) have developed the only model that appears to work with large numbers of people. They exist everywhere and they are free. This is a great sign. But they are not preventative organizations. I expect that the next stage of activity to emanate from the people gaining insight and commitment via these thousands of self-help groups will be public efforts such as:

- Solid, empirically based public education programs to reduce demand for drugs and alcohol. These will likely include, for example, boycotts of media that accept advertisements that glorify drinking.
- More effective Mothers Against Drunk Driving–type, forceful advocacy activity, which will begin really having an affect on the legislative and justice systems, expressing points of view that are absolutely intolerant of chemically based violations of the community, and insisting on the end of gestures in these arenas, in favor of successes. Leadership from self-help sources could mold these forces into positive channels, including national prevention and treatment modes.
- A straightening of legislators' and candidates' backs on these issues, as is now largely being done only in favor of economic-issue groups, by political action committees and labor and corporate lobbyists.

DISRESPECT FOR THE LAW

One hundred years ago, before he sat on the Supreme Court, Oliver Wendell Holmes opined that criminal law postulated the likelihood of criminals being apprehended, speedily and fairly being tried, found guilty or not, and, if guilty, punished. The law, thus postulated, presumes that the public knows such processes are dependably in place, and generally supports them. Knowing this, those contemplating crime are given pause.

Today, the prospective criminal's calculations are being interfered with because a large percentage of local jails are full, and criminals, especially misdemeanants, are simply being released without charges filed. The scofflaw contingent is growing. We need jails. We need to let our intolerance of crime be known by means of intelligent action. Americans need, particularly, to increase the interest in citizen participation in police work, via neighborhood-watch programs, Crime Stoppers–type programs (citizen tips to the police via confidential channels), and other, similar means. Criminals need to know they are being watched, likely will be reported on, and that their violations will likely result in arrest, prosecution, and both punishment and, where possible, reform.

Secondly, Americans heavily using drugs or drinking cannot be depended upon to make rational calculations about much of anything, except, perhaps, how to get more drugs and alcohol. The many citizens using illegal drugs have rationalized their own criminality. Preposterously, some public officials and media leaders honor such rationalizations. Furthermore, the media has continued a vastly antisocial drumbeat of themes: that justice is unavailable, that idiots run the justice system, that police are a type of enemy, and that citizen cooperation in crime-stopping is un-American "snitching" (in fact, this is squarely within our legal traditions: the English felony of misprision—failure of a citizen to report a felony—is one example). Those responsible for the media need to wake up to their dedication to truth.

HOSTILITY TOWARD THE YOUNG; NEGLECT OF EDUCATION

Being psychologically children themselves and envying carefree childhood, many Americans do not really like children. This has been expressed in the eroding of our once fierce support for high-quality, free public education. The flight to suburban school districts has heightened an "us and them" psychology wherein city-center schools have suffered. And as Detroit and the Bronx have learned (to name but two examples), without good schools, neighborhood rejuvenation is impossible.

Teachers' salaries plummeted compared with those of other learned professionals after World War II, although there was a rebound of nearly 20 percent in real terms, to a national average of $28,044, in 1988. This is still ridiculously low. Somehow, our nation needs to start talking of educators as heroes, as wonderful counselors, as a revered corps on whom we all gratefully depend.

Illiteracy is common on the streets, and the prices we pay, teaching a person to read after neglecting to teach the child two or three decades earlier, are staggering. "I would assume those who are not well-educated may not be well-trained for jobs, and therefore have a difficult time making ends meet, especially with housing costs as they are today," noted Vance Grant, a senior statistician for the U.S. Education Department.

Voters are starting to demand excellence in the schools, but, except in a handful of districts, such as Grossmont Union High School District near San Diego, few demand academic excellence and at the same time systematically suppress drug use and other antischolastic activities. Few districts care enough for *each child*.

We don't like kids much today. We fear them. We don't reach out to them. And in our increased selfishness and isolation, we don't give them what they need: contact, communication, truth, love, a decent education.

LACK OF INTEGRITY

The word of many Americans is no longer their bond, and the same sad fact holds true today for too many of our institutions. People and institutions who keep their word are adult. Such people take for granted the daily price of pain and inconvenience that responsibility always entails. They also work to solve problems rather than massaging them. They aim to achieve goals rather than to merely do tasks. The worker "building a cathedral" rather than "laying bricks" exemplifies this. What is the remedy for lack of integrity? The only consistent source of integrity is knowledge of the profound, sacred relationships one shares with the Creator, with the universe, and with other people.

> The crisis is far worse than anyone knows because the adults who parent their children were also abandoned and are separated from their own true inner selves.
> So the crisis is not just about how we raise our children; it's about a hundred million people who look like adults, talk and dress like adults, but are actually adult children. These adult children run our schools, our churches and our government.
>
> —John Bradshaw

But then, in the midst of all that optimism about reason [in the 1920s, with the "reasonable" writings of G. B. Shaw, A. Huxley and H. G. Wells], democracy, socialism, and the like, there appeared a work that was disturbing: Oswald Spengler's *The Decline of the West*. Other writings of uncertain import were also appearing in those happy years, from unexpected quarters: Thomas Mann's *The Magic Mountain,* James Joyce's *Ulysses,* Marcel Proust's *Remembrance of Things Past,* and T. S. Eliot's "The Waste Land." In a literary sense, those were very great years indeed. But what certain of its authors seemed to be telling us was that with all our rational triumphs and progressive political achievements, illuminating the dark quarters of the earth and so on, there was nevertheless something beginning to disintegrate at the heart of our Occidental civilization itself. And of all these warnings and pronouncements, that of Spengler was the most disquieting. For it was based on the concept of an organic pattern in the life course of a civilization, a morphology of history: the idea that every culture has its period of youth, its period of culmination, its years then of beginning to totter with age and of striving to hold itself together by means of rational planning, projects, and organization, only finally to terminate in decrepitude, petrifaction, what Spengler called "fellaheenism," and no more life. Moreover, in this view of Spengler's, we were at present on the point of passing from what he called the period of Culture to Civilization, which is to say, from our periods of youthful, spontaneous, and wonderful creativity to those of uncertainty and anxiety, contrived programs, and the beginning of the end. When he sought for analogies in the classical world, our moment today corresponded, he found, to that of the late second century B.C., the time of the Carthaginian Wars, the decline of the culture-world of Greece into Hellenism, and the rise of the military state of Rome, Caesarism, and what he termed the Second Religiousness, politics based on providing bread and circuses to the megalopolitan masses, and a general trend to violence and brutality in the arts and pastimes of the people.

Well, I can tell you, it has been for me something of a life experience to have watched the not so gradual coming into fulfillment in this world of every bit of what Spengler promised.

—Joseph Campbell (*The Power of Myth*)

SUGGESTED READING

The Hideous Strength, C. S. Lewis, McMillan, 1975. (Science fiction—disembodied intelligence defined as evil.)

Coming to Our Senses, Morris Bernan, Simon & Schuster, 1989.

American Journey: Traveling with Tocqueville in search of Democracy in America, Richard Reeves, Simon and Schuster, 1982.

The Closing of the American Mind, Allen Bloom, Simon & Schuster, 1988.

The Culture of Narcissism, Christopher Lasch, Warner Books, 1979.

Bradshaw on the Family: A Revolutionary Way of Self-Discovery, John Bradshaw, Health Comm., 1989.

Molecules of the Mind, Jon Franklin, Laurel, 1987.

Myths to Live By, Joseph Campbell, Bantam, 1972.

Wonderful Life: The Burgess Shale and the Nature of History, Stephen Jay Gould, Norton, 1989.

IV
Empowerment

18

The *Sine Qua Non:* Leadership

"Listen, man-cub," said the Bear, and his voice rumbled like thunder on a hot night. "I have taught thee all the Law of the Jungle for all the peoples of the jungle—except the Monkey Folk who live in the trees. They have no law. They are outcast. They have no speech of their own, but use the stolen words which they overhear when they listen, and peep, and wait up above in the branches. Their way is not our way. They are without leaders. They have no remembrance. They boast and chatter and pretend that they are a great people about to do great affairs in the jungle, but the falling of a nut turns their minds to laughter and all is forgotten. We of the jungle have no dealings with them."

—Rudyard Kipling, *The Jungle Book*

The leader is committed to developing a wide arsenal of skills and a keen capacity to know the uses and limitations of each. The competent leader is also ruthlessly self-reflective and honest. The "path to enlightenment consists," Buddha allowed, "of passing judgment on each thought as it flows through one's consciousness." The statesman/leader must, as Lord Chesterton observed, live the truth.

America's homeless problem today calls for its own peculiar form of leadership. Courage, vision, and the ability to create excellent teamwork are central. The capacity to communicate forcefully about homelessness as a *moral* issue is a tall strength. Homelessness presents a test of each city's capacity to recognize and analyze problems and to organize itself to confront them.

Seattle, Washington, the nation's twenty-fifth-largest city, may be the best model now available for how a great city's leadership could decide to face up to its homeless dilemma and organize itself to do something about it. Seattle's is not a well-known story, but it deserves to be.

In most American cities consistent leadership regarding adult, integrated responses to the challenge of homelessness has emanated from the so-called "social service providers," agencies both public and private, often operating more or less in concert through a United Way or other structure, many of which are church-sponsored or church-inspired. A different leadership example is presented in Seattle, where an elected, political leader appeared who was popular enough, clear-seeing enough, and courageous enough to orchestrate his community's advantages while reaching out, step by step, for new resources. Seattle thereby successfully rode out the "Reagan storm" that tattered the existing safety net of social services everywhere else, halting new, low-income housing construction and catapulting hundreds of thousands of Americans onto the streets.

Mayor Charles T. Royer had remarkable local advantages on which to build. Foremost among these was a vigorous local economy that remained unblemished by the pockets of ill health common to so many other locales in the 1980s. The economy was anchored by a great port (second only to New York's), a healthy fishing industry, high-technology biomedical and computer industries, and a gigantic aerospace industry (Boeing, alone, boasts an $80-billion work backlog) The city has a well-educated populace and a "deep bench" of intelligent leaders from the top levels down to the neighborhood PTAs, and it has nurtured its sense of commitment and teamwork. This is easier to do within a buoyant economy.

Royer was elected mayor in 1977, served Seattle twelve years, and then moved to Boston, where he now heads the Harvard Institute of Politics, part of Harvard's Kennedy School of Government. He is preparing the "next generation." When Royer came aboard, Seattle was doing little in the way of human services. County government presided over troubled mental health and jail systems. Royer told his staff he was determined to wage a guerrilla war to get human services delivery" back into the public mainstream." He sent the city after the Nixon-era community block grant federal monies in a big way, and in 1984 (by a five-to-four vote) the City Council augmented those funds with $500,000 of city money, which grew to $7.2 million by 1989.

Seattle's 1984 Task Force on Street People and the Homeless embodied Royer's strategy as the "new homeless" began to arrive. He put in one room leaders of the community representing the two major viewpoints on the homeless—that they were "homeless" (and thus a group of needy humans to be helped), and that they were "street people" (and thus a shiftless crew of generally undeserving ne'er-do-wells harming the business climate). Seattle's civilized instincts prevailed and these diverse leaders hammered out plan after plan together, in the context of an initial three agreed goals: 1) to build a consensus on the nature of a problem and its practical solutions; 2) to obtain the resources to solve the problem; and 3) to coordinate implementation of the solution.

The city government functioned as a focal point for the layers of networks, lubricating their interaction with funds and assistance—most strategically, grant preparation help for state and federal funding requests. In 1981, when it became clear that a key Reagan agenda item was to gut the half-century-old, federal low-cost housing construction efforts, the city went to the ballot and gained 76-percent voter approval for a $50-million bond issue, the first in U.S. history initiated by a local government for low-cost housing. A thousand units were planned, but it turned out that the bond monies could enable construction of a great many more, so four hundred units with particularly low rents were added to the project: a two-hundred-unit, downtown SRO (half elderly, half mentally ill, with federal rent support), and the rest for frail elderly and elderly American Indians.

As homelessness increased and became a major issue in Seattle, the city went to the voters again in 1985, and it was again resoundingly successful. Sixty percent approved another $50-million bond issue, this time for low-income housing for families with children. These units are now being built. Additional low-income housing will be built with contributions from a "height bonus" system in which developers earn the right to construct higher buildings by paying into a fund earmarked for the construction of low-income housing. A reluctant partner at first, business has become more and more enthusiastic about playing a role in reducing homelessness. Small business leaders, fully involved from the beginning, are now the ones bringing the biggest businesses and business leaders on board, along with their added clout.

During the twelve years Royer was mayor:

- A total of $220 million in public funds has been spent on low-income housing and other services aimed at responsibly meeting the challenges of homelessness.
- Seattle doubled its public housing stock from nine thousand units to eighteen thousand units.
- City funding of human services began in 1985 and now amounts to $7.2 million annually, including $4.8 million in community block grant funds (on which the federal government has now placed a limit). We have here made much of the strength of Seattle's local economy, but a remarkable irony is that, for every dollar paid in taxes to state, federal, or local government by the citizens of Seattle, only seven cents stays with Seattle's city government.
- With its intact, functioning leadership and service networks, Seattle was ready when the McKinney Act federal funds came on line, and its veteran grant writers pieced together dozens of plans that made sense. Seattle made off with a tenth of all the monies available to the entire nation in the act's first year.

The Seattle example stands as a monument to the courage, civility, and commitment of a group of city leaders, in a city bursting with leadership and civility. In April 1990 Mayor Norman B. Wright accepted the Public Sector Achievement Award of the National Alliance to End Homelessness on behalf of the city. Seattle's example shows what can be accomplished as problems and opportunities are spotted early and faced up to unblinkingly by able problem-solvers. It proves that homelessness can be responsibly addressed and solved. Visitors to Seattle invariably remark on that port city's loveliness and on its warmth and civility. Increasingly, they also notice that the city's streets are not crowded with the homeless.

LEADERSHIP SHOULD NOT EMANATE FROM THE MAYOR'S OFFICE ALONE

> It is the function of the citizen to keep the government from falling into error.
>
> —U.S. Supreme Court Justice Robert Jackson

Two years ago, a wonderful, thoughtful San Diego leader died of cancer. She was not an elected official or a corporate or foundation mogul. Instead, she was simply a staff employee of the Chamber of Commerce. Dot Migdal staffed the key local government section of the chamber for over a decade and was renowned for her clear-mindedness, her personal courage, her caring for people, and her commitment to problem-solving, to leadership, and to truth. Two weeks before she passed on, Midgal gave an interview to Gary Shaw, a reporter for the local legal and business newspaper, the *San Diego Daily Transcript*. These are some of the things she had to say:

Suburban Leadership

What we have now are career politicians and it just puts a different spin on everything. They aren't community people who come in and try to look at governmental oversight. They don't have their businesses they run every day to bring some reality to what they're doing. Their full job is being a politician and it brings a different perspective. When they don't have an outside job they don't have anything else.

Loss of Philosophy

It's also single-issue politics. Everyone wants what they want. You don't have any political philosophy there. There's no predictability, consistent in their behavior. It doesn't necessarily mean they're bad, but they're trying to respond to everybody and they spend a lot of time working out compromises or consensus so nobody will dislike them. So there are no leaders. The public will turn them out of office if they don't act this way. If their goal is to stay in office, they don't have long-term goals for the community. They have short-term goals to stay in office. The business community pretty much gave up its role in leadership when Pete Wilson came in and took charge. There's very little business leadership in this town. There's very little courage in this town. Nobody wants to stand up and put his head above the crowd. Everyone wants something from government, but no one wants to hurt anyone's feelings by speaking up.

Remembering Courage

There was a time when I felt that when we took good government issues up at the chamber, that I could always get the support of the business community. They were very brave and courageous on things we stuck our necks out on. But I find more and more that people become more reluctant to stand up and be counted because of retaliation. Everybody wants a contract or they want to go to the right parties. They aren't big things that they want, but they want to be on the inside. In that respect, we're still such a small town. It makes the town nice, but it's not providing the leadership that's needed. People aren't rewarded for being courageous anymore. You're left off of the social list or advisory committee list or what have you. The press doesn't help. The media covers things in a pretty shallow fashion.

In every great city there is a cadre of people, a dozen or two, no more. They're intelligent, very intelligent, and they care, they care about their city. These men and women achieve no recognition, this is the only thing they don't care about. The recognition is being at the seat of power, and the self-satisfaction in helping move the city forward. They create the vision for us to strive toward. Some are more effective than others, to be sure. And some are more charismatic than others. But all have one thing in common—uncompromising integrity. These are the people we should honor. These are the people who deserve our plaudits, these unsung, quiet but strong leaders. It is to them we should erect statues.

A CULTURAL PRODUCT

The leadership shouldn't just come from the mayor's office. It makes it a lot easier when you have that. But if you don't have a community that really cares, other than for their own canyon or their own particular project, there is really no incentive for politicians to behave any differently. That is why I am reluctant to overly criticize a particular mayor or anyone else for not showing leadership. Leadership isn't rewarded much in this country. America now does have has a cadre of leaders with respect to the homeless, but, for the most part, they remain little known. They ought to be identified, city by city, thanked, and acknowledged as the important municipal assets, heroes, and heroines that they in fact are. People should get their mayors to establish monthly awards programs to publicly recognize the "Heroine/ Hero for the Homeless for the Month," with appropriate fanfare.

A few national figures who have helped focus America on its dilemma with the homeless come to mind in this respect.

The late Mitch Snyder first riveted the nation's attention on the homeless, in the nation's capital, labeling the issue always as a *moral* one and putting himself on the line, time after time, Ghandi-like, with lengthy and purposeful fasts. His passion for justice was undeniable.

A lawyer associated with the National Coalition for the Homeless shares Snyder's passion for justice. In 1983, Harvard-educated Bob Hayes squeezed in a *pro bono* ("for free," taken on for the good of justice and the community) case into his upscale securities law practice. With that case he made history. The city of New York, in settling the case, acknowledged the legal right of homeless New Yorkers to housing. Almost incidentally, Hayes founded the National Coalition for the Homeless, now a growing force with emphasis on legal advocacy and information sharing.

Simultaneously with Hayes's early work in New York, another skillful professional was at work in Los Angeles. The Los Angeles Legal Aid Foundation's Gary Blazi was piecing together the hardest-hitting legal team of homeless litigators in the nation. The "Los Angeles Homeless Litigation Team" needed added force because of the vastness of the Los Angeles problem, with its estimated fifty thousand homeless in eleven discrete concentrations countywide (see the appendix on legal rights of the homeless.) Early on the team consisted of attorneys from seven public interest law firms with help from innumerable volunteer attorneys and a few large law firms. Blazi has been the pioneer of the use of such complex legal teams on behalf of the homeless, and of thinking strategically on behalf of a region's homeless. He now chairs the National Coalition for the Homeless.

These three men, to me, exemplify the quality in intellect, passion, and stamina required in the national moral effort to right the wrong of American homelessness. I salute them each, and thank them for what they have done, including Hayes and Blazi for help with this book.

LEADERSHIP BY A FOUNDATION

The Robert Wood Johnson Foundation of Princeton, New Jersey, has stalked American homelessness doggedly since 1983. Its systematic health-related grants have been responsible for much of the good research that is known about homelessness. From it has developed consensus on many types of "model homeless programs." Many who know have reflected that the Mc-Kinney Act itself—cornerstone of Federal government's involvement—would not exist, without the foundation's brilliant work.

A $3.5 billion entity, the Robert Wood Johnson Foundation is one of the largest of American foundations focused on health care. Its namesake was one of the founding "Johnsons" of Johnson & Johnson Co. (yes, Band-Aids!). He directed that its efforts be catalytic and leveraged, that they "change systems" for the better and with as much permanence as is rational, and that this be done by creating excellent models and gathering and publishing top-of-the-line research. Its directors are leading doctors, and, at any given moment, the range of its existing grant programs tends to inform its officials as to medical frontiers.

Thus, in 1983, Robert Wood Johnson launched the first of three major grant "initiatives" (its term) relative to the health dilemmas posed by America's homeless. The initial grants funded health programs for the homeless in nine cities, each of which received about $5 million, under the heading of "the Homeless Health Care Project," for four years. The grants were structured to create or strengthen local coalitions, institutionalized cooperation, and programs appropriate to the scale of needs.

These grants gave birth to the Stuart B. McKinney Act, which now makes $100 million available annually for homeless programs, nationwide.

The second Robert Wood Johnson initiative was much more ambitious, aiming at positive, nationwide changes for good in America's sagging state mental health systems. In 1985, nineteen cities received these grants, to extend over three years. To be selected, cities had to agree to make major changes and to commit themselves to *results*. Many did not, therefore, apply.

The third Robert Wood Johnson initiative relates to homeless families, the fastest growing and most portentious subgroup of the homeless. The resulting studies and models are expected to be definitive.

Dr. Rodger Farr says that the Robert Wood Johnson Foundation, aiming explicitly at system changes, was boldly doing what the federal and state government ought to have been doing. At the time, he says, "It was about as popular as poison ivy."

But it worked.

It created—and is continuing to create—the necessary, credible and elegant models.

It provided the cradle of the historic Stewart B. McKinney Act initiatives, and such actions are continuing to "spin off" of its solid work.

Relative to America's homeless, Mr. Johnson, the foundation you laid is far more significant than a Band-Aid!

QUOTATIONS

A true leader always keeps an element of surprise up his sleeve, what others cannot grasp but which keeps his public excited and breathless.

—Charles de Gaulle

Go into emptiness, strike voids, bypass what he defends, hit him where he does not expect you.

—Ts'ao Ts'ao (A.D. 155–220)

Never shake your fist and then shake your finger.

—Theodore Roosevelt

Be nice, feel guilty, and play safe. If there was ever a prescription for producing a dismal future, that has to be it.

—Walter B. Wriston

The very essence of leadership is [that] you have to have a vision. It's got to be a vision you articulate clearly and forcefully on every occasion. You can't blow an uncertain trumpet.

—Theodore Hesburgh

As a general marches at the head of his troops, so ought wise politicians . . . to march at the head of affairs. . . . They ought not to await the event, to know what measures to take, but the measures which they have taken ought to produce the event.

—Demosthenes

No Captain can do wrong if he places his ship alongside that of the enemy.

—Admiral Horatio Nelson

In all debates, let Truth be thy Aim, not Victory, or an unjust interest: And endeavor to gain, rather than to expose the Antagonist.

—William Penn

Yield to a man's tastes and he will yield to your interests.

—Edward Bulwer-Lytton

So nigh is grandure to our dust, so near is God to man, when duty whispers low, "thou must," the youth replies, "I can!"

—Ralph Waldo Emerson

Never doubt that a small group of thoughtful, committed citizens can change the world. Indeed, it's the only thing that ever has.

—Margaret Mead

There is no good reason why we should fear the future, but there is every reason why we should face it seriously, neither hiding from ourselves the gravity of the problems before us nor fearing to approach these problems with the unbending, unflinching purpose to solve them aright.

—Theodore Roosevelt (Inaugural Address, March 4, 1905)

Where there is no vision, the people perish.

—Proverbs 29:18

It is not the critic who counts, not the man who points out how the strong man stumbled or where the doer of deeds could have done them better. The credit belongs to the man who is actually in the arena; whose face is marred by dust and sweat and blood; who strives valiantly; who errs and comes short again and again; who knows the great enthusiasms, the great devotions, and spends himself in a worthy cause; who, at the best, knows the triumph of high achievement; and who, at the worst, if he fails, at least fails while daring greatly, so that his place shall never be with those cold and timid souls who know neither victory nor defeat.

—Theodore Roosevelt

There are men, who, by their sympathetic attractions, carry nations with them, and lead the activity of the human race.

—Ralph Waldo Emerson (1860)

The final test of a leader is that he leaves behind him in other men the conviction and the will to carry on.

New York Herald Tribune on the death of FDR

A leader is a dealer in hope.

—Napoleon I, *Maxims* (1804–15)

A decision is the action an executive must take when he has information so incomplete that the answer does not suggest itself.

—Arthur William Radford

> And find
> What wind
> Serves to advance an honest mind.

—John Donne

> So came the Captain with the mighty heart;
> And when the judgment thunders split the house,
> Wrenching the rafters from their ancient rest,
> He held the ridgepole up, and spikt again
> The rafters of the Home. He held his place—
> Held the long purpose like a growing tree—
> Held on through blame and faltered not at praise.

And when he fell in whirlwind, he went down
As when a lordly cedar, green with boughs,
Goes down with a great shout upon the hills,
And leaves a lonesome place against the sky.
                                —Edwin Markham, *Lincoln*

SUGGESTED READING

"City of Seattle Homeless Priority Agenda," Seattle Human Services Strategic Planning
     Office, 1989.

19

Ethics

Ethics, too, are nothing but reverence for life. That is what gives me the
fundamental principle of morality, namely, that good consists in maintaining,
promoting, and enhancing life, and that destroying, injuring, and limiting
life are evil.

—Albert Schweitzer, *The Philosophy of Civilization*

Ethics is important because ethical ideas have power. Historically, this has
been peculiarly true in America, and although the grip of ethical thought
may have loosened recently in the lives of Americans, ethical considerations
remain powerful potential motivators. Ethical concepts help fill the quiver
of arguments available to those who find themselves thrust into the role
of recruiter or motivator relative to solving homelessness. Although anyone
can fit the role, it fits a mayor, member of Congress, city manager, public
health director, United Way or Chamber of Commerce official, or church
leader. A concerned person with no particular title can also play an important
role in the struggle, of course. We can each write our leaders embark on
speaking campaigns, and make suggestions. The constitutional right to petition
the government (or almost anybody else) still stands tall.

While it is true generally that Eastern ethical traditions emphasize
acceptance of life as it is much more than Western traditions (for example,
"yin and yang" versus "right and wrong"), Greek philosophy and the Judeo-
Christian tradition also emphasize acceptance and realism. Both Eastern and
Western thought have been strongly ethical in context.

"Why help the homeless?" can be answered with, "Why *not* help the
homeless?" This is especially true because there are so many reasons to do
so, ranging from the humanitarian to the purely practical, such as the state
of public health, the functioning of streets and parks, good business conditions,
and aesthetic values. Most convincingly to me, we need to set an example
to our children. As an educational opportunity for us, America's homeless
afford the chance to reveal to our children that they belong to a responsible,

capable—and, most importantly, *competent*—species.

Almost uniquely among the traditions of the planet, those of the Western world, from apparent origins in the Mosaic Laws and in Greek thought, have exhibited a preoccupation with "right action." Called ethics, this preoccupation has largely consisted of a sincere effort to be thoughtful, aware, and responsible in one's life. It has also sometimes looked like a nervous glance over a determinedly sinful society's shoulder—at what it felt it ought to be doing (or have been doing), as opposed to its actual behavior. Ethics has also been described as the thought processes by which the alienation from nature and the natural (paleolithic) state of mankind (and of its nervous system, which was "designed" for such a life) might be thought through, and mankind led back, perhaps through action, to the oneness or resolution toward which all religions and philosophies aim.

For America, ethical considerations have been a big factor from the earliest colonization. The story of the ethical debates in Spain occasioned by Cortez's fabulous return—with Indians, galleons full of stolen gold and promises of more—makes instructive reading. The lead advocate of the winning side of these debates, a priest named Juan Gins de Sepulveda, skillfully pieced together an ethic of plunder, conjoining Aristotle's concept of "natural slave classes" with St. Thomas Aquinas's idea of a "just war" (to expand Christendom, which concept may have been adopted from the very aggressive Islam). The same ethical patterns were used to rationalize English- and French-speaking modes of getting and exercising domination over other continents and their inhabitants. The point is not that ethics can be misused. The point is that ethics must be used in order to win any argument. While nihilism, or denial of the relevancy and power of ethics, may be on the rise, in America ethics has always been a powerful, necessary prelude to action. Among our decision-makers and leaders, at least a semblance of ethical justification is necessary for all actions and policies.

Building on the thinking of Locke, Mill, and Jefferson, our pluralistic society has encouraged and required free speech and debate. Up through the time of Martin Luther King, moral and ethical concerns have been common fare in consideration of public issues. This history has admittedly dimmed in the 1980s, with the advent of the political action committees, "sound bite" television politics, and the loosening of community ties. There has been a corresponding increase in raw lunging for power, but even here the weapons used by the opposition have largely been ethical arguments, appeals to "right." Ultimate success has often consisted, quite simply, of turning the debate into an ethical discussion of what is right (as opposed to who should win). This, then, is the prime assignment for those concerned with America's expanding armies of homeless: how to turn general discussion about homelessness into talk about it as a moral issue.

Why help the homeless? The most obvious reasons involve self-interest. Perhaps it is part of one's job to provide benefits, to create or sponsor social programs, to solve problems relating to homelessness. One might be motivated by concern over the public health problems that will inevitably result from growing populations of sick, homeless people packed into areas of already high density. One might be motivated by concern for the health of one's city's downtown business climate. Other concerns might include the potential harm to citizens of the community or to one's family at the hands of someone driven to desperation, the loss of easy use of parks and other public areas because they have been "taken over" by homeless people, the loss to society of the economic contribution that could be made by the homeless, and the general psychological damage done by a decline in the quality of the social environment. One might be motivated by genuine and deep feelings of compassion and charity ("It feels good to help"). Some might be seeking the appearance of charity for promotional purposes or to impress others.

What is it that causes some individuals and groups to feel a greater obligation to their fellow human beings and to the world as a whole? Since human beings have begun reflecting upon their own behavior and that of their social institutions, there have been many attempts to explain why people act altruistically, apparently counter to immediate self-interest, and also to explain the basis for the proliferation of moral codes that are so ingrained in human cultures. This is the study called ethics.

The difference between a committed and a complacent person can be traced to that person's degree of aliveness, and also to the existence, nature, and origins of the individual (or his or her group's) ethical philosophy. This philosophy will come from the group's history and social perspective. Ethical philosophies are often based upon a particular cosmology or worldview. Thus, a person whose job it is to motivate people to work for homeless people cannot fully grasp the nature of the problem without some under-standing of the ethical philosophies already in place within the individual or collective minds of those solicited for aid. For example, one would want to think carefully before basing one's appeal solely on the New Testament when addressing people who are not Christians. A knowledge of the context in which a quotation from it would be received would be indispensable. Since a group's individuals often behave inconsistently with the group's offi-cial ethical line, it is obviously not enough merely to quote such a line back to people. An appeal must be made to those sensibilities that are genuine motivators. Trial and error, and sensitivity, cannot be avoided. As an added dimension of complexity in our modern society, there are an ever-increasing number of sources of ethical codes or guidelines, some of which overlap. Languages represent viewpoints and, as a symptom of the strains on our American "melting pot," the Los Angeles Police Department now has translator capacity in ninety-two languages.

The traditional religions, of course, provide ethical codes. Each school of philosophy develops its own ethical approach. Political party platforms have ethical underpinnings. The learned professions regulate themselves with ethical codes. Some businesses develop "corporate cultures" that include elements of ethical philosophy. There is also the plethora of service organizations, volunteer groups, youth groups, and clubs. Finally, there are grassroots sources of ethical attitudes, such as folk wisdom and street etiquette. Some of these ethical sources conflict or contradict one another, or simply represent alternative approaches and points of view. Some are internally inconsistent. Some are proud of their inconsistency.

Unfortunately, there also seem to be increasing numbers in our society at all levels who are deprived of the most basic ethical values, who have replaced the Golden Rule with the law of the jungle, either through the absence of exposure to any coherent ethical system or through a somewhat conscious rejection of ethics. There is an intensifying perception on the part of the public that those in positions of American leadership and authority share this ethical vacuum. Advocacy on behalf of the homeless necessarily involves the task of awakening many people's sensitivity to ethical issues both in their lives and in the world around them.

BIOLOGICAL ORIGINS OF ETHICS

Biologists have identified two forms of altruistic behavior in nonhuman species that are readily recognizable as rudimentary possible bases for much of human ethical thought. The first is kinship altruism. Many species of animals act in ways apparently counter to self-interest, in order to protect or advance members of the family or group. Social animals have an inherent need for cooperative behavior patterns, and one way of achieving cooperation has been through developing a capacity to recognize and be concerned with the welfare of the closest genetic relatives. The closer the relationship, genetically, the greater the concern. The more refined the animal's apparatus of intuition and communication, the more forceful are these demands. An example of this type of behavior is the protection adult birds or mammals will provide offspring against dangerous predators, often using themselves as decoys. The nervous systems of human beings contain vast areas of "altruistic wiring." We love naturally. Some say we are "made of love, but tend to forget."

Moral duty is derived from kinship in every human society. One hardly needs to mention the obligation of parent to child, of provider to dependent, as well as traditional obligations of obedience and respect for parents and for the elderly generally. Much of human history can be viewed as an expansion of the boundaries defining those within the kinship group. Family loyalties develop into tribal and clan loyalties, ultimately evolving into nationalism. Biologically, mankind is, as we know, a single unit, a species.

The challenge for an advocate for the homeless is to present the homeless as people decidedly inside these boundaries, *inside* the group, deserving of concern and assistance as coequal members of the community, nation, or family of humanity.

Reciprocity is the other identified form of nonhuman altruistic behavior known to biologists. There are many examples of animals who act selflessly, in exchange for similar treatment. Monkeys take turns grooming each other. This behavior also arises out of the need for cooperation, and notions that cheating at a bargain is morally wrong would seem to have their origins in the development of reciprocal forms of altruistic behavior. The roots of this are, of course, deep in "the wiring," the nervous system.

Although many today may see the homeless as completely devoid of resources, and thus hardly candidates for mutually beneficial relationship's with them, there are many direct reciprocal benefits from assisting the homeless and reclaiming them as social insiders. The abilities of all human beings to contribute to social and economic achievement are in fact incalculable.

ETHICS FROM RELIGIONS

"Virtually every human society has some form of myth to explain the origin of morality," says the *Encyclopaedia Britannica* in its discussion of ethics. In the Jewish account, God gave Moses the Ten Commandments, a moral code fundamental to Western society. Its contents are primarily prohibitive in nature, rather than creating an affirmative duty of benevolence toward others. Nonetheless, charitable acts are considered part of a good life in Jewish ethical and moral philosophy and tradition. In the Talmud, the section on the teachings of the rabbis begins with a passage called, simply, "Benevolence."[65] Charity is viewed as a species of benevolence, but inherently inferior because it can only be practiced toward the poor, and the poor are deprived of practicing it themselves, whereas "benevolence" can be shown toward all people (true reciprocity?).

Christianity takes on so many forms, and is such a complex subject, being the dominant religion in the Western world for many centuries, that an entire chapter is devoted to it elsewhere in this book. However, central to all of Christianity is the belief in the divinity of Jesus of Nazareth, and his role both as savior and teacher. Some of the most profound and broadly sweeping ethical propositions ever to have been set into language are found in Jesus' teachings, as contained in the New Testament. In Mark 12:30–31, Jesus proclaims,

> And thou shalt love the Lord thy God with all thy heart, and with all
> thy soul, and with all thy mind, and with all thy strength: this is the first
> commandment. And the second is like, namely this. Thou shalt love thy
> neighbor as thyself. There is none other commandment greater than these.

And in John 2:9–10, Jesus declares,

> He that saith he is in the light, and hateth his brother, is in darkness even
> until now. He that loveth his brother abideth in the light, and there is
> none occasion of stumbling in him.

Charity is the supreme ethical imperative of Christianity.[66] Christians
are urged, without haughty judgments, to serve individual people and humanity
selflessly, as symbolized by Jesus' washing the feet of his disciples, and by
the parable of the Good Samaritan. Jimmy Carter once declared that, "We
should live our lives as though Christ was coming this afternoon." How
is it that people calling themselves Christians can sleep in houses with empty
rooms while their fellow human beings, their *neighbors*, are sleeping on streets
or in dumpsters? Christian charity insists on personal involvement.

The central figure of Islam, the prophet Mohammed, was born in Mecca
around the year 570. About 610 he had a vision of a being, later identified
as the angel Gabriel, and he heard a voice saying to him "You are the
messenger of God." Thereafter, until his death, Mohammed received frequent
revelations, which he and his followers believed came directly from God.
He never heard a voice during the revelations, but rather found a message
in his "heart." It is the collection of these messages that make up the Koran,
the sacred writings of Islam. At the time of Mohammed Mecca was a rich
trading city, and wealth was for the most part in the hands of a few merchants.
Traditional tribal order was breaking down, and these merchants were viewed
by Mohammed as ignoring their responsibilities to the less fortunate. These
duties have traditionally been viewed as tribal obligations, but under Mohammed's new preaching such duties became divine edicts. The Koran opens
by declaring the goodness and power of God, demonstrated by the wonders
of nature and by the prosperity that was being experienced in Mecca at
the time. The Meccans are called upon to be grateful. Such gratitude is
to be expressed through worship and generosity. It is emphasized that on
the Last Day, humanity will be judged by its deeds, and individuals will
be sent either to heaven or hell.

When a Westerner thinks of Eastern religion and philosophy, the tendency
is to imagine the mystic, monk, or ascetic who has renounced all involvement
with the world, sitting passively and meditating, seeking inner harmony and
higher consciousness, but ignoring the strife and suffering of ordinary people.

This image is entirely too limited in scope, and it ignores much of the cosmology of Eastern thought, in which all existence is interconnected and immutable, giving rise to philosophies grounded in an immense respect for all of creation. The Hindu, for example, will not eat meat out of respect for all life. Certainly human beings are part of all life and all creation and are to be accorded the same respect. Eastern thought deemphasizes ego, and emphasizes openness to and acceptance of things as they are. Its views can therefore yield an unprejudiced assessment of reality that can produce great power when conjoined with a passion for problem-solving.

To lie is unethical. To distort the truth is unethical. With a greater commitment to realism, Americans would be seeing the homeless without distortions. Indeed, many would be actually seeing the homeless for the first time. According to Lao Tsu,

> Carrying body and soul and embracing the one,
> Can you avoid separation?
> Attending fully and becoming supple,
> Can you be as a newborn babe?
> Washing and cleansing the primal vision,
> Can you be without stain?
> Loving all men and ruling the country,
> Can you be without cleverness?
> Can you play the role of woman?
> Understanding and being open to all things,
> Are you able to do nothing?
> Giving birth and nourishing,
> Bearing yet not possessing,
> Working yet not taking credit,
> Leading yet not dominating,
> This is the Primal Virtue.[67]

Perhaps the most socially conscious Eastern thought is found in the teachings of Confucius. In summary,

Everything he wrote, taught, and practiced was aimed at restoring the loving, respectful stability of the family pattern. As a historian, he wrote to show the proper family relations of the dynasty. . . . As a teacher of ethics he taught men to look into their hearts and find there, before the pulls of self-interest had distorted it, the basic will to be good, and to be just and kind to others. He found this goodness operating naturally in the family, and again showed how it could be carried up into the relations of friends, towns and empire. For, having looked into his heart to find the good path, the follower of Confucius, as a son, a brother, a friend, a governor, a lord or a king, would then be governed by the rules of propriety or (to give a less narrow translation) of "right conduct." The rules of right conduct advocated by Confucius were not mere arbitrary social conventions but that good pattern of manners and ritual that grew out of and were designed to maintain the loving, respectful balance of the family and super-family system.[68]

ETHICS FROM PHILOSOPHY

Since philosophers, unlike prophets and religious leaders, do not have faithful followers down through the centuries, modern ethical thought from the study of philosophy, although based on centuries of work from predecessors, can best be exemplified by modern philosophers. It was the German philosopher Immanuel Kant who, in the Western world at least (excepting Moses and Jesus), first proposed the idea that actions possess moral worth only when duty is done for its own sake. He distinguished between "hypothetical" imperatives, which can be ignored when an individual rejects their underlying hypotheses, and "categorical" imperatives, which must be followed regardless of the individual's feelings or wants. Morality, Kant insisted, was the totality of categorical imperatives. Kant also figured that we must be prepared to apply any such imperatives universally. Kant's Categorical Imperative was, "So act, that you would be willing that the principles upon which you act should be universalized." What is right for one must be right for all.

Kant's Categorical Imperative has much going for it. It is easy to remember. It makes sense, at least superficially. And it is useful. But it can get one into trouble. Applying a rule universally can be dangerous for anyone who does not have a universal understanding of the facts, of cause and effect, of the outcome of our acts. No one does have all those things. The Categorical Imperative is just about as useful as is the opinion that the Earth is flat. For most situations, it works well, but, if one were to use it all the time, ruthlessly, one would get into deep trouble. For one thing, it lacks compassion. For another, it presumes one has all the facts before action begins. In actual practice, one must adjust plans when one meets the unexpected. A more pragmatic, heuristic approach is necessary when dealing with a complex issue like homelessness.

Jeremy Bentham was perhaps the first philosopher to confront urban homelessness in England at the beginning of the Industrial Age. This led him to found a school of philosophy known as utilitarianism, an attempt to work backwards, philosophically, from a desired result. Bentham figured that human beings are driven by pleasure and pain, and he concluded that anything that decreases the total aggregate of human pain and increases the total aggregate of human pleasure must be good. In addition to having been "only the most influential English philosopher" (as a philosophy professor once archly told me) Bentham was a philosopher who did things in the real world. He spearheaded the movement that lead to the first social welfare laws in England in the early nineteenth century. Observing the hardships of the working class occasioned by the Industrial Revolution, he conceived the then-novel notion that a "moral" government must account for the welfare of its citizens. That some wealth might be passed from the rich to the poor through the government—particularly to enhance public health, safety, and education—made sense in the context of his utilitarian ethic. Today there are few nations that do not recognize that as a basic objective of government. St. Augustine, earlier, declared that, "Any government, the purpose of which is other than Justice, is but a robber band, enlarged."

Bentham and his followers represent the classic communitarian values of modern Anglo-American liberal philosophies. Other modern philosophies have taken a different tack. European continental philosophies have paid great attention to the alienation of the modern individual, giving rise to existentialist philosophies that embrace subjectivism and relativism. The thinking of some of these, like Nietzsche and Heidegger, have been used, and misused, by totalitarian political movements. But more recent continental philosophers, such as Jürgen Habermas and several philosophical psychologists and sociologists, including the critical studies movement, have sparked a renewed interest in the fate and suffering of the common man. They disdain the view that power and wealth somehow indicate ethical propriety. In fact, they find most political systems, which help maintain wealth and power in the hands of the few, to be unwittingly unethical.

Subjectivism is the theory that individual conscience is the only valid standard of moral judgment. Subjectivism can lead to tolerance and to the ultimate political manifestation of that viewpoint, democracy and constitutionalism. The free choice implicit in subjectivism can be made to work politically only within a constitutional framework. Subjectivism also embraces and exalts the individual. In a caste, class, or other hierarchical system thought to be part of the natural order, members at higher levels have little incentive to lend aid to the less fortunate who find themselves within the lower strata. However, the view holding that each person's moral choices have equal validity is necessarily grounded in the notion that all human beings are of equal worth.

SCIENCE AND BEYOND

According to Hume, science can never lead us to a positive determination of normative ethical principles, since science has traditionally confined itself to a description of what is, and avoids any speculation regarding what ought to be. Yet science has the potential of bringing together much of the disparate cosmologies of the peoples of the world because of the objectively verifiable nature of the scientific method. Modern archeological and paleoanthropological evidence is fleshing out the details of the conclusion that all human beings share a common origin.[69] Perhaps general acceptance of the uncontrovertible evidence of our common origin will help enlarge our definitions of kinship to include all of humanity, strengthening our biologically driven ethical imperative to alleviate the suffering of our brother and sister humans.

APPLICABLE ETHICS AND
SERVICE CLUB PHILOSOPHIES

While the ethical thinking of European philosophers, from the Enlightenment to Bertrand Russell and Ludwig Wittgenstein, has been of interest to American intellectuals, it has not retained much influence, if any at all, in modern America. Before the advent of television, in fact, the prime sources of American ethical thought remained the Bible, the dependable "moral" endings of each section of McGuffy's readers (which were used by essentially all of the nation's school children for decades), and, above all, the moral examples being lived by parents and grandparents, the great majority of whom were rural people (and, therefore, presumably more grounded in the physical basis of reality). Sports, especially baseball, which Reinhold Niebuhr once declared to have had more spiritual influence over Americans "than all the churches combined," with its emphasis on individual virtuosity serving the team, hustle (giving one's all), fair play, and honoring one's opponent. There are still "basics" as sources of morality in America, even though there has been a rise in narcissism, individualism (sometimes bordering on anarchism), and nihilism, since World War II. The ethical themes that retain the most power today—and to which the wise mobilizer of power will turn, continue to be those of:

1. Fairness to all. ("Fair's fair.")
2. Concern for the health of the community, of its neighborhoods and families.
3. Concern for the future, and how we leave it to our children and their children.
4. Concern for perceived self-interest; good management planning; professionalism and prudence. ("Is inaction stupid?")
5. Fear, or anticipated fear.
6. Concern for the cost of proposed actions, or of inaction.

7. Striving for a better life for our children than we have had.
8. This is crucial: the thought (particularly when held by those with power or wealth) that a personal debt is owed the community that can never be fully repaid, partly for what one has been so fortunate to have received, partly on the theory that all life is held in trust ("From those unto whom much is given, much will be required.")

Today in America there are several generally understood and respected principles. These include:

1. The Ten Commandments and, to a much lesser extent, some of the general concepts of the Mosaic laws.
2. Jesus' second law: "Love thy neighbor as thyself."
3. Cause follows effect, and ethical right action begets right actions in others. Some say it quaintly as, "What goes around comes around."
4. "Stewardship"—the relation of an ethical person to everything over which he or she has authority.
5. Being humane is deeply etched in the American character. "He ain't heavy, he's my brother."
6. Americans consider themselves a sort of modern "chosen people." They can and do solve problems, and it is their duty to be a shining example to the world.

These themes, together with the Golden Rule and a generous sense of the general reciprocity of life and of assisting others and one's community, are far more powerful moral reference points than all the technical philosophy in the world. These are what the mobilizer on behalf of the homeless needs to master, and to use. These ethical thoughts have found form in a number of well-known mottos, such as the Boy Scouts' "Do a good deed daily," "Leave it better than you found it," and "Be prepared," and "A Scout is trustworthy, loyal, helpful, friendly, courteous, kind, obedient, cheerful, thrifty, brave, clean, and reverent" (the Scout Law).

Service clubs abound, and they all express and embody moral creeds. A few are:

- *Rotary.* Motto: "Service above self." Rotary Four-Way Test: "Is it the truth? Is it fair to all concerned? Will it build goodwill and better friendship? Will it be beneficial to all concerned?"
- *Kiwanis.* Motto: "Serving the world. Achieve by believing." Six Permanent Objects include: "To give primacy to the human and spiritual, rather than to the material values in life."
- *Lions.* Motto: "We serve." Aims: "To create understanding and pro-

mote principles of social welfare of the community and to provide a forum for mutual understanding."

To be effective motivators we have to care genuinely about the people we are attempting to influence. It was said of Theodore Roosevelt that the more different someone was from him, the more interested in that person he became. Leaders must care with a deep passion to learn about the people around them, about their inevitably fascinating cultural backgrounds, social positions and perspectives, political views, and aesthetic tastes. To be an effective leader one must learn, responsibly, to touch people at their deepest moral cores, perhaps deeper than they (or we) have ever before had occasion to delve. No one gets to that point without presenting themselves openly, honestly, with love.[70]

A simple ethic is that people ought to have a continuous state of truthfulness between each other (a condition without which paleolithic tribal members could not long survive, occupied as they were with the high teamwork of the Great Hunt and pitted against the surrounding elements). The second "at bottom" element I believe we owe each other is *acknowledgment* of each other. It helps if this is in a context of acknowledging our common humanity, our relatedness. I believe that there can be no ethics without these.

Ethical considerations are important because ethical ideas have power. The would-be recruiters to causes aiding the homeless must *live* a powerfully compelling ethic, or they court failure. Even so, life is inexorable and coercive. It rushes at us, demanding correct action before we have figured it all out. Humans are a familial and tribal species and as the veil lifts, slowly, from the mysteries of our ancient origins and our biology, what is being discovered on all sides is what we already know: we are one. What is being discovered is that we humans care, utterly. And we are also all capable of laziness and of elegantly lying about the fact of our caring. Helen Keller wrote, "Security is mostly a superstition. It does not exist in nature, nor do the children of men as a whole experience it. Avoiding danger is no safer in the long run than outright exposure. Life is either a daring adventure or nothing."[71] Further, duty eventually merges, as one matures, with enjoyment, with a permanent position of joy and gratitude. As Ursula LeGuin put it in one of her novels, "As a man's real power grows and his knowledge widens, ever the way he can follow grows narrower: until at last he chooses nothing, but does only and wholly what he must do."[72]

Buddha is supposed to have noted that as a person's enlightenment grows, the person becomes less and less capable of creating an evil result, regardless of his or her behavior. People are powerful. To act powerlessly is to be dishonest. To do other than to empower others is to lie about them and one's relation to them. "Power corrupts, and lack of power corrupts absolutely," observed Adlai Stevenson. The result of insight about life is, ultimately, a certain wildly joyful passion to be part of life and engaged in its service.

> This is the true joy in life, the being used for a purpose recognized by yourself as a mighty one; the being a force of nature instead of a feverish selfish little clod of ailments and grievances complaining that the world will not devote itself to making you happy. I am of the opinion that my life belongs to the whole community and as long as I live it is my privilege to do for it whatever I can. I want to be thoroughly used up when I die, for the harder I work the more I live. I rejoice in life for its own sake. Life is no "brief candle" to me. It is a sort of splendid torch which I have got hold of for the moment, and I want to make it burn as brightly as possible before handing it on to future generations.
>
> —George Bernard Shaw

20

Mobilizing Religious Congregations and Religious People

If the salt hath lost its savour, wherewith shall it be salted?
—Matthew 5:13

In 1835 Alexis de Tocqueville noted America's nearly universal religiosity and the commonality of viewpoints it generated, the bonding it created between people, and the ease of public problem-solving that it enabled. Today, government has nearly yielded the field of dealing with America's homeless to the United Way and church-associated agencies. More than 90 percent of the money being spent on the homeless is flowing through such groups. This represents solid commitment—and it may also represent a form of cooptation or quieting of an otherwise potential source of advocacy for true solutions to pieces of the homeless dilemma. Without such an exceedingly powerful and intelligent source of moral advocacy, it is certain that there will never be the analysis, action, and sacrifice needed to push ahead the two most looming fronts of this dilemma: the crisis in affordable housing, and the urgent need for a viable national program to care for the hundreds of thousands of Americans who are chronically, permanently mentally ill.

A number of religious beliefs, traditions or attitudes can motivate, hinder, or inform social activism:

- Believers are "justified by faith."
- Believers are "justified by action."
- Believers must have faith and also live lives consistent therewith.
- Ecumenicism is important.
- Do (not) get involved in politics.
- Love your neighbor as yourself.
- There are "worthy" and "unworthy" poor.
- Everyone who wishes to can raise themselves up.
- Mental illness is a myth, or a product of sinfulness.

Because an author writes from his experience, this chapter is more limited in scope than I would have wished. I have not wanted to presume into the affairs of religions not Judeo-Christian, and I heartily apologize for being unable to present, here, the full range of religious thought, potentially bearing on homelessness, that exists in America.

With great respect, the following passages from the Koran are offered, followed by ones from the Bible.

KORAN

To spend of your substance out of love for Him, for your kin, for orphans, for the needy, for the wayfarer, for those who ask, and for the ransom of slaves; to be steadfast in prayer and practice regular charity.

—Sura II, Verse 177

They ask thee what they should spend. Say: whatever ye spend that is good, is for parents and kindred and orphans and those in want and wayfarers; whatever ye do that is good—God knoweth it well.

—Sura II Verse 215

BIBLE—OLD TESTAMENT

Blessed is he that considereth the poor: the Lord will deliver him in time of trouble.

—Psalms 41:1

Defend the poor and fatherless: do justice to the afflicted and needy.

—Psalms 82:3

He that hath pity upon the poor lendeth unto the Lord; and that which he hath given will he pay him again.

—Proverbs 19:17

Whoso stopeth his ears at the cry of the poor, he also shall cry himself, but shall not be heard.

—Proverbs 21:13

You shall not harden your heart or shut your hand against your poor brother, but you shall open your hand to him, and lend him sufficient for need whatever it may be.

—Deuteronomy 15:7–8

He that giveth unto the poor shall not lack: but he that hideth his eyes shall have many a curse.

—Proverbs 28:27

There is a generation, whose teeth are as swords, and their jaw teeth as knives, to devour the poor from off the earth, and the needy from among men.

—Proverbs 30:14

He that hath a bountiful eye shall be blessed; for he giveth of his bread to the poor.

—Proverbs 22:9

Blessed is he who considers the poor!

—Psalms 41:1

Learn to do good; seek justice, correct oppression; defend the fatherless; plead for the widow.

—Isaiah 1:17

The stranger who sojourns with you shall be to you as the native among you, and you shall love him as yourself.

—Leviticus 19:34

He has showed, Oman, what is good; and what does the Lord require of you but to do justice, and to love kindness, and to walk humbly with your God.

—Micah 6:8

And thou shalt not glean thy vineyard, neither shalt thou gather every grape of thy vineyard; thou shalt leave them for the poor and stranger.

—Leviticus 19:10

And if thy brother be waxen poor, and fallen in decay with thee; then thou shalt relieve him: yea, though he be a stranger, or a sojourner; that he may live with thee.

—Leviticus 25:35

If there be among you a poor man of one of thy brethren within any of thy gates in thy land which the Lord thy God giveth thee, thou shalt not harden thine heart, nor shut thine hand from thy poor brother: But thou shalt open thine hand wide unto him, and shalt surely lend him sufficient for his need, in that which he wanteth.

—Deuteronomy 15:7–8

The stranger did not lodge in the street: but I opened my doors to the traveler.

—Job 31:32

He that oppresseth the poor reproacheth his Maker: but he that honoureth Him hath mercy on the poor.

—Proverbs 14:31

And the old man said, Peace be with thee; howsoever let all thy wants lie upon me; only lodge not in the street.

—Judges 19:20

Woe unto them that decree unrighteous decrees, and that write grievousness which they have prescribed; to turn aside the needy from Judgment, and to take away the right from the poor of my people, that widows may be their prey, and that they may rob the fatherless!

—Isaiah 10:1-4

BIBLE—NEW TESTAMENT

And whoever give to one of these little ones even a cup of cold water because he is a disciple, truly, I say to you, he shall not lose his reward.

—Matthew 10:42

Jesus said to him, "If you would be perfect, go, sell what you possess and give to the poor."

—Matthew 19:21

Every one whom much is given, of him will much be required; and to him to whom men commit much they will demand the more.

—Luke 12:48

He who has two coats, let him share with him who has none; and he who has food let him do likewise.

—Luke 3:11

For I was hungered, and ye gave me meat: I was thirsty, and ye gave me drink: I was a stranger, and ye took me in.

—Matthew 25:35

JESUS' ATTITUDE TOWARD THE POOR

Bishop George Dallas McKinney supplied the following about the founder of the Christian faith.

Christ modeled a life and ministry of compassion to the poor. He was forever mingling with them (Luke 5:1–11), eating with them (Luke 5:27–32), comforting them (Luke 12:22–34), feeding them (Luke 9:10–17), restoring them to health (Luke 5:12–16), and ministering to them (Luke 7:18–23). He even went so far as to use the dramatic words of Isaiah to summarize and epitomize his life's purpose: "The Spirit of the Lord is on me because He has anointed me to preach good news to the poor. He has sent me to proclaim freedom for the prisoners, and recovery of sight for the blind, to release the oppressed, to proclaim the year of the Lord's favor" (Luke 4:18–19).

It is not surprising, then, that His disciples, those called to "conform themselves to his image" (Romans 8:29), would similarly place a high priority on the care of the poor. Even a cursory glance through the New Testament "hall of fame" after Jesus' death reveals a startling level of commitment to ministries of compassion.

Tabitha, for example, was a godly woman whose chief occupation was "helping the poor" (Acts 9:36–41), and Barnabas was a man of some means who made an indelible mark on the early Christian communities, first by supplying the needs of the poor out of his own coffers (Acts 4:36–37), and later by spearheading relief efforts and taking up collections for famine-stricken Judeans (Acts 11:27–30).

Titus was the young emissary of the Apostle Paul (II Corinthians 8:23) who organized a collection for the poor Christians in Jerusalem (II Corinthians 8:3–6). Later, he superintended further relief efforts in Corinth, and delivered Paul's second letter to the church there, all on his own initiative (II Corinthians 8:16–17). When last we see Titus, he has taken over the monumental task of mobilizing the Gretan Church of similar "good works" (Titus 2:3,7; 12:3:8).

The Apostle Paul himself was a man deeply committed to "remembering the poor" (Galatians 2:7–10). His widespread ministry began with a "poverty outreach" (Acts 11:27–30) and ultimately centered around coordinating the resources of churches in Greece and Macedonia for relief purposes (II Corinthians 8–9). In the end, he willingly risked his life for this mission of compassion (Acts 20:17–35).

The Good Samaritan is the unnamed lead character in one of Christ's best-loved parables (Luke 10:25–37). When all others, including supposed people of righteousness, had skirted the responsibility of practical charity, the Samaritan took up its mantle. Christ concluded the narrative, saying, "Go and do likewise" (Luke 10:37).

These early Christian heroes fully comprehended that the religion our God and Father accepts as pure and faultless is this: "To look after orphans and widows in their distress, and to keep oneself from being polluted by the world" (James 1:27). They knew that true repentance evidenced itself in sharing food and sustenance with the poor (Luke 3:7–11). And they understood that selfless giving would be honored and blessed (Luke 6:38; II Corinthians 9:6–8) as a sign of genuine faith.

Biblical teaching concerning the believer's obligation to the poor permeated Old Testament thinking also. It was an ancient teaching that if people were kind and generous to the poor, they would themselves be happy (Proverbs 14:21). God would preserve them (Psalms 41:1–2). They would never suffer need (Proverbs 18:27). They would prosper (Proverbs 11:25). They would be raised and restored from beds of sickness (Psalms 41:3).

On the other hand, to refuse to exercise charity to the poor would have meant hurling contempt upon the name of the Lord (Proverbs 14:31). And for such an offense, they knew that their worship would have been rendered useless (Isaiah 1:10–17) and their prayers would have gone unanswered (Proverbs 21:13). They knew that they would in no wise escape punishment (Proverbs 17:5).

As a result, every aspect of their lives became shaped to some degree by this high call to compassion *in action* from the ordering of their houses (Romans 12:13) to the conducting of their businesses (Ephesians 4:28), from the training of their disciples (Titus 3:14) to the character of their worship (James 2:2–7), they were compelled by the Author and Finisher of their Faith to live lives of charity.

Today, there is stark poverty in the shadow of plenty. World hunger is on the rise. Poverty and starvation are critical problems facing much of the world. In spite of widespread economic recovery, the poorest of the poor continue to live in grave deprivation. The same cry of despair that rose above the stench of Babylon's slums and Warsaw's ghettos rises today above America's Urban Sprawl. The poor are with us still: more and more of them. Jesus said, "The poor will be with you always." If we didn't believe him before, we are compelled by the weight of evidence to believe Him now.

Our obligation to the homeless and displaced poor is indisputable. As believers in the power of Christ, we must work to minimize the injustice in the world. We must strive to feed the hungry and clothe and house the poor. We must share the necessary skills that will enable them to reach their full human potential, and we must forge the institutions—private and governmental—to meet these tasks as adults.

As Christians, we must live in the light of the saving grace of Christ our Lord, ministering to those in need and loving our neighbor as ourselves. As Mother Theresa wrote, in the faces of the poor and hungry, we will see the face of Christ. For as He said, "I assure you that whatever you did for the humblest of my brothers, you did for me."

Needless to say, McKinney's church is "up to its waist" in programs aiding the poor and the homeless. McKinney added the following small section on the subject of biblical messages for the recovering homeless.

The poor, like all others, need to be instructed in the life-transforming tenants of the Gospel of grace (Matt 28:19–20), and be told and to hear the Good News (Luke 4:18). They, like all of us, need to comprehend that their gravest obstacle to a full and abundant life is poverty of the soul

(John 10:10). Secondly, the poor must be taught Biblical principles of personal finances. Show them what the Bible has to say about the tithe (Malachi 3:8–12), about budgeting (Luke 14:28), about saving (Proverbs 6:6–11), goals and priorities (Proverbs 1:8–19), co-signing (Proverbs 6:1-5; 11:15), and indebtedness (Romans 13:8), and with this assistance, they will more likely become good stewards, and more economically independent. Third, the poor must be taught Biblical principles of providence. Their families need to plan ahead, to prepare. They need to know that it is supremely advantageous to prepare. Fourth, the poor must be taught scriptural principles of health and hygiene. The Bible's emphasis on cleanliness (Lev. 14–15; Numbers 19; Deuteronomy 23), diet (Leviticus 11), and rest (Exodus 20:8-10), makes it clear that our bodies are to be respectfully taken care of. Fifth, the poor must be taught the godly concepts of industry and craftsmanship. Not only should they learn about the work ethic, they should learn skills of how to implement it. According to an old Hebrew proverb, "He who does not teach his son a trade, teaches him to steal."

A CONCRETE CHURCH SHELTERING MODEL

Led by Mayor Ed Koch of New York City, churches in many cities have been refining a shelter model often called the "interfaith church/shelter network." Mayor Maureen O'Connor transplanted the idea to San Diego after a visit to New York, and San Diego's version of the network won a 1987 Valley Forge Freedom's Foundation Award after it linked together 115 congregations (almost a quarter of all the congregations in the county) to take homeless people into church buildings for short periods, and assist them.

This is the model: divide the city into regions and find churches willing to take in a well-screened group of homeless people, a dozen or two at a time, for two-week periods, cycling them from church to church. Other neighborhood churches then get recruited to help with meals, hygiene kits, bus tokens to get to job interviews, and people to spend time "supervising" the shelter of the moment, which is usually a church recreation hall. A batch of cots follows the homeless group (which continually "loses" members into jobs and housing settings) from church to church. In sunny San Diego, unfortunately, the network operates only from late fall to spring.

The problem for city planners is the issuance of conditional-use permits to allow actual living in the church. San Diego's city attorney, perhaps not atypically, opined that sheltering homeless people was "not a church function." No matter how much Martin Luther, John Wesley, or St. Francis might have argued against this modern, legal argument, city councils can cut this Gordion knot by passing, as San Diego's did pass, a blanket conditional-use permit that now covers the entire city for such purposes.

Initially criticized as a "silk stocking" effort benefiting only the "upper 3 percent" or so of the homeless, the program has actually accomplished much. It does generally deal only with the "situationally homeless," people with whom most congregation members can easily identify. But the program boasts a high percentage of participating churches, a remarkably high job placement record (67 percent of the adults after three weeks in the program), and some three hundred volunteers with a total of fifteen thousand volunteer hours worked by parishioners in 1989. Perhaps the program's greatest value is in getting church members together with people who have problems to sit around over meals just to talk. This tends to break down people's myths and get the church people engaged with real human beings who have fascinating stories to tell and unique, real problems to solve. It gets homelessness out of the theoretical and into the concrete. Best of all, it generates great public policy support for homeless causes, person to person, one at a time. People wind up feeling great about helping—and wanting to help more.

> Wherefore, the Lord said, forasmuch as this people draw near me with their mouth, and with their lips do honor me, but have removed their heart far from me, and their fear toward me is taught by the precept of men; therefore, behold, I will proceed to do a marvelous work among this people, even a marvelous work and a wonder: for the wisdom of their wise men shall perish, and the understanding of their prudent men shall be hid. Woe unto them that seek deep to hide their counsel from the Lord, and their works are in the dark, and they say, Who seeth us? and who knoweth us?
>
> —Isaiah 30:13–15

SUGGESTED READING

Myths to Live By, Joseph Campbell, Bantam, 1972.
Modern American Religions: The Irony of It All, Martin E. Marty, University of Chicago Press, 1986.
Awash in a Sea of Faith: Christianizing the American People, Jon Butler, Harvard University Press, 1989.
The Holy Bible.
The Koran.
City Streets, City People: A Call for Compassion, Michael J. Christensen, Abingdon Press, 1988.
The Protestant Establishment: Aristocracy and Caste in American, E. Digby Baltzell, Vintage Books, 1964.
The Broken Covenant: American Civil Religion in Time of Trial, Robert N. Bellah, Seabury Press, 1974.

21

Economics . . .

Unless one can describe a phenomenon using numbers, one knows very little about it.

—René Descartes

How does one quantify the economic impacts of homelessness on a community? It is not enough to add up all the dollars spent on programs directly designed to benefit the homeless—the soup kitchens, temporary shelters, job training programs, and myriad other services discussed elsewhere in this book. The economic impacts of homelessness go much deeper into the fabric of a community than these dollar figures indicate. What follows is a single outline, listing categories representing likely cost areas occasioned by the presence of a city's homeless population. This analysis is commended to city leaders in hopes that some may be moved to launch studies, to fill in numbers for themselves, and, usefully for all, to publish the results.

What follows is an outline, with numbers crudely filled in with the most informed estimates I could produce. More refined models, created by professional economists, would be useful to government, business, and the homeless alike. With clarity as to what it is costing—and who is bearing the costs—all players in downtown development and downtown life will be able to make more rational decisions.

Economic Factors Occasioned by a City's Homeless

1. *City Budget*

   a. Social services
   b. Redevelopment
   c. Housing commission
   d. Police (not available for burglaries, etc.)
   e. Eviction of the public from parks, streets

    f. Remodeling, re-tooling, iron-plating (parks)
    g. Ambulance services
2. *County Budget*
    a. Welfare
    b. Health, mental health
    c. Jail
    d. Courts, defenders, prosecutors
    e. Social services
    f. Housing
    h. Burial
3. *United Way and Social Service Agencies*
    a. Shelters (especially operating costs)
    b. Food
    c. Medical, social work, etc.
    d. Legal aid
    e. Communications and meetings
4. *School District Costs*
    (Mandated to educate all children.)
5. *Impact on Business*
    a. Architectural additions
    b. Guards, lighting, thefts, cleaning, painting
    c. Lost business, business failures
    d. Increased insurance
    e. Arson
6. *Federal/State Monies*
7. *Tax Losses*
    a. Sales tax
    b. Property tax (cities, schools, etc.)
    c. Hotel/motel occupancy tax
8. *Imponderables*
    a. Risk of epidemics
    b. Risk of major fires
    c. Loss of labor and capital

    In quantifying the impacts of homelessness, numbers cannot be attached to the deepest impacts—the moral and societal damage done by the growing presence of the homeless on our streets. How do you put a number on the brutalization of the homeless themselves from life on the street, or the brutalization of a society increasingly inured to their presence; or on the moral damage done to our young people who notice that society seems incapable—and/or unwilling—of living up to its most basic responsibilities. Who can assess the cost of the loss to our future because homeless children are being deprived of the educational and societal skills that would make them contributing members?

This chapter is included, also, in the hope that economic theorists are, at the end of the day (as they say) correct that it is true that many people's attention *is* gained when their pocketbooks are threatened. It is said that it isn't enough for people to hear and see that homelessness exists and is a cancer eating out the heart of our society. As long as they pay their taxes and make the occasional charitable donation, people (they say) feel they have "done their part." With some help from the churches and the other dogooders?[73]

To get the attention of these people, who may be able to step over the homeless on the street with a clear conscience because, after all, it's the government's job to solve the problem, the direct impact of homeless populations on their businesses, their profits, their overhead costs, and their bank accounts needs to be demonstrated.

Homelessness as an economic problem is costing our communities millions of dollars in added police, jail and court costs, lost tax revenues from properties devalued by the presence of the homeless, rising insurance costs because the presence of the homeless poses an increased threat of arson, petty burglaries, accidental fires, and vandalism, increased maintenance costs for areas in which the homeless congregate, frequently the loss of the use of swaths of public parks and recreational areas to the general public because the homeless have "taken over," and lost sales and tourist-oriented revenues suffered by businesses in areas frequented by the homeless. The very citizens who are the most difficult to motivate to join the fight against homelessness for moral reasons may be the easiest to motivate for economic reasons.

SAN DIEGO: A CASE STUDY

In 1986, homelessness in San Diego County cost a minimum of $10,848,000 in governmental funds; the actual cost may have been as high as $15,987,000. Included in these sums are $310,000 allocated to the Downtown Homeless Project, and $1,420,000 that went to the county exclusively for the treatment of the mentally disabled homeless.

The City of San Diego that year allocated $165,000 and $278,400 for, respectively, the San Diego Rescue Mission and St. Vincent de Paul Center for capital improvements. For the period including fiscal years 1984 through 1987, the city allocated $410,000 to its Downtown Transient Jobs Center. For the same period, the city provided the Travelers' Aid Society with $92,915 to assist homeless people and, since 1984, the city has provided $75,000 per year to fund the Neighborhood House Food Bank. In 1986, $500,000 was spent by the city to steel-plate all parking meters, after two enterprising homeless people were caught after smashing some one hundred of them with sledge hammers (to steal some $50,000 or so in nickels, dimes and quarters).

Total city governmental expenditures directly for the homeless through fiscal year 1987 were $1,871,315. When added to funds provided by the federal government and spent by the city, the total expenditures for the homeless through fiscal year 1987 were $2,993,922.

San Diego County government contributes millions of dollars more on an annual basis to the equation in direct expenditures because of homeless individuals as a part of general social services budgets. The following table presents a breakdown of some of these.

Estimated Annual Cost to San Diego County of Services to the Homeless

Program	Total Direct Cost	Estimated Percent to Homeless	Estimated Cost
Protective Services		%	
Adult	$11,425,481	9	$914,000-$1,142,000
Child	20,000,956	3.75	500,000-1,000,000
AFDC/Foster Care	27,074,546	4	812,000-1,353,000
Food Stamps	3,228,336	17.5	484,000-650,000
General Relief	9,896,158	9	792,000-990,000
Mentally Disabled Homeless	1,420,000	100	1,420,000
Downtown Homeless Project	310,000	100	310,000
Alcohol Program	4,337,419	6.5	217,000-347,000
Drug Program	3,065,199	4	92,000-153,000
Mental Health Program	46,853,506	2.5	937,000-1,405,000
Rental Assistance	10,196,000	2.5	204,000-306,000
Probation			
Adult Field Services	10,261,254	3.5	205,000-513,000
Adult Institutions	7,928,748	7.5	396,000-793,000
Juvenile Institutions	8,469,249	3.5	169,000-424,000
Sheriff's Detention Facilities	32,240,867	12.5	3,224,000-4,836,000
Nutrition Meals Program	3,445,000	7.5	172,000-345,000

Homelessness has other dollars-and-cents costs which, though often hidden, have no less significant impact on the local governments' annual budgets. These costs often take the form of resources intended for some sector of the community other than the homeless, which, due to the failure to address the needs of the homeless directly, are expended on the homeless indirectly. These include added downtown and park police foot patrols, park restroom maintenance, indestructible architectural features of buildings (which may sacrifice aesthetics) and personnel costs for added clean-up in public facilities and to "sit" in public restrooms, easing the fears of non-homeless that the facility may be used by them.

Some expenditures go directly to solving problems caused by the increased presence of the homeless in the City of San Diego. For example, in 1984, the city council felt compelled to spend $500,000 to replace existing parking meters with new meters with stronger casings much more resistant to breakage and theft. The City Council also allocated $500,000 for temporary "Johnny-on-the-Spot" temporary toilets and to build a permanent public restroom in downtown San Diego, largely to serve homeless people. This restroom, in turn, occasioned annual costs to maintain and staff.

Other budget items that have increased due to the presence of the homeless include downtown street and sidewalk maintenance and cleaning, janitorial maintenance costs for comfort stations in the many city parks frequented by the homeless, and building maintenance, security, and repair costs necessitated by a rise in vandalism.

The San Diego County jail system provides an excellent illustration of the indirect expenditures on the homeless. At any given time in 1984–85, 10 to 15 percent of the county's jail population consisted of homeless people, most of whom had been incarcerated for public drunkenness, sleeping in restricted areas, or other nuisance-type offenses. In other words, a significant number of county inmates are being held by the county because they have no private place to sleep, to get drunk, or do something that would not be illegal if it were done in an appropriate place. Providing the community with shelters would lift a significant burden from the county budget and jail system simply because homeless people would more rarely be jailed for these petty offenses. Weeding out these minor offenders from the jails would obviously create more space for more serious offenders.

The county jails are of course required by law to provide for the medical, dental, and psychiatric needs of their inmates. Regardless of whether the homeless have access to such assistance from social service agencies in the county, the jails have to provide these services when necessary, for any inmate. For the homeless, these services are necessary more often than not. Therefore, the jail system, as the county agency that cannot avoid contact with the homeless, becomes the caretakers of many of the homeless by default. This is not bad in and of itself. At least some of the homeless will get some of the care that they need. But this way for providing social services has untoward consequences.

First, such care costs the jail system money and personnel resources that it certainly could use in fulfilling its main job. More importantly, providing these services only when the law requires that they be provided is neither the most effective nor the most efficient use of resources. If people must wait until they are arrested before they can get medical, dental, or psychiatric services, their health conditions become more complicated and expensive to address. A localized infection can become generalized, a dental cavity can become an abscessed tooth, and a psychosis can cause physical deterioration. More ominously for the general public, public health doctors warn that intermittently treated infections (such as tuberculosis, which is common in today's streets) is developing treatment-immune strains of disease. That is, intermittent treatment of the homeless is creating a threat to the public health of the general population. Perhaps one cannot place a dollar estimate on the costs of a potential epidemic or two, but, should they occur, they will be costly.

Another governmental victim of the hidden costs of homelessness is the police department. The San Diego Police Department estimated in 1985 that police contacts with the homeless in the downtown area alone cost approximately $1.8 million per year in officers' time, vehicle use, etc. To this must be added a standard factor of 60 percent overhead used in calculations of all police functions. On top of this, according to the department's Central Division management, a realistic assessment would include the training, disability, and other costs of high turnover from resulting low officer morale, since a huge percentage of this kind of work is seen by intelligent officers as purposeless movement of people through two less than intelligent, revolving-door systems: jail and the mental health department.

The police department also gets caught in the political games played with the homeless. For example, about a year before the opening of the huge and creative Horton Plaza shopping center in downtown San Diego—a cornerstone of the downtown redevelopment plan—a specially trained detachment of twenty-four volunteer police officers was added to foot patrols in the downtown business district. Their mission: to be utterly courteous and constitutionally respectful with all people . . . while issuing citations for every conceivable violation of the city's code, from spitting on the sidewalk to discarding a cigarette butt or gum wrapper. The intent: to drive the homeless out of the area before the grand opening of the shopping center. City officials were then able to say, with relatively straight faces, that no police were added because of the opening of Horton Plaza. True. The police were already there.

COSTS OF HOMELESSNESS TO LOCAL BUSINESSES

In a recent survey of businesses operating in San Diego's Gaslamp Quarter, a downtown shopping district with a highly visible homeless population, the shopkeepers and business people made it clear that their enterprises were suffering because of the presence of the homeless. Of those who responded to the survey, 74 percent said that street people constituted a problem for their businesses, costing their businesses money. Fourteen percent said that the homeless were a problem for their employees. Among those who identified expenditures for cleaning, repairs, vandalism, and other problems directly related to the homeless, the average monthly cost was $85. Although the amount is impossible to determine with complete accuracy, respondents who felt they had lost business due to the presence of the homeless estimated an average of $1,765 per month in lost sales. Respondents frequently asserted that the homeless population made it difficult to attract customers to the downtown area. One respondent wrote, "Most old San Diegans do not like downtown because of transients, bums and crazy people." Another respondent declared, "We are estimating that 100 people per month make a decision not to visit our business because of its location in an area populated by many homeless." Another wrote, "Most customers we talk to seem to resent this display of people." Another commented, "We are told every day that people will not come downtown unless they absolutely have to because of the street people. So, anyone who can shop elsewhere will do so." Some businesses have added iron fences; some, guards. These all cost money.

Another, much more scientific survey was conducted by the San Diego Chamber of Commerce on the enthusiasm or lack thereof on the part of suburban San Diegans for visiting downtown. This study was never released in full to the press or public, but its conclusions stated that fully 82 percent of those responding were very reluctant to venture downtown for any reason. Four factors were mentioned as being of nearly equal weight to the respondents: 1) presence of "street people"; 2) fear for personal safety; 3) mounting traffic concerns; and 4) difficulty in finding affordable parking.

Further, the study indicated which groups will or will not visit the downtown area: those who will tend to visit downtown are men, those who live close to downtown, those with a family member who works downtown, younger people, home renters, relative newcomers, executives, government workers, and blue-collar technicians. Those tending not to visit downtown are women, those who live ten or more miles from downtown, those who have no family members who work downtown, older people, home owners, long-time residents, retired people, and housewives.

New businesses and entire buildings near downtown areas where temporary meal outlets are, often find themselves cut off from potential customers by a disquieting barrier of street people waiting in line. Intimidation by the homeless is a problem not only for customers of businesses located near homeless populations, but also for employees of those businesses. Common is the example of the woman who drove to downtown San Diego to interview for a job as a secretary. She called her interviewer forty-five minutes late to say that she could not make it to the interview or take the job because she did not feel safe getting out of her car once she got downtown. Similarly, a San Diego architect who set up his office in the Gaslamp Quarter personally loved and significantly upgraded the premises but eventually moved to a quieter business district after female employees were accosted, on several occasions, when leaving the offices after dark.

The manager of a large shopping center in downtown San Diego indicated that security spends about 20 percent of its time escorting the homeless off the premises.

Owners of several landmark businesses were interviewed, and they offered some unique insights:

1. A major upscale hotel estimated a total loss in revenues plus expenses occasioned by the presence of the homeless around the immediate area at above $1 million per year. The bottom eight feet of the hotel's exterior had been repainted four times in a year and a half; there had been assaults on guests, room burglaries, car thefts, and much aesthetic consternation. The hotel manager initiated a reorganization of his business under the Bankruptcy Act (which he says would have been unnecessary, absent street people), and now sends, every month, copies of all of his guests' comment sheets, filled out on check-out, to the city's mayor and members of the City Council who represent downtown. The sheets graphically demonstrate the frustration of vacationing and convention-attending tourists with street people in a city that emphasizes tourism yet de-emphasizes low-income housing, glosses over mental health needs and has inadequate social services and jail space. The San Diego downtown business community, instead of being a clear source of clarion calls for remedies, has so far vacillated between silence and an occasional, ineffectual yelp of surprise that the unattended street populations are not healthy for business. Do tell!

The manager of the hotel provided some graphic examples of the impacts of the homeless on the beautifully restored but bankrupt downtown landmark. Walls were defaced, windows broken, property stolen. Transients urinated in the doorways and hallways. All of this contributes to higher maintenance, repair, and personnel costs. Over a six-month period in 1989, he estimated that the presence of the homeless increased the hotel's operating expenses by $88,525 for addition personnel costs and $4,000 for supplies. He estimated that during the same period the presence of the homeless deprived the hotel of three thousand room-nights of occupancy, or $389,500 in potential revenues.

2. A major, popular, sixty-year-old retail store has barred its windows, considered hiring guards, and experienced much higher petty theft rates over the past decade since the arrival of the homeless. Its owner/manager estimated

a loss of 25 to 40 percent of the store's business because of apprehension by potential customers that if they even walk to the store they'd be harmed physically, or scared. This latter factor was universally mentioned in 1986 responses to a poll of retail business managers in the areas of downtown populated by the homeless. As noted, the suburban polls support this idea strongly.

3. Vacancy rates in upscale condominiums remain high, contradicting projections prepared before construction.

4. One tourist-oriented, bayfront concentration of shops, restaurants, and entertainment businesses, called Seaport Village, reports having spent hundreds of thousands of dollars on architectural features (fences, lighting, gates, etc.) designed to discourage entry by street people, on high all-night lighting bills, and on eight extra guards. Seaport's manager said that his insurance costs are higher because of the homeless and that he has had to spend prodigious sums on a skillful, longer-term promotional campaign in order to succeed (as he has) in carving out an exception in the minds of suburban San Diegans, so that they do not think of Seaport as part of "downtown."

As these business cost factors mount, the costs of *solving* at least the component parts of the homeless phenomenon impacting these businesses so severely ought to be juxtaposed with the prices now being paid. Business is not being harmed by all homeless people. The chronic drunks, the deeply mentally ill, the substance abusers, and the young louts among the homeless are those who hurt business. In San Diego, a routine effort to suppress chronic public drunkenness and panhandling could be easily done with more jail space. The business community is finally advocating this, and, in fainter terms, supporting an added $10 million in the county budget to service the city's homeless mentally ill more humanely. The bearers of the present costs, once shown these costs, might well be persuaded to accept a (property-based?) tax to shift funds to pay for some really effective answers.

HIGHER INSURANCE COSTS

Another direct impact on businesses located in areas populated by the homeless is the soaring cost of insurance. The presence of the homeless translates into a higher risk of vandalism, petty theft, and burglaries. The homeless also are prone to entering buildings at night in search of warmth and a dry place to sleep. They don't always restrict their entries to vacant or abandoned properties, and often they build fires. The San Diego Arson Strike Force counted eight major blazes in eight years that it attributed to the homeless. The result for businesses in areas frequented by the homeless is higher insurance premiums, both for theft coverage and for coverage on the property and structures themselves.

Stanford F. Hartman, Jr., vice president of Commercial Insurance for the real property firm of John Burnham & Co., offered some personal observations on the effects of the homeless on insurance rates in San Diego. He pointed out that the homeless tend to gravitate to areas occupied by older, less well-maintained buildings, the "run down" neighborhoods where property values are already lower. As a result, insurance rates are higher, even before the presence of the homeless is factored in. Hartman sees an increase in rates attributable to the increased exposure to losses such as vandalism, theft and fire due to the presence of the homeless, but he sees a more noticeable impact on insurance premiums for buildings under construction. San Diego has suffered several major fires at construction sites in recent years caused by transients burning scrap wood or other materials in the buildings to keep warm. Underwriters and carriers now require guard services on the construction sites during non-working hours to protect against both fire and theft. Others also require that the site be securely fenced. While most insurance carriers have become reluctant to insure construction sites without guard services and fencing, insurance is still available without these precautions—at double the premiums.

Captain Larry Carlson of the San Diego Metro Arson Strike Team says that every day there are several "small fires set by transients," citywide. Partly because of fire retardant commercial carpeting and other materials, most of these just burn themselves out without involving structural damage; but

> at least thirty fires per year over the past decade, set by transients, are fully investigated because they do involve structural or major fire damage. Half of these occur in the greater downtown area. Most of these are not technically arsons. They are recklessly set by people to get warm. Their numbers are a lot higher in winter. I could take you to several vacant buildings, right now, where we'd see lots of fire evidence, all over carpeted floors, surrounded by empty bean cans and soup cans. These are like campsites. It's happening all over, and the major fires we see reported every year in the newspapers, attributed to "transients" or "homeless," are only the tip of the iceberg.

Property values in the areas in which the homeless are located are significantly affected by their presence—and the adverse effects increase with time. Moving the homeless from one location to another doesn't solve the problem; it just spreads the impact to new sections of the community.

In San Diego, a large number of homeless people currently spend their days in the Gaslamp Quarter, an area of downtown gradually being renovated as a shopping and restaurant district in hopes that it will attract the dollars brought in by the nearby Convention Center. Once renovation of the area is completed, it is likely that private security forces and political pressure on the police department will operate, not necessarily to solve the homeless problem, but to try to move it elsewhere. The process has, in fact, already begun with approaches ranging from police crackdowns on "vagrants" to elimination of fortified, 20-percent-alcohol, cheap wine downtown.

One arena in which San Diego has led has been in restructuring its homeless shelter system. Many homeless people often do not receive medical care until they are found in a completely debilitated condition. Emphasis on early treatment could result in significant savings in both money and personnel to county hospitals. The homeless face both emergency and chronic illnesses that can be treated easily and successfully in their early stages but, when neglected, can cause permanent, irreversible harm and, finally, death. Treating people in a shelter clinic at the onset of illness or disease is a more efficient use of scarce resources than later placing them in hospitals and other institutions once the disease has reached an advanced stage.

The medical disorders of the homeless are often common illnesses such as colds or influenza that are exacerbated by unsanitary living conditions, exposure to extremes of heat and cold, bizarre sleeping accommodations and overcrowding in shelters. A disease that significantly affects the homeless population is pulmonary tuberculosis. People living in shelters and single-room-occupancy hotels are at a high risk. Unless treated, many people temporarily placed in shelters will ultimately carry the infection back to their families, the workplace and elsewhere in the community at large.[73] Medical attention at early stages would not only prevent the consumption of scarce and costly inpatient resources necessary to treat diseases in advanced stages, but would also tend to prevent the spread of diseases both among the homeless and throughout the larger community.

CONDUCTING A LOCAL ECONOMIC STUDY

To be able to show a community that it cannot afford *not* to solve homelessness, one must gather statistics and data from local sources. Every community is, of course, different, and the economic impacts of homelessness will vary.

Where to start? Every community, no matter how large or how small, has much of the needed information already collected. The problem is recognizing it for what it is. The right police commander can tell what percentage of downtown cops' time is spent responding to problems created by the homeless. Businesses can estimate the impact of the homeless on their customers and their sales. The local government knows how many tax dollars are spent on the homeless each year—and can calculate how much revenue is lost due to their presence. Insurance underwriters and arson experts in the fire department know the cost of increased risk due to homelessness. Health care professionals know the scope and cost of providing medical, dental and psychiatric treatment for the homeless, and the added public health risks. Parks administrators will happily estimate both costs occasioned by the homeless and percentages of park usage lost because homeless people scare others away. A local advocate's job (or the mayor's or councilman's, perhaps) is to collect this information and put it to use.

Below is an outline listing suggested agencies, groups and individuals one might approach in collecting the data for one's own community. Sources may not exist in every community, or may have different names, and some sources may prove more cooperative than others. Some data will be neatly analyzed and ready to distribute, while others will not be aware that they have the information wanted until you help them put it together. A novel idea would be for a city to get a foundation grant and hire a source of economic expertise, such as the Rand Corporation.

Governmental Sources

Local tax dollars being expended on the homeless, and in reaction to the presence of the homeless, will show up somewhere in the local city and county government budgets. Few items will be listed as "homeless expenses," but an understanding of the scope of the budget and an examination of the "big budget items" will give you a starting place in approaching other government offices such as the police.

We found that most city or county department heads, when asked the costs to their department occasioned by the homeless, had not the foggiest idea and would produce inaccurate numbers unless the questioners (ideally, staff people from the city manager's or county chief administrator's office, doing a "routine study") came with the authority of a real inquiry from "the boss" and was empowered to question the personnel at the bottom of the order—the jail commanders, welfare intake workers, and so on. These lower-on-the-totem-pole estimates are based on actual experience, on facts. Thus can an approximation of the truth be approached.

United Way and Social Service Agencies

It might appear that these data could be obtained at a single source, such as your local United Way. This is, I suppose, possible; but it is much more likely that dependable numbers will be as difficult to root out as on the government side, and will need to be "interviewed" painstakingly, agency by agency, budget element by budget element. It ought to be a very profitable exercise, by the way, to track and graph flows of particular state, federal, and foundation sources (FEMA emergency housing funds, for example) over time. Perhaps these can be used more effectively, or perhaps broader sources, upon examination, could be identified.

Surveys of Impacted Businesses

These can be tailored to your needs and targeted by area. Door-to-door polls of businesses in impacted areas, collecting reactions from customers and employees as well as owners and managers, will yield much. Volunteers and universities might be enlisted to cut costs, and a pooling of costs across interested groups could yield a more complete survey, broader attention to its results, and financial feasibility.

Just go get the data where it is. Data banks will include those of local government, federal agencies, United Way and its member agencies, chambers of commerce, libraries, and universities. Many agencies (the courts, for example) consider it their duty and function to meet citizens' information requests and retain data in astonishingly accessible form on computers.

Do not forget that people respond best to questions coming *down* an administrative ladder, and better yet, when they perceive their own interest in giving good, detailed, check-able answers. Have the city manager direct the "city" part of the study, and so forth. Go to experts; and double check by finding more experts. Get to the "brains of the outfit." Each outfit. Check it out like a detective.

Economic Disincentives to Solving Homelessness

Be alert. There may be some people coming to volunteer service on certain "homelessness" committees who do *not* want to see the committee's work succeed. These perceive their own economic interests to be served best by the persistence of homelessness, and they quietly act to assure that persistence.

Two types of these have been observed, but surely there must be many more:

Short-term downtown investors. These investors specialize in the downtown area, and as long as homeless people roam certain areas and suppress property values and taxes, such market-oriented individuals can continue to "buy cheap." We have seen them thus join business organizations and become placed on key committees where they can help assure that nothing intelligent or really effective ever happens, that homelessness is continually "studied."

Businessmen at the rim of the city. The second example may sometimes be found where there is a metropolitan area's chamber of commerce (or other such entity), which once served as a bastion of downtown interests as well as a source of strong leadership on major problems, but serves as such no more. Today, boards of such entities may contain a majority of business people from areas "where the action is"—in the suburbs, the industrial parks, and the shopping centers that ring the city's aging central core (with maybe a token "downtowner" or two). These leaders may not want to see downtown homelessness effectively addressed. They may be well trained as corporate loyalists, possibly both upwardly and geographically mobile, with their MBAs gleaming, and may owe no great loyalty to this particular city, as the old aristocracies once did. These new gentry have to view the prospect of a healthy, economically viable retail-emphasizing downtown as the prospect of a nascent competitor. Why not thwart or, at best, delay such competition? Or, cloak one's supposed benign neglect with an ineffectual generous-looking gesture on occasion? Who would be the wiser?

These lists, obviously, are not all-inclusive. Organizations and entities like these may not exist in your community, but being alert for the potential for such counter-motivations may help avoid some pain, and some needless efforts.

Most importantly, eschew discouragement. Some groups and agencies may not initially want to talk. Others may feel like sharing only that information that they feel justifies their refusal to help. Still others will refuse to listen, no matter how many facts and figures are presented to them, no matter how eloquently the case is pled. Don't give up. Many *will* listen. A difference will ultimately be made, and the major media and leaders will respond. Homelessness did not come into being overnight, and it will not be solved instantly, either. The longest journey begins with a single step; and as light is shed, denial becomes impossible.

> *What happens to a dream deferred?*
> Does it dry up
> like a raisin in the sun?
> Or fester like a sore—
> And then run?
> Does it stink like rotten meat?
> Or crust and sugar over
> like a syrupy sweet?
> Maybe it just sags
> like a heavy load.
>
> *Or does it explode?*
> —Langston Hughes

SUGGESTED READING

Publications of:

The Joint Center for Housing Studies of the Massachusetts Institute of Technology and Harvard University, 53 Church St., Cambridge, MA 02138.

The National Association of Housing and Redevelopment Officials, 1320 18th St. NW, Washington, D.C., 20036, 202-429-2960.

The Urban Land Institute, 1090 Vermont Ave. NW, Washington, D.C., 20005, 202-289-8500.

22

"How Can I Help?"

Who is my neighbor, Lord?
          —Luke 10:29–37 (put to Jesus, to which he responded
          with the parable of the Good Samaritan)

We humans instinctively respond to the cry of a hungry child. No response is more universal. In America, a deep tradition of volunteerism and problem-solving exists, with roots far back into our frontier heritage. De Tocqueville wrote of us, "Americans are an unusual people; when they see a problem come up, they immediately form a group or committee—whatever is necessary to get the job done." Encountering some piece of the homeless dilemma, people today instinctively ask, "How can I help?" This is an important question and a clear answer to it is needed. Nonetheless, I find it a difficult question to answer clearly. I cannot always know the individual questioner's peculiar talents or predilections. Every person must search his or her own mind and heart.

Officials at all levels, with all types of responsibilities, also ought to be thoughtfully wrestling with how people might answer the question. They need to identify the types of volunteers who would be the most helpful. Then they need to create cunning strategies designed to bring those volunteers on board with enthusiasm. They might have answers to the question, "How can I help?" that their own ideal volunteers could give to other potential volunteers. At this psychological moment, the polls show us that people want to volunteer. Agencies therefore must develop sophistication in recruiting and sensitively handling volunteers.

No battalion of experts can solve homelessness alone. What will solve it will be an uprising, a harnessing of passion and power, ultimately expressing itself as a mighty tide of political will. In the interim, we need huge gains in the resources available to help the homeless. We need Americans rolling up their sleeves and plunging into work, acting in the tradition of their frontier heritage.

An early 1989 *Newsweek* poll showed that solving America's homeless dilemma has become the number-two demand of the American public, second only to handling the federal deficit. This represented a major turnaround in public opinion. It meant that "How can I help?" was no longer an academic question.

People want answers *now*.

A 1987 national survey by America's United Way (funded by J.C. Penney) revealed that, of the 50 percent of Americans who do volunteer work, 23 percent now do volunteer work dealing with poverty and hunger. Thus, about twenty-five million American adults are presently working as volunteers, dealing in some way with hunger and poverty issues. Of the non-volunteers, 76 percent said they would be interested in doing volunteer work relative to alleviating hunger and poverty.

As for those who do not yet volunteer, the report concluded that, "To make it easier for non-volunteers to become involved, agencies must develop short-term projects; structure activities so that volunteers can involve their families in them; and assist in providing or locating low-cost day care." If we and our institutions turn out to be receptive and subtle in making room for waves of varied volunteers, we will multiply the power being applied to the solutions we come up with.

Those in charge must be careful not to "hide the ball." It ought to be made easy for any citizen to discover present needs. Much can be done by the local mayor's office, homeless task force, United Way, Council of Churches or other organization with explicit or implicit responsibility for solving the homeless dilemma.

To reiterate Descartes' advice: unless a phenomenon is described in numbers, one knows little about it. Publicize the numbers. Use talk shows, newspaper editorials, speakers' bureaus, state-of-the-city addresses, television documentaries, public utility mailings, billboards, and radio and television public-service advertisements.

The information disseminated needs to communicate where and how to volunteer for each agency and each piece of the problem, and it need to go out through many channels. We Americans speak different languages. I am referring here to sociology rather than mother tongue. We speak (and often only listen to) the languages of lawyers, laborers, doctors, Methodists, Catholics, Pentecostals, farmers, Republicans, the elderly, or whatever group or groups we may belong to.

POTENTIAL VOLUNTEERS

People considering becoming volunteers should first, or early on, become informed, see the problems of the homeless directly and in close detail, talk with homeless people to some depth, let their reality sink in. A new volunteer might do some harm out of his or her uninformed enthusiasm. This cannot be avoided. Volunteers must remain determined that mere barriers will not keep them from delivering their service. A marathoner's motto reads: "Press on. Regardless."

Most importantly, volunteers can touch people with their humanity. Here, one cannot do harm. This is, after all, the most profoundly correct way to help anyone. Here, heart touches heart. The touch brings solace, kindliness, cheer, company, and that greatest of all tonics, acknowledgement. The world does not really need more love. There is plenty of love out there. The world needs more *acknowledgment*. What is deeply needed is the simple, cheerful courage to express oneself.

WHAT SHOULD I DO?

Do what you are good at. Better yet, do what you feel like doing. Follow your instincts. Sure, one ought to think about it. Do some research. Ask smart and good people. Maybe get a friend or two to join you (or, you join them). But get out there and *do*. Do something that feels good, especially at first. Maybe even plan some good feedback for yourself. (The missions are good at this. They specialize in warmth, in thank-yous. So do churches putting up the homeless.) Decide to have a great time, to be inspired, to learn, and to deliver yourself to some people. How can you lose? God bless you. Get involved.

CREATIVE USE OF VOLUNTEER EFFORTS

Shelter managers in San Diego noticed that people kept volunteering specialized skills, ranging all over the map—from bricklaying to fundraising—but they didn't want to be misused. So the shelters set up a central clearinghouse for listing the specialist/volunteers and the specifics of their availability (hours, etc.), on a computer, which all agencies could access.

Other San Diego activists did something similar for the *things* people wanted to give away (dishes, laundry baskets, forks, etc.). They listed them on a computer "bulletin board," making the information available at any time to shelter staffs citywide.

Another nice idea was the use of teenaged shelter staff to identify homeless kids who needed to live in transition houses, then matching them with donors willing to contribute $500 for furnishings. The volunteer donor then went *with the kid* and taught him or her how to find things for next to nothing.

This is a several-directioned, win-win idea! Kids learn how to learn from a responsible role model, and how to scheme to stretch resources—and the adult gets the thrill of being (helpfully!) with a kid who desperately needs learning from a parent figure.

BRAINSTORM LIST OF WAYS TO HELP

1. Hire a homeless carpenter to remodel your garage or house.
2. Let a homeless person live in the spare room.
3. Write a check.
4. Peel potatoes.
5. Organize your activity club's first annual breakfast at the local YWCA homeless women's shelter.
6. Find out the present needs of an agency—forty lockers for the Work Center, for example, or a washer-dryer set for the Women's Shelter, shower curtains or doors or shower heads, mattresses, bags of beans and rice, bus tokens, reading materials. Schedule a visit of your church group, or just a bunch of friends, for a survey of such needs, then take one on.
7. Discover a way to leverage your action. A group of San Diego businessmen found that $100,000 was the final element needed to establish a Homeless Day Center. They threw a black-tie dinner with the mayor and wrote checks totalling $184,000.
8. Donate a van (or four) for the county mental health department's homeless outreach program. Transportation is a chronic problem.
9. Give crates of apples.
10. Make apartments available to be rented by screened parents with children on welfare, but without requiring payment of a security deposit or payment of the last month's rent.
11. Get some typewriters to use for teaching typing at skills classes.
12. Get your fellow church members and leaders to care more. Tell them. Mobilize them.
13. Search for things. For example, large lots of samples can often be discovered at post offices: giveaway soap, tampons, medicines, even glasses and hearing aids.
14. If you insist on giving food, find out what will really help. Get a supermarket chain to donate dented cans, or contact big food distributors and growers. Food gathered for distribution is generally not a problem. But if you bring in three little cans of peas, you create a problem.
15. Be creative. I know a lawyer who makes it his practice to carry

nutritious granola bars in his suit coat pocket. He will offer one to a scruffy, needy-looking individual he meets on the streets, trying to accompany it with a deep, friendly look. "Hi, pal. Want a granola bar?" He likes to depart quickly, imagining himself to be a Lone Ranger, leaving his shabby friend wondering, "Who was that masked man?" On other occasions, this gentleman can be found engaged in conversations with such a recipient, or accompanying him to a shelter. These are his ways of sharing himself.

16. Supply paper goods to local centers for the homeless.
17. Volunteer to paint a facility or to clean carpets.
18. Donate videos to be shown at local day centers.
19. Donate rolls of postage stamps or bus tokens to centers for client use.
20. If your company or church does large mailings, hire homeless people from your local homeless centers to do your mailing for you.
21. If you are a technical professional, make a generous offer of architectural, structural engineering, medical, legal and/or other services.
22. Think more elegantly. One nice idea has teenaged shelter staff identifying homeless kids ahead of time who will get to live in transition houses, and also a donor willing to contribute $500 for furnishings. This volunteer donor then gets to go *with the kid* and teach the kid how to find things for next to nothing. This is a several-directioned, win-win idea because the kids learn how to learn from a responsible role model, and how to scheme to stretch resources and the adult gets the thrill of being with a kid who desperately needs to learn from a parent.
23. Think on a grander scale—who would write a huge check to donate a ranch in the country; who would persuade the governor to help, or bring a major foundation into the effort? Go for it!
24. After doing one or two of the above, begin to communicate with elected officials charged with handling the homeless dilemma. Let them know you expect them to solve the homeless problem, to lie awake sweating and praying over the moral weight of their responsibility. Offer to help them, but keep holding their feet to the fire.

One thing I know. The only ones among you who will be really happy are those who have sought and found how to serve.

—Albert Schweitzer

23

We Can Handle It!

But we have faith that we shall not prove false to the memories of the men of the mighty past. They did their work, they left us the splendid heritage we now enjoy. We in our turn have an assured confidence that we shall be able to leave this heritage unwasted and enlarged to our children and our children's children. To do so we must show, not merely in great crises, but in the everyday affairs of life, the qualities of practical intelligence, of courage, of hardihood, and endurance, and above all the power of devotion to a lofty ideal, which made great the men who founded this Republic in the days of Washington, which made great the men who preserved this Republic in the days of Abraham Lincoln.

—Theodore Roosevelt (Inaugural Address, 1905)

Is not this the fast that I have chosen? To loose the bands of wickedness, to undo the heavy burdens, and to let the oppressed go free, and that ye break every yoke? Is it not to deal thy bread to the hungry, and that thou bring the poor that are cast out to thy house? When thou seest the naked, that thou cover him; and that thou hide not thyself from thine own flesh? Then shall thy light break forth as the morning, and thine health shall spring forth speedily: and thy righteousness shall go before thee; the glory of the Lord shall be thy reward.

—Isaiah 58:4–8

The "how did we get here" portions of each chapter of this book are, logically enough, descriptions of failures. The solutions prescribed are descriptions of American courage and realism in action. They are attempts to list assets that can be drawn upon: monetary resources, ideas that have been applied and shown to work, self and community interests, available institutional resources and those of institutions that may be "committed but not yet enlisted," the power of volunteerism in all its forms, and the human resources that keep this country rich.

What I have not done so far is to attempt a catalogue of over-all strengths. Whenever I have done that mentally, I have always concluded that although homelessness in America is certainly not a trivial difficulty (it is certainly one of our top moral challenges), it is, in terms of both the difficulty and the dollar costs of its resolution, not a problem I would place among the nation's top twenty.

The examples of solutions given heretofore are simply a few almost random ones from among the thousands of remarkable efforts that have arisen over this nation, meeting the challenge of American homelessness. These fine efforts are powered by tens of thousands of Americans, as human and frail as many presented here, and also as stalwart, determined and courageous. These people are obeying the first requirement of life and health: participation. They are learning that the arena of homelessness is a place of historic, pivotal consequence. To work to end homelessness is to reconnect to the fundamentals of human life: relationship, truth, physicalness, learning and growth, love and community, humility, humankind's oneness. These fundamentals are, of course, everywhere under assault today. Involvement with homelessness and the homeless can serve as a tonic both to individuals and, possibly, to our civilization.

Theodore Roosevelt wrote:

> It is not the critic who counts, not the man who points out how the strong man stumbled or where the doer of deeds could have done them better. The credit belongs to the man who is actually in the arena; whose face is marred by dust and sweat and blood; who strives valiantly; who errs and comes short again and again; who knows the great enthusiasms, the great devotions, and spends himself in a worthy cause; who, at the best knows the triumph of high achievement; and who, at the worst, if he fails, at least fails while daring greatly, so that his place shall never be with those cold and timid souls who know neither victory nor defeat.[75]

America is a country in which, over the brief span of two hundred years, dozens of tough challenges have been confronted: of colonialism, of wide ethnic and cultural diversity, of a wild frontier, of cultural clashes with a native population, of slavery, secession and the Civil War, of waves of immigrants, of the challenges of purist capitalism and labor's place, of the world wars and the Great Depression, all amidst the evolution of freedom, conflict and poverty worldwide, and a mounting ecological crisis.

Through this, our people have maintained a pragmatism and common sense, and a cheerful notion of human dignity and decency that are unique in history. With our blemishes of pride and willful ignorance, of greed and insensitivity and of a startling capacity (in the short term) to deceive ourselves and ignore problems, we have an awesome history of accomplishment and great strengths on which to draw.

Is it not obvious that we can responsibly handle this challenge of homelessness? It may help to list our nation's strengths and clear incentives.

- A pragmatic, frontier heritage that has colored our religions and philosophies with a tradition of realism and a commitment to problem-solving.
- An enduring form of government that is designed (in the long run, at least) to foster experimentation, acknowledgement of difficulty, insight, self-correction, recovery.
- A tradition of volunteerism that rewards and honors people who lead with courage and who take responsibility for community needs.
- We appear to stand today at an auspicious point on the thirty-year political cycle of social activism postulated by Arthur Schlesinger, Jr., *The Cycles in American History*. Public opinion polls have, over the past two years particularly, shown an incoming tide of public awareness of homelessness and determination to see it responsibly confronted.
- The moment also seems auspicious internationally, with the prospects of relaxation of the drumbeats for more arms. Military spending succeeded in siphoning off a staggering percentage of our national wealth and much of its potential for problem-solving for a decade.
- However, we're still rich. The U.S. gross national product for 1989 was over $4.5 trillion!
- A recognition that local attempts to isolate, segregate and thereby hide homelessness have failed and are doomed to failure.
- Homelessness must be responsibly confronted, we are realizing, or else the quality of our nation's urban life, and the civilized lives of their neighborhoods and of each of us, cannot be sustained.
- We now know that homelessness (like water supply for southern California early in this century, the solution of labor strife late in the last, or of any of dozens of dilemmas that realistic struggling with, facing up to and ultimately resolving, we now breezily take for granted) must be faced up to, or ignored at our great peril.

This book is simply an effort to speed the process and an expression of the hope that in our rush, we leave nobody out. Being responsible to any crisis—on any scale, from personal to national to international—involves facing up to new, inconvenient, and irritating truths. It also generally takes time to rationalize one's way through such new experiences and perceptions, and if there is a little light, kindly shed during this process in the tunnel, it might help disproportionately.

I beg and urge each reader to be a part of the truth-seeking process—that cheerful, pain-enduring, light-shedding process we must live through as people beginning to deal with the degrading, scandalous realities of American homelessness. I beg each reader to approach the tasks of beginning to deal with healing homelessness with all of the prayerful cheer and humility and commitment that is our national heritage. I hope that we can all come to see the present homeless dilemma as actually one of the mighty opportunities that life, in its random wisdom, places before most human generations, so that we can approach the work of solving homelessness with gratitude and joy, aware of our adulthood and power and community. And I beg that all of us ask our Creator to keep holding us in the hollow of His hand, sweetly informing and correcting us, infusing us with the power and truth and sweetness we need, as we roll up our sleeves and get about this fascinating labor.

> Not like the brazen giant of Greek fame,
> With conquering limbs astride from land to land;
> Here at our sea-washed, sunset gates shall stand
> A mighty woman with a torch, whose flame
> Is the imprisoned lightning, and her name
> Mother of Exiles. From her beacon-hand
> Glows world-wide welcome; her mild eyes command
> The air-bridged harbor that twin cities frame.
> "Keep, ancient lands, your storied pomp!" cries she
> With silent lips. "Give me your tired, your poor,
> Your huddled masses yearning to breathe free,
> The wretched refuse of your teeming shore.
> Send these, the homeless, tempest-tost to me.
> I lift my lamp beside the golden door!"
> —Inscription, Statue of Liberty
> (Emma Lazarus, "The New Collossus")

SUGGESTED READING

The Cycles in American History, Arthur Schlesinger, Jr., Penguin, 1989.
More Like Us: Making America Great Again, James Fallows, Houghton Mifflin, 1989.

Appendices

Appendix A

Legal Rights of Homeless Americans

This appendix was originally published in the *University of San Francisco Law Review* vol. 24, pages 297-362 (Winter 1990), as part of a symposium on "The New Property and the Individual—25 Years Later," but was written specifically for this book. The author gratefully acknowledges the lavish assistance rendered in production of this article by the following persons: Marianne Lachman, Nancy Mintie, Rebecca Heldt, J.W. Harrott, Robert Hayes, Gary L. Blasi, James Preis, Richard G. Shouse, Margaret L. Coates, Michael C. Spata, Karen R. Di Donna, Lali Villaoicencio, Michael Crosby, David B. Himelstein, and Russell D. Ward. Attorney Mark Regalbuit and Charles R. Dyer, the Director fo the San Diego County Law Library, gave indispensable and tireless efforts to the editorial works.

INTRODUCTION

For every wrong, the Law will provide a remedy.

—Ancient Legal Maxim

Vice is a Monster of so frightful mien, As to be hated needs but to be seen. Yet seen too oft, familiar with her face, We first endure, then pity, then embrace.

—Alexander Pope

The National Coalition on the homeless estimates that there are 3 million homeless Americans.[1] The author accepts this as the best estimate available. However, many of these are only homeless part of the time, and sub-populations of the homeless are expanding rapidly.[2] The homeless are, of course, the poorest of the nation's poor.

Auspiciously, the American public is increasingly aware of homelessness. In urban centers the subject now receives a steady, if muted, drumbeat of media coverage, and 1988 polls showed that the American people strongly want to see homelessness responsibly addressed.[3] The phenomenon is impossible to ignore, but the 1988 presidential candidates of both parties, in contrast with the silent, but hostile, departing administration, were required to speak only if faintly to the existence of homelessness.

Some think there may be a double-edged sword to the increasing public awareness of American homelessness, because although homelessness' rising tide has, on the one hand, captured much public attention, this has not yet led to broad awareness of available solutions; and overexposure, combined with the methodically repeated falsehood that we are collectively helpless vis-à-vis homelessness, has made us hapless. There remain hundreds of thousands of people roaming American streets and parks, living in alleys and canyons, under bridges and on street grates, being victimized by criminals, and too often being left to rummage through trash cans for sustenance.[4]

Increased public awareness is a step forward. However, in the United States, the type of public attention paid to major issues seems to be cyclic in nature.[5] Homelessness, too, may crest and then decline in terms of public concern; and one fear is that our citizenry may become inured to homelessness. This may be correct. There is therefore an immediacy to the need for forceful advocacy on behalf of the homeless. And if the rights of the homeless are to be championed effectively, lawyers must be their champions.

Observers of the homeless wonder where our systems have failed and what legal rights repose in these hundreds of thousands of shuffling, shabby human beings, haunting each American city. What follows is a survey of an evolving body of case law and litigation concerning the legal rights that lawyers have struggled to secure for homeless Americans. More pointedly, the purpose of this article is to outline the litigation strategies that lawyers can and must use to assist the homeless while also effecting overall solutions to homelessness.

This grave national problem is receiving remarkably scant attention in the mainstream media, particularly as to its solutions. This void of information is even more puzzling, given the fact that the increasing incidence of homelessness says much about our society. Professor Charles Reich has written,

> Vitally important ideas, ideas that contain the explanations and answers to our most dire social problems, can be effectively denied access to the marketplace. A few powerful voices, which endlessly repeat a highly ideological picture of reality, can gain a degree of market domination enabling them to shut out their competitors, silencing them instead of having to debate them.[6]

For Reich, the problem of homelessness has become obfuscated to the advantage of the small percentage of the American public whose own position on the economic ladder is secure and stable. As to the poorest of today's Americans, however, Jefferson's ideal of a mass of equally powerful and assertive voters/citizens is simply not applicable. They have lost the power to be heard by the government, and by other large and powerful institutions as well;[7] and these institutions, together with the press, largely shape what the public's perception of society will be.[8] The treatment, so far, is doing violence to the truth, and to rational evaluations of the public interest as well. To say nothing of the homeless.

Much of the article is devoted to litigation in California, New York, New Jersey, and Massachusetts. More emphasis is placed on developments in California and New York. The article examines in particular detail statutory provisions in California that provide the homeless with only a semblance of the legal rights which most other Americans take for granted.

Part one of this article provides a brief overview of the present underlying and pervasive resistance of our society to the devising of a thorough and genuine solution to homelessness. Secondly, litigation strategies useful to lawyers representing the homeless are presented. In part three, results of specific litigation concerning the right to shelter, adequacy and availability of shelter, various barriers to assistance, and the right to vote are examined. Part four deals with the major issue of the inadequacy of general relief systems of California, recognizing that such a problem exists in all states. Part five of the article focuses on litigation on behalf of the hordes of America's mentally ill who are homeless and the specialized needs of this most dysfunctional sub-group of homeless Americans. Part six similarly concentrates on litigation aiming at keeping families with children together and problems faced by this rapidly growing sub-group of the homeless population. Part seven deals with the very real problem of locating facilities to handle the homeless. Part eight points out areas into which advocacy for the homeless might expand. The article concludes that lawyers and litigation are crucial to efforts to assist otherwise powerless homeless Americans. More importantly, these heroes may be providing an essential foundation to resolving a national scandal that is indeed solvable.

I. LEGAL OVERVIEW

Most states have imposed upon themselves or their political subdivisions the duty to care for poor inhabitants.[9] The amount of federal and state funding for homeless programs is, however, feeble,[10] considering the scale of the condition and the imperiled lives these people lead on the streets.[11] In many cities in the early 1980s, local government officials' first general reaction to growing local homelessness was either to refuse to extend help, or grudgingly to offer below-subsistence assistance.[12] A second phase of official stinginess has taken the form of erecting sophisticated barriers between the applicants and the assistance that the law mandates.[13]

Why has the response to homeless people been so uncompassionate? One expects local officials to muster more decency and vigor—and a firmer regard for the law—than so far shown in providing assistance for their homeless constituents. Unfortunately, homeless people are seen as nobody's constituency; they have no market power and no voting power.[14]

Providing aid to the homeless sometimes boils down to intelligent management and commitment; but at the crux are also questions of money and the allocation of resources. When the question of the costs of programs to ameliorate homelessness arises, the answer is almost always: "That's too much." Local elected officials tend to short-change aid to the homeless, so that resources can go to more politically productive areas.

The efforts of legal advocates of the homeless have begun to bring relief to America's homeless people. Victories, however, have been hard won and constantly challenged. Legal advocacy on behalf of the homeless is one conduit through which these American citizens can participate in democracy. According to Professor Reich, "Without a home, a person cannot effectively be a citizen, or vote. The homeless cannot take part in democracy."[15]

Allegations of sweeping deprivations of procedural due-process rights to life, liberty and property are standard for legal pleadings filed to assist the homeless. Professor Reich has suggested that, "We should establish a right to have a home because that . . . was something that was within the reach of most people when the Constitution was adopted and it is no longer in the reach of everyone today."[16] He argues that the American life conditions have changed, and our justice systems have not kept pace.

Remarkably, there has been little comprehensive study or planning to address the problem of homelessness. Shelter is an obvious need shared by a heterogeneous and steadily expanding homeless population. Yet ". . . [t]o place highest priority on sheltering the homeless is to treat the problem after it has already occurred. . . ."[17] Shelterization does not treat the underlying causes of homelessness. Shelter is not the only important need of the homeless. This should not, however, diminish the significance of early litigation that focused on the right to shelter.[18] Such litigation has provided a framework for other advocates to bring a variety of actions on behalf of the homeless.

A prime cause of American homelessness is our dwindling supply of affordable low-income housing. Ultimately, the net loss of 1.5 million lowest-income housing units over the past ten years needs to be replaced,[19] and some form of problem-solving national housing policy reinstituted. Meanwhile, individuals at local levels must determinedly do their ethical, professional and human duties as practically and well as they can—with the tools at hand in each circumstance. And they must work to create better tools, else our system of justice may lose its claim as the basis of a civil society in respect for the law.

Social and health service bureaucracies are too often today bending or ignoring statutory mandates in the interest of controlling costs and caseload numbers.[20] Only aggressive legal advocacy can straighten the backs of such entities, and simultaneously strike a powerful blow for respect for the law.

There is little self-help a homeless person can pursue when confronted by a monolithic bureaucracy. Absent legal counsel, a recalcitrant local government can successfully ignore constitutional and statutory duties. Litigation is an ancient and honorable tool that can prod such an entity to institute reform.

The law exists to serve justice.[21] No matter what an attorney's sense of justice may be, the existence of a burgeoning homeless population in this country and in one's own community does violence to any notion of justice. Homelessness smacks of injustice, of the unraveling of the foundations of civil society, and of a dysfunctional society. Lawyers, through the centuries, have operated under general, ethical duties to perform *pro bono* legal services and to see that persons who are "oppressed or downtrodden" may obtain legal assistance without fear or favor.[22]

As Erickson and Wilhelm have pointed out, "Policy and program options to help the homeless generally fall within four areas: 1) prevention; 2) short-term emergency shelter and other life and health sustaining services; 3) transitional services such as longterm residential placement, health care, employment training and assistance, and 4) temporary and permanent housing."[23] Litigation can also be a curative strategy.[24] Although litigation cannot address the many causes of homelessness, ameliorating the agony of the homeless cannot today take place without it.[25] Advocates can also focus attention on legislative proposals under which local authorities might face homelessness issues head-on.

II. APPROACHES TO LITIGATION— THE LAWYER'S DILEMMA

Practicing poverty lawyers focus on the desperate daily existence of homeless persons. They believe that, in general, litigation for the homeless should be aimed at the immediate and life-threatening needs of the homeless—in other words: shelter, food, clothing, personal security and health care.[26] It is fairly easy for an honest observer to make a list of what one's community ought to be doing for its homeless members. Lawyers, however, can address difficulties only where a cognizable legal right is involved.

In the midst of litigation for the homeless, lawyers have lost some innocence with the discovery that they cannot always use *legal* tools to accomplish what needs to be done. Further, umpire-like trial judges are likewise often constrained to respond only to "yes" or "no" propositions. As a result, courts can rarely devise comprehensive solutions to societal problems. Litigation is, moreover, time-consuming, and implementation of judicially imposed remedies can often be difficult.[27]

Despite such limitations, there have been many successful lawsuits brought by Legal Aid and other public-interest lawyers in the last decade.[28] Courts have recognized and enforced governmental duties under state laws to provide shelter and other life-sustaining services to those in need.[29] Moreover, these lawsuits themselves—when conducted with dignity and based on solid facts, and when publicly discussed— continue to contribute to raising the public consciousness, potentially attracting the attention of decision-making public officials.[30]

Litigation can thus play a central role in helping those homeless who can least help themselves. What strategies should concerned lawyers devise in view of the limitations of litigation?[31] Successful litigation on behalf of the homeless has often involved bringing a series of carefully targeted cases challenging particularly egregious local practices. Litigators have been careful to select those practices that clearly result in severe harm to homeless people, and are so obviously onerous and unfair that decent persons, when apprised of them, react with sympathy, if not outrage.

Regardless of what right is being pressed or what governmental practice is being challenged, the first and most critical step for a litigation strategy is the development of a detailed and comprehensive understanding of the present and local welfare, shelter, and health systems by the litigators themselves. Counsel must then focus on local or state statutes requiring counties to "relieve and support" the indigent.[32] All fifty states have such statutes on their books.[33]

Litigators must be cognizant of the extent to which the judicial system is a part of the overall political system, because the outcome of a case might depend to some degree upon a trial judge's assessment of community values and the community's desired solutions to homelessness. For example, if the local media negatively portray homeless people, the lawyer's task in persuading a judge in that community for a court order may become more difficult. Succeeding in educating the middle-class and decision-makers in one's community about the realities of homelessness is crucial, in the long run, to successful litigation.

Here, the litigator is called upon to help build "teams" among those concerned with the homeless—teams working to raise issues and to educate both the public and individual decision-makers. The San Diego Mayor's Interfaith Shelter Network (a church/shelter program) was initially criticized because it assisted only the "upper 3 percent" of the homeless—in other words, the most presentable and least needy. But this program has now been recognized as a highly useful program because it has sensitized suburban church leaders, turning some into effective champions of the homeless, and many into educated voters.

Attorneys must similarly devise ways to bring the reality of their city's streets into the courtrooms. Life on the streets contains realities utterly outside of the life experience of many judges and jurors. This difficulty has been overcome by homeless advocates' filing numerous affidavits wherein homeless people graphically declare that they are victims of the particular governmental action or inaction challenged by the lawsuit.[34] These affidavits can give the judge a better idea of what life is like in the streets, and of the multitude of problems which besiege homeless individuals.[35] They have proven to be essential exhibits attached to a complaint.[36] Attorneys, with their law clerks, volunteer law students and others, must collect such affidavits themselves. Videos and photos, admissible under most state's Evidence Codes, can also be important ways to present facts.

A victory in the courtroom may not immediately translate into benefits for the homeless. Success can ultimately only be judged by impacts in the lives of real people. Litigators for the homeless live with the knowledge that courtroom reality can contrast sharply and paradoxically with reality "on the streets." Court orders are frequently not self-enforcing; therefore, vigilant monitoring is usually necessary to ensure that courtroom victories are not lost in the coming days in the local Welfare office or shelter. The starkest, pragmatic definition of "law" is helpful here: "The law is what is done to you in your individual case by the public official involved."[37]

To gain their understanding of actual conditions and needs, to gather evidence, and to build the teamwork necessary for better relations, lawyers for the homeless must maintain good communications with shelter managers and others working with the homeless. Having done all these things, such lawyers will nonetheless often find it necessary to go back to court to vindicate rights upheld in early victories.[38]

2A. Litigation Techniques

Homeless advocacy is thought of as occurring on two levels: 1) service cases, and 2) impact litigation. In service cases lawyers may represent individuals with individual problems. However, if an entire system refuses to provide legally mandated assistance, any amount of individual advocacy will be in vain. In response, Legal Aid and public interest attorneys have filed legal challenges to system-wide denials of rights to the homeless. This latter type is called *impact* litigation. In reality, legal issues affecting poor and homeless people can be effectively addressed only by a combination of both impact and service case work.[39] Impact litigation is too often neglected because it requires more creativity, resources, staying power, and bravery. But only impact litigation can clean up systems in need of such.

In utilizing their skills to secure homeless peoples' rights into forms of helpful governmental action, lawyers now have available a growing body of case law. This has been the product of nearly a decade of advocates' confrontations with federal, state, and local bureaucracies. These bureaucracies have tended to bend the intent of statutory and constitutional law in order to achieve other political and budgetary goals. To be successful, advocates for the homeless have had to develop an empirical sophistication concerning the systems and institutions which are creating and perpetuating homelessness.

Lawsuits brought on behalf of the homeless can be classed by litigation objectives. Some litigation has concerned breaking down barriers to access forms of assistance needed by the homeless. Other actions have focused on a "right to shelter" for homeless individuals. Others focus on the adequacy of the relief that may be supplied; the homeless' right to vote; various rights of the homeless mentally ill[40] (an area with many possibilities); and rights to aid that would be supportive of the integrity of homeless families,[41] or of children.

This body of case law exposes techniques and theories that litigators may apply. First, it is useful to review general legal principles involved in state court actions against government entities to enforce individual rights. To date, case decisions have challenged bureaucratic interpretations of state constitutions and statutes that have transformed systems, initially designed to help people and prevent harm, into systems that affirmatively cause harm while at the same time denying homeless people certain basic rights.

Lawyers challenging such governmental activities may resort to extraordinary writs or to requests for injunctive relief or mandamus, unless a procedure for particular judicial review is prescribed by a statute. Plaintiffs seeking an injunction must generally establish four elements: (1) a violation of a clear legal right, or an imminent threat of such violation; (2) threat of irreparable injury; (3) no adequate remedy at law, and (4) a balance of equities in his or her favor.[42] Although a plaintiff may establish these four elements, a court may still refuse injunctive relief if it is not considered to be in the public interest."[43]

There are two varieties of injunctions. Prohibitory injunctions command one to *refrain* from performing a particular action, while mandatory injunctions *compel* the performance of an action or duty. Historically, courts have been reluctant to issue mandatory injunctions, especially against a governmental authority or official. This reluctance is significant in cases on behalf of the homeless, where the plaintiff's desired result would be a mandatory injunction compelling a governmental authority to act. Confronted with a justiciable controversy, however, courts may issue mandatory injunctions against the government only when a public official or governmental entity fails to perform a non-discretionary, clear duty *and* when the defendant's conduct amounts to an abuse of discretion or is arbitrary and capricious.[44]

A writ of mandamus is a legal remedy commanding a governmental official to perform a duty imposed by law. The basic requirements for obtaining such a writ are: 1) a clear legal right on the part of the plaintiff; 2) a corresponding duty that the defendant must perform; and 3) the absence of an adequate, alternative remedy at law.[45] An important difference between a mandatory injunction and a writ of mandamus is an injunction's ability to prescribe a detailed course of action. In litigation for the homeless, either remedy can be issued to order governments to comply with their legal duties toward the poor, but only an injunction may provide detailed directives ordering governments what to do and how to do it.[46]

Individuals on the streets who require help from a government typically encounter many barriers in securing the assistance to which they are legally entitled. The homeless often have many questions regarding their legal rights. For example: Do their lack of homes make them nonresidents of the community and thus ineligible for aid? How much aid are they entitled to? How quickly can they get it? What type of identification is required to secure aid? If terminated from aid or otherwise sanctioned, do they have a right to a hearing? What rights will be upheld regarding getting evidence and otherwise preparing for the hearing? What rights will be afforded in the hearing itself? Can officials relegate homeless people to political nonexistence by denying them even the right to vote?

These questions and others have arisen out of the implementation of the "General Relief" systems that all states have established to provide basic minimal support for destitute people. The administration of relief programs will likely be vested in a County Board of Supervisors, a Director of Welfare, an Overseer of the Poor, or contracted to social services officials. All states have undertaken the duty to care for their poor either by adopting constitutional provisions or by enacting statutes; such duties are usually delegated to cities or counties, townships or municipalities.[47] It was this duty that homeless advocates initially focused on when asserting a "right to shelter."[48]

III. SPECIFIC AREAS OF LITIGATION

2A. Right to Shelter

Early cases brought on behalf of the homeless focused on the right to shelter. The seminal case establishing a right to shelter for the homeless was filed in New York in 1979 by Hayes' National Coalition for the homeless. *Callahan v. Carey*[49] is a paradigm of impact litigation on behalf of the homeless.

Plaintiffs in *Callahan* were the estimated ten thousand homeless men inhabiting New York City.[50] The complaint alleged (1) a critical shortage of available shelters; (2) that available shelters were unhealthy and dangerous; and (3) that this state of affairs violated the New York State Constitution and statutes requiring state and city officials to provide adequate care, aid and support for the needy.[51] The plaintiffs' argument relied heavily on Article XVII, section 1 of the State Constitution, which provides: "The aid, care and support of the needy are public concerns and shall be provided by the state and by such of its subdivisions, and in such manner and by such means, as the legislature may from time to time determine."[52]

The New York State Supreme Court issued a preliminary injunction directing state and city officials to furnish meals and lodging to homeless men of the Bowery District in New York City "who applied for shelter."[53]

Since *Callahan,* many suits have sought to improve shelter standards.[54] New York courts have generally been able to provide relief to homeless parties. However, they have avoided deciding the question of whether shelter is a fundamental right under the New York State Constitution.[55] A declared constitutional right to shelter in New York would ensure that that state's government would provide housing for the homeless, and that subsequent courts hearing such matters in other states might endorse this approach. The questions of whether a state's constitution guarantees a right to shelter is important, but without enforcement it becomes an abstract right.[56]

A constitutional provision like New York's permits counsel to buttress and offer arguments aimed at filling a myriad of urgent human needs. Further, even where an explicit constitutional claim may not be available, similar *statutory* claims may be raised.

In *Maticka v. City of Atlantic City,*[57] New Jersey plaintiffs were homeless men and women who had been refused emergency shelter assistance upon application to the municipal Welfare Department. Plaintiffs sought both a declaratory judgment of the city's violation of the right to "safe and suitable emergency shelter," guaranteed by the state constitution,[58] and preliminary and permanent injunctions ordering defendants to provide such emergency shelter. Plaintiffs also sought a declaratory judgment that defendants' refusal to "provide emergency shelter" violated plaintiffs' rights to immediate assistance under the New Jersey General Public Assistance Law.[59]

The plaintiffs prevailed on the basis of their statutory claim, and the court issued a temporary restraining order prohibiting state and local governments from denying General Assistance to the homeless when based solely on their inability to furnish a permanent address.

Maticka did not establish a constitutional right to shelter for the homeless in New Jersey. However, in granting the plaintiffs' injunction, the court ordered the defendants to develop and prepare a comprehensive plan for the provision of emergency shelter in Atlantic City.[60] The court did not need to reach the constitutional issue because the statutory grounds provided adequate relief.[61] *Maticka* illustrates the utility and necessity of raising both constitutional and statutory claims when litigating on behalf of the homeless. Purely constitutional arguments may not be fully persuasive. Yet, constitutionally based arguments can help to buttress and strengthen statutory claims because they tend to highlight the justiciability of issues concerning the plight of the homeless plaintiffs. Therefore, these two-pronged arguments can be extremely useful in persuading a judge whose life experiences are quite likely to be far removed from life on the streets.

2B. Actual and Adequate Shelter

In *Ross v. Board of Supervisors of Los Angeles County,*[62] the issue of the adequacy of shelter provided by the government was raised.[63] Plaintiffs challenged the county's practice of issuing $8 checks and referring homeless general-relief recipients to cheap hotels. A survey revealed that only seven such hotels used rate structures low enough to accommodate the homeless, and only four vacancies were found over a three-day period. The plaintiffs also challenged the county's failure to fund shelters, and submitted evidence from a developer demonstrating that the county could have saved twenty-five percent of the costs of the check system by providing money to private providers of shelter, instead of issuing $8 checks. A preliminary injunction issued, and, since then, the county has ceased issuing checks and instead has increased the number of voucher hotel rooms available. *Ross* illustrates successful litigation on behalf of the homeless. The preliminary injunction had the immediate effect of compelling the county to provide more beds for the homeless.[64] This concrete result directly affects homeless people.[65]

2C. Barriers to Assistance

While some homeless are not willing to accept any type of public assistance, many other homeless people, especially the mentally ill, are unaware of, usually afraid of, and generally incapable of dealing with bureaucracies providing public benefits.[66] Moreover, homeless people often find themselves barred from taking advantage of general assistance or shelter benefits because of the imposition of arbitrary pre-conditions such as lack of identification and/or address. The most common barrier to assistance facing a homeless person is that an applicant for general assistance is often required to provide a permanent address: often it is claimed the address of a shelter will not be sufficient. Legal advocates have been universally successful in eradicating these barriers.[67]

2C1. A Lack of Identification

In *Eisenheim v. Board of Supervisors of the County of Los Angeles*,[68] it was alleged that the County was denying emergency shelter to eligible homeless applicants by requiring each homeless individual to produce documentary identification.[69] Additionally, people were being required to wait a week after initial contact to "schedule" an appointment to "apply" for emergency relief. Moreover, they were usually required to wait even longer after application to receive aid. Further, at the scheduled appointment, the homeless applicant would have to produce formal proof of identification. Many homeless people have been robbed of or have otherwise lost their identification papers. An organized homeless person could often take four to five life-threatening months to secure a new birth certificate or similar proof.[70] Homeless people from rural areas, for example, socially dislocated and finding themselves in a big city like Los Angeles, were often born with the assistance of midwives, and birth certificates were never issued. Other individuals are from Latin America. Some do not have enough information about their own background even to apply for a copy of their birth certificates. Thus, the remarkable bureaucratic impediments thrown up by Los Angeles County proved nearly insurmountable, especially as applied to those mentally ill individuals who compose forty percent of the entire Los Angeles homeless population.[71]

In *Eisenheim*, plaintiffs pointed out that section 17000 of the State Welfare and Institutions Code required that each California county and city "relieve and support the needy," and that the federal and state due process clauses mandate that this to be done both reasonably and fairly. The Los Angeles Superior Court issued an order temporarily restraining the County from its practices. A stipulated settlement was filed shortly thereafter, whereby Los Angeles County agreed to stop requiring a birth certificate, driver's license, or other documentary proof of identification as a condition to receiving emergency housing benefits. The county was also required to make such benefits available to eligible applicants on the *same day* as their application.[72]

Los Angeles Legal Aid's Gary Blasi, coordinator of the multi-law firm Los Angeles Homeless Litigation Team,[73] points out that Los Angeles County's strategy has been "to litigate every aspect of each case in the most hardball way one can imagine." Revealing of the County's approach was that, after it had settled the General Relief grant amount case for a gross increase totaling $33 million, the County was at that very moment devising five new internal programs.[74] The net effect of these internal programs was to reduce the total numbers of persons on general relief, thereby negating the positive gains for homeless persons on general relief that had ostensibly been achieved through the settlement.

Blasi cites another example which illustrates Los Angeles County's approach in defending litigation brought by the homeless. The situation occurred when the Homeless Litigation Team filed one hundred affidavits signed by homeless general relief recipients, all essentially claiming that they could not possibly sustain civilized life on $228 per month. The County had welfare workers contact these individuals and direct them to appear at the Welfare Office at a certain time and date "to pick up a check." When sixty-seven of these individuals did appear, instead of a check they received subpoenas directing them to come back another day for depositions. Upon appearing for deposition, these people were "herded into offices which contained welfare-fraud investigators."[75] The depositions thus taken were significantly costly to the County, and the information obtained therein was useless in the litigation. Blasi concluded that the only possible purpose of this charade was to retaliate against and to intimidate the homeless who complained. Having revealed such tactics to the Court, the Homeless Litigation Team hopes that its efforts, in the future, will be less like "shoveling flies across an open room"[76] and, at least to some extent, more like cornering an opponent in a chess match and announcing checkmate."[77]

2C2. Lack of an Address

Another barrier having drastic consequences for the homeless is the often-imposed requirement that one have a fixed dwelling address in order to receive any benefits. Since these benefits are often the person's only source of sustenance, under such a requirement, absent an address, an applicant would be summarily denied income. It stands to reason, of course, that in order to pay rent to establish an address, one must have an income, and, if these people had income, they would probably also have an address.[78] The absurd, circular character of such regulations makes them an appealing target for litigation.[79]

Before challenging such regulations, however, attorneys should first investigate local welfare statistics to find out how often their county might be denying assistance to homeless persons because of lack of an address. Secondly, counsel needs to discern whether challenging such regulations locally will have an effect that would really benefit homeless persons. Address requirements ought to be challenged if there is a significant denial of assistance and if courtroom challenges would lead to actual benefits for some homeless.

In Los Angeles, the Homeless Litigation Team decided that such a challenge would do little to benefit homeless people concretely.[80] On the other hand, in San Diego, Legal Aid attorneys concluded that a significant number of individuals were locally denied benefits solely because they had no address, and thereupon filed a lawsuit.

In *Nelson v. San Diego County Board of Supervisors*,[81] plaintiffs successfully challenged, as constitutionally and statutorily invalid, a county's regulations terminating general relief (welfare) payments to any recipient not obtaining a valid address within sixty days.[82] The court of appeal found that the general relief statutes did not require a valid dwelling address as an element of "residence."[83] Holding that these regulations violated a statutory mandate to aid the indigent,[84] the court further found that, as a matter of law, the county had not met its burden of showing the absence of other available, possible cost-cutting methods to limit total general relief payments to the available financial resources.[85]

Plaintiffs also contended that the county's regulations violated their rights to equal protection under the California Constitution by authorizing general relief aid to indigents with fixed addresses, while denying such benefits to equally or more needy homeless people. Plaintiffs urged the court to apply a strict scrutiny standard of review to the regulation strictly because the right to shelter is fundamental.[86] Plaintiffs also asserted that such regulations were invalid under the "rational basis" standard of review, "because denying aid to the homeless is irrational, and inconsistent with the goal of the general relief statutes and not in furtherance of any legitimate governmental interest."[87] In the absence of any trial court finding, the reviewing court did not get to the merits of these constitutional claims.[88] Therefore, the advocate should make clear offers of proof and demand findings.

In California at least, *Nelson* might indicate that courts are increasingly unwilling to countenance a county's attempts to shirk statutory responsibility to assist the homeless. The *Nelson* court's refusal to address the merits of the plaintiffs' equal protection claims does not mean that such claims are not viable. If anything, *Nelson* suggests that such claims should still be pursued. There is no apparent reason that such advocacy can hurt the case, and pressing such claims may provide an additional degree of dignity for the challenges homeless advocates make to local practices. The federal Constitution's insistence on fundamental fairness must be reapplied to the unique dilemmas of each generation.[89]

2D. The Right to Vote

Ultimately, the homeless need a political voice in order to challenge the consequences of homelessness effectively. In several states, homeless individuals have been denied the right to vote on grounds that they have no bona fide residence.[90] For the most part, however, the homeless have lacked the organization and support necessary to have any political influence. In *Clark v. Community for Creative Non-Violence*,[91] Justice Marshall, in dissent, pointed out that the homeless need political power if they are to attain and preserve civil liberties.[92] Indeed, in any democracy, the ability to vote is the ultimate voice through which citizens can preserve and protect their civil liberties. The right to vote is that much more crucial for the homeless because they do not have any financial resources that commonly multiply others' political clout.

The right to vote will not, of course, necessarily lead to quick, measurable benefits on the streets. In fact, some veteran homeless advocates opine that voter registration projects among the homeless uniformly result in increasing the number of voters who "vote wrong," because they identify with the prevailing rhetoric and want to "identify with the non homeless."[93]

But some issues may become litigation priorities simply as matters of democratic faith and principle. In any true democracy, "all must vote or none can remain free."[94] In the short run, the right to vote may be a purely symbolic first step in securing for the homeless some political voice. Voter registration cards might also help homeless people to establish their identification at welfare offices and the like, thereby solving the problems incident to lack of identification discussed above.[95] Moreover, having this form of identification may help to prevent indignities suffered by "non-persons," such as being prodded along by officials. Establishing a homeless-voter base might help dispel the damaging myth that homeless people are "transients" who swarm from city to city.[96] Unmasking these stereotypes facilitates breaking down barriers to assistance because it changes a community's view of the homeless. Getting a community concerned with its homeless population can heighten the prospects of successful litigation as the courts become attuned to the community's desired solution to homelessness. Furthermore, it would be difficult for a City Council member to blithely ignore a block of 6,000 to 50,000, or even 500, registered voters.

A highly visible voter registration program, enrolling homeless citizens (along with more prominent, supportive citizens), could be used to make a major impact on local public sentiment and, therefore, impact on elected public officials.

In the 1984 case of *Pitts v. Black*,[97] homeless plaintiffs brought a class action seeking to enjoin the New York City and State Election Boards from applying regulations that defined the "residence" required to vote as "that place where a person maintains a fixed, permanent and principal home, and to which he, wherever temporarily located, always intends to return."[98] The plaintiffs offered an alternative definition of bona fide residence: "The act of being in one geographic locale, where one performs the usual functions of sleeping, eating, and living in accordance with one's lifestyle, and a place to which one, wherever temporarily located, intends to return."[99] Applying a strict scrutiny standard, the district court reasoned that although the state's regulations served to prevent fraud and to ensure an individual's stake in the community, less restrictive procedures were available that could serve to protect these state interests without abridging the more fundamental right to vote.[100] To qualify for voter registration, the court opined that homeless individuals must at least identify a "specific location within a political community which they consider their 'home base', to which they return regularly, manifest an intent to remain for the present, and a place from which they can receive messages and be contacted."[101] The residence test adopted in *Pitts* may serve as a model for the redefinition of bona fide residence requirements in other contexts such as public assistance. Furthermore, *Pitts* has provided the authority used by homeless advocates in California and elsewhere to secure voting rights for the homeless.[102]

In *Collier v. Menzel*,[103] the plaintiffs, three homeless Santa Barbara individuals, submitted voter registration applications listing a local public park as their residence.[104] The applications were rejected by the County Registrar of Voters as having given an insufficient residence address for the purpose of voting.[105] The trial court denied plaintiffs' petition for a writ of mandamus to compel the Registrar to accept their applications. On appeal, the plaintiffs successfully argued their compliance with statutory requirements for voter registration, and that failure to process their applications violated the constitutional right to equal protection of the law.[106] The court found that the park dwellers satisfied the statutory residentiary requirements of having: (1) a fixed habitation, and (2) an intention of remaining at that place and of returning to it after temporary absences.[107] The court further held that homeless appellants' interest in voting on an equal basis with other citizens represented a fundamental right in our democratic society.[108] The court concluded that the appellants were entitled to a writ of mandamus directing the respondents to allow the appellants to register to vote on the ground that their submitted affidavits of registration complied with State registration laws.[109] The court further observed that the respondents' refusal to register the appellants was not necessary to promote the goals of preventing fraud and was violative of the appellants' right to vote under equal protection standards.[110]

In litigating a homeless individual's right to vote, the focus is on a proper construction of the residency requirement. In *Collier*, it was argued that "permitting the 'homeless' to vote will impart a sense of responsibility to those people by giving them a political stake in their future and a sense of caring about their community."[111] Thus, an unduly restrictive residency requirement would only serve to hinder the possibility of reintegrating homeless people back into society, in addition to violating citizens' fundamental right to vote.

IV. INADEQUACY OF GENERAL RELIEF AMOUNTS

Another difficulty general relief schemes may pose is that the monthly allocation an individual receives may not be enough to cover local food, clothing, and shelter expenses adequately. This problem becomes more significant when officials attempt to reduce an already insufficient allocation. In *Boehm v. Superior Court of Merced County*,[112] the plaintiffs sought to enjoin the county's July 1983 reduction of General Assistance for indigent residents[113] from $198.00 to $175.00 per month for individuals, with proportional reductions for larger family units. On appeal, the court held that the county's act of reducing general assistance without basing the reduction on an empirical study to determine the minimum local subsistence needs of indigent residents was arbitrary and capricious. Subsequently, Merced County conducted two studies of minimum subsistence needs that considered only the minimum need for housing and food and, after which, the county raised the level by $10.00 to $185.00. The county's studies did not account for transportation, clothing, or medical costs. Petitioners then sought a preliminary injunction to stop this reduction,[114] which was denied by the Superior Court. In response, the petitioners sought a writ of mandate to enjoin the reduction and to order retroactive payments at the 1983 level, along with cost of living increases from the date of the reduction.[115] In granting this relief, the court declared that if a General Assistance program failed to provide for the aforementioned needs, the omission must be based on a study demonstrating that the needs omitted will be satisfied by some other program available to General Assistance recipients.[116]

The facts of *Boehm* revealed an egregious attempt by a county to control its costs while ignoring law and human reality. Such a situation is, regrettably, not atypical. *Boehm* has been used as a springboard for legal challenges to increase General Assistance benefits. If advocates can demonstrate that a county's General Assistance level is predicated upon either no study or a study that does not adequately consider the core necessities of life (shelter, food, clothing), they may argue that General Assistance is inadequate as a matter of law.

Indeed, homeless advocates in Los Angeles, San Diego, and Sacramento have chosen to use the county's statutory obligation under California Welfare and Institutions Code sections 10000, 17000, and 17001 to relieve and support those who lack minimal income or resources as the basis for increases in general relief benefits. Under section 10000, the California Legislature has sought to "provide for protection, care and assistance to people of the state in need thereof and to promote the welfare and happiness of all the people of the state by providing appropriate aid and services to all of its needy and distressed."[117] Section 17000 imposes a duty upon the counties to relieve and support all incompetent, poor, indigent persons and those incapacitated by age, disease, or accident . . . when such persons are not supported . . . by their own means."[118] Section 17001 imposes a further duty to adopt standards of aid and care."[119] All American states have similar statutes.[120]

Because of vigorous litigation on behalf of the homeless, both San Diego and Los Angeles Counties have now established their general relief programs to meet these statutory obligations.

In August 1986, San Diego County had set general relief grants at $225 per month for qualifying individuals. The grant was intended to provide for food, shelter and personal needs. One hundred thirty dollars of the grant was designated for obtaining shelter. Recipients were receiving their grant via two payments per month, making it especially difficult to accumulate necessary funds for deposits and monthly rents to secure housing.[121] San Diego's county government was claiming that $130 monthly was enough to allow one indigent person to share housing with another person or persons, or to rent a room at a single room occupancy hotel (SRO).

In 1988, homeless plaintiffs in *Bell v. Board of Supervisors of San Diego County*[122] sought declaratory relief based on California Welfare and Institutions Code section 17000 and on federal and state constitutional grounds, claiming that the relief grants provided were inadequate. Plaintiffs predicated their statutory violation by alleging that the defendant county had: (1) failed to conduct a proper study to determine the minimal cost of housing in San Diego County; (2) failed to provide general relief recipients with a housing allowance sufficient to obtain housing; (3) provided such allowance in two payments for employable recipients; and (4) failed to determine and provide a utilities allowance for any recipients and a transportation allowance for non-employable recipients.[123]

Plaintiffs further alleged that by basing the housing portion of the grant primarily on the amount paid for housing by a small, atypical subset of general relief recipients, most of whom rented housing from relatives or friends at below market rates, defendants were violating the due process and equal protection clauses of both the California Constitution[124] and the fourteenth amendment to the federal Constitution and, in addition, had acted arbitrarily and capriciously.[125]

Plaintiffs sought preemptory writs and permanent injunctions ordering the county to make an adequate study of housing, utilities and transportation costs so as to provide plaintiffs with aid sufficient to meet those discovered needs.[126]

In both *Bell* and *Blair v. Board of Supervisors of Los Angeles County*,[127] legal advocates successfully attacked California counties' faulty determination of general relief payment amounts, and the cases resulted in each defendant county entering into a stipulation agreeing to increase general relief monthly amounts significantly.[128] In March 1988, the defendants in *Bell* agreed to increase the monthly allocation by $50.00 to $275.00, effective April, 1988. Moreover, this became available in one payment at the beginning of each month if the employable general relief recipient gave the Department of Social Services (DSS) a written statement from a landlord that the general relief recipient could rent the premises for the month and that the landlord agrees to accept the rent directly from DSS. The immediate benefit of this arrangement was that these general relief recipients gained guaranteed shelter for an entire month. This step has some practical benefit for disabled individuals: the mentally ill, persons of low intelligence, alcoholics, and shell-shocked veterans, for example. Some individuals so assisted were able to find jobs, gain some dignity, and work themselves off of the general relief rolls. Furthermore, in *Bell*, the DDS was ordered to evaluate the policy of providing a transportation allowance to non-employable general relief recipients as a special need only.[129] In both *Bell* and *Blair*, as in *Callahan*, the court never reached the merits of the plaintiff's suit because a stipulated judgment was entered.[130]

Initially, the lawsuits in both *Bell* and *Blair* were successful in that they had a measurable effect on the streets where, as a result, people gained money on which to live. However, homeless advocates are quick to point out that grant level increases alone may not have a lasting effect.

2A. The *Poverty Resistance* and *Guidotti* Cases

In August 1989, advocates were successful in persuading a court that the Sacramento County Board of Supervisors breached statutory duties imposed on it by Welfare and Institutions Code sections 17000, 17001 and 10000 in setting the levels of aid for county recipients of general assistance.[131] In *Poverty Resistance Center v. Hart*, plaintiff's complaint for declaratory, injunctive and monetary relief alleged that the County breached its aforementioned statutory duty because the standard of aid was not supported by ". . . adequate studies of the actual cost of maintaining a minimum standard of living in Sacramento County."[132] The trial court sustained defendant's demurrer on the ground that plaintiffs had not shown a failure by the Board of Supervisors to review evidence of the minimum subsistence needs of the indigent residents within Sacramento County.[133] It reasoned that a trial court should not inquire into the relative validity of the various studies conducted to determine these minimum subsistence needs.[134]

In reversing, the appellate court did inquire into the validity of such studies. It reasoned that the materiality of the "factual grist" of such studies depended on the standards of aid and care mandated by Welfare and Institutions Code sections 17000 and 17001 and were subject to review.[135]

The court criticized plaintiffs' claim that they were entitled to an "independent adjudication of the cost of subsistence in Sacramento County,"[136] and held that only the facts considered by the County in setting the grant levels and the statutory compliance and rationality in setting such standards were reviewable.[137]

On the other hand, the court found defendant's perception of the standard of review too narrow. Defendants claimed there should be no review of the factual underpinnings of their action.[138] The court declared that defendants incorrectly viewed ". . . the adoption of standards of aid and care as a part of the County's budgetary process."[139] Instead, the court reviewed the County's actions in light of the statutes governing the administration of general assistance. More specifically, the court considered whether the County adhered to the factors of subsistence mandated by section 17000, in adopting standards pursuant to the mandate by section 17001, and whether there was an evidentiary predicate for their action in setting the grant levels.[140]

Following *Mooney v. Pickett*,[141] the court found that, "Section 17000 imposes a mandatory duty upon the counties to support 'all incompetent, poor, indigent persons, and those incapacitated by age, disease, or accident.' "[142] The court further noted that, in carrying out that duty, section 17001 imposes a further duty to adopt standards of aid and care."[143] Following *Boehm v. Superior Court*, the *Poverty Resistance* court also posited that challenges to general assistance grant level standards, which were insufficient by comparison with other government indices of poverty, had to be justified by an identified factual predicate detailing the actual costs of subsistence within the county.[144] Because the terms of such standards turned on factual issues—the subsistence studies—the court found that the County needed to demonstrate reasonable support in the administrative record for the factual determinations it made in setting grant levels, and that the decision makers (here, members of the elected County Board of Supervisors) had a duty personally to consider the actual studies.[145] The court declared that such standards must be consistent with not only sections 17000 and 17001 but also with section 10000, which requires that aid be provided "promptly and humanely."[146]

In sum, the court found in *Poverty Resistance Center* that the governing statutes and information concerning actual subsistence living costs set discretionary boundaries that a county must find before setting grant levels.[147] Thus, under the statutory scheme, the adequacy of General Assistance grants promulgated by counties become questions of law.[148]

The defendants' misperception of the standard of review caused them to fail to join issue with some of the plaintiff's allegations of inadequacy in the standards of aid. Nevertheless, in order to resolve the appeal as presented, the court went on to consider the actionability of specific matters put in issue by the complaint.[149]

The plaintiffs alleged that no studies considered by the county supported the amount allocated to defray shelter costs. The court declared that the grant level standard adopted by the county for shelter costs was actually *lower* than costs of shelter set forth in the studies upon which the county based such grant,[150] and concluded that, "This presents an apparent failure of the adopted standard to find support in the evidence considered by the Board (County), warranting judicial relief."[151] The Board explained this discrepancy on the grounds that cost-of-living surveys are only hypothetical data in regard to actual costs incurred by the homeless. The court found this extrapolation unreasonable given the available data,[152] pointing out that, "Persons cannot eat hypothetical food nor live in hypothetical houses."[153] Thus, the plaintiffs were found to have stated an actionable claim for relief for insufficient standards of aid and care under section 17001.[154]

The plaintiffs unsuccessfully argued that grant levels were improperly set if done without including amounts for the purchase of clothing, newspapers, bedding utensils and other goods they deemed essential to subsistence.[155] The court found such items to be beyond the core subsistence elements of food, shelter and medical care. A county's judgment about what constitutes subsistence is discretionary unless unreasonable. Counties are not restricted to making an individual-needs assessment for each recipient. Nor are the needs of some classes of recipients removed from the county's statutory obligation merely because they are not common to all recipients.[156] It is very instructive to litigators that the court declared that counties are not required ". . . to address every conceivable need via the monthly flat grant."[157] The court noted that other deficiencies in the county's failure to provide general relief under section 17000 ". . . must be sought under a pleading which identifies the county regulation or practice that facially or as applied occasions the alleged unlawful result."[158]

The lesson to be gleaned from *Poverty Resistance Center* may be that it is fruitless to challenge a county's standard grant for General Assistance by seeking an adjudication of the actual costs of subsistence in the county. Courts at both the trial and appellate level may be simply unwilling to consider such problems, and defer to the county's discretion in such matters. Rather, it appears that a more narrowly framed pleading may be more successful in challenging General Assistance grants.

Seemingly, allegations that a county's evidentiary predicate for a General Assistance grant violates the statutory framework of Welfare and Institutions Code sections 17000, 17001 and 10000 are more likely to be found actionable and less subject to demurrer. Thus, it may be argued that General Assistance is inadequate as a matter of law.

On the heels of *Poverty Resistance*, it appears that judicial review of General Assistance grants by a county may be strictly limited to the record of proceedings before the Board of Supervisors. It should be noted that the *Poverty Resistance* court rejected the plaintiff's argument that *Boehm* stood for the proposition that the issuable facts in a judicial proceeding are the costs of a subsistence living within the particular county.[159] Specifically, the *Boehm* opinion was criticized as accepting ". . . without examination or analysis the assumption that . . ." the adequacy of a housing survey in that case was triable fact.[160] Apparently the *Poverty Resistance* court was not convinced that the *Boehm* court sufficiently considered whether the county's utilization of the housing survey as a factual basis for the grant level satisfied the requirements of sections 10000, 17000 and 17001. The *Poverty Resistance* court reviewed only the lawfulness of a Board's action in setting a General Assistance grant on the basis of the evidence before the Board under the relevant statutory provisions.[161]

It is noteworthy that, subsequently, an important aspect of the *Poverty Resistance* ruling has been limited by the *Guidotti v. County of Yolo* decision.[162] In *Poverty Resistance*, the appellate court accepted the county's use of rent-averaging in formulating the amount for shelter costs to be included in general assistance grants.[163] In *Guidotti*, however, the same appellate court found that the DSS study, which averaged the housing costs of different groups of general assistance recipients, many of whom shared housing and paid below market rent, was impermissibly flawed.[164] The *Guidotti* court specifically ruled that averaging, whether for shelter or food costs, must be fair and reasonable.[165] Averaging was only found reasonable if it represented the price at which a person could purchase food, housing, or other necessities.[166] The court concluded there was insufficient evidence before the Board that there was housing available at a cost commensurate with the housing allotment of its General Relief grant.[167]

Advocates for the homeless believe that the effect of the *Guidotti* decision is to limit the court's ruling in *Poverty Resistance*, which accepted rent averaging, to those circumstances where no contrary evidence is presented to the local County Board of Supervisors. On remand, the trial court presumably will have to order the Board to conduct another study on the housing assistance portion of the grant.[168] *Guidotti* underscores the utility of drafting pleadings directed at attacking the factual predicate upon which a county bases its General Relief grants.

2B. Advocacy Regarding Inadequate Medical Benefits

While this issue has thus far hardly been touched by litigation, the physical health problems of the homeless are stark. Dermatological and podiatric problems afflict essentially all homeless people. The incidence of respiratory diseases, including tuberculosis, is the highest of any sub-population ever recorded in American health history, and the difficulties in sustaining care for serious and even life-threatening conditions are universal.[169]

One recent case established a right to dental care. In *Cook v. Superior Court*,[170] the California Third District Court of Appeal ruled that a county must provide a humane level of dental care under California Welfare and Institutions Code section 17000.[171] While the court ruled that dental care services need not be equivalent to California's present standard for state-provided medical services to the indigent, the court strongly rejected the county's contention that Welfare and Institutions Code section 10000[172] did not apply to the amount, scope and duration of dental services. The court noted:

> In its brief, the County contends section 10000's command that "aid shall be administered as services provided promptly and humanely," does not refer to the *kind* of services to be provided but only to the *manner* in which they are provided. Thus, according to the County, section 10000 does not mandate the provision of any services at all so long as any services provided are provided humanely. Reduced to its practical consequences, the County's contention would mean it could satisfy section 17000 obligations by providing an aspirin to an indigent person dying of malaria so long as the provider said, "Sorry about the aspirin. It's all we've got. We *do* hope it helps you die with dignity."
>
> We think the county's construction of 10000 leads to absurdity which must be avoided.[173]

V. THE MENTALLY ILL

The chronically mentally ill are the most visible and dysfunctional sub-group of the homeless populations.[174] There is no precision on the percentage of the homeless who suffer some mental disability, although a greatly disproportionate number, and surely a majority of homeless, suffer from mental illness.[175] Experts have estimated that at least forty percent of the homeless suffer from severe, and in most cases permanent and completely disabling, mental disorders.[176]

The deinstitutionalization of perhaps one million previously hospitalized state psychiatric patients was the initial factor in the growth of the United States' homeless mentally ill population.[177] The loss of supportive "after (hospitalization) care," and of SSI total disability, Social Security, and other benefits has been a "cruel after-shock."[178] As thousands of disabled individuals exited the state hospitals (or, later, were never taken there in the first place), there was no clear consensus as to what community treatment for these individuals should consist of. For a quarter century, legislatures and governors carved away at program element after program element. In California, for example, the allocation for mental health care is less than one fourth the money that was being allotted twenty-five years ago. In addition, local communities have often resisted the establishment of clinics and half-way residences in their residential neighborhoods.[179]

That homeless persons lack a support system and face great difficulty in meeting basic subsistence needs of food, shelter and clothing is axiomatic.[180] A fortiori, the homeless who are mentally ill face the greatest difficulties in meeting these basic subsistence needs. The application processes to obtain resources to meet *any* of these needs, even those for emergency shelter, are often so complex and daunting that individuals with significant mental impairment have no chance of successfully negotiating these processes.[181]

Living in hostile environments inevitably resulted in relapses into more severe mental illness. When these people were ultimately hospitalized, further mental deterioration had occurred; therefore, they were hospitalized in costly facilities[182] for longer periods of time, only to be discharged once again on to the debilitating streets.[183] This outrageous circumstance relative to profoundly mentally ill Americans exists across the nation. Probably as many as twenty percent of *all* Americans who are permanently mentally disabled are homeless.[184]

Unlike other areas of litigation on behalf of the homeless, case law regarding legal efforts to assist the homeless mentally ill has been slow to develop. However, in *Klosterman v. Cuomo*,[185] the Coalition for the Homeless filed a class action suit against New York state officials seeking supportive housing in the community for an estimated 6,000 former state psychiatric patients who were homeless.[186] The suit alleged that the plaintiffs were being denied the right to appropriate community-based residences, and, as a result, they were being subjected to a vicious cycle of life on the streets; in and out of jail and in public shelters; then back to the streets. The bases for the *Klosterman* suit were the constitutional, statutory and regulatory framework of the New York mental health system. By law, the State of New York is under an affirmative duty to develop appropriate community housing, but at the time of filing, it had developed only 3,000 community residence beds in the entire state. This was supposed to be serving an estimated 108,000 chronically mentally ill New Yorkers.[187]

On appeal, the *Klosterman* court declared that it was proper for a court to intervene in this legislatively based bureaucratic allocation of resources. To do so was merely "a declaration and enforcement of rights that have already been conferred by the executive and legislative branches and, thus, not an interference with the decision-making function thereof."[188] In a subsequent ruling, the trial court dismissed certain counts of the complaint, which were based on federal constitutional and statutory rights to receive adequate treatment in the least restrictive environment.[189] The court declared it could not find a constitutional right to such treatment unless plaintiffs were confined and a liberty interest was threatened.[190] Nevertheless, the right to treatment has been recognized elsewhere even absent such pre-conditions.[191]

A recent decision, however, has proved devastating to the interests of California's homeless mentally ill. In *Mental Health Association v. Deukmejian*, plaintiffs/appellants sought declaratory and injunctive relief to compel state and local officials to create and fund community-based, mental health residential and rehabilitative programs.[192] However, the court did not agree with plaintiffs that ". . . in the absence of the deprivation of constitutional rights, this court has the power to dictate (1) how the mental health system should be structured, and how much money the legislature should appropriate to accomplish the changes."[193] Instead, it was the court's position that setting up a bureaucracy to supervise a new mental health system with least restrictive care alternatives was better left to the legislature and executive.[194] Given this predisposition, it is hardly surprising that the court held that while the Lanterman-Petris-Short Act[195] (the "LPS" act), Community Residential Treatment Act[196] ("CRT") and Short-Doyle Act[197] created a clear legislative preference for the provision of mental health treatment in the least restrictive alternative, they established no right to this.[198] Further, these three legislative acts create a statutory framework for the administration and implementation of the California Legislature's mental health program.[199]

The court denied the statutory claim, focusing on the appellant's reliance on

California Welfare and Institutions Code section 5325.1, which provides in part, "Treatment *should* be provided in ways that are the least restrictive of the personal liberty of the individual."[200] Similarly, the court found that, by enacting Welfare and Institutions Code section 5450.1, the Legislature was concerned with promoting, rather than mandating, the least restrictive form of treatment.[201] That section provides, in pertinent part, ". . . counties *may* implement the community residential treatment system described in this chapter either with available county applications or, as new moneys become available, by applying for funds to the State Department of Mental Health."[202] Further, the Short-Doyle Act sets up a mechanism for sharing state and county responsibilities in mental health services, and the court found that the only part of Short-Doyle that referred to least restrictive treatment only directed that such "services shall be developed."[203] In sum, the court found that the Short-Doyle Act and LPS did not together mandate such facilities.[204]

The court also held that the State Legislative scheme concerning treatment of "gravely disabled" persons provides adequate due process. Appellants characterized gravely disabled persons as both "hard core" and "revolving door" patients. Appellants claimed that the legislative scheme included a least restrictive treatment for the revolving door population, and did not challenge the state and county's treatment of hard-core patients.[205] The trial court found that, as a result of deinstitutionalization and civil commitment statutes, patients capable of community treatment had, in fact, been removed to the community.[206] Hard-core patients theoretically remained in the hospitals twenty-five years ago, but what of the "new hard core?"[207] Both the trial and appellate courts followed the "professional judgment standard" set forth by the U.S. Supreme Court in *Youngberg v. Romeo.*[208]

Appellants' last claim was that Article I, section 13, of the California Constitution ensures gravely disabled persons treatment in a least restrictive environment. Appellants argued that section 13 guaranteed that no person could wrongfully be deprived of his fundamental liberty interests without due process of law. The court, however, refused to recognize a state constitutional right to least restrictive treatment because the California statutory scheme under LPS established due process protection of all the rights of the involuntarily committed mentally disordered person.[209]

In *Deukmejian*, the Court of Appeal found the prospect of a court setting up and running a mental health system unworkable. The *Deukmejian* decision dealt another blow to California's mentally ill, because, in it, California parted company with most modern states. In California, there is no longer a statutory or constitutional right to mental health treatment in the least restrictive alternative.

After the Court of Appeal decision, the California Supreme Court, using a provision of the California Constitution,[210] ordered the *Deukmejian* opinion depublished, which technically means that it cannot properly be cited to a court as case authority.[211] Nevertheless, all the principals in the case (advocates for the mentally ill homeless, advocates for the counties, and the county governments themselves) are reported to presume that the California Supreme Court would uphold the ruling, but disapproved of the logic of the argument of the Court of Appeal, and thus depublished.[212] The depublished *Deukmejian* decision, therefore, has had a peculiarly forceful effect, as if it were law.[213] Counsel for California Governor George Deukmejian of course attended all hearings as the *Deukmejian* case proceeded through the courts. During this period Governor Deukmejian approved of budget increases for mental health purposes on every occasion presented; since the depublishing of the opinion, however, the Governor has vetoed every proposed increase.[214]

On the other hand, the decision engendered howls of protest from a remarkably wide range of political groups. According to Jim Preis, Director of Mental Health Advocacy Services, "A tide is building. I believe the Governor helped focus it. When California gets a new governor in 1991, from either party, and new Mental Health Department leadership, this wave of demand for a common sense care system for California's chronically mentally ill will be irresistible."[215] Grasping the larger hope, it may be that, in the long run, the interests of the plaintiffs were served by counsel's pressing needs of plaintiff's claims in *Deukmejian*. Advocacy in this arena will be bracing, since it is done on the stage of history.

2A. Strategy

Today, advocates for the homeless mentally ill wage an especially tough and challenging uphill battle on their clients' behalf. Faced with typically slow and cumbersome bureaucratic processes and reticent courts, it is essential that the advocate forcefully pursue all possible causes of action.

Persistent challenges to deliberately placed, bureaucratic obstacle courses, via litigation, in effect "papering" bureaucracies, are essential to realize and sustain victories for the homeless. This is especially true with regard to the homeless mentally ill. Without forceful advocates these persons will be the 1990s' lowest priority when a county formulates its fiscal budget.

City of Los Angeles v. County of Los Angeles[216] is an ongoing consolidation of actions designed to address the systemic failure of the General Relief program to meet the county's statutory obligation to provide for *all* homeless persons. In that case, the court recognized the city's legal right to petition the court for an interpretation of State laws regarding government responsibilities for mentally ill residents.[217] The Los Angeles Homeless Litigation Team's consolidation of this litigation illustrates a strategy that must be considered by advocates confronted by a recalcitrant bureaucracy. The Team's rationale behind consolidation was that every time they had won a piecemeal reform of the general relief system, the county simply had adjusted another part of the system to exclude as many persons as it had been improperly excluding by the devices complained of before a litigation victory.[218] Litigation had become analogous to "punching a soft beach ball."[219]

2B. Other Homeless Mental Health Cases

Subsequent California litigation involving the homeless mentally ill raises the issue of whether California Welfare and Institutions Code section 17000, requiring relief for the poor and incapacitated, imposes a mandatory duty on counties to assist the homeless mentally ill. The question, as if from *Alice in Wonderland*, then becomes: Is a homeless mentally ill individual "indigent' for purposes of section 17000?

Remarkably, courts have so far been unwilling to construe the seemingly clear statutory mandate so "broadly."[220]

Filed in 1986, *Rensch v. County of Los Angeles* was consolidated with, but in August 1989 severed from, *City v. County of Los Angeles.*[221] *Rensch* addresses issues concerning the practical inability of homeless mentally ill persons to gain access to county general relief services. Essentially, plaintiffs argued that the county must refrain from all actions that have the practical result of denying General Relief Benefits to the mentally ill homeless.[222]

The plaintiff's general theory in *Rensch* is that, beginning at the federal level, discrimination against mentally ill individuals is prohibited by section 504 of the United States Rehabilitation Act of 1973.[223] It follows that, since the County Department of Public Social Services ("DPSS") receives federal funding, DPSS cannot discriminate and must reasonably accommodate the special needs for such disabled people so that they can make use of the federal benefits.[224]

In *Rensch*, homeless plaintiffs challenged the constitutionality of an application process designed for general relief that they saw as so complex and arbitrary that it functioned as an insurmountable barrier for the mentally ill homeless. Recalling that Welfare and Institutions Code section 17000 mandates public assistance for California's indigent, one realizes that barriers thus presented are as real for mentally disabled persons as a physical stairway would be to a person in a wheelchair.[225]

The plaintiffs challenged these "improperly and arbitrarily" imposed requirements as breaches of the county's affirmative statutory duty "to relieve and support the indigent" under section 17000.[226] Given the Court's encouraging directive that the plaintiffs amend and expand their complaint,[227] the plaintiffs are now alleging that Los Angeles County is under a duty to identify individuals who need special assistance in order to get through the application process successfully, and then to provide such people with appropriate assistance.[228]

Whether the section 17000 claim in *Rensch* is ultimately successful will undoubtedly be influenced by the appellate decision in *Board of Supervisors of the County of Los Angeles v. Los Angeles Superior Court (Comer).*[229] This case, following *Deukmejian*, has been the second major judicial blow to the interests of California's mentally ill homeless. *Comer* challenged a $16.7 million reduction in the County of Los Angeles' Mental Health budget during the 1988-89 fiscal year.[230] These reductions would force the closing or curtailing of the services of thirteen clinics operated or funded by the County; many mentally ill persons with no other source of care would experience psychotic episodes requiring emergency hospitalization,[231] with regrettable results that would have been equally as burdensome to the county's limited resources.

In a strained opinion, the appellate court in *Comer* rejected plaintiffs' Section 17000 claim. Instead, it held that Welfare and Institutions Code section 5709 permits counties to limit their mental health obligations to the minimum amount required.[232] Welfare and Institutions Code section 5705 (a) gives the minimum, stating in relevant part, "The net cost of all services specified in the approved county Short-Doyle plans shall be financed on the basis of 90 percent state funds and 10 percent county funds. . . ."[233] The court reasoned that the ". . . only reasonable reading of these statutes is that 5709 absolutely limits any duty imposed by Section 17000."[234] Interestingly enough, research by both parties and the court failed to reveal any legislative intent materials that spoke to the relationship between the Short-Doyle Act and Welfare and Institutions Code section 17000. Thus, the court's reaction is best reflected in its statement, "Were section 17000 construed to require counties to fully meet the need for mental health services without regard to the Short-Doyle limits, sections 5705 and 5709 would be nullified, and county obligations in this area would be open-ended."[235]

Comer represents another major loss for advocates for the mentally ill homeless in California. *Comer* today stands for the principle that section 17000 provides no statutory mandate for a county to provide the chronically ill with adequate mental health services.[236] This decision will undercut a plaintiffs' ability to argue that California counties are not honoring statutory duties to assist their homeless mentally ill. The policy underlying *Comer* and *Deukmejian* today allows counties wide discretion to determine how they will fund and administer programs for the mentally ill. Some advocates of the homeless mentally ill believe that *Comer* will stand as a strong precedent.[237] However, *Comer* only involved section 17000 in the context of a county's obligations to *fund* mental health care for the homeless mentally ill.[238]

Unlike *Comer*, in *Rensch* the County of Los Angeles clearly violated a court order. Therefore, despite *Comer*, the discretionary argument raised by counties ought not to be ultimately impenetrable. It may be that *Comer* will be narrowly construed to its own facts, affecting funding only. Presumably, a county's only legitimate interest in refusing to provide such relief in such circumstances is fiscal. A fiscal interest is arguably not, under settled case law, a sufficient interest to justify violations of rights which are guaranteed by either or both the state or federal Constitutions.[239] Moreover, such an interest cannot possibly outweigh the extensive suffering of the thousands of California's individual mentally ill homeless persons.[240]

Advocates for the homeless find themselves cast, in circumstances like these, as adversaries of their county officials and, perhaps, of the courts themselves. Courts are traditionally disinclined to impose affirmative mandates on local governments where enforcement will unduly burden the courts, or prove impossible. Judges are guided by the legal maxim that, "Courts may not ethically engage in vain acts,"[241] especially when long-term supervision of a case may be needed. In many cases involving the homeless, judges are faced with the prospect of telling a county how to exercise its discretion in allocating resources. As *Comer* and *Mental Health Association* illustrate, courts are hesitant to do this. Courts incline to defer to the legislative branch and the local government's administrative decisions;[242] sadly, even when the defendant may be blatantly ignoring statutory guarantees and constitutional rights.

Following the major losses in *Deukmejian* and *Comer*, homeless advocates had to consider whether pursuit of these ill-fated lawsuits had in fact improved their clients' positions. Short term, the decisions are devastating defeats, and the advocates' only justification is faith in democracy's tendency toward health and justice. These cases raised the issues—which are now etched in some relief—for the people and their legislature to see.

Legal advocates will nevertheless continue to press the evil non-systems now besetting America's homeless. Someone needs "to comfort the afflicted and afflict the comfortable."[243] *Rensch* serves as an example that vigilance for the uncomfortable is not the only quality required to secure benefits for the homeless. Although ordered by the court to attend to specific needs of the homeless mentally ill, the County of Los Angeles dragged its feet and a second amended complaint had to be filed.[244]

East Coast courts have examined the relationship between voluntary mental health treatment and homelessness. Most recently, the *Joyce Brown*[245] case in New York City gained national attention. Joyce Brown was a homeless mentally ill woman to whom Mayor Ed Koch referred while launching Project HELP. This program provided for detention of the most severely mentally ill homeless, with little regard for due process or, it seems, medicine.[246] The New York trial court found that Ms. Brown was not dangerous to herself or others and therefore could not be involuntarily committed.[247] The appellate court reversed a trial court order permitting the City to continue to confine Ms. Brown.[248] The *Brown* case caused many to conclude, erroneously, that defining mental illness is difficult.[249] It also led many to the baseless conclusion that involuntary imposition of mental health care must, of necessity, ignore due process and that life on the streets does not constitute an inability to provide for one's basic personal needs.[250]

Some advocates for the mentally ill homeless believe that *Brown* served to mask the true problem in providing adequate assistance to the homeless mentally ill.[251] There was no immediate legislative response to *Brown*. In effect, the New York City government did not have to change the laws to justify involuntary commitment, but rather, "They just purported to 'informally redefine' who was gravely disabled. They picked them up and they provided them some service."[252] Indeed, between 1984 and 1988, the New York State Legislature rejected six bills proposing procedures for emergency detention and civil commitment of "gravely disabled" individuals.[253]

The legislative response to homelessness and mental health around the country has typically been to create a service called "Involuntary Outpatient Services" ("IOS").[254] This development ignores a fundamental defect of most of America's mental health systems for the poor—that they are coercive. Would it not make more sense to offer adequate regular services, free from burdensome application procedures? Society could more clearly evaluate whether mentally ill homeless individuals were truly unwilling to seek assistance. As the situation now exists, state-funded mental health services nationwide are woefully underfunded,[255] coercive, and largely inaccessible. Arguably, an adequate array of voluntary services has never been offered; and thus, to argue for creation of a whole new involuntary system of providing mental health services to people, when the money to do so is unavailable, is a disingenuous response to the lack of resources.[256]

The acute care mental hospital beds are full in Los Angeles,[257] San Diego, and all major California cities.[258] Effective additional treatment cannot be provided simply by changing the criteria for involuntary commitment. The first logical step is to recognize that new resources have to be infused into the system before one can helpfully consider changing criteria. Otherwise, all that might be accomplished would be to shift some voluntary patients to "involuntary" status. This would accomplish nothing. Ultimately, great savings may be realized via modest expenditures because it is agreed that an excellent "aftercare" program could prevent the expensive rehospitalizations now seen.[259]

The problem of homelessness among the mentally disabled stems from a break-down in the mental health system that has been created by a total underfinancing of the system. Basic necessities for the mentally disabled are not now being provided. It is not, today, a question of people saying "no" to a system that works. They are saying "no" to a system that is not workable. Chronically, desperately disabled mentally ill Americans are at best today offered treatment only in the form of medication. This seems cost effective to some in the near term, but medications are no substitute for shelter, or for real treatment inside of civilized settings.

There is no visible attempt to deal with other issues within the mental health budget, such as shelter, support, and supportive housing. The options do not exist today. To say people are "choosing not to participate in the mental health system" is simply untrue. Any change in the mental health system has to focus on creating alternatives and developing resources before one can rationally talk about forcing people into treatment, because treatment right now does not lead anywhere. It leads patients right back onto the streets. A street is not a home. Or a treatment system.

Mental Health Advocates' Jim Preis' bottom line reads: "There will be no good treatment system for the homeless mentally ill until citizens really care, and then forcefully demand that their legislative and executive officials allocate money."[260]

Because the homeless mentally ill comprise an estimated forty percent of all homeless, litigation on their behalf is crucial. The current system is unable to provide anything close to effective relief. As a result, homeless mentally ill individuals "fall through the cracks" much more frequently than other sub-groups of the larger homeless population.

More often than not, the "fall" is into jail. Our jails have become our modern mental institutions—albeit institutions neither designed nor able to provide the required care these thousands who were cut loose during the deinstitutionalization of our state mental hospitals need. In 1986, the National Association of Counties estimated that of the 8 million Americans incarcerated for over 30 days, 600,000 (13.3 percent) were severely mentally ill.[261] Our justice systems are intimately involved. The homeless are appearing in our criminal courts by the hundreds and thousands.[262]

This does not mean that the homeless are not impacting other elements of the justice system. Urban police forces spend millions annually interfacing with the homeless. Similarly, our urban jail holding tanks contain many homeless persons charged with misdemeanors (including failure to appear on an infraction, such as spitting on the sidewalk or tossing a cigarette). Many are ejected a few hours after arrest, never to see arraignment and a judge. The niceties of due process are absent. In effect, there exists a vicious cycle through which the homeless, especially those who are mentally ill, go from the street, to jail, receiving little or no mental health care, and back to the street. Repeatedly.

As a Municipal Court judge in the County of San Diego, California, I have seen hundreds of homeless individuals appear before me. With what are these people generally charged? The huge majority are charged with trespassing-type offenses—sleeping in public parks and beaches or in stairwells of buildings that are dry when it's raining. Camping in one's own car is also a commonly seen offense—and, of course, there are the prostitutes and the chronic, skid-row drunks. Very rarely is a theft case seen; and I have been surprised, frankly, at the almost total dearth of homeless defendants being charged with felonies.

I recall one piteous old man, into his sixties, his eyes blurry and his face sad, looking emaciated from starvation, quivering intelligently before me. Charged with second degree burglary, he had been found in a commercial building basement where he had crawled to get warm. It was obvious to me that this man was here as a result of a "mercy arrest" by the police, who are silently hollering at us in such a case, "Please help this gentleman! Please take notice. Please do the right thing. We have nowhere else to take him!"

Do the civil courts see the homeless? About forty percent of the 25,000 civil filings in San Diego are landlord-versus-tenant, unlawful-detainer cases.[263] The subject is eviction, and for some, this court appearance (or sadly, default judgment, rendered in 85 percent of such cases) is the "last stop before the streets" for the hapless defendant(s). As one who handled the bulk of this portion of the civil calendar for more than a year, I saw many disabled people—disabled by recent surgery, loss of limbs, military action, mental illness, alcoholism, drug abuse, marginal intelligence, or a combination of these—getting tossed out on their ears. Not infrequently, this ejection was from federally subsidized (section 8) housing:[264] housing specifically designed by the Congress to serve the most disabled of our populations. Sometimes, it involved parents with disabled children; sometimes, disabled parents with children.

Ejected and homeless, these folks become financially costly to society, and as to the children (who are monstrously terrified and brutalized by life on the streets), they represent a grave threat to the community's and the nation's future.[265] The justice system is burdened by them, along with the other elements of society's tattered human care infrastructure. It would clearly be in the interests of prudence (as well as justice) to prevent these people's entry into the ranks of the homeless, if possible. But how?

Well, this Judge often found himself back in chambers after ordering such an eviction, on the phone telephoning shelters, "emergency specialists," social workers, and fellow Rotarians, finding avenues to new shelters. Landlords' attorneys often pitched in, and they were discovered to have done so, preventively, in dozens of cases that never made their way to court. Obviously, Legal Aid and other tenant counsel learned that this had become part of their fiduciary duty to improve their clients' lot.

VI. KEEPING FAMILIES WITH CHILDREN TOGETHER

> But a bold peasantry, their country's pride,
> When once destroy'd, can never be supplied.[266]
>
> —Oliver Goldsmith

The fact that we know that many families have been turned out into America's streets the last few years probably explains why we Americans have not yet become resigned to homelessness. Nightly news broadcasts conveying the plight of homeless families and children have struck a responsive cord in American hearts. Who could turn away and become inured to such barbarism, embodying the future of the nation, its children, without confessing to having cast away all of his or her humanity?

Today, estimates are that as many as twenty to thirty percent of the entire homeless population is comprised of families with children.[267] Three years ago, the public seemed to be able easily to stereotype the homeless as a crew of the shiftless, drunk, or crazy, somehow on the streets by choice and thus estopped to complain. The significant increase of families living in their cars, and children being separated from their parents, is changing public opinion about homelessness;[269] to what extent is not yet clear. Middle class Americans' increased concern about homeless families serves as a new type of foundation for successful litigation; judicial decisions may occasionally and to some extent reflect a judge's assessment of the community's desires as well as interests.

Indeed, the legislative as well as the judicial branches of state and federal governments have expressly recognized the importance of keeping families together. Under United States Code section 625(a)(1), a defined purpose of the child welfare services is to prevent "the unnecessary separation of the children from their families by identifying family problems, assisting families in resolving their problems. . . ."[269] In *Lehr v. Robertson*,[270] the United States Supreme Court found that, "The intangible fibers that connect parent and child have infinite variety. They are woven throughout the fabric of our society, providing it with strength, beauty, and flexibility."[271]

Courts have recognized that "the unique ability of a parent to give love, guidance, protection and encouragement to his or her child lies at the very heart of the parental relationship."[272] Yet, familial bonds have been weakened or destroyed because of homelessness. "The typical consequence of homelessness of families with dependent children is the separation of the family and the placement of the children in foster care. . . ."[273] Generally, courts have held that parents have a constitutionally protected interest in retaining custody of their children.[274] Courts have required a showing of "paternal fault or unfitness" before it will interfere with the parent-child relationship.[275]

Too often, homelessness is today a situation beyond a family's control. For families, "homelessness functions not as a freely chosen option but as a tragic, inexorable destiny."[276] Taking an abused child out of a dangerous home environment is clearly necessary. However, the fact that a family is homeless should not be a carte blanche justification for placing the children in foster care.

Why not help the family, and try to hold it together, as most state welfare schemes command?

New York has had some significant litigation on behalf of homeless families. In *Martin A. By Aurora A. v. Gross*[277] (*"Martin A."*), plaintiffs were homeless families in New York City who were denied emergency shelter. The only available alternative was to place children from these homeless families in foster care. Advocates brought an action against the city and state for failure to provide sufficient services to homeless families so as to avoid having to place their children in foster care.

Citing to a New York State law, the court stated, "The State's first obligation is to help families with services to prevent its break up. . . ."[278] In *Martin A.*, the court found that "Families shall not be separated for reasons of poverty alone," and ordered that families be provided services to maintain and strengthen family life.[279]

The defendants in *Martin A.* moved for dismissal on the grounds of mootness, claiming that the plaintiffs had been subsequently provided with preventive services. The court, however, found that these services were not actually provided until after plaintiffs commenced the suit. To avoid a reccurrence of such actions, the court denied the defendants' motion to dismiss. Instead, the plaintiffs were granted injunctive relief requiring the city to provide preventive services and a plan to assist homeless families consistent with its statutory obligations.[280] The *Martin A.* court stressed the city's duty to provide help for the needy. Making a point which California courts might be advised to consider, it emphasized that neither limited resources nor a shortage of staff was a "proper justification for denial of services."[281] The court noted that the last resort of foster care usually cost more than the preventive services.[282]

Other homeless families in New York have not been as fortunate. In *Grant v. Cuomo*,[283] the plaintiffs faced similar circumstances as those in *Martin A.* The lower court in *Grant* found the language of the Child Welfare Reform Act—"shall provide"—created a nondiscretionary statutory duty among its officials to provide the preventive services.[284] Notwithstanding such language, the appellate court held that the provision of these services was discretionary and required professional judgment. Remedies for failure to render such services could, the court held, only be decided on a case by case basis. The court found that a social services official could not reasonably believe that the preventive services would or should avoid foster care in all circumstances. Some children faced foster care placement due to abuse, death of parents or abandonment. In most of these situations preventive services would not help.[285] Presumably, absent such factors, a mandatory duty exists.

Massachusetts decisions, on the other hand, have found similar statutory language mandatory. In *Massachusetts Coalition for the Homeless v. Secretary of Human Services*,[286] advocates for homeless families sought declaratory and injunctive relief. Plaintiffs were Aid to Families with Dependent Children ("AFDC") recipients who alleged that the state was not furnishing the funds provided for under Massachusetts General Laws c. 118, 2, which provides in relevant part, "the aid furnished shall be sufficient to enable such parents to bring up such child or children properly in his or her own home."[287] There, the court held that a mandatory statutory duty existed to provide sufficient funds for mere shelter, as well as a "permanent residence" where children could be raised by their own relatives.[288] In so doing, the *Massachusetts* court went a step further than New York decisions. It required not only that the family should be kept together, but also that a permanent home be provided.[289]

In New Jersey in 1988, advocates for homeless families challenged termination of the plaintiffs' emergency assistance due to a five-month maximum regulation.[290] In *Franklin v. New Jersey Department of Human Services*, the plaintiffs argued that this termination of assistance was arbitrary and charged that such practice violated the right to shelter guaranteed to their children by the State's AFDC program.

The defendants emphasized that two bills directing funds for the homeless had recently been enacted by the New Jersey Legislature and that a new, untried program had been designed to prevent homelessness.[291] The court expressed some doubt as to the Department of Human Services' policy, which suggested that "shelter of last resort for children be foster care."[292] The court found that this policy "would not only result in break up of families but would further burden an already overloaded foster-care system."[293] Nonetheless, the *Franklin* court held that it would give the recently designed program an opportunity to be tested before invalidating it, stressing that it did not want these children to become "bureaucratic orphans."[294]

In California, litigation on behalf of homeless families has also involved state AFDC provisions. *Hansen v. Department of Social Services* involved, in part, a class action suit filed in Los Angeles County by a state-wide consortium of Legal Aid and public interest law firms.[295] The plaintiffs challenged a Department of Social Services ("DSS")[296] practice of denying emergency shelter to "neglected, abused, or exploited" homeless children unless they had been separated from their parents.[297]

The DSS responded that the regulation restricting emergency shelter care to homeless children who had been removed from their families was consistent with the legislative intent. The DSS argued that such "emergency shelter care" be provided to a neglected child only during the period that the child is initially removed from the home to evaluate the child's need for state protection. The DSS asserted that intact homeless families were not entitled to any financial assistance, beyond their monthly AFDC grant, to secure safe and adequate shelter.[298] In opposition, the plaintiffs contended that the plain meaning of Welfare and Institutions Code section 16504.1 was that "emergency shelter care" be provided to all homeless children, regardless of whether they remained with or were separated from their families.[299]

The DSS replied that the legislature did not intend to provide emergency shelter care to homeless families because child welfare services are available to families regardless of wealth.[300] The court rejected this argument on the grounds that an affluent family would fail to qualify for any emergency shelter under the statutory scheme.[301]

Similarly, the DSS also argued that the legislature did not intend that the DSS provide emergency shelter care to homeless families because such aid was available under other components of the Child Welfare Services Program.[302] These components were Family Reunification[303] and Permanent Placement,[304] which take effect after the child has been removed from his or her parents. Social services provided through these two components were expressly limited to "children who cannot safely remain at home."[305] However, the court found that there was no such limitation contained in the other statutory language controlling the Preplacement Preventive Services components, which required DSS to provide emergency shelter care for homeless families and children.[306] The court concluded that "the Legislature's failure to include similar limitations upon homeless children who are at risk, but still residing with their parents, is a manifestation of its intent that all children be intended beneficiaries of emergency shelter care."[307]

In reaching this conclusion, the court found that both state and federal legislatures intended that the preservation of the family unit was of primary importance. The court found that the subject DSS regulation controverted these important legislative goals. Application of the regulation was found to have the potential of forcing homeless families into child dependency proceedings, which would ultimately split up the families.[308] Further, the court noted that "the plight of the homeless AFDC family often considerably worsens once their children are removed to foster care, in that loss of AFDC eligibility follows the loss of custody."[309] This eventuality often resulted in permanent separation of the parent from the child. The court concluded that child welfare services must be provided in all instances where the child is at risk, without regard to whether the child has or lacks shelter.[310]

The *Hansen* court went on to outline the legislature's repeated statutory enactments concerning the dearth of housing for low-income families, and further noted that the California Legislature had enacted a body of law to assist homeless families.[311] Thus, the court held that the DSS had to act in conformity with the intent of this legislation. Therefore, the plaintiffs were granted a preliminary injunction compelling the DSS to provide emergency shelter care for homeless children, regardless of whether they remained with their parents, guardians or caretakers.[312]

Strategy-wise, plaintiffs' counsel in *Hansen* did not hope for relief for homeless children through the Child Welfare Service program, despite the fact that such relief was clearly available. Such relief would have done nothing to keep homeless families intact and provide emergency shelter. As previously discussed, two components of Child Welfare Services program, California Welfare and Institutions Code sections the 16507.1 and 16508.1, take effect only after a child has been removed from the parents.

The importance of *Hansen* does not lie in the fact that the court held that the preplacement preventive services component required the DSS to provide emergency shelter care for homeless families and children. Instead, the case was important because it caused the California Legislature to take action toward resolving the dispute as to whether Welfare and Institutions Code sections 16500 *et. seq.* provides relief for children only, or also for their parents, guardians, caretakers and others.[313] In early 1988, the legislature set up a new program to assist homeless families by providing special needs allowances for temporary and permanent shelter through the AFDC program.[314] Welfare and Institutions Code section 11450(f)(2) defines homeless families as those families which lack a fixed and regular nighttime residence.[315]

Although *Hansen* stirred the California Legislature to act, the predicted bureaucratic response of diluting the effects of such legislation was swift. County of Los Angeles DSS Director McMahon first enacted emergency regulations to implement the statute prior to its effective date of February 1, 1988.[316] These regulations were to be effective through July 1, 1988. Under these DSS regulations, families who were sharing housing on a temporary and emergency basis were considered homeless and therefore eligible for homeless assistance benefits. However, McMahon planned to implement a revised homeless assistance regulation that was to take effect July 1, 1988. The new regulation would have barred any family that was sharing housing with others from eligibility for the program, even if the family was truly homeless.[317]

In July 1988, Legal Aid attorneys filed a complaint for injunctive and declaratory relief in *Merriman v. McMahon*.[318] The complaint was filed to prevent the DSS from modifying the February 1 regulations.[319] The gravamen of the complaint was that because the new regulation denied benefits to families lacking fixed, regular nighttime residences and who were entitled to relief under the statute, it was inconsistent with Welfare and Institutions Code section 11450(f)(2).[320]

Unlike *Hansen*, *Merriman* was not a class action. Rather, the plaintiffs were several single homeless mothers with children.[321] The plaintiffs alleged that a primary purpose of DSS regulations was "to provide a consistent detailed interpretation of the applicable provisions of controlling state and federal law for the benefit of the county welfare departments and to ensure their compliance with the law."[322]

The amended DSS regulations differed significantly from the emergency regulations. The final regulation provided that "an [assistance unit] is not considered homeless when it is sharing housing."[323] In effect, the regulation would have cut off aid to those homeless individuals who shared housing with relatives and friends on a temporary and emergency basis. Families living on the edge of destitution would have had necessary benefits arbitrarily slashed.

On October 5, 1989, the Alameda Superior Court entered judgment enjoining the DSS from implementing its amended regulation or from any other similarly designed regulation.[324] The court also ordered the DSS to notify and secure the compliance of each of California's fifty-eight county welfare departments with the provisions of its judgment.[325]

Hansen and *Merriman* underline, again, the need for vigilance in preserving gains secured for the homeless through litigation. Although *Hansen* engendered legislation favorable to the homeless, bureaucratic machinations attempting to stymie, negate, and nullify such gains instantly appeared. The lesson of *Merriman* for advocates for the homeless is that they can never relax after achieving an apparent victory.

Hansen was litigation that prompted a legislature to act. Counsel for the Hansens there did not wish relief that would have required their clients to proceed through the child welfare system. Such relief would not have had a measurable positive effect on homeless families. The legislative response to *Hansen* spawned an $80 million program that has allowed 6 to 7 thousand families per month since February 1988 to receive assistance. Plaintiffs' counsel in *Hansen* were elegantly creative in its approach to securing tangible benefits for homeless families. Lead counsels' theory forced the state to provide care for children, which resulted in more money being allocated towards permanent housing.

Although litigation can seem overly time consuming, when properly targeted, and well executed, litigation can indeed produce life-saving benefits for the homeless.

VII. THE "NOT IN MY BACK YARD" SYNDROME ("NIMBY")

Everybody has to be someplace. So do social service agencies, such as job centers, missions, barracks, schools, half-way houses and the like, which serve the homeless. But today, looking at the political behavior of citizens of America's largest cities, one finds that Alexis de Tocqueville's most terrifying nightmare has come true: The healthy tension between the two American poles of individualism, on the one hand, and a powerful sense of commitment to the community, on the other, has at long last broken down. Individualism has won.[326]

Thinking people generally acknowledge the need for locating those social service agencies that serve the halt, lame, disabled, and poor" somewhere, but today they rise up in extremely effective political prevention action when the proposal is to locate a vital social service facility in their neighborhood. And the NIMBY Syndrome is acutely harming many efforts to ameliorate homelessness in the United States.

The following examples from Los Angeles were supplied by attorney Nancy Mintie, homeless advocate who directs the Los Angeles Inner City Law Center:

A reputable [Los Angeles] local program, Law Familias, which operated a drop-in center for poor and homeless families, had the funding and governmental approval to run a small shelter for homeless women and children. The organization tried for many years to come up with a site that would be acceptable to the community. After several years, the funding had to be returned because opposition to the establishment of such a shelter was so great. One suggested location had been in the hills near Dodger Stadium, and this was opposed by the Dodger establishment. They seemed to feel that the sight of a few poor women and children would be bad for ballpark business.

Another example achieved national publicity. Mayor Tom Bradley secured a small group of trailers to be used to house homeless families around the city of Los Angeles. Tremendous opposition was generated among the city council members to the placement of the trailers in their respective districts. Though the trailers were obtained a number of years ago, to this day some of them remain unused because the thought of housing a homeless family (usually a woman with one or more small children) was too threatening for most communities in Los Angeles.

Another example concerned a highly touted drop-in and social services center for the homeless called LAMP. After a great deal of planning and some legal advocacy around zoning issues, LAMP received the funding and governmental approval to run a shelter, sheltered workshop and cottage industry for its homeless clients in an empty city-owned warehouse in the Skid Row district. Even though Skid Row has been the traditional service site for the homeless through the reputable and long established private missions, the local industries and businesses in the area mounted tremendous opposition to the project, fighting it every step of the way through the zoning appeal process. This was an example of the local business community wanting to "have its cake and eat it, too." These businesses moved into the area taking advantage of the low rents that resulted because of the presence of the homeless. However, once there, the businesses have attempted to drive the homeless out by opposing service programs for them.

Planning for the LAMP project was begun in early 1987 and the program was supposed to begin in mid-1988. However, due to the opposition of the local Skid Row business community, the estimated start up date is now mid-1990, an additional delay of two years.

Another rather astounding example of the NIMBY phenomenon occurred recently when the State of California erected a new state office building (The Ronald Reagan State Building) across the street from one of the largest and oldest missions in downtown Los Angeles. As part of the construction, the city agreed to spend approximately ten million of its scarce social services dollars on moving the mission from its original location on the border of Skid Row to a new location a few blocks away in the heart of Skid Row. The concerns prompting this move were purely NIMBY-related. It was feared that the sight of the homeless would spoil the view from the Ronald Reagan State Building and disturb the state employees who would be working there. Instead of creating new housing or shelter beds with this large sum of money, it instead is being spent on what is largely a cosmetic purpose.

Though these are local examples, the pattern is being repeated nationally. Unfortunately, the callousness of our elected representatives toward the homeless is mirrored by that of the populace. I believe that the new national reaction to the homeless is not one of compassion, but one of distancing by stereotyping. This reaction seems to arise out of the general population's feelings of powerlessness to change the problem and from the middle class' fear of its own economic vulnerability.[327]

Of course, lawyers can and should "act like attorneys" in these dramas, representing clients at the various zoning hearings, for example. But here, as elsewhere, legal problem-solving may require more strategic thinking, including advance planning, as well as building both relationships and coalitions, and a reservoir of public good will. These can translate into political force at a crucial time.

There is no good antidote to NIMBY. But the advocate has to work with what is available. First and foremost there is de Tocqueville's answer: heightened commitment to community. Beyond that, a strategy of "sprinkling" small agency centers all about a city have been successful, because it is hard to argue against a small entity, particularly when all neighborhoods are equally "sharing the load."

Finally, does not the logic of the federal Constitutional right to travel contain within it a concomitant "right to be somewhere?"[328] If so, a persuasive legal argument, useful against NIMBY claims, can perhaps be pieced together.[329]

VIII. THE MODERN HOMELESS ADVOCATE MUST BE AWARE OF THE LEGAL HORIZONS

As with attorneys for corporations, government agencies, or other clients, attorneys for the homeless cannot properly do their jobs merely by keeping their "nose to the grindstone."

While the day-to-day workload can be all-consuming, real progress lies in using the imagination to search for and discover the latent threats and opportunities looming on the legal horizon, and in timely recognition and molding of new developments to serve the interests of one's homeless clients. The following examples illustrate a belatedly perceived threat to low-income housing, an interesting missed opportunity, and a newly developing area.

2A. Growth Management, City Planning, and Housing

To be homeless, in its barest terms, means not to have a roof. And if a locale's supply of low income housing is permitted to decline,[330] the homeless will be harmed, and will multiply. So, efforts to increase such housing must be fostered by the homeless' advocates, while actions seen as further eroding the low-income housing stock must be thwarted where possible.

The general land-use plans of modern cities are typically required to contain an analysis and plan section called "the housing element."[331] In some states[332] this section must include specific plans for meeting the housing needs of the homeless. If the general plan does not specify such goals, policies, and action programs designed to ameliorate the shelter needs of the homeless, then homeless advocates may have a viable ground upon which to attack the general plan and compel the affected city or county to adopt and implement programs to come to grips with this fundamental cause of American homelessness. If homeless advocates determine that the housing element of the general plan is deficient, they should then consider bringing a writ of mandamus proceeding to establish that the affected city or county has abused its discretion by not complying with its statutory mandate.

Drawbacks to such litigation are that homeless advocates will need to find a basis to establish relevance between some individual land use project and the allegedly deficient aspect of the plan's housing element; and most importantly, they must further show they have already exhausted all available administrative remedies by appearing and lodging all objections, and proferring evidence, to avoid any subject matter jurisdiction defense that may be asserted by the city or county. The advocates should therefore bring witnesses to testify during the relevant administrative hearings and should submit evidence in the nature of national, state, and local studies or reports documenting the points to be made and answers to counter-points. This is, of course, arduous.

In regions of rapid residential growth, citizens and local governments frequently attempt to limit such growth.[333] In contexts dealing with this by city ordinance[334] and initiative,[335] the provision of California Evidence Code section 669.5[336] has been upheld, requiring counties to include provision for adequate "affordable" (low-income) housing, or such a growth control plan will not withstand attack.

2B. Applications for Disaster Relief

In a 1985 burst of both logic and creativity, the Los Angeles County Grand Jury recommended to its County Board of Supervisors that they formally declare the Skid Row area of downtown Los Angeles a "disaster area," and make application for federal emergency assistance.[337] With estimates of Los Angeles' homeless then ranging upwards from thirty-five thousand,[338] could anyone seriously argue that the "Homeless Disaster" was not more momentous than the destruction and suffering following Mt. St. Helen's eruption in 1979 or the devastation caused by Hurricane Hugo in late 1989? But the unimaginative Los Angeles Supervisors failed to act and thus, like the thousands of mentally ill homeless Americans who neglect to request federal assistance (in the form of Social Security Income), the Supervisors and their homeless received nothing. Perhaps a timely nudge to the local Taxpayers Association and Chamber of Commerce by attorneys for the homeless could have made a difference here. Perhaps an idea like this is applicable wherever significant numbers of Americans are homeless. Why not? And if Disaster Aid could apply to the homeless, what of other "ordinary," but large, federal or state funding sources, such as the Veterans Administration budget, low interest student loans, Vista volunteer or state CCC camp status for homeless individuals, and so on.

2C. Tort Claims of the Homeless

It is, of course, possible for a homeless person to be run down in a crosswalk—or to suffer almost any other type of personal wrong recognized by our tort law. But representation of the homeless has not yet become a chic activity among plaintiff's lawyers.

From the preceding, a lay person might conclude that homeless individuals might be able to assert breaches of individual rights against local and state governments in the courts. In keeping with ancient tradition, and for excellent reasons, states have, however, made most types of acts or omissions by government about which homeless individuals might complain, immune from lawsuits.[339]

Plaintiffs' opportunities may nevertheless exist. Intentional torts may not be blanketed by the immunities, and plaintiffs are probing for other openings. In San Luis Obispo, a *Tarasoff*-type[340] negligence case has been filed against the county and a doctor, alleging (1) that foreseeability of homicide if a certain medicine were not properly administered; (2) that it was not so administered; and (3) that the threatened killings took place.[341] If such a theory holds against any of these defendants, would not a similar suit brought by survivors of a suicide-prone homeless person, released by a county because "beds were full," also lie?

A New York Federal District Court recently held that panhandling constitutes federally protected free speech under the First Amendment;[342] and thus, persons whose rights are abridged by such wrongful arrests would appear to have potential causes of actions, including one under 42 U.S.C. section 1983.

Plaintiffs' lawyers do become remarkably imaginative when the possibility exists of a large dollar recovery.[343]

Conclusion

There has been mass homelessness in this country before, but never during such a period of general economic prosperity. There has been an explosion of homelessness in the United States since the beginning of the eighties. As the decade began, an era of the massive deinstitutionalization of state mental hospital patients had come to a close, and Americans were seeing more and more people in downtown areas and transportation terminals who were visibly mentally disturbed. The 1981 recession and the international flight of blue-collar jobs[344] squeezed young people with inadequate schooling out of a tight job market and onto the streets. Slashes in SSI disability rolls (one third of a million in 1981-83 alone) and of unemployment, welfare, and other "safety net" structures contributed to the increase in homelessness, as did the rapid disintegration of both white and black family structures.[345] Today the new homeless are typically families. America's homeless are a steadily expanding heterogeneous population.[346]

Litigation must be a central tool in the 1990s battle against American homelessness and poverty—recognizing that the widespread existence of unasserted rights and injustice foil the rule of law in civil society. Although litigation for the homeless has tended to focus on mere subsistence needs, without it homeless people would be much worse off. Litigation has, at the very least, prompted begrudging bureaucracies into providing legally mandated subsistence assistance to the homeless. More importantly, it has simultaneously had the effect of helping to raise the public consciousness, since litigation can be a stark appeal against lawless government and for justice. However, because of the diverse needs of homeless Americans, litigation has developed in a seemingly piecemeal fashion. More accurately, perhaps, strategies of advocates for the legal rights of the homeless have developed in response to the reality that there has often been a system-wide denial of these people's rights. To counter this denial, and to break down barriers erected by local governments, advocates have had to analyze how the process of denial works in reality, at a local level. This can only be determined by spending days at the Welfare or Social Security office, and on the streets.

Advocates for the homeless must also do something alien to most lawyers: they must develop models of the institutions that are victimizing their clients. These models must be developed on the basis of objective and accurate information. Only by having a comprehensive perspective of the bureaucratic machinery that denies the homeless dignity can litigators successfully prompt such machinery to work in ways that provide tangible benefits for those sentenced to the streets.

Litigation has helped to ameliorate norms engendered in various systems that would do nothing but exacerbate the problem of homelessness, if left unchallenged. Litigation has served as an educational tool, teaching Americans what homelessness is about and, most importantly, showing that homelessness is not an insoluble problem. In addition, advocates are experiencing increasing success in the courtrooms. Yet, local governments have too often seemed ready to counter such victories with additional bureaucratic roadblocks. American citizens need to make one threshold political demand of their local governments, namely that these entities obey the laws!

Nonetheless, the pure force of litigation cannot fully address the causes of homelessness, although some litigation efforts have focused on causes, such as failed mental health and housing policies. It will take time to reverse the tide of homelessness in America; piece-by-piece, however, the situation is solvable. As Victor Hugo observed: "An invasion of armies can be resisted, but not an idea whose time has come."[347] Recent surveys reveal that solving homelessness is an idea whose time is nearly upon us.[348]

Litigation serves as a public reminder that homelessness is not incurable. Perhaps the most rudimentary and essential function of litigation on behalf of the homeless has been to prevent people from *accepting* homelessness. This is enormously important. Innocent though many a normal American may be, when he or she strolls a city street and encounters a person without a place to live, a normal response is to want to do something about it. This is as normal as our reflex start at the cry of a hungry baby. Litigation, therefore, helps to remind people—judges and bureaucracies in particular—that there is somebody out there skillfully trying to do something to assist these startling, homeless people, and that citizens need to be supportive of such efforts. Litigation is essential in that it plays an integral role in making communities carefully consider details of how they will treat their respective homeless populations.

Moreover, litigation on behalf of the homeless must include legislative and regulatory proposals in order to provide more thorough-going solutions to the problem. In the end, political power and legal precedents cannot prevent all levels of government from turning their backs on the homeless. The hope can be raised, though, that our leaders may wake up one fine day and recognize what a sad commentary on American life (and on its leaders) it is that the richest nation on the Earth again has millions of people with no roof over their heads. Justice Brandeis' words are as valid today as when he commented: "publicity is justly commended as a remedy for social and industrial diseases. Sunlight is said to be the best of disinfectants; electric light the most efficient policeman."[349]

Litigation on behalf of homeless Americans will be an indispensable arena in the looming drama wherein solutions to the American Homeless Dilemma will be created. Litigators in this arena will be engaged in one of the great adventures of their age; such endeavors always call for heightened courage, culture and moral perception. It is fitting, I believe, to close this offering with words from that great champion of forgotten Americans, Clarence Darrow, who through his life ably placed his cases into historic perspective—as homeless advocates will, over and over, also be called upon to do:

> Your verdict means something in this case. It means something more than the fate of this boy. It is not often that a case is submitted to twelve men where the decision may mean a milestone in the progress of the human race. But this case does. And I hope and I trust that you have a feeling of responsibility that will make you take it and do your duty as citizens of a great nation, and, as members of the human family, which is better still. . . . Gentlemen, what do you think is your duty in this case? I have watched day after day, these black, tense faces that have crowded this court. These black faces that now are looking to you twelve whites, feeling that the hopes and fears of a race are in your keeping. This case is about to end, gentlemen. To them, it is life. Not one of their color sits on this jury. Their fate is in the hands of twelve whites. Their eyes are fixed on you, their hearts go out to you, and their hopes hang on your verdict. This is all. I ask you, on behalf of this defendant, on behalf of these helpless ones who turn to you, and more than that—on behalf of this great state, and this great city which must face this problem, and face it fairly—I ask you, in the name of progress and of the human race, to return a verdict of Not Guilty in this case![350]

Appendix B

Housing and Homeless Bond Act of 1988

OFFICIAL TITLE AND SUMMARY
PREPARED BY THE ATTORNEY GENERAL

Housing and Homeless Bond Act of 1988. This act provides for a bond issue of three hundred million dollars ($300,000,000) to provide funds for a housing program that includes: (1) emergency shelters and transition housing for homeless families and individuals, (2) new rental housing for families and individuals including rental housing which meets the special needs of the elderly, disabled, and farmworkers, (3) rehabilitation and preservation of older homes and rental housing, and (4) home purchase assistance for first-time homebuyers.

FINAL VOTE CAST BY THE LEGISLATURE ON SB 1693 (PROPOSITION 84)

Assembly:
Ayes 54
Noes 16

Senate:
Ayes 27
Noes 3

ANALYSIS BY THE LEGISLATIVE ANALYST

Background

The state administers various housing programs to help meet the need for affordable and decent housing. Most of these programs provide either low-interest loans or grants for the construction or rehabilitation of housing for low-income persons.

Proposal

This measure authorizes the state to sell $300 million in general obligation bonds to provide funds for six housing programs administered by the state. General obligation bonds are backed by the state, meaning that the state will use its taxing power to assure that enough money is available to pay off the bonds. The state's General Fund would be used to pay the principal and interest costs on the bonds. General Fund revenues come primarily from the state corporate and personal income taxes and the state sales tax.

The $300 million in bond proceeds would be used entirely to assist low-income persons by providing assistance for the development or rehabilitation of affordable rental housing and temporary housing for the homeless, and by providing financial assistance to first-time home buyers. The state would use specific definitions of "low-income" and "affordable" to administer the programs.

Rental Housing Construction Program ($200 Million). The state would use $200 million to provide affordable rental housing for low-income households. Under the existing program, the state may make a variety of loans and grants to public and private developers to provide this housing. In the past, the state has made "deferred-payment" loans to develop and finance affordable housing and grants to reduce the amount of rent collected from low-income tenants. If the state continues to operate the program in a similar manner, the state would make loans, at no or low interest, for periods of at least 40 years. The borrowers would begin repaying principal and interest after 30 years. In return for the low-interest loans, the state would require borrowers to rent at least 30 percent of the units to low-income households at affordable rents. In some cases, the loans would not provide enough assistance to keep rents affordable to the targeted households. In these instances, the state could make grants on an ongoing basis to ensure affordability.

Special User Housing Rehabilitation Loan Program ($25 Million). The state would make $25 milliion in loans for the purchase and rehabilitation of residential hotels. These hotels typically rent rooms to low-income individuals on a month-to-month basis. The state would lend the money at low interest rates—up to 3 percent—for periods ranging from 20 to 30 years. During that time, home owners could not raise rents on units rehabilitated purchased with program loans above levels affordable to the low-income tenants. Borrowers could postpone payment of principal and interest until the end of the loan period.

Emergency Shelter Program ($25 Million). The state would make $25 million in grants to nonprofit agencies and local governments to provide emergency shelters for the homeless.

Migrant Housing Program ($10 Million). The state would spend $10 million to construct rental housing developments for migrant farmworkers and their families. The housing units would be owned by the state and operated by local governments using other state funds and rent receipts. These units would be available at affordable rents to farmworkers when they are working at local farms.

The measure also provides $40 million for two new housing programs:

Home Purchase Assistance Program ($25 Million). The state would provide

$25 million in loans and mortgage insurance to help low-income persons buy their own homes. This program would supplement low-interest loans provided under two existing state programs to assist California veterans and low- and moderate-income households in buying homes. The loans under the new program could be used, among other things, for: (a) additional interest-rate subsidies; (b) low-interest second mortgages; or (c) down payment assistance. The state would make the loans under this program for periods up to 30 years, and the borrowers would repay principal interest at the end of the loan period or when they sell or refinance their homes.

Family Housing Demonstration Program ($15 Million). The state would provide $15 million in loans, at 3 percent interest, for the construction or rehabilitation of two "nontraditional" forms of housing.

- Congregate Housing. Twenty-five to 35 percent of the funds would be allocated for "congregate housing" developments. These projects would house 2 to 10 families within a single large unit and provide common living areas.
- Community Housing. The remaining funds would go to "community housing" developments, which would have 20 or more rental or cooperative units and provide various support services (such as child care, job training and placement) to the residents.

Both of these housing developments would be aimed at serving the needs of low-income single-parent households and households with both parents working outside the home. Rents or payments on units would be kept low and affordable. The state would make loans for periods ranging from 20 to 30 years, and the borrowers could postpone payment of principal and interest until the end of the loan term.

Fiscal Effect

Direct Cost of Paying Off the Bonds. The state would receive loan repayments under the four loan programs discussed above. These repayments, however, would be used for additional loans, not for repayment of the general obligation bonds. As a result, the state's General Fund would be responsible for the bond principal and interest payments, which typically would be paid off over a period of about 20 years. If all of the authorized bonds were sold at an interest rate of 7.5 percent, the cost would be about $535 million to pay off both the principal ($300 million) and interest ($235 million). The average payment would be about $25 million each year.

Borrowing Costs for Other Bonds. By increasing the amount that the state borrows, this measure may cause the state and local governments to pay more under other bond programs. These costs cannot be estimated.

State Revenues. The people who buy these bonds are not required to pay state income tax on the interest they earn. Therefore, if California taxpayers buy these bonds instead of making taxable investments, the state would collect less in income taxes. This loss of revenue cannot be estimated.

TEXT OF PROPOSED LAW

This law proposed by Senate Bill 1693 (Statutes of 1988, Ch. 48) is submitted to the people in accordance with the provisions of Article XVI of the Constitution.

This proposed law adds sections to the Health and Safety Code; therefore, new provisions proposed to be added are printed in *italic type* to indicate that they are new.

Section 1. Part 9 (commencing with Section 53150) is added to Division 31 of the Health and Safety Code, to read:

Part 9. Housing and Homeless Bond Act of 1988

Chapter 1. General Provisions

53150. This part shall be known and may be cited as the Housing and Homeless Bond Act of 1988.

53151. As used in this part, the following terms have the following meanings:

(a) "Committee" means the Housing Committee created pursuant to Section 53172.

(b) "Fund" means the Home Building and Rehabilitation Fund created pursuant to Section 53160.

Chapter 2. Home Building and Rehabilitation Fund

53160. The proceeds of bonds issued and sold pursuant to this part shall be deposited in the Home Building and Rehabilitation Fund, which is hereby created. Moneys in the fund shall be allocated and utilized in accordance with Part 8 (commencing with Section 53130), as added by Senate Bill No. 1692 of the 1987-88 Regular Session.

Chapter 3. Fiscal Provisions

53170. Bonds in the total amount of three hundred million dolars ($300,000,000), exclusive of refunding bonds issued pursuant to Section 53170.5, or so much thereof as is necessary, may be issued and sold to provide a fund to be used for carrying out the purposes expressed in this part and to be used to reimburse the General Obligation Bond Expense Revolving Fund pursuant to Section 16724.5 of the Government Code. The bonds shall, when sold, be and constitute a valid and binding obligation of the State of California, and the full faith and credit of the State of California is hereby pledged for the punctual payment of both principal of, and interest on, the bonds as the principal and interest become due and payable.

53170.5. Any bonds issued and sold pursuant to this chapter may be refunded by the issuance of refunding bonds in accordance with Article 6 (commencing with Section 16780) of Chapter 4 of Part 3 of Division 2 of Title 2 of the Government Code. Approval by the electors of the state for the issuance of these bonds shall include the approval of any bonds issued to refund any bonds originally issued or previously issued refunding bonds.

53171. The bonds authorized by this part shall be prepared, executed, issued, sold, paid, and redeemed as provided in the State General Obligation Bond Law (Chapter 4 (commencing with Section 16720) of Part 3 of Division 4 of Title 2 of the Government Code), and all of the provisions of that law apply to the bonds and to this part and are hereby incorporated in this part as though set forth in full in this part.

53172. (a) Solely for the purpose of authorizing the issuance and sale, pursuant to the State General Obligation Bond Law, of the bonds authorized by this part, the Housing Committee is hereby created. For purposes of this part, the Housing Committee is "the committee" as that term is used in the State General Obligation Bond Law. The committee consists of the Controller, the Treasurer, the Director of Finance, the Director of the Department of Housing and Community Development, and the Executive Director of the California Housing Finance Agency, or their designated representatives. A majority of the committee may act for the committee.

(b) For purposes of the State General Obligation Bond Law, the Department of Housing and Community Development is designated as the "board" for programs administered by the department and the California Housing Finance Agency is designated as the "board" for programs administered by the agency.

53173. The committee shall determine whether or not it is necessary or desirable to issue bonds authorized pursuant to this part in order to carry out the actions specified in Part 8 (commencing with Section 53130) as added by Senate Bill No. 1692 of the 1987-88 Regular Session, and, if so, the amount of bonds to be issued and sold. Successive issues of bonds may be authorized and sold to carry out those actions progressively, and it is not necessary that all of the bonds authorized to be issued be sold at any one time.

53174. There shall be collected each year and in the same manner and at the same time as other state revenue is collected, in addition to the ordinary revenues of the state, a sum in an amount required to pay the principal of, and interest on, the bonds maturing each year, and it is the duty of all officers charged by law with any duty in regard to the collection of the revenue to do and perform each and every act which is necessary to collect that additional sum.

53175. Notwithstanding Section 13340 of the Government Code, there is hereby appropriated from the General Fund in the State Treasury, for the purposes of this part, an amount that will equal the total of the following:

(a) The sum annually necessary to pay the principal of, and interest on, bonds issued and sold pursuant to this part, as the principal and interest become due and payable.

(b) The sum which is necessary to carry out the provisions of Section 53176, appropriated without regard to fiscal years.

53176. For the purposes of carrying out this part, the Director of Finance may authorize the withdrawal from the General Fund of an amount or amounts not to exceed the amount of the unsold bonds which have been authorized to be sold for the purpose of carrying out this part. Any amounts withdrawn shall be deposited in the fund. Any money made available under this section shall be returned to the General Fund, plus interest that the amounts would have earned in the Pooled Money Investment Account, from money received from the sale of bonds for the purpose of carrying out this part.

53176.5. The board may request the Pooled Money Investment Board to make a loan from the Pooled Money Investment Account, in accordance with Section

16312 of the Government Code, for purposes of carrying out the provisions of this chapter. The amount of the request shall not exceed the amount of unsold bonds which the committee has by resolution authorized to be sold for the purpose of carrying out this chapter. The board shall execute any documents which are required by the Pooled Money Investment Board to obtain and repay the loan. Any amounts loaned shall be deposited in the fund to be allocated to the board in accordance with this chapter.

53177. All money deposited in the fund which is derived from premium and accrued interest on bonds sold shall be reserved in the fund and shall be available for transfer to the General Fund as a credit to expenditures for bond interest.

53178. The Legislature hereby finds and declares that, inasmuch as the proceeds from the sale of bonds authorized by this part are not "proceeds of taxes" as that term is used in Article XIII B of the California Constitution, the disbursement of these proceeds is not subject to the limitations imposed by that article.

ARGUMENT IN FAVOR OF PROPOSITION 84

Homelessness. It's a California tragedy. Over 100,000 Californias are homeless and the number grows daily.

Who are they?

Many are frail elderly, Vietnam veterans, families with small children, single mothers, mentally ill, disabled men and women.

They all have one thing in common. They can't find affordable housing.

Anyone can end up without shelter.

Serious illness or injury, low wages, a sudden layoff, a house fire, mental illness, loss of a spouse. Any of these can spell devastation for someone barely able to balance the cost of food, clothing, medical bills and shelter.

The forecasts are unsettling.

While the holes in the safety net of low-income housing are getting bigger and homelessness grows, federal housing subsidies are ending.

California, the sixth largest economic power in the world, has a severe shortage of affordable homes and rental units. Homeless shelters throughout the state are overcrowded and turning people away.

There is something we can do.

Simply stated, Proposition 84 is the most important action to fight homelessness in 10 years. After a decade of neglect, this responsible and effective measure can help communities and citizens groups solve local housing problems.

This program will produce 33,000 new emergency shelter beds, 22,000 rehabilitated residential hotel units, 8,000 rental units for low-income tenants and 300 farm-worker housing units.

And Proposition 84 contains provisions for child care, job training and other support services to help break the cycle of homelessness and hopelessness.

This bond act will do a lot of good.

For many in need of emergency shelter: a bed in a secure place and the chance to stop the humiliation of living on the street, to seek out new or improved employment.

For the elderly: the chance to live in an affordable home or apartment without fear of eviction or premature nursing home institutionalization.

For single parents and couples with children: the chance to leave a neighbor's couch or the family car to find decent housing, child care and jobs.

For the growing number of homeless children: the chance to go to school regularly.

For veterans: the chance for job training, affordable rental housing and the possibility of owning a home.

Proposition 84 is the right thing to do and the right way to do it.

Help bring the homeless inside. Help restore the sense of community and family. Help break the cycle of hopelessness that threatens so many Californians.

Please vote "yes" on Proposition 84.

DAVID ROBERTI
State Senator, 23rd District
Senate President pro Tempore

PETER T. CHACON
Executive Director, Vietnam Veterans of California

CARL JONES
Director, Congress of California Seniors, Inc.

ARGUMENT AGAINST PROPOSITION 84

Public housing projects quickly become the ugliest, worst maintained, and most blighted part of any neighborhood in which they are found. England is selling its public housing to the tenants, recognizing that public housing projects are not only inefficiently managed by government bureaucracies but demoralizing to the occupants. Those senior citizen housing projects which are planned and operated by churches and other private organizations are more attractive, more responsive to the needs of senior citizens, and less costly to operate. A White House commission, after studying the problem of housing, recently urged the use of direct subsidies to individuals for housing rather than pouring any more money into public housing projects.

There are alternative solutions to housing shortages. One is to stop the influx of illegal immigrants into California, competing for low-cost housing with our citizens who have lived, worked, and paid taxes in this country all their lives.

Another alternative is to chop in half federal spending on "defense," by pulling our troops out of Germany, Japan, and Korea, our ships out of the Persian Gulf, and all the other spots in the world where we are trying to maintain the roles of world policeman and world banker. By abandoning our policies of worldwide intervention and the arms race in space we could balance the budget, start paying off the national debt, and free up hundreds of billions of dollars for construction and mortage loans. Interest rates would drop back to where they were in the '50s, at 4% or 5% for mortgage loans. The construction industry would boom, providing jobs and housing for all.

There is no surplus in the state budget this year. The $27 million needed to pay off these bonds will have to come from a tax increase or a cut somewhere else in future state budgets.

Payments of principal and interest on outstanding bonds totaled $515 million in the 1987-88 budget. Bonds already authorized but not yet sold will add $372 million when sold. The nine bond issues on this ballot would add $295 million, for a total of $1.1 billion each year. On a pay-as-you-go basis $1.1 billion would finance all of the projects in the nine bond issues, schools, prisons, housing, etc. in only three years.

Vote NO on the housing bonds!

William McCord
Retired State Administrator

REBUTTAL TO ARGUMENT
IN FAVOR OF PROPOSITION 84

If you vote for this measure you may temporarily feel like a nice person, but don't think that you will solve the problems of the poor or homeless. Government efforts to help the poor inevitably produce the opposite result. Today's government-subsidized housing becomes tomorrow's human-demoralizing slum. The proponents to this measure hope to pull at your heartstrings, but they do not, and cannot, show you that government housing subsidies make any significant dent in the problems of the poor or homeless. In fact, government housing projects typically destroy potential repairable homes, and then erect instant slums in their place.

Studies have found that exclusionary zoning and onerous building codes and regulations add up to 25% to the cost of new construction and can delay and even discourage new residential building. These are the major causes of housing shortages, not a lack of of government spending.

In June of this year voters approved $1.7 billion bonds. This ballot proposes $3.3 billion more—$5 billion just this year alone! At this rate, before these bonds are paid off in 20 years, we will have a bonded indebtedness of $100 billion and annual payments of $9 billion, a quarter of today's entire state budget. Politicians know that voters don't want their taxes raised. They have chosen instead to address genuine humanitarian concern by mortgaging ours and our children's future for programs which won't work to solve the problems which the politicians have created.

Vote No on 84!

JUNE R. GENIS
Libertarian Candidate for State Assembly, 20th District

MICHAEL TEJEDA
Businessman

DAVID M. GRAPPO
Attorney

REBUTTAL TO ARGUMENT AGAINST PROPOSITION 84

Proposition 84 is the right thing to do, and the right way to do it. Mr. McCord's opposition suggests no solutions. It is also inaccurate.

This bond act is *not* a public housing program. Churches and private organizations will be eligible to build, own and manage low-income housing financed under this bond act. Private and public, nonprofit and profit-motivated sponsors will all participate in building the housing.

Apartments built under the bond act will *not* be managed by government bureaucracies, but in most cases will be run by private management companies.

In addition to housing and temporary shelters, this bond act provides child care, job training and other support services for families and single parents. This innovative program is supported by housing experts as the way to fight homelessness on a permanent rather than "band aid" basis.

Mr. McCord's scare tactics are an attempt to cover the truth. This bond act will help thousands of people at a minimal cost to taxpayers. The annual debt service will be approximately $1 per Californian per year.

Support for Proposition 84 is widespread. Nearly 100 public and private organizations throughout California have joined the fight against homelessness by supporting the Housing and Homeless Bond Act. They include: the Congress of California Seniors, the Vietnam Veterans of California, the California Council of Churches, the California Homeless Coalition, the Salvation Army, Jewish Family Services, Catholic Charities, and the League of Women's Voters of California.

Please join us in support of Proposition 84.

PATTI WHITNEY-WISE
Director, California Council of Churches

DAVID P. RILEY
Lieutenant Colonell, the Salvation Army

SHELLEY HANCE
Cochairperson, California Homeless Coalition

Appendix C

Assistance to Homeless Persons

CHAPTER 1. GENERAL PROVISIONS

15290. This part shall be known and may be cited as the Homeless Relief Act of 1986.

15290.5. The Legislature finds and declares all of the following:

(a) Many persons residing in this state lack sufficient income or capacity to provide daily shelter, food, and clothing for themselves or their families.

(b) Federal, state, local, and private efforts to assist these homeless persons are not well coordinated and data concerning these shelterless residents are not kept in a consistent manner.

(c) Local and state efforts to help homeless persons have not fixed overall coordination responsibility with individuals in either county or state government.

(d) To feed the hungry, to clothe the naked, and to house the homeless consistent with this part is a priority for this state.

15290.8. As used in this part, unless the context otherwise indicates:

(a) "Office" means the Office of Homeless Services.

(b) "Director" means the Director of the Office of Homeless Services.

CHAPTER 2. OFFICE OF HOMELESS SERVICES

15291. There is hereby established in the Governor's Office an Office of Homeless Services. The office shall be headed by a director, who shall be appointed by, and shall serve at the pleasure of, the Governor.

15291.5. The functions and duties of the office shall include all of the following:

(a) Allocating funds for services to homeless persons as provided in this part.

(b) Submission of a report to the Governor and the Legislature on or before January 1, 1989, of a housing production study of the causes of homelessness in this state, and the appropriate steps, including production of low-income housing, which would be sufficient to minimize the state's future problems in providing shelter for all its citizens. This report shall include recommendations on solving the problems confronting displaced workers, recommendations as to modification of existing local zoning laws, and recommendations on the creation of incentives for private production of low-income housing which will produce conditions for reducing this state's future potential homeless population.

(c.) Submission to the Governor and the Legislature of a report by December 31 of each year, on the implementation of this part.

In implementing subdivisions (b) and (c), the office shall include recommendations of county coordinators of, and county advisory committees on, services to the homeless and detailed information about the homeless population in the state.

15292. The Governor shall appoint an advisory committee to the office. The advisory committee shall make recommendations to the director on the most effective methods for implementation of this part.

15292.5. The director shall allocate funds to each county for the establishment of emergency services centers for homeless persons. The director shall develop an equitable allocation formula for distribution of funds to the counties.

CHAPTER 3. HOMELESS SERVICE CENTERS

15293. Funds for homeless service centers shall be awarded to each county, or to a group of consenting counties, pursuant to a plan which shall be submitted to the director by the board of supervisors of each county. Prior to submitting a plan to the director, the board of supervisors of each county shall appoint a county coordinator for services to homeless persons, who shall assist the board of supervisors in formulating the proposed plan.

A proposed county plan shall include at least all of the following:

(a) To the extent that this information is available, information on the number of homeless persons in the county and the currently unmet needs of these homeless persons.

(b) The number of homeless service centers which would be needed in the county to adequately serve homeless persons, and whether the county intends to administer the service centers directly or to contract with private nonprofit agencies for their establishment.

(c) The services to be provided by the emergency centers in order to meet the unmet needs of homeless persons, including both mandatory and optional services.

(d) Methods for coordinating the county's efforts with other governmental entities, businesses, and nonprofit organizations, in order to ensure not only that necessary services are provided to homeless persons, but also to prevent the duplication of services.

(e) The method of appointment to, and composition of, a county advisory committee on services to homeless persons, which shall make recommendations to the county coordinator for services to homeless persons concerning services to homeless persons.

15293.5. Each county, or county contractor, operating a homeless service center shall provide at least all of the following services:

(a) Food.

Appendix C: Assistance to Homeless Persons   331

(b) Clothing.

(c) Emergency shelter, in accordance with Section 15294.

(d) Transportation services to a place of permanent residence, in accordance with Section 15294.5.

(e) Case management services, including an evaluation of the client's needs and the making of referrals to other entities that provide services needed by the client.

15294. (a) In providing emergency shelter services under this part, the county or its contractor may utilize either direct services or a voucher system.

(b) A single individual shall be entitled to stay in a particular emergency shelter for an annual period of 10 days, and the individual shall be entitled to an annual stay in not more than three shelters.

(c) A couple shall be entitled to stay in a particular shelter for an annual period of 20 days, and the couple shall be entitled to an annual stay in not more than three shelters.

(d) A family shall be entitled to stay in a particular shelter for an annual period of 30 days, and the family shall be entitled to an annual stay in not more than three shelters.

(e) Notwithstanding subdivisions (c) and (d), if approved by the county or its contractor, a couple or a family may be allowed to remain in a particular shelter longer than the allotted period, so long as the total stay in the shelter does not exceed the maximum amount of time which a couple or a family is permitted to stay in emergency shelters pursuant to subdivision (c) or (d), whichever is applicable.

(f) In order for a single individual, a couple, or a family to be eligible for emergency shelter services in excess of the initial 10, 20, or 30-day period, as provided for in subdivisions (b) to (d), inclusive, prior to the end of the initial 10, 20, or 30-day stay, whichever is applicable, the single individual, couple, or family shall participate in case management services, as provided for in subdivision (e) of Section 15293.5.

15294.5. Whenever a homeless person can demonstrate that he or she will be able to establish a permanent residence in another state, such as with relatives, friends, or through the acceptance of a pending job offer, the county, or its contractor shall, if consistent with cost-effectiveness guidelines which shall be adopted by the director, provide the individual with funding for transportation to the out-of-state residence. The county or its contractor may purchase the necessary services rather than provide the homeless person with cash assistance. The director shall adopt regulations specifying the manner in which an individual would have to verify his or her potential permanent residence in order to receive services under this section.

15295. Each county or its contractor, may also provide job placement services, including job counseling, to homeless persons. If the county contracts with other entities to provide job services under this chapter, the county shall utilize incentives to reward agencies that successfully place homeless individuals in unsubsidized employment.

A county or its contractor may also provide, or arrange for the provision of, counseling services and nonpsychiatric mental health services.

15295.5. If consistent with cost-effectiveness guidelines which shall be adopted by the director, a county may utilize funds allocated pursuant to this chapter in order to provide loans to individuals placed in employment for first and last month's rent and for cleaning deposits. Any loan made pursuant to this section shall be approved by the county coordinator of services to homeless persons, or his or her designee.

CHAPTER 4. ALTERNATIVE FACILITIES FOR PUBLIC INEBRIATES

15296. The director shall allocate funds to six consenting counties for the establishment of alternative facilities for the housing of public inebriates. Funds shall be awarded pursuant to proposed plans which shall be submitted by a county seeking funding pursuant to this chapter.

15296.5. A person who is charged with a violation of subdivision (f) of Section 647 of the Penal Code may be placed by an authorized peace officer, subject to the individual's right to bail, in a facility funded pursuant to this chapter. If a person is convicted of a violation of subdivision (f) of Section 647 of the Penal Code, a judge may elect, as an alternative to placing the individual in the county jail, to place the individual in a facility funded under this chapter for a period not to exceed 90 days.

15297. Each pilot project funded under this chapter shall provide to its residents counseling and other nonpsychiatric mental health services.

CHAPTER 5. DURATION OF CHAPTER

15298. This part shall remain in effect only until January 1, 1990, and as of that date is repealed, unless a later enacted statute which is enacted prior to January 1, 1990, extends or deletes that date.

SEC.2. Section 647 of the Penal Code is amended to read:

647. Every person who commits any of the following acts is guilty of disorderly conduct, a misdemeanor:

(a) Who solicits anyone to engage in or who engages in lewd or dissolute conduct in any public place or in any place open to the public or exposed to public view.

(b) Who solicits or who engages in any act of prostitution. As used in this subdivision, "prostitution" includes any lewd act between persons for money or other consideration.

(c) Who accosts other persons in any public place or in any place open to the public for the purpose of begging or soliciting alms.

(d) Who loiters in or about any toilet open to the public for the purpose of engaging in or soliciting any lewd or lascivious or any unlawful act.

(e) Who loiters or wanders upon the streets or from place to place without apparent reason or business and who refuses to identify himself or herself and to account for his or her presence when requested by any peace officer so to do, if the surrounding circumstances are such as to indicate to a reasonable person that the public safety demands such identification.

(f) Who is found in any public place under the influence of intoxicating liquor, any drug, controlled substance, toluene, any substance defined as a poison in Schedule D of Section 4160 of the Business and Professions code, or any combination of any intoxicating liquor, drug, controlled substance, toluene, or any such poison, in such a condition that he or she is unable to exercise care for his or her own safety or the safety of others, or by reason of his or her being under the influence of intoxicating liquor, any drug, controlled substance, toluene, any substance defined as a poison in Schedule D, of Section 4160 of the Business and Professions Code, or any combination of any intoxicating liquor, drug, toluene, or any such poison, interferes with or obstructs or prevents the free use of any street, sidewalk, or other public way.

(ff) (1) When a person has violated subdivision (f), a peace officer, if he or she is reasonably able to do so, shall place the person, or cause him or her to be placed, in civil protective custody. The person shall be taken to a facility, designated pursuant to Section 5170 of the Welfare and Institutions Code, for the 72-hour treatment and evaluation of inebriates. A peace officer may place a person in civil protective custody with that kind and degree of force which would be lawful were he or she effecting an arrest for a misdemeanor without a warrant. No person who has been placed in civil protective custody shall thereafter be subject to any criminal prosecution or juvenile court proceeding based on the facts giving rise to such placement. This subdivision shall not apply to the following persons:

(A) Any person who is under the influence of any drug, or under the combined influence of intoxicating liquor and any drug.

(B) Any person who a peace officer has probable cause to believe has committed any felony, or who has committed any misdemeanor in addition to subdivision (f) of this section.

(C) Any person who a peace officer in good faith believes will attempt escape or will be unreasonably difficult for medical personnel to control.

(2) A person who is charged with a violation of subdivision (f) may be placed by an authorizd peace officer, subject to the individual's right to bail, in a facility funded pursuant to Chapter 4 (commencing with Section 15296) of Part 6.6 of Division 3 of Title 2 of the Government Code. If a person is convicted of a violation of subdivision (f), a judge may elect, as an alternative to placing the individual in the county jail, to place the individual in a facility funded under Chapter 4 (commencing with Section 15296) of Part 6.6 of Division 3 of Title 2 of the Government Code for a period not to exceed 90 days.

(g) Who loiters, prowls, or wanders upon the private property of another, at any time, without visible or lawful business with the owner or occupant thereof. As used in this subdivision, "loiter" means to delay or linger without a lawful purpose for being on the property and for the purpose of committing a crime as opportunity may be discovered.

(h) Who, while loitering, prowling, or wandering upon the private property of another, at any time, peeks in the door or window of any inhabited building or structure located thereon, without visible or lawful business with the owner or occupant thereof.

(i) Who lodges in any building, structure, vehicle, or place, whether public or private, without the permission of the owner or person entitled to the possession or in control thereof.

In any accusatory pleading charging a violation of subdivision (b) of this section, if the defendant has been once previously convicted of a violation of that subdivision, the previous conviction shall be charged in the accusatory pleading; and, if the previous conviction is found to be true by the jury, upon a jury trial, or by the court, upon a court trial, or is admitted by the defendant, the defendant shall be imprisoned in the county jail for a period of not less than 45 days and shall not be eligible for release upon completion of sentence, on parole, or on any other basis until he or she has served a period of not less than 45 days in the county jail. In no such case shall the trial court grant probation or suspend the execution of sentence imposed upon the defendant.

In any accusatory pleading charging a violation of subdivision (b) of this section, if the defendant has been previously convicted two or more times of a violation of that subdivision, each such previous conviction shall be charged in the accusatory pleading; and, if two or more of such previous convictions are found to be true by the jury, upon a jury trial, or by the court, upon a court trial, or are admitted by the defendant, the defendant shall be imprisoned in the county jail for a period of not less than 90 days and shall not be eligible for release upon completion of sentence, on parole, or on any other basis until he or she has served a period of not less than 90 days in the county jail. In no such case shall the trial court grant probation or suspend the execution of sentence imposed upon the defendant.

This section shall remain in effect only until January 1, 1990, and as of that date is repealed, unless a later enacted statute which is enacted prior to January 1, 1990, extends or deletes that date.

SEC.3. Section 647 is added to the Penal Code, to read:

647. Every person who commits any of the following acts is guilty of disorderly conduct, a misdemeanor:

(a) Who solicits anyone to engage in or who engages in lewd or dissolute conduct in any public place or in any place open to the public or exposed to public view.

(b) Who solicits or who engages in any act of prostitution. As used in this subdivision, "prostitution" includes any lewd act between persons for money or other consideration.

(c) Who accosts other persons in any public place or in any place open to the public for the purpose of begging or soliciting alms.

(d) Who loiters in or about any toilet open to the public for the purpose of engaging in or soliciting any lewd or lascivious or any unlawful act.

(e) Who loiters or wanders upon the streets or from place to place without apparent reason or business and who refuses to identify himself or herself and to account of his or her presence when requested by any peace officer so to do, if the surrounding circumstances are such as to indicate to a reasonable person that the public safety demands such identification.

(f) Who is found in any public place under the influence of intoxicating liquor, any drug, controlled substance, toluene, any substance defined as a poison in Schedule D of section 4160 of the business and Professions Code, or any combination of any intoxicating liquor, drug, controlled substance, toluene, or any such poison, in such a condition that he or she is unable to exercise care for his or her own safety or the safety of others, or by reason of his or her being under the influence of intoxicating liquor, any drug, controlled substance, toluene, any substance defined as a poison in Schedule D of Section 4160 of the Business and Professions Code, or any combination of any intoxicating liquor, drug, toluene, or any such poison, interferes with or obstructs, or prevents the free use, of any street sidewalk, or other public way.

(ff) When a person has violated subdivision (f) of this section, a peace officer, if he or she is reasonably able to do so, shall place the person, or cause him or her to be placed, in civil protective custody. Such person shall be taken to a facility, designated pursuant to Section 5170 of the Welfare and Institutions Code, for the 72-hour treatment and evaluation of inebriates. A peace officer may place a person in civil protective custody with that kind and degree of force which would be lawful were he or she effecting an arrest for a misdemeanor without a warrant. No person who has been placed in civil protective custody shall thereafter be subject to any criminal prosecution or juvenile court proceeding based on the facts giving rise to such placement. This subdivision shall not apply to the following persons:

(1) Any person who is under the influence of any drug, or under the combined influence of intoxicating liquor and any drug.

(2) Any person who a peace officer has probable cause to believe has committed any felony, or who has committed any misdemeanor in addition to subdivision (f) of this section.

(3) Any person who a peace officer in good faith believes will attempt escape or will be unreasonably difficult for medical personnel to control.

(g) Who loiters, prowls, or wanders upon the private property of another, at any time, without visible or lawful business with the owner or occupant thereof. As used in this subdivision, "loiter" means to delay or linger without a lawful purpose for being on the property and for the purpose of committing a crime as opportunity may be discovered.

(h) Who, while loitering, prowling, or wandering upon the private property of another, at any time, peeks in the door or window of any inhabited building or structure located thereon, without visible or lawful business with the owner or occupant thereof.

(i) Who lodges in any building, structure vehicle, or place, whether public or private, without the permission of the owner or person entitled to the possession or in control thereof.

In any accusatory pleading charging a violation of subdivision (b) of this section, if the defendant has been once previously convicted of a violation of that subdivision, the previous conviction shall be charged in the accusatory pleading; and, if the previous conviction is found to be true by the jury, upon a jury trial, or by the court, upon a court trial, or is admitted by the defendant, the defendant shall be imprisoned in the county jail for a period of not less than 45 days and shall not be eligible for release upon completion of sentence, on parole, or on any other basis until he or she has served a period of not less than 45 days in the county jail. In no such case shall the trial court grant probation or suspend the execution of sentence imposed upon the defendant.

In any accusatory pleading charging a violation of subdivision (b) of this section, if the defendant has been previously convicted two or more times of a violation of that subdivision, each such previous conviction shall be charged in the accusatory pleading; and, if two or more of such previous convictions are found to be true by the jury, upon a jury trial, or by the court, upon a court trial, or are admitted by the defendant, the defendant shall be imprisoned in the county jail for a period of not less than 90 days and shall not be eligible for release upon completion of sentence, on parole, or on any other basis until he or she has served a period of not less than 90 days in the county jail. In no such case shall the trial court grant probation or suspend the execution of sentence imposed upon the defendant.

This section shall become operative on January 1, 1990, unless a later enacted statute which is enacted prior to January 1, 1990, extends or deletes that date.

SEC.4. The sum of _____ dollars ($_____) is hereby appropriated from the General Fund to the Office of Homeless Services for purposes of implementing this act, including: reimbursement to counties for costs mandated by this act.

Notes

CHAPTERS 1 TO 23

1. Richard C. Tessler, Ph.D., and Deborah L. Dennis, M.A., *A Synthesis of NIMH-Funded Research Concerning Persons Who Are Homeless and Mentally Ill*, for the Office of Programs for the Homeless Mentally Ill, National Institute on Mental Health, February 1989, pp. 20–22. See also Peter H. Rossi, *Down and Out in America: The Origins of Homelessness*, University of Chicago Press, 1989.

2. Tessler and Dennis, p. 47, citing E.L. Bassuk, L. Rubin, and A. Lariat, "Characteristics of Sheltered Homeless Families," *American Journal of Public Health*, vol. 76, 1986, pp. 1097–1100.

3. *Ibid.* p. 47–48.

4. Jonathan Kozol, *Rachael and Her Children: Homeless Families in America*, 1988.

5. *Monthly Review*, Bureau of Labor Statistics, March 1989.

6. Charles Hoch of the University of Illinois School of Urban Planning and Policy recently finished a study of this for the city of Chicago. He concluded that housing codes must be loosened, for we are losing both renter- and owner-occupied housing stock.

7. R. Bratt, *Rebuilding a Low-Income Housing Policy*, Temple University Press, 1989, p. 319.

8. Henry Pringle, *Theodore Roosevelt, A Biography*, Harcourt, Brace & World, 1931, p. 108.

9. Lilia Reyes and Laura DeKoven Waxmen, *Report from the U.S. Conference of Mayors*, Washington, DC, annual reports for 1988 and 1989.

10. Section 501(a), 42 U.S.C. 114111(a).

11. See *National Coalition for the Homeless* v. *U.S. Veterans' Administration*, 695 F. Supp. 1226 (D.D.C. 1988).

12. P.L. 93-383, 88 Stat. 734, 12 U.S.C. 1706e.

13. *San Diego Union*, March 18, 1990.

14. San Diego's 1987 Vintage Baltic Inn is a modern, 208-unit SRO hotel. Its low rates ($210 to $320 per month) and creative design have won it a raft of awards: Finalist, Ford Foundation and John F. Kennedy School of Government, Harvard University, for "Innovation in State and Local Government 1998"; Honor Award, American Institute of Architecture, 1987; and Presidential Recognition Award for Community Service, 1988.

Another Lincoln Properties SRO, the "J Street Inn," received another AJA Honor Award in 1990 following a feature story in *Architecture* magazine.

15. Telephone interview with Ronald W. Manderscheid, Ph.D., National Institute of Mental Health, Division of Biometry and Applied Sciences, August 3, 1990.

16. The American Public Health Association now publishes a 52-page booklet, *Helping Homeless Mentally Ill People: A Model for Shelter Workers*, Mary E. Stefl, Ph.D., ed. 1989.

17. Farr's friend, Bud Mayer, was at that time director of ADAMHA (Administration

of Drug Abuse, Mental Illness and Alcohol Programs, National Institute of Mental Health) and an assistant surgeon general. During the Great Depression, Mayer had "been on the bum" for a year, and this helped him to empathize with the situation of the homeless. He started NIMH's first initiatives vis-à-vis America's homeless mentally ill. Conversation with Rodger Farr, July 25, 1990.

18. See Tessler and Dennis, pp. 38–39.

19. In 1939, German Lutheran pastor Dietrich Bonhoeffer, soon to be martyred by the Nazis, declared from the pulpit, "Silence in the face of evil is complicity with evil."

20. See San Diego Union, July 13, 1990, p. A1, by Cheryl Clark.

21. Access, monthly publication of the National Resource Center on Homelessness and Mental Illness, NIMH, June 1989, vol. 1, no. 2.

22. The Homeless Mentally Ill: A Task Force Report of the American Psychiatric Association, edited by H. Richard Lamb, American Psychiatric Association Press, 1984.

23. Tessler and Dennis, pp. 21–31.

24. Ibid., p. 38.

25. Ibid.

26. Letter from Janlee Wong, Public Conservator, San Diego County Department of Social Services, to the author, July 18, 1990.

27. Ibid.

28. Rebecca T. Criag and Barbara Wright, Mental Health Financing and Programming: A Legislature's Guide, National Conference of State Legislatures, p. 54.

29. Ibid., p. 98.

30. Ibid., p. 103.

31. Ibid., p. 96

32. Ibid., pp. 99–113.

33. Tessler and Dennis, p. 41, quoting Barrow, et al., 1988, p. 1.

34. Ibid., p. 42.

35. The Homeless Mentally Ill, Task Force Report of the American Psychiatric Association, 1984, pp. 132–133.

36. Robert Hayes, "Ethics," Time, September 17, 1987.

37. A full discussion of the procedural and substantive due process considerations arising from the involuntary commitment procedure is beyond the scope of this chapter. For further discussion of this issue, see Strobos, The Constitution and the Rights of the Mentally Ill: An Analysis and Proposal, 10 J. Legal Med. 661 (1989); Comment, The Liberty Interest in the Right to Refuse Psychiatric Medical Treatment: A Need for Balance of the Competing Interests, 24 Gonz. L. Rev. 333 (1989); Kaufman, "Crazy" Until Proven Innocent? Civil Commitment of the Mentally Ill Homeless, 19 Colum. Hum. Rts. L. Rev. 333 (1988); Brown and Smith, Mental Patients' Rights: An Empirical Study of Variation Across the U.S., 11 Intl. J.L. & Psychiatry 157 (1988).

38. Conservatorship of Roulet, 23 Cal. 3d 219, 223, 152 Cal. Rptr. 424, 590 P. 2d 1 (1979).

39. O'Connor v. Donaldson, 422 U.S. 563 (1975).

40. See Tessler and Dennis, pp. 41–42.

41. California Welfare and Institute Code sections 5000 et seq. (West 1984).

42. Ibid. at section 5008(h).

43. Ibid. at section 5008(h)(1).

44. See Ariz. Rev. Stats. Ann. section 36-535 (1987 Supp.); Ark. Stats. Ann. sections 59-1406 (1985 Supp.); Conn. Soc. and Hum. Services Law Sections 17-178(c), 17-183 (1987); Colo. Rev'd Stats. section 27-10-105(1)(a) (1987 Supp.); Idaho Code section 66-326 (Michie, 1987 Supp.); La. Rev. Stat. Ann. section 28-53 (West 1987 Supp.); Mass. Ann. Laws section

123-12 (1987); N.C. Gen. Stat. section 122C-262 (1987); Wash. Rev. Code Ann. section 71.05.210 (1988).

45. Plummer v. Murphy, 134 Cal. App. 15, 184 Cal. Rptr. 363 (1982).

46. *Ibid.*, p. 17.

47. *Ibid.*, pp. 17–18.

48. *Ibid.*, p. 19.

49. 180 Cal. App. 3d 1030, 226 Cal. Rptr. 33 (1986). But see *Conservatorship of Walker,* 206 Cal. App. 3d 1572, 254 Cal. Rptr. 552 (1989), wherein the court narrowly read *Benvenuto* and *Murphy* in sustaining the reappointment of a conservator.

50. *Ibid.* at 1034.

51. Matter of Boggs, 136 Misc. 2d 1082, 522 N.Y.S. 2d 407 (Sup. Ct. 1987).

52. *Boggs* v. *N.Y. City Health and Hosp. Corp.,* 132 A.D. 2d 340, 523 N.Y.S. 2d 71 (1987).

53. Conservatorship of Roulet, 23 Cal. 3d 219, 590 P.2d 1, 152 Cal. Rptr. 425 (1979).

54. *Ibid.* at 228.

55. *Ibid.* at 225.

56. *Addington* v. *Texas,* 441 U.S. 418 (1979).

57. See Ga. Code Ann. section 37-3-1(9.1) (Supp. 1987); Mich. Comp. Laws Ann. section 330.1401 (West 1980); Neb. Rev. Stat. section 83-1009 (Supp. 1986); Okla. Stat. Ann. Tit. 43A, section 1-1-03(n) (West Supp. 1986); In re Harris, 98 Wash. 2d 276, 284, 654 P.2d 109, 112-13 (1982).

58. See Ariz. Rev. Stat. Ann. section 36-524(c) (1986); Md. Health-Gen. Code Ann. section 10-622 (1982); Minn. Stat. section 253B.05 (1982).

59. Ky. Rev. Stat. Ann. section 202A.026 (Michie/Bobbs-Merrill 1982); Mo. Ann. Stat. section 632-305 (Vernon Supp. 1987); Ohio Rev. Code Ann. section 5122.10 (Anderson 1981).

60. Cal. Welf. and Inst. Code sections 5351 and 5352 (West 1984).

61. For a list of local conservatorship agencies, see Johnstone and House, *California Conservatorships* section 8.4 (California Continuing Education of the Bar, 2d ed., 1989 Supp.).

62. See Ga. Code An. section 37-3-81.1 (Supp. 1987). For a fuller discussion of this statutory change, see Comment, *1986 Amendments to Georgia's Mental Health Statutes: The Latest Attempt to Provide a Solution to the Problem of the Chronically Mentally Ill,* 36 Emory L.J. 1313 (1987).

63. Tessler and Dennis, p. 21.

64. See also "Homelessness: Halting the Race to the Bottom," 3 *Yale Law & Policy Review,* 1985, pp. 551–559; and HUD Report on the Homeless: Hearing before the Subcommittee on Housing and Community Development of the House Committee on Banking, Finance and Urban Affairs, 98th Congress, 2d Session 2, 1984, p. 348.

65. Abraham opened his house to passing travelers and entertained them in a hospitable manner. When his guests thanked him for his attention, Abraham replied, "Do not thank me, for I am not the owner of this place; thank God, who created heaven and earth." In this manner he made the name of God known among the heathens. Therefore he gave us an example of hospitality that we should follow, as it is written in the proverbs of the fathers, "Let thy house be open wide as a refuge, and let the poor be cordially received within the walls." When they enter thy house, receive them with a friendly glance, and set immediately before them bread and salt.

66. In I Corinthians 13, St. Paul says, "Though I speak with the tongues of men and of angels, and have not charity, I am become as sounding brass, or a tinkling cymbal. And though I have the gift of prophecy, and understand all mysteries, and all knowledge; and though I have all faith, so that I could remove mountains, and have not charity, I am nothing. And though I bestow all my goods to feed the poor, and though I give my body to be

burned, and have not charity, it profiteth me nothing. Charity suffereth long, and is kind; charity envieth not; charity vaunted not itself, is not puffed up. Doth not behave itself unseemly, seeketh not her own, is not easily provoked, thinketh no evil; rejoiceth not in iniquity, but rejoiceth in truth; beareth all things, believeth all things, hopeth all things, endureth all things. Charity never faileth: but whether there be prophecies, they shall fail: whether there be tongues, they shall cease; whether there be knowledge, it shall vanish away. . . . And now abideth faith, hope, charity, these three; but the greatest of these is charity."

67. Lao Tsu, Verse Ten from the Tao Te Ching.

68. *The Philosophy of Confucius*, James Legge, trans., Peter Pauper Press, 1970.

69. Peter Johansen, *Lucy's Child*, Morrow Publishing, 1989, and *Lucy: Beginning of Mankind*, Warner Books, 1989.

70. For more on what it means to "help," see the works of John Bradshaw, *Bradshaw on the Family*, Health Community Publications, 1988, and Ram Dass, *How Can I Help*, Knopf Publishing, 1985.

71. Helen Keller, *Helen Keller's Journal*, Doubleday, 1938.

72. Ursula K. LeGuin, *A Wizard of Earthsea*, Parnassus Press, 1968, p.77.

73. I felt it appropriate to add here a famous dialogue from Charles Dickens' *A Christmas Carol*, wherein Ebeneezer Scrooge is solicited on behalf of the poor: *A Christmas Carol*, Charles Dickens, Macmillian Co., 1963, pp. 9–11.

"At this festive season of the year, Mr. Scrooge," said the gentleman, taking up a pen, "it is more than usually desirable that we should make some slight provision for the Poor and destitute, who suffer greatly at the present time. Many thousands are in want of common necessaries; hundreds of thousands are in want of common comforts, sir."

"Are there no prisons?" asked Scrooge.

"Plenty of prisons," said the gentleman, laying down the pen again.

"And the Union workhouses?" demanded Scrooge. "Are they still in operation?"

"They are. Still," returned the gentleman, "I wish I could say they were not."

"The Treadmill and the Poor Law are in full vigour, then?" said Scrooge.

"Both very busy, sir."

"Oh! I was afraid, from what you said at first, that something had occurred to stop them in their useful course," said Scrooge. "I'm very glad to hear it."

"Under the impression that they scarcely furnish Christian cheer of mind or body to the multitude," returned the gentleman, "a few of us are endeavouring to raise a fund to buy the Poor some meat and drink, and means of warmth. We choose this time, because it is a time, of all others, when Want is keenly felt and Abundance rejoices. What shall I put you down for?"

"Nothing!" Scrooge replied.

"You wish to be anonymous?"

"I wish to be left alone," said Scrooge. "Since you ask me what I wish, gentleman, that is my answer. I don't make merry at Christmas and I can't afford to make idle people merry. I help to support the establishments I have mentioned—they cost enough; and those who are badly off must go there."

"Many can't go there and many would rather die."

"If they would rather die," said Scrooge, "they had better do it, and decrease the surplus population. Besides—excuse me—I don't know that."

"But you might know it," observed the gentleman.

"It's not my business," Scrooge returned. "It's enough for a man to understand his own business, and not to interfere with other people's. Mine occupies me constantly. Good afternoon, gentleman!"

74. P.W. Brickner *et al.*, "Homeless Persons and Health Care," 104 *Annals of Internal*

Medicine, 1986, 405–406, citing J. McAdam *et al.*, "Tuberculosis in the SRO/Homeless Population," found in P.W. Brickner *et al.*, *Health Care of Homeless People*, Springer Publishing Co., 1985, pp. 155–175.

75. Theodore Roosevelt, "To the Man in the Arena."

APPENDIX A

1. R. Hayes, *Pushed Out—America's Homeless,* summary, at II (1987).

2. *Status Report on Hunger and Homelessness in American Cities* (27 City Survey, U.S. Conference of Mayors, Dec. 1989), pp. 2–3.

3. Matthews, "What Can be Done?," *Newsweek,* March 21, 1988, pp. 57–58.

4. Blasi, "Litigation Concerning Homeless People," 4 *Pub. L.F.* 433 (1985).

5. See generally A.M. Schlesinger, Jr., *The Cycles in American History* (1986).

6. Reich, "Affirmative Action for Ideas," 38 *Case W. Res. L. Rev.* 632, 634 (1988).

7. Reich, "Constitutional Transformation: New Wrongs, New Rights," 22 *U.S.F. L. Rev.* 189, 190 (1988).

8. *Ibid.,* see generally M. McLuhan, *Understanding Media,* 1964, especially chapters 23 (Ads), 31 (Television), and 22 (Weapons).

9. Chackes, "Sheltering the Homeless: Judicial Enforcement of Governmental Duties to the Poor," 31 *Wash. U.J. Urb. & Contemp. L.* 155 (1987).

10. Hombs, "Social Recognition of the Homeless: Policies of Indifference," 31 *Wash. U. J. Urb. & Contemp. L.* 143 (1987).

11. Werner, "On the Streets: Homelessness—Causes and Solutions," 18 *Clearinghouse Rev.* 11 (1984).

12. *Ibid.*

13. Blasi, "Litigation on Behalf of the Homeless: Systematic Approaches," 31 *Wash. U.J. Urb, & Contemp. L.* 137, 138 (1987).

14. "Building a House of Legal Rights: A Plea for the Homeless," 59 *St. John's L. Rev.* 530, 552 (1985). Further, despite a slightly uplifted public consciousness, images of the stereotypical drunk, shiftless "ne'er-do-well," and undeserving bag lady are still lodged with opprobrium in many American minds: Products of the intellectual dogma of the "Age of Greed," as the 1980s was recently named, Barol, "The Eighties Are Over," *Newsweek,* Jan. 4, 1988, p. 40 (cover story). The dogma still echoes: "They chose their lives. Let them raise themselves." *Ibid.,* p. 42.

15. Reich, *supra* note 7, p. 198.

16. *Ibid.* p.

17. Swanstrom, "No Room at the Inn: Housing Policy and the Homeless," 35 *Wash. U.J. Urb. & Contemp. L.* 81, 102 (1989).

18. See *infra* notes 49–61 and accompanying text.

19. C. Dolbeare, *Out of Reach. Why Everyday People Can't Find Affordable Housing,* 1989, p. 3.

20. Blasi, *supra* note 13, pp. 139–40.

21. St. Augustine declared that any government, the purpose of which is other than justice, is but a robber band, enlarged. *City of God,* Book II. (This statement is attributed by scholars to Book II. However, a direct quotation from the Latin cannot be found. This seems to be an accepted crystallization of one of the important themes of Book II.) Justice O.W. Holmes' concept was a bit different. He once declared: "This is a court of law, young man, not a court of justice." *Peter's Quotations,* p. 276 (11th ed. 1979).

22. "Model Rules of Professional Conduct" Rule 6.1 states: "Pro Bono Publico Service: A lawyer should render public interest legal service. A lawyer may discharge this responsibility by providing legal services at no fee or at a reduced fee to persons of limited means or to public service or charitable groups or organizations, by service in activities for improving the law, the legal system or the legal profession, and by financial support for organizations that provide legal services to persons of limited means." *Ibid., Law. Man. on Prof. Conduct* (ABA/BNA) 01:162 (August 1983). "Model Code of Professional Responsibility" EC 2-25 states, "Historically, the need for legal services of those unable to pay reasonable fees has been met in part by lawyers who donated their services or accepted court appointments on behalf of such individuals. The basic responsibility for providing legal services for those unable to pay ultimately rests upon the individual lawyer, and personal involvement in the problems of the disadvantaged can be one of the most rewarding experiences in the life of a lawyer. Every lawyer, regardless of professional prominence or professional workload, should find time to participate in serving the disadvantaged. The rendition of free legal services to those unable to pay reasonable fees continues to be an obligation of each lawyer, but the efforts of individual lawyers are often not enough to meet the need. Thus it has been necessary for the profession to institute additional programs to provide legal services. Accordingly, legal aid offices, lawyer referral services, and other related programs have been developed, and others will be developed, by the profession. Every lawyer should support all proper efforts to meet this need for legal services." *Ibid., Law. Man. on Prof. Conduct* (ABA/BNA) 01:308-09 (1980).

23. Erickson and Wilhelm, *Housing the Homeless,* pp. xxvii–xxix (1986). See also, Chackes, *supra* note 6, p. 157, n. 11.

24. Erickson & Wilhelm, *supra* note 23.

25. The need of shelter for humans is fundamental. As the Coalition for the Homeless' founding attorney Robert Hayes has said (possibly more for effect than for scientific accuracy), "There are three causes of American homelessness: lack of housing, lack of housing, and lack of housing." Conversation with Robert Hayes, director, The Coalition For The Homeless, New York (December 4, 1986).

26. Blasi, *supra* note 13, p. 138.

27. Chackes, *supra* note 9, p. 157.

28. See *infra,* parts III through VI, for a discussion of leading cases.

29. *Ibid.*

30. Collin, "Homelessness: The Policy and the Law," 16 *Urb. Law.* 317, 328-29 (1984).

31. Confronted with a resistive bureaucracy, one might be tempted simply to utilize all available legal hammers and simultaneously pound as hard as possible on all apparently vulnerable pieces of the local system. This would be the legal equivalent of applying General Foch's flawed maxim, "Attacke! Attacke!" This French general's army was smashed by superior German firepower and strategy during World War I. His maxim proved ridiculous.

32. See *Hodge* v. *Ginsburg,* 303 S.E.2d 245 (W. Va. 1983). "The Department of Welfare . . . [was established] 'to the end that residents of the State who are subject to the recurring misfortunes of life may continue to have such aid and encouragement as . . . [the government] may provide.' W. Va. Code § 9-1-1 (1979 Replacement Vol.)." *Ibid.* at 248. The court in *Hodges* held that the indigent fall within the category of "incapacitated adults" intended by the legislature to be assisted by the Social Services for Adults Act. *Ibid.* at 250 (citing W. Va. Code § 9-6-1). Subsequent amendments to the West Virginia Social Services for Adults have, if anything, expanded the rights of the homeless. W. Va. Code §§ 9-6-1 through 9-6-15 (Supp. 1989). See also *Canady* v. *Koch,* 608 F. Supp. 1460, 1466-7 (D.C.N.Y.), *aff'd,* 768 F.2d 501 (2d Cir. 1985) (homeless right to shelter under N.Y. Const. art. 17, § 1). In *Mooney* v. *Pickett,* 4 Cal. 3d 669, 483, P.2d 1231, 94 Cal. Rptr. 279 (1971), Welfare and

Institutions Code section 17000 was found to have imposed a mandatory duty on California counties to relieve and support the homeless. *Cal. Welf. & Inst. Code* § 17000 (West 1980).

33. Blasi, *supra* note 4, p. 435.

34. *Ibid.* pp. 437–438.

35. *Ibid.*, p. 440.

36. Affidavits attached to complaints present facts and may also help kindle a judge or jury's active empathy for the plaintiffs. Bombarding the court with thousands of pages of affidavits from 170 homeless depositions describing poor conditions was critical in persuading a judge to issue a temporary restraining order and eventually lead to an overhaul of the Los Angeles County hotel voucher system. To obtain these affidavits, the private law firm of Irell & Manella sent their own employees into streets, welfare offices, and poverty clinics. Interview with G. Blasi, director of the Homeless Litigation Team, Los Angeles Legal Aid Foundation (November 10, 1988); interview with John Davidson, Esq., of the law firm of Irell and Manella, Los Angeles (October 11, 1987).

37. One of the oft-repeated sayings of Robert K. Castetter, dean emeritus of the author's alma mater, the California Western School of Law, San Diego, California.

38. Blasi, *supra* note 13, p. 142.

39. Werner, "Homelessness: A Litigation Round Up," 18 *Clearinghouse Rev.* 1255 (1985).

40. Comment, "The Duty of California Counties to Provide Mental Health Care for the Indigent and Homeless," 25 *San Diego L. Rev.* 197, 203–212 (1988).

41. Chackes, *supra* note 9, p. 158.

42. *Ibid.* pp. 157–159.

43. *Ibid.* p. 159.

44. *Ibid.* pp. 159–160.

45. *Black's Law Dictionary*, p. 866 (5th ed. 1979).

46. Chackes, *supra* note 9, p. 160.

47. *Callahan* v. *Carey*, Index No. 42582 (N.Y. App. Div. Dec. 5, 1979), at 79 N.Y.L.J., Dec. 11, 1979, at 10, col. 4, and *The Rights of the Homeless*, pp. 223–237 (PLI Litigation Handbook Series No. 366, R.M. Hayes, chair.) (1988).

48. Interview with Robert Hayes, attorney for plaintiffs, *Callahan* v. *Carey*, No. 42582 (N.Y. App. Div. Dec. 5, 1979), and founder of the Coalition for the Homeless (August 15, 1985).

49. No. 42582 (N.Y. App. Div. Dec. 5, 1979).

50. The *Callahan* rationale was expanded to women and children in *Eldridge* v. *Koch*, 118 Misc. 2d 163, 459 N.Y.S.2d 960 (N.Y. Sup. Ct.); *rev'd. in part*, 98 A.D.2d 675, 469 N.Y.S. 744 (1983).

51. *Callahan*, *supra* note 47.

52. *Ibid.*, New York Const. art. XVII, § 1.

53. The court did not explain its reliance on the constitutional article. Somehow, the court did not feel a need to clarify the preliminary injunction's unexplained finding of a right to shelter in New York City. Note, "A Right to Shelter for the Homeless in New York State," 61 *N.Y.U. L. Rev.* 272, 281–82 (1986).

54. *Callahan* opened the door to homeless litigators. Subsequent litigation met mixed success. See *Wilkins* v. *Perales*, 128 Misc. 2d 265, 487 N.Y.S.2d 961 (Sup. Ct. 1985) (complaint that Department of Social Services violated shelter capacity regulations was dismissed because the department was deemed to have waived such regulations without strict adherence to waiver procedures); *Lamboy* v. *Gross*, 129 Misc. 564, 493, N.Y.S.2d 709 (Sup. Ct. 1985), *aff'd*, 126 A.D.2d 265, 513 N.Y.S.2d 393 (1987) (Action to enforce the right to adequate emergency shelter; court granted preliminary injunction to prohibit sheltering families with children in welfare offices without beds, food, or showers); *Weiser* v. *Koch*, 632 F. Supp.

1369 (S.D.N.Y. 1986) (court denied standing to request established eviction procedures to protect "homeless from midnight ejection" and to guarantee access to personal property: (1) No standing to seek equitable relief in federal court; (2) Abstained to state court, issue not settled by state high court; (3) U.S. Const. amend. XI bars damage claim against a state.); *Slade* v. *Koch,* 135 Misc. 2d 283, 514 N.Y.S.2d 847 (Sup. Ct. 1987), *modified by* 136 Misc. 2d 119, 517 N.Y.S.2d 389 (Sup. Ct. 1987), (challenge to segregate pregnant women and children from those with infectious diseases); *Kennedy* v. *Allen,* No. 19238 (N.Y. Sup. Ct. 1985) (individuals denied right to be housed in motels instead of mass shelters); *Petroff* v. *Black,* 85 Cir. 7099 (GLG) (S.D.N.Y., filed Sept. 5, 1985) (challenge to city to provide either low-salt meals or food stamps to residents on special diets); *Barnes* v. *Koch,* 136 Misc. 2d 96, 518 N.Y.S.2d 539 (Sup. Ct. 1987) (right to emergency shelter includes provision of environment free of potentially significant health dangers such as lead-based paint, asbestos insulation, and lack of sprinkler system and of lavatory facilities). One conclusion from these post-*Callahan* suits is that the court has been willing to narrowly expand the rights of sheltered homeless people, favoring families with children.

55. "A Right to Shelter for the Homeless in New York State," *supra* note 53, p. 284.

56. Blasi, *supra* note 10, p. 137.

57. 216 N.J. Super. 434, 524 A.2d 416 (1987).

58. N.J. Const. art. I, § 1. See Connell, "A Right to Emergency Shelter for the Homeless Under the New Jersey Constitution," 18 *Rutgers L.J.* 765 (1987).

59. Complaint in Lieu of Prerogative Writ at 19, *Maticka* v. *City of Atlantic City,* No. L-8306-84E (N.J. Super. Ct., Law Div., Atlantic City, filed Feb. 7, 1984). See also Connell, *supra* note 58, p. 797.

60. The statutory claim prompted the city to submit a comprehensive plan for emergency shelter services in December 1985. This litigation was thus instrumental in encouraging a previously unhelpful bureaucracy to assume a more positive stance, on its own. Connell, *supra* note 58, p. 797, n. 230.

61. Connell, *supra* note 58, p. 797.

62. No. C 47953 (Los Angeles Superior Court, June 11, 1984).

63. *Ibid.*

64. *Ibid.*

65. New York advocates are looking to the California *Ross* rationale, hoping that it will serve as the basis for an attack on the startling morass of New York family hotels. For example, a mother with two children may be put up in a run-down hotel at a cost to the city of upwards of $3,000 per month. These hotel owners are reported to be contributing millions to city council and mayoral campaigns in a city that continues to have no alternate policies. J. Kozal, *Rachel and Her Children* 36–37 (1988).

66. Schneider, "Food Research and Action Center, Food Stamps Benefits and the Homeless," 18 *Clearinghouse Rev.* 31, 34 (1984); Tuttle, Jacobs & Hosticka, "The Plight of the Homeless," 18 *Urb. Law.* 925, 927 (1986).

67. Tuttle, Jacobs & Hosticka, *supra* note 66, pp. 927–28. See e.g., *Lake* v. *Illinois Dept. of Pub. Aid,* No. 79 Ch. 3434 (Ill., Cook Co. Cir. Ct., July 10, 1979). In one of the earliest "no address" cases, homeless advocates successfully persuaded the court to strike down the state regulation requiring a verifiable address as a prerequisite to receiving assistance. Since then, other courts have followed suit. See *Martin* v. *Milwaukee Co.,* No. 656–770 (Wis., Milwaukee City Cir. Ct., Jan. 9, 1985); *Shirley* v. *County of Contra Costa,* No. 277550 (Cal. Contra Costa Super. Ct., filed Sept. 25, 1985); *San Luis Obispo Coalition for the Homeless* v. *Bd. of Super.,* No. 58261 (Cal. San Luis Obispo Super. Ct., filed Jan 23, 1984); *Ehlers* v. *Bates* (N.Y. App. Div. filed Aug. 3, 1983) and (N.Y. Sup. Ct. Feb. 15, 1984).

68. Cal. App. Dep't Sup. Ct. filed Dec. 19, 1983, *Eisenheim* v. *Los Angeles Superior*

Court, No. C 479453 (Cal. Los Angeles Super. Ct., Dec. 20, 1979).

69. Werner, *supra* note 39, p. 1259.

70. *Ibid.*

71. Statistic comes from R.K. Farr, P. Koegel, and A. Burnam, "A Study of Homelessness and Mental Illness in the Skid Row Area of Los Angeles," 1986.

72. *Eisenheim* No. C479453.

73. The Los Angeles Homeless Litigation Team is composed of seven public service law firms: the Legal Aid Foundation of Los Angeles, Mental Health Advocacy Services, Inc., the Inner City Law Center, the Center for Law and the Public Interest, the American Civil Liberties Union Foundation of Southern California, San Fernando Valley Neighborhood Legal Services, and the Western Center on Law and Poverty, Inc. Many private attorneys and law firms assist, *pro bono publico.* These include the 160-attorney Century City law firm of Irell & Manella, a general business litigation firm, with roots in tax and entertainment law, which has alone been handling the litigation raising the issue of the "habitability" (for human occupation) of some two hundred elderly hotels to which Los Angeles general relief recipients have being referred by the county. Interview with Gary Blasi, coordinator of the Los Angeles Homeless Litigation Team (Nov. 1, 1987).

74. *Ibid.*

75. *Ibid.*

76. *Ibid.*

77. *Ibid.*

78. See J. Heller, *Catch 22,* p. 129, 1961.

79. Blasi, *supra* note 13, pp. 139–40.

80. *Ibid.,* p. 140.

81. 190 Cal. App. 3d 25, 235 Cal. Rptr. 305 (1987).

82. *Ibid.* at 27, 235 Cal. Rptr. at 306.

83. *Ibid.* at 30, 235 Cal. Rptr. at 308.

84. *Ibid.* at 32, 235 Cal. Rptr. at 310.

85. *Ibid.* at 32, 235 Cal. Rptr. at 310.

86. *Ibid.* at 34, 235 Cal. Rptr. at 311.

87. *Ibid.* at 34, 235 Cal. Rptr. at 312.

88. *Ibid.*

89. Thomas Jefferson, letter to James Madison, September 6, 1789, in *The Papers of Thomas Jefferson,* vol. 15, p. 396 (Boyd, J.P., ed., 1958). See also B.N. Cardozo, *The Nature of the Judicial Process,* pp. 150–152, 1921; Holmes, "The Path of the Law," 10 *Harv. L. Rev.* 457, 458, (1897).

90. "Building a House of Legal Rights," *supra* note 11, p. 547.

91. 468 U.S. 288 (1984) involving the First Amendment rights of political protesters wishing to stage a sleep-in demonstration in support of the Homeless in Lafayette Park. The rights of the Homeless themselves were not at issue.

92. *Ibid.* at 304, n. 4 (Marshall J., dissenting). Justice Marshall stated, "Though numerically significant, the homeless are politically powerless inasmuch as they lack the financial resources necessary to obtain access to many of the most effective means of persuasion. Moreover, homeless persons are likely to be denied access to the vote since the lack of a mailing address or other proof of residence within a State disqualifies an otherwise eligible citizen from registering to vote." *Ibid.* (citing brief for National Coalition for the Homeless as *amicus curiae,* at 5).

93. Letter from Nancy Mintie, Director of Los Angeles' Inner City Law Center, to the author 4 (Jan. 2, 1990).

94. See Aristotle, "Politics," bk. 1, ch. 2, in *Great Books of the Western World,* Aristotle, vol. 2, 446 (B. Jowett, trans., R. Hutchins, ed., 1955).

95. Werner, *supra* note 39, p. 1260. See *supra* notes 68–77 and accompanying text.
96. *Pitts* v. *Black,* 608 F. Supp. 696 (D.C.N.Y. 1984).
97. *Ibid.* at 698.
98. *Ibid.* at 698, quoting N.Y. Election Law § 1-104 subd. 22 (McKinney).
99. *Ibid.*
100. *Ibid.* at 709.
101. *Ibid.* at 710.
102. See *Collier* v. *Menzel,* 176 Cal. App. 3d 24, 221 Cal. Rptr. 110 (1985).
103. *Ibid.*
104. *Ibid.* at 29, 221 Cal. Rptr. at 111.
105. *Ibid.* at 30, 221 Cal. Rptr. 111–12. Plaintiffs were told they could register under their former addresses until they had established new residences. *Ibid.*
106. *Ibid.* at 32–37, 221 Cal. Rptr. at 113–17.
107. *Ibid.* at 31, 221 Cal. Rptr. at 112. The court also noted that Cal. Elec. Code, 207 includes trailers or vehicles, public camps or camping grounds within the term "domicile." The court found that the park would fit into the same grouping because a person could sleep and otherwise dwell there, though perhaps not legally. The court supported the plaintiffs' argument that they intended to remain at the park because they had signed the affidavit of registration to that effect; no further written proof is required under Cal. Elec. Code §§ 301 and 500 (j). Also, the plaintiffs had provided a post office box number to fulfill the mailing address requirement under Cal. Elec. Code § 500(d). *Collier,* 176 Cal. App. 3d at 31–32, 221 Cal. Rptr. at 112–113.
108. *Collier,* 176 Cal. App. 3d at 32, 221 Cal. Rptr. at 113. Relying on *Pitts,* the court found that the respondents presented no evidence that appellants were more likely to vote fraudulently than persons who were not homeless. *Ibid.* at 34, 221 Cal. Rptr. at 115. The court also reasoned that the *type* of place people call home was irrelevant to their eligibility to vote if compliance with statutory residence requirements had been achieved. *Ibid.* at 35, 221 Cal. Rptr. at 115. The court stated,

> First of all, there is no statutory authority for the proposition that a residence cannot be a place where there are no living facilities. In other words, the old adage, "A man's home is where he makes it," is not statutorily proscribed. We therefore agree with appellants that whether people "sleep under a bush or a tree or in the open air is immaterial regarding their right to vote." The type of place a person calls home has no relevance to his/her eligibility to vote if compliance with registration has been achieved, that is, the designation of a fixed habitation, the declaration of an intent to remain at that place and to return to it after temporary absences, and the designation of an address where mail can be received. (Elec. Code § 200, subd. (b), 500.)

Ibid. Although a park had no building numbers, it fit within an identifiable election precinct. *Ibid.* at 35–36, 221 Cal. Rptr. at 116.
109. *Ibid.* at 35–36, 221 Cal. Rptr. at 115–116.
110. *Ibid.* at 34–35, 221 Cal. Rptr. at 115.
111. *Ibid.* at 36, 221 Cal. Rptr. at 116. The court continued,

> Unlike other minority groups or disadvantaged persons, the "homeless," by the very nature of their living circumstances, have been unable to experience any political influence in order to make their particular problems and needs known.
> It is patently unjust that society ignores the homeless and yet also denies them the proper avenues to remedy the situation. Even more compelling, the denial of the vote to the "homeless" denies them electoral power. Powerlessness breeds apathy, and apathy is the greatest danger to society.

112. 178 Cal. App. 3d 494, 223 Cal. Rptr. 716 (1986).

113. *Ibid.* at 497, 223 Cal. Rptr. at 717.

114. *Ibid.* at 497, 223 Cal. Rptr. at 718.

115. *Ibid.*

116. *Ibid.* at 502, 223 Cal. Rptr. at 721. The court declared, "Nothing less will satisfy the requirements of sections 10000, 17000 and 17001 when fairly and equitably construed as required by section 11000."

117. Cal. Welf. & Inst. Code § 10000 (West 1980).

118. Cal. Welf. & Inst. Code § 17000 (West 1980).

119. Cal. Welf. & Inst. Code § 17001 (West 1980).

120. See e.g., Mass. Gen. Laws Ann. ch. 450 (West 1987); N.J. Stat. Ann. § 52:27C-24 (West 1984).

121. *Bell v. Board of Supervisors of San Diego County,* No. C 593846 (Cal. San Diego Super. Ct., Mar. 9, 1988).

122. *Ibid.*

123. *Ibid.*

124. Cal. Const., art. I, § 7.

125. U.S. Const. amend. XIV.

126. *Bell* at 8.

127. No. C 578184 (Cal. Los Angeles Super. Ct., Sept. 27, 1985).

128. *Ibid.; Bell.*

129. Order on Stipulation by the Parties for Dismissal, *Bell.* Nancy Mintie, chief counsel for the Inner City Law Center in Los Angeles, has noted that,

There is a problem with the portion of the *Bell* solution that provides that a general relief recipient will be given his or her full payment at the beginning of the month if a statement from a landlord is provided saying that the landlord will accept payment directly from the Department of Social Services. Many landlords, particularly those relatively few low income residential property owners who keep their premises habitable, discriminate against welfare recipients. Requiring [general relief] recipients to disclose the fact that they are on welfare often eliminates them from consideration for the few habitable low income rentals that are available, even with the guarantee of direct payment from DSS.

Letter from Nancy Mintie, p. 3, January 2, 1990.

130. Concerning *Blair,* attorney Mintie states,

The General Relief grant increase obtained in *Blair* was rendered virtually useless by uncontrolled rising rents in the low income housing market. These rent increases absorbed the GR increase, leaving the homeless with no real net gain.

When the first *Blair* increase went into effect, I and Jim Preis and Mike Bodaken drafted an ordinance that instituted vacancy decontrol in the Single Room Occupancy Hotels, which constitute the entry level housing market for the homeless. This was a very important addition to the Los Angeles Rent Stabilization Ordinance. Because of the transient nature of many of the occupants in these hotels, the landlords were free to raise the rent every time a person moved out or was evicted, prior to the effective date of our ordinance. After the ordinance went into effect, such raises were limited to the once per year increase allowed for inhabited units. Consequently, these units remained affordable for the GR recipients seeking entry into housing with our *Blair* increase.

However, after a time, the city permitted the vacancy decontrol provision of the ordinance to lapse. Once again, the landlords in the Single Room Occupancy Hotels began to raise their rents every time a tenant moved on. As a result, the rents quickly rose to, and then surpassed, the new GR levels.

  This illustrates the absolute necessity of coupling low income housing rent control measures with grant level increase legal advocacy for our litigation gains to have any real effect.

Letter from Nancy Mintie pp. 3–4, January 2, 1990.

  131. *Poverty Resistance Center* v. *Hart,* 213 Cal. App. 3d 295, 261 Cal. Rptr. 545 (1989), *review granted,* Nov. 16, 1989. Since the California Supreme Court granted review, this case may not be properly cited as authority to a California court.

  132. *Ibid.* at 300, 261 Cal. Rptr. at 548.

  133. *Ibid.* at 313, 261 Cal. Rptr. at 557.

  134. *Ibid.* at 301, 261 Cal. Rptr. at 548.

  135. *Ibid.* at 301–302, 261 Cal. Rptr. at 548.

  136. *Ibid.* at 302, 261 Cal. Rptr. at 549.

  137. *Ibid.*

  138. *Ibid.* at 303, 261 Cal. Rptr. at 549.

  139. *Ibid.*

  140. *Ibid.* at 303–304, 261 Cal. Rptr. at 549.

  141. 4 Cal. 3d 669, 676, 94 Cal. Rptr. 279, 283 (1971).

  142. *Ibid.*

  143. *Poverty Resistance Center,* 213 Cal. App. 3d at 304, 261 Cal. Rptr. at 550.

  144. *Ibid.* See also *Boehm* v. *County of Merced,* 163 Cal. App. 3d 447, 452, 209 Cal. Rptr. 530, 532–3 (1985) (hereinafter cited as *Boehm I*); *Boehm* v. *Superior Court,* 178 Cal. App. 3d 494, 223 Cal. Rptr. 716 (1986) (hereinafter cited as *Boehm II*). *Boehm II* represented a second look at the same case by the Fifth District Court of Appeal, and the court therein noted that the legislative purposes of Welfare and Institutions Code section 10000 include the intent that "aid shall be so administered and services so provided . . . as to encourage self-respect, self-reliance, and the desire to be a good citizen, useful to society." *Boehm II,* 178 Cal. App. 3d at 500, 223 Cal. Rptr. at 720 (quoting Cal. Welf. & Inst. Code § 10000). It added a further, helpful refinement to those of *Boehm I* that a general assistance grant cannot fail to provide for any of the enumerated subsistence needs—for housing, food, utilities, clothing, transportation, and medical care—or the need satisfied by some other program. 178 Cal. App. 3d at 501, 223 Cal. Rptr. at 720.

  145. *Poverty Resistance Center,* 213 Cal. App. 3d at 304, 261 Cal. Rptr. at 550. "This means that the factual premises which underpin a standard adopted under Section 17001 must be supported by evidence before the Board and by reasonable inferences drawn therefrom." *Ibid.* at 305, 261 Cal. Rptr. at 551.

  146. *Ibid.*

  147. *Ibid.*

  148. *Ibid.* The court went on to state, "If the Board has gone outside these boundaries plaintiffs are entitled to judicial relief. . . . These assessments, with due deference to the Board, ultimately present questions of law for the court." *Ibid.* at 305, 261 Cal. Rptr. at 551.

  149. *Ibid.*

  150. *Ibid.* at 306, 261 Cal. Rptr. at 551.

  151. *Ibid.,* 261 Cal. Rptr. at 552.

  152. *Ibid.*

  153. *Ibid.*

  154. *Ibid.* at 307, 261 Cal. Rptr. at 553. The majority also disagreed with the dissent's position that "this and other shortcomings . . . are cured because the Board allocates funds in its welfare budgeting scheme to 'multidimensional' supplemental services made available to general assistance recipients." *Ibid.* at 306–07, 261 Cal. Rptr. at 552. These "services" included

county budget allotments funding soup kitchens, homeless shelters, and the salaries of social workers assisting general assistance recipients. The majority, however, found that there was nothing permitting an inference that these services filled the identified gaps between the minimal cost-of-living survey and the grant levels adopted by the board.

155. *Ibid.*

156. *Ibid.* at 308–09, Cal. Rptr. at 553.

157. *Ibid.* at 309, 261 Cal. Rptr. at 554.

158. *Ibid.* The plaintiffs also alleged that the standard of the grant levels were unjustified because the survey of shelter costs relied upon by the county was "grossly inadequate." *Ibid.* at 310, 261 Cal. Rptr. at 554–55. The plaintiffs argued that the survey was inadequate because it was erroneously premised on the assumption that recipients presently lived in habitable housing, it took no account of future inflation in shelter costs, and it failed to consider the need of some recipients for security deposits to obtain housing. The court rejected this claim in its entirety. *Ibid.*, 261 Cal. Rptr. at 555.

159. *Ibid.* at 302–03, 261 Cal. Rptr. at 549.

160. *Ibid.*

161. See Cal. Welf. & Inst. Code §§ 10000, 17000, and 17001 (West 1980).

162. 214 Cal. App. 3d 1552, 263 Cal. Rptr. 262 (1989).

163. *Poverty Resistance Center,* 213 Ca. App. 3d at 306, 261 Cal. Rptr. at 552.

164. *Guidotti,* 214 Cal. App. 3d at 1565–66, 263 Cal. Rptr. at 270.

165. *Ibid.* at 1565, 263 Cal. Rptr. at 270.

166. *Ibid.* at 1565–66, 263 Cal. Rptr. at 270

167. *Ibid.* at 1566, 263 Cal. Rptr. at 270.

168. Letter from Nancy Mintie 5 (Jan. 2, 1990).

169. Conversation with Dr. Rodger Farr, citing the experience of the Los Angeles Robert Woods Johnson Health Clinics, February 22, 1988.

170. Cal App. 3d, 261 Cal. Rptr. 706 (1989). While the case was in litigation, Butte County adopted a resolution that the "dental services to be provided will be those procedures necessary to alleviate substantial pain, to treat infection, to maintain basic function, to maintain adequate nutrition, and to care for dental conditions which present a serious health risk." *Ibid.,* 261 Cal. Rptr. at 715. The Court of Appeal declined to issue a writ, finding that if the county provided the level of services specified in the resolution, no order of compulsion would be necessary. *Ibid.,* 261 Cal. Rptr. at 716.

171. Cal. Welf. & Inst. Code § 17000 (West 1980).

172. Cal. Welf. & Inst. Code § 10000 (West 1980).

173. *Cook,* 261 Cal. Rptr. at 714 (emphasis in original).

174. "The Homeless Mentally Ill: A Task Force Report of the American Psychiatric Association" (H.R. Lamb ed. 1984) (hereinafter 1984 Task Force Report). Dr. Rodger Farr, a contributor to the 1984 Task Force Report, noted that the report has become a model for later reports in other jurisdictions because, as he said, "It has a hundred pages on methodology, which, when followed, keeps the findings from being biased. Often politicians fashion the criteria for determining mental illness in order to come out with the answer they want." Interview with Dr. Rodger Farr, (January 20, 1990). In 1984, a study by the city of New York found that 90 percent of the homeless were mentally ill, while a study by the State of New York found that only 10 percent of the homeless were mentally ill. Perhaps it is not coincidental that the state is responsible for those homeless who are mentally ill, while the city is responsible for those homeless who are merely economically deprived, and specifically not for the mentally ill homeless. Interview with Dr. Rodger Farr, (January 20, 1990).

175. Werner, *supra* note 39, p. 1263.

176. *Ibid.*

177. "1984 Task Force Report."

178. "1984 Task Force Report."

179. "Building a House of Legal Rights," *supra* note 14.

180. Mentally ill homeless can be seen clothed in a bizarre array of dirty rags, protecting themselves from the elements, stumbling along, mumbling in reaction to visions and to voices heard. Often carting meager possessions in shopping carts, muttering to themselves, they find warmth over street grates. These deeply mentally ill, neglected citizens haunt all of America's cities. They have become blatant manifestations of our society's recent failure to care for those who are most unable to care for themselves.

181. "1984 Task Force Report."

182. As Los Angeles' County Mental Health psychiatrist and founder of the now famous Skid Row Mental Health project of Los Angeles, Dr. Rodger Farr declares relapse is inevitable, usually once yearly: "Like the birds coming back to Capistrano." Conversation with Dr. Rodger Farr, July 15, 1988.

183. Werner, *supra* note 39, p. 1264.

184. R. Lamb, *The Mentally Ill Homeless* (1979). Note that Dr. Richard Lamb served as chair of the task force for the American Psychiatric Associations which produced the seminal tool cited above as the "1984 Task Force Report."

185. 61 N.Y.2d 525, 463 N.E.2d 588, 475 N.Y.S.2d 247 (1984).

186. *Ibid.*

187. *Klosterman.*

188. *Ibid.*

189. *Klosterman* v. *Cuomo,* Index No. 11270182 (N.Y. Sup. Ct. App. Div., filed May 20, 1982.

190. Werner, *supra* note 39, p. 1264.

191. *L.A. Daily Journal,* March 9, 1988, § 2, p. 1.

192. *Mental Health Association* v. *Deukmejian,* 233 Cal. Rptr. 130 (Ct. App., 2d Dist. 1986), *depublished by the California Supreme Court when denying review* on March 5, 1987. They alleged that State law mandated these and that state and local agencies had been illegally neglecting to establish them. These proposed programs would have served the needs of certain "gravely disabled" individuals as "kinder" alternatives to treatment in state hospitals. *Ibid.* at 130, 135.

193. *Ibid.* at 133. But see *Newman* v. *Alabama,* 466 F. Supp. 628 (M.D. Ala. 1979). In *Newman,* the United States District Court for the Middle District of Alabama in 1979 "took over" the Alabama prison system via an appointed "temporary receiver" and ran it for several years. However, that situation involved an *existing* statewide system, violations of federal constitutional rights (precipitating a plaintiffs' supporting *amicus* brief from the U.S. Attorney General), and doubtless one of less complexity than a varied-patient county and state mental health system. See also *Landman* v. *Royster,* 354 F. Supp. 1302 (E.D. Va. 1973). *Cf.* for enforcement by contempt, *Landman* v. *Royster,* 354 F. Supp. 1292 (E.D. Va. 1973).

194. *Deukmejian,* at 133. While "least restrictive care" is a jargon term in the mental health industry, the statutory definition of "least restrictive environment" for California is found at Cal. Welf. & Inst. Code § 9123 (West 1984). The prospect urged by plaintiffs was more daunting even than the school desegregation cases, such as *Morgan* v. *Kerrigan,* 401 F. Supp. 216 (D. Mass.), *stay denied,* 523 F.2d 917 (1st Cir. 1975), *aff'd,* 530 F.2d 401 (1st Cir.), *cert. denied, White* v. *Morgan,* 426 U.S. 935 (1976). See J. Lukes, *Common Ground,* 1985, for the story of that case, well told.

195. Lanterman-Petris-Short Act, Cal. Welf. & Inst. Code §§ 5000–5585.59 (West 1984 & Supp. 1990).

196. The Community Residential Treatment Act, 1978 Cal. Stat. 3978, amended the Lanterman-Petris-Short Act. Now codified at Cal. 'Welf. & Inst. Code §§ 5450–5466 (West 1984 & Supp. 1990).

197. Cal. Welf. & Inst. Code §§ 5600–5770.5 (West 1984 & Supp. 1990).

198. *Deukmejian* at 132.

199. *Ibid.* at 135.

200. Cal. Welf. & Inst. Code § 5325.1 (West 1984). (Emphasis added.)

201. *Deukmejian* at 136.

202. Cal. Welf. & Inst. Code § 5450.1 (West 1984). (Emphasis added.)

203. *Deukmejian* at 136.

204. *Ibid.* at 137.

205. *Ibid.* at 134.

206. *Ibid.* at 139.

207. However, Dr. Rodger Farr, *supra* note 67, has told the author, September 9, 1988, "85,000 mental patients would be in California state mental hospitals if the 1960s system were in place today. But in 1988, there were only some 2,200 patients, not counting the 2,000 criminally insane."

208. *Deukmejian,* at 139 (the court found "community treatment for this hard-core population because of limited land space of community facilities, negative community reaction, and victimization of patients would not be less restrictive than hospital treatment and, in fact, would be more restrictive."). See also *Youngberg* v. *Romeo,* 457 U.S. 307 (1982).

209. *Deukmejian* at 140.

210. Cal. Const. art. VI, § 14, implemented by Cal. R. Ct. 976(c)(2). For a good explanation of depublication, see Grodin, "The Depublication Practice of the California Supreme Court," 72 *Cal. L. Rev.* 514 (1984). In recent years, the practice of depublication has become commonplace in California. A record 125 cases were depublished in 1988 (the first year of the "Lucas Court"), only to be surpassed with 142 in 1989. Uelmen, "Mainstream Justice," 9 *Cal. Law.* no. 7, p. 37 at 40 (July 1989).

211. *Cal. R. Ct.* 977(a).

212. Conversation with Jim Preis, Esq., Director of Mental Health Advocacy Services, Inc. (Oct. 2, 1989).

213. *Ibid.*

214. *Ibid.*

215. *Ibid.*

216. No. C 655274 (Cal. Los Angeles Super. Ct., filed July 22, 1987), still pending.

217. Order, *City of Los Angeles* v. *County of Los Angeles,* No. C 614380 (Cal. Los Angeles Super. Ct., March 8, 1988) (J. Vogel).

218. Letter from Nancy Mintie, Esq., of the Inner City Law Center, Los Angeles, to the author, August 30, 1989 (discussing litigation strategies for the homeless).

219. Conversation with Nancy Mintie, August 10, 1989.

220. *Board of Supervisors of Los Angeles County* v. *Superior Court of Los Angeles County,* 207 Cal. App. 3d 552, 254 Cal. Rptr. 905 (1989) (hereinafter referred to as *Comer*).

221. *Rensch* v. *County of Los Angeles,* No. C 595155 (Cal. Los Angeles Super. Ct., Second Amended Complaint, July 10, 1988, p. 2).

222. See generally *Rensch,* 1. On August 6, 1986, the court granted plaintiffs' preliminary injunction ordering Los Angeles County to prepare a plan for the identification and special assistance of mentally disabled persons seeking aid under the General Relief Program. Since then, the court found that the county failed to comply with the court's order, and ordered plaintiffs to file a broader supplemental amended complaint. This the plaintiffs did file on July 10, 1989, *Ibid.* at 1, and this situation continues with the severely mentally ill plaintiffs

(still alone, in pain, untreated, in grave danger today, on the streets) appearing to be "closing in" on their own county government, which, by a straightforward reading of section 17000, is obligated to support all indigents. Cal. Welf. & Inst. Code § 17000 (West 1980).

223. P.L. 93–112, Title V 504 stat. 394 (Sept. 26, 1973). Conversation with Jim Preis, Esq., Director of Mental Health Advocacy Services, Inc., October 2, 1989.

224. *Rensch* at 3, 16.

225. Preis, *supra* note 223. The plaintiffs pointed out that the county's arduous application process continues to require potential recipients to meet unreasonably detailed administrative application requirements, including documentation and verification requirements concerning identity. Additionally, applicants were required to undertake work assignments, job searches, employment registration, and medical and psychiatric examinations. Failure to comply with any of these requirements resulted in denial of all public assistance benefits. *Rensch* at 6.

226. *Ibid.* at 10, 11.

227. *Ibid.* at 2.

228. *Ibid.* at 6.

229. *Ibid.* at 2, 11.

230. *Comer,* 207 Cal. App. 3d at 552, 254 Cal. Rptr. at 905.

231. *Ibid.* at 556–57, 254 Cal. Rptr. at 907–08.

232. *Ibid.* at 556–57, 254 Cal. Rptr. at 907–08. Section 5709 provides, "In no event shall counties be required to appropriate more than the amount required under the provisions of this chapter." Cal. Welf. & Inst. Code § 5709 (West Supp. 1990).

233. Cal. Welf. & Inst. Code § 5705(a) (West Supp. 1990).

234. *Comer,* 207 Cal. App. 3d at 560, 254 Cal. Rptr. at 910.

235. *Ibid.* at 560–61, 254 Cal. Rptr. at 910.

236. See generally *Comer.*

237. Preis, *supra* note 223.

238. See generally *Comer.*

239. See *Chackes, supra* note 9.

240. See also Note, "The Duty of California Counties to Provide Mental Health Care for the Indigent and Homeless," 25 *San Diego L. Rev.* 197 (1988).

241. This common sense proposition, which is familiar to all law students, is first attributed (in English law) to Lord Coke in *Laughter's Case,* 5 Rep. 1; Co. Litt. 127b, cited in *Marson* v. *Short,* 2 Bing. N.C. 118, 121, 42 Rev. Rep. 544, 547 (1835); Wing. Max. 600. Another elderly English decision cited for the proposition is *Bell* v. *Midland Ry. Co.,* 10 C.B.M.S. 287, 306, 128 Rev. Rep. 719, 729 (1861) (Willes, J.).

242. *Comer,* 207 Cal. App. 3d at 564, 254 Cal. Rptr. at 913.

243. The well-known quotation has often been attributed to H.L. Mencken, but in fact was merely included by him in his *A New Dictionary of Quotations on Historical Principles from Ancient and Modern Sources,* p. 852 (H.L. Mencken, ed., Knopf, 1960). In *The Harper Book of American Quotations,* p. 300 (Gorton Carruth, ed., 1988), it is attributed to Peter Finlay Dunne's "Mr. Dooley," from his book *Observations of Mr. Dooley.*

244. *Rensch* at 1, 2.

245. *In the Matter of Billie Boggs,* 136 Misc. 2d 1082, 522 N.Y.S.2d 407, 410 (Sup. Ct. N.Y. City), *rev'd sub nom., Boggs* v. *New York City Health and Hosp. Corp.,* 132 A.D.2d 340, 523 N.Y.S.2d 71 (1987), *appeal dismissed,* 70 N.Y.2d 972, 520 N.E.2d 515, 525 N.Y.S.2d 796 (1988).

246. 19 *Colum. Hum. Rts. L. Rev.* 333, 342 (1988).

247. *Boggs,* 136 Misc. 2d at 1089–90, 522 N.Y.S.2d at 412.

248. *Boggs* v. *New York City Health and Hosp. Corp.,* 132 A.D.2d 340, 366, 523 N.Y.S.2d 71, 87 (1987).

249. *Ibid.* at 343, 523 N.Y.S.2d at 72.

250. In California, the definiton of "gravely disabled" means "A condition in which a person, as a result of a mental disorder, is unable to provide for his basic personal needs for good, clothing, or shelter," Calf. Welf. & Inst. Code § 5008(h)(1) (West Supp. 1990).

251. Preis, *supra* note 223.

252. *Ibid.*

253. 19 *Colum. Hum. Rts. L. Rev.* at 341. In reality, many homeless, mentally ill New Yorkers *wanted* services from the Department of Mental Health in New York, but were not getting them because they were unavailable. Thus, in a sense, the Brown/Koch affair appears in retrospect to have been almost a publicity stunt, designed to get Americans to conclude that "these people don't want services!" Preis, *supra* note 223.

254. Cal. A.B. 1714, 1989–90 Reg. Sess. Preis, *supra* note 223.

255. California now has one-fifth of the level it had twenty-five years ago, in real terms. Conversation with Dr. Rodger Farr, Los Angeles psychiatrist and founder of the Skid Row Mental Health Project, on July 10, 1988.

256. Preis, *supra* note 223.

257. Conversation with Dr. Rodger Farr, Los Angeles psychiatrist and founder of the Skid Row Mental Health Project on January 20, 1990.

258. *Ibid.*

259. Possibly one-third of the present $1 billion in state and county funds spent on mental health care could be saved if re-hospitalizations (some of which are "annual") could be avoided. Farr, *supra* note 255. See generally "Report of the California Economic Development Commission on the Chronically Mentally Ill" (1987).

260. Preis, *supra* note 223.

261. This figure was also disseminated to California judges at a C.J.E.R. Institute on Mental Health Law, Clairmont Hotel, Oakland, CA, January 21–26, 1990.

262. The "flow of homeless" into San Diego Courts has now largely "dried up" because of overcrowded, crisis conditions in our jails. But the jail-crowding crisis will ultimately be resolved, and the homeless will be "welcomed" once again.

263. Monthly Reports of the Court Administrator to the Judges of the San Diego Municipal Court, San Diego, CA (1989).

264. "Section 8 housing" is the name commonly given to housing made available through largesse provided under 42 U.S.C.A. § 1437f (West Supp. 1989) and HUD Regulations, 24 C.F.R. part 883 (1989).

265. See generally D.P. Moynihan, *City and Nation* (1987).

266. From Oliver Goldsmith's poem, "The Deserted Village," lines 55–56, quoted in *The Oxford Dictionary of Quotations,* p. 224 (2d ed. 1959).

267. *Hansen* v. *Department of Social Services,* 193 Cal. App. 3d 283, 297–98, 238 Cal. Rptr. 232 (1987); "The Continued Growth of Hunger, Homelessness and Poverty in America's Cities," p. 2 (United States Conference of Mayors study, 1986).

268. T. Mathews, "Homeless in America: What Can Be Done?" *Newsweek,* March 21, 1988, pp. 57–58.

269. 42 U.S.C. § 625(a)(1)(C) (1982).

270. 463 U.S. 248, 256 (1983).

271. *Ibid.*

272. *Hansen,* 193 Cal. App. 3d at 289, 238 Cal. Rptr. at 235. See also *Lehr,* 436 U.S. 248, 261.

273. *Maticka* v. *City of Atlantic City,* 216 N.J. Super. 434, 447, 524 A.2d 416, 423 (App. Div. 1987).

274. Cal. Civ. Code § 197 (West 1971 & Supp. 1990) and § 4600 (West 1984 & Supp.

354   Notes

1990). See, e.g., *Meyer* v. *Nebraska,* 262 U.S. 390, 399 (1923); *Quillim* v. *Walcott,* 434 U.S. 246, 255 (1977), *reh. denied,* 435 U.S. 918.

275. *Stanley* v. *Illinois,* 405 U.S. 645, 649–657 (1972).

276. Connell, "A Right to Emergency Shelter for Homeless Under the New Jersey Constitution," 18 *Rutgers L.J.* 765, 769 (1987).

277. 138 Misc. 2d 212, 524 N.Y.S.2d 121 (Sup. Ct. 1987).

278. *Ibid.* at 217, 524 N.Y.S.2d at 125 (quoting *New York Soc. Serv. Law* § 384–b[1][a][iii]).

279. *Martin A.* 138 Misc. 2d at 217–18, 524 N.Y.S.2d at 125 (quoting *New York Soc. Serv. Law* § 397[1][b]). In New York, before a child may be placed in foster care, the Department of Social Services must make an assessment of the child and family circumstances. A service plan is then established identifying the needs and services warranted, which are designed to keep the family intact. *Ibid.* These services include "day care, homemaker services, parent training and aid, transportation, clinical services and 24 hour access to emergency services such as shelter, cash and goods." *Ibid.* at 219, 524 N.Y.S.2d at 125. Once the state determines that these preventive services are warranted, section 423.4(a) of the New York State Department of Social Services Regulations requires that they "shall be provided according to the needs of the child and his family." *Ibid.* at 218, 524 N.Y.S.2d at 125.

280. *Ibid.*

281. *Ibid.* at 224, 524 N.Y.S.2d at 128–29.

282. *Ibid.* at 224, 524 N.Y.S.2d at 129.

283. 130 A.D.2d 154, 518 N.Y.S.2d 105 (1987).

284. 134 Misc. 2d 83, 509 N.Y.S.2d 685 (Sup. Ct. 1986).

285. *Grant,* 130 A.D.2d at 164–72, 518 N.Y.S.2d at 112–16.

286. 400 Mass. 806, 511 N.E.2d 603 (1987).

287. *Ibid.* at 809, 511 N.E.2d at 606.

288. *Ibid.* at 821, 511 N.E.2d at 612.

289. *Ibid.*

290. *Franklin* v. *New Jersey Dept. of Human Services,* 111 N.J. 1, 543 A.2d 1 (1988).

291. *Ibid.* at 13–14, 543 A.2d at 7.

292. *Ibid.* at 18, 543 A.2d at 9.

293. *Ibid.*

294. *Ibid.* at 17–18, 543 A.2d at 9.

295. 193 Cal. App. 3d 283, 238 Cal. Rptr. 232 (1987).

296. The DSS is the single state agency supervising the administration of California public social services including the provisions of the AFDC and homeless assistance programs. *Merriman* v. *McMahon,* No. 640362–5 (Cal. Alameda Super. Ct., June 29, 1988). See also *Hansen.*

297. *Merriman.*

298. *Hansen,* 193 Cal. App. 3d at 290, 238 Cal. Rptr. at 236.

299. *Ibid.*

300. *Ibid.* at 291, 238 Cal. Rptr. at 237; Cal. Welf, & Inst. Code §§ 16504, 16506 (West Supp. 1990).

301. *Hansen,* 193 Cal. App. 3d at 291, 238 Cal. Rptr. at 236.

302. *Ibid.*

303. Cal. Welf, & Inst. Code § 16507.1 (West Supp. 1990).

304. Cal. Welf. & Inst. Code § 16508.1 (West Supp. 1990).

305. *Hansen,* 193 Cal. App. 3d at 291, 238 Cal. Rptr. at 237.

306. *Ibid.* at 291–92, 238 Cal. Rptr. at 237.

307. *Ibid.* at 292, 238 Cal. Rptr. at 237.

308. *Ibid.* at 293, 238 Cal. Rptr. at 238. The U.S. Supreme Court has stated: "The preven-

tion of . . . abuse of children constitutes a government objective of surpassing importance." *New York* v. *Farber*, 458 U.S. 747, 757 (1982) (unanimous opinion in an obscenity case).

309. *Hansen,* 193 Cal. App. 3d at 294, 238 Cal. Rptr. at 239.

310. *Ibid.* at 295, 238 Cal. Rptr. at 240.

311. *Ibid.* at 296–97, 238 Cal. Rptr. at 240–41.

312. *Ibid.* at 296, 238 Cal. Rptr. at 240.

313. See Cal. Welf. & Inst. Code § 16500.5(c) (West Supp. 1990). For instance, Welfare and Institutions Code section 11450(f)(2) creates a homeless assistance program that provides temporary shelter benefits of $30 a night for three to four weeks while an eligible homeless family is seeking permanent housing. Cal. Welf. & Inst. Code § 11450(f)(2) (West Supp. 1990). This program also supplies such families the move-in costs to secure permanent shelter. *Ibid.* To qualify for benefits, a family must be homeless, apparently eligible for or receiving AFDC, and have less than $100 in liquid resources. *Ibid.* The statute defines a family as homeless when it lacks a fixed and regular nighttime residence, when it is residing in a public or private shelter, or when it is residing in a public or private place that is not intended as a sleeping accommodation for human beings. *Ibid.* A family may qualify for homeless assistance no more than once per twelve-month period. *Ibid.*

314. *Merriman,* at 1.

315. Cal. Welf. & Inst. Code § 11450(f)(2) (West Supp. 1990).

316. *Merriman,* at 1.

317. *Ibid.*

318. See generally *Merriman,* at 1.

319. *Ibid.*

320. *Merriman* at 5; California Department of Social Services Regulation MPP 44–211.512 (final) (quoted in *Merriman*).

321. *Merriman* at 4.

322. Citing Cal. Welf. & Inst. Code § 10600 (West 1963).

323. California Department of Social Services Regulation MPP 44–211.512 (final) (quoted in *Merriman*). Plaintiffs' claim for injunctive relief barring such new regulations alleged that Welfare and Institutions Code section 10000 required that public social services be administered and provided in a humane fashion. *Merriman* at 9. Plaintiffs further alleged that denial of benefits under the new DSS regulations was inhumane and contrary to the purposes of the welfare program, *Ibid.,* and that defendants had violated Welfare and Institutions Code sections 10000 and 11450(f)(2), and were making illegal expenditures of public funds. *Ibid.* at 9–10.

324. Judgment, *Merriman* v. *McMahon,* No. 640362-5 (Alameda Super. Ct., October 5, 1989) (J. Girard).

325. *Ibid.*

326. A. de Tocqueville, *Democracy in America,* pp. 121–28 (New American Library, Heffner, ed., 1956); A. de Tocqueville, *Journey to America,* pp. 51–52, 252–53 (Yale University Press, George Lawrence, trans., 1960). See also, for sociologists' views of the state of modern America, R.N. Bellah, *et al., Habits of the Heart,* 1986, preface, p. 7.

327. Letter from Nancy Mintie, director of Los Angeles' Inner City Law Center, to the author on January 2, 1990, pp. 1–3.

328. See *United States* v. *Guest,* 383 U.S. 745, 757–58 (1966).

329. See the discussion of the work of the Coalition on the Homeless in *Callahan* v. *Carey.*

330. "Pushed Out: America's Homeless," Report by the National Coalition for the Homeless, 1987, pp. 75–76.

331. *Cf. Camp* v. *Board of Supervisors,* 123 Cal. App. 3d 334, Cal. Rptr. (1981); *Buena*

Vista Gardens v. *City of San Diego*, 175 Cal. App. 3d 289, Cal. Rptr. (1985), on the "housing element," but no relation to the homeless issue.

332. See, *e.g.*, Cal. Gov't Code § 65583 (West Supp. 1990).

333. *Construction Industry Association* v. *City of Petaluma*, 522 F.2d 897 (9th Cir. 1975), *cert. denied*, 424 U.S. 934 (1976).

334. *Lee* v. *City of Monterey Park*, 173 Cal. App. 3d 798, 219 Cal. Rptr. 309 (1985).

335. *Building Industry Association of Southern California, Inc.* v. *City of Camarillo*, 41 Cal. 3d 810, 718 P.2d 68, 226 Cal. Rptr. 81 (1986) (citing *Lee*).

336. Cal. Evid. Code § 669.5 (West 1966 & Supp. 1990).

337. Report lodged with Los Angeles County Board of Supervisors by the Los Angeles County Grand Jury Social Services Committee (January 15, 1985). Current U.S. Code sections have been gathered at 50 U.S.C.A. App. §§ 2251, et. seq.

338. R.K. Farr, P. Koegel, and A. Burnam, *supra* note 71.

339. See, *e.g.*, *Thompson* v. *County of Alameda*, 27 Cal. 74, 614 P.2d 728, 167 Cal. Rptr. 70 (1980). But see *Myers* v. *Morris*, 810 F.2d 1437 (8th Cir. 1987) (government psychologists held to be immune from suit as long as they were doing their job, even if they were acting with malice toward the plaintiff).

340. *Tarasoff* v. *Board of Regents of the University of California*, 13 Cal. 3d 177, 529 P.2d 553, 118 Cal. Rptr. 129 (1974) and 17 Cal. 3d 425, 551 P.2d 334, 131 Cal. Rptr. 14 (1976).

341. *McClare* v. *County of San Luis Obispo* (1989). This lawsuit is about to be filed. Attorney for plaintiff is Robert Kirkpatrick, Esq., of San Luis Obispo. The claim against the county is on file.

342. *San Francisco Chronicle*, Jan. 25, 1990, p. A1, col. 6.

343. *Royal Globe Ins. Co.* v. *Superior Court*, 23 Cal. 3d 880, 592 P.2d 329, 153 Cal. Rptr. 842 (1979).

344. See Chackes, *supra* note 9, at 155–58.

345. See generally D.P. Moynihan, *supra* note 265.

346. See Chackes, *supra* note 9, at 155–157.

347. Victor Hugo, *Histoire d'un Crime*, conclusion (1852). Yogi Berra once conversely observed: "If the people don't come out to the park, noboby's going to stop "em." B. R. Sugar, *The Book of Sports Quotes*, 1979.

348. Mathews, *supra* note 268, at 58. A substantial number indicated that the government should guarantee enough to eat and a decent place to sleep.

349. L.D. Brandeis, *Other People's Money*, p. 92 (1914).

350. Darrow's closing argument in *People* v. *Sweet*, Detroit 1926, reprinted in *Attorney for the Damned*, Arthur Weinberg 3d, ed., 1957, pp. 260, 262–63.